MICHAEL A. BABCOCK, PH.D

THE STORY OF
WESTERN CULTURE

SECOND EDITION

The Story of Western Culture
Michael A. Babcock

HPS Publishing

Copyright © 2011 Michael A. Babcock
Cover art by Matthew D. Pamer

First Printing: June 2011

Second Edition Printing: June 2012

Printed in the United States of America

ISBN-13: 978-0-9857507-0-1

Contents

Foreword

In the pages that follow, we'll be recounting the story of western culture. This won't be a simple recitation of facts—a litany of dates and names and technical jargon. Rather, it will be an interpretation of the underlying values that have defined western culture from the start and continue to give it shape in the present. It's a great story—and I encourage you to plunge into it with enthusiasm and curiosity. I encourage you as well to adopt the attitude of Terence, a Roman poet who said: "I am a man, and whatever concerns humanity is of interest to me." This story should interest each one of us, because it's *our* story.

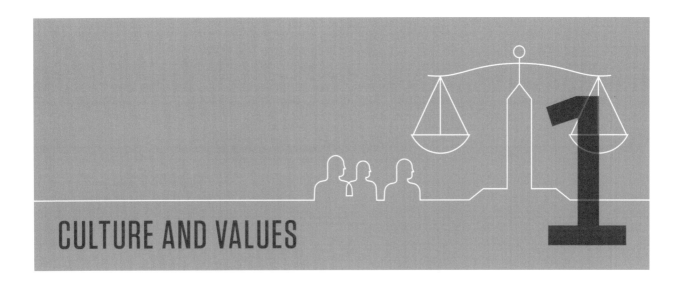

CULTURE AND VALUES

Chapter Objectives

- Define what the humanities is—and what it's not.
- Articulate why studying the humanities should matter to you.
- Explain the crucial connection between culture and values.

What are the humanities all about? Here's a definition for us to reflect on at the outset:

The study of the humanities is the study of how a culture expresses its values through the creation, preservation, and transmission of ideas and works of art.

There's a lot in that definition. One of the key words to highlight would certainly be "culture." **Culture** is the sum total of the common things that bind people together in a society—and this is what we're specifically interested in trying to understand when we study the humanities. We will be looking closely at culture because we want to understand how people organize their lives and their societies around things that matter strongly to them.

Another key word in this definition is **values**. This word, with all its depth of meaning, will be central to the approach we'll take in our study of western culture. "Val-

ues" is a familiar word to us; at first glance we feel we know what it means. Certainly in Christian circles, it's a word that's used often—as in "family values," "Judeo-Christian values," and "traditional values." But what does any of that really mean? We may know how to use the word in everyday discourse, but we find that it's a little more difficult to pin down in a concrete definition. If you take the word back to its original meaning, the word "value" has to do with weighing something. We still speak of valuing (or weighing) precious metals and gold. To determine the weight of something like gold is to fix its value. Think of gold miners in nineteenth-century California. At the end of a long day, miners would "assay" the value of the gold from that day's work. That's a concrete way of visualizing what values ultimately come down to.

REPRESENTATION OF MINERS WEIGHING THEIR GOLD.

Here's another way to think about it. Our deepest values are the things we believe are *worth living for and worth dying for*. When we define values that way, then a lot of things suddenly fall into perspective. The gold in the mine is *valued* by the miner, because he's risking his life to get it.

What does a nation go to war for? Things they believe are worth living for and dying for. What are the essential things in our own lives that are worth fighting for and defending? For the Christian, this question should bring things into focus as well. What should a follower of Christ mean when he or she says, "These are my values"? Well, we should mean what the apostle Paul meant when he said in Philippians 1:21, "For to me to live is Christ and to die is gain." And right there, in that one verse, we have a beautiful definition of biblical Christian values. What's worth living for? Christ. What's worth dying for? To gain the promise of all we have in Christ, the promise of all He has given us—eternal life through Him.

Why, then, are the humanities an important subject to study? We can see clearly just from that initial definition that this is something we should consider deeply, not just as an abstract idea, but as something that really does affect the way we live our lives.

Let's look a little more closely at the rest of that definition. Of course, a culture expresses its values—but just how does it do that? Three ways, through "the creation, the preservation, and the transmission of ideas and works of art." The creation of art involves the productive, creative process that the artist engages in. It's a mystery to us how the artist creates the masterpiece. We don't really understand the psychology of that. One of the beautiful things about how God created us is that we ourselves have the instinct, the desire, and even the *need*, to create things and thereby give expression to our lives, to society, and to the world around us. We'll be looking at quite a few art objects as we study western culture, because they're such concrete examples of what culture produces. But culture also involves the creation of institutions in every sphere of life—political, social, philosophical, educational, and economic. The study of the humanities, then, is not just the study of art. It's the study of all the things that a culture produces as an expression of its values and beliefs.

Once we've made an art object, or developed an institution within culture, we seek to preserve it. Anything important enough to create in the first place is worth preserving. A culture seeks to maintain those things that it sees as valuable. It wouldn't make sense for an artist to create a work of art, and then say, "That's one of the best paintings I've ever done. Now, I think I'll stoke the fire with it." That wouldn't make any sense at all! After expending that kind of effort to make something in the first place, you want to preserve it. And not just preserve it, but also to transmit it to future generations. And that's really the process that we'll be looking at and trying to understand in greater detail as we study the culture and values of the western world.

Look again at the last phrase of the definition. What exactly is created, preserved and transmitted within a culture? Two things: "ideas and works of art." This definition clearly suggests that we can divide the humanities into two broad categories. And so let's give a label to each one of those very briefly, because we are going to be working through each one of these, emphasizing some more than others.

First, culture expresses itself through ideas. The first category of the humanities, then, is what we call the **reflective arts**. That's a fairly descriptive term, referring as it does to the process of reflection, analysis, and contemplation. What are some of the academic disciplines that we associate with the reflective arts? Philosophy, history, and theology should come to mind. What does a philosopher do, if not try to understand values by reflecting on them? *Who am I as an individual? What is the nature of freedom? What are the limits of freedom for an individual in society? What is the nature of reality in the world? What is expected of me in this life?* These great philosophical questions are fundamentally questions about values. We're going to see this point illustrated well by the ancient Greeks as we study the philosophical legacy of Socrates, Plato, and Aristotle. These great questions motivated the Greeks to reflect on the nature of reality, the meaning of the cosmos, and how we fit into the whole picture as individuals. They reflected long and hard—and they came up with some remarkable answers to those questions.

History, too, is a reflective art. We often think that history is simply "what happened in the past." Ask a hundred people on the street what history is, and ninety-nine will probably tell you that. But history is really best understood as "what people write down about the past" as they reflect upon its meaning and significance for us today. Here's an example. If you take three scholars and give each of them the same set of facts about a historical event (say, the French Revolution), then you can expect three entirely different histories to be written. Give ten pieces of historical data to a feminist historian, the same data to a Marxist historian, and the same data to a conservative Christian historian; tell them to "Write the history of the French Revolution using only this data." What will you get? You should expect the feminist to write a gender-based history, emphasizing the struggle for equality. You would expect the Marxist historian to emphasize economic factors and the distribution of material wealth in France. You should expect the conservative historian to emphasize, perhaps, the great themes of freedom and liberty. In other words, these historians are going to write history out of their understanding of the world; and that understanding will be filtered through the framework of their values. That's why we can say that history, as a discipline, is a reflective art like philosophy.

According to our definition, culture also expresses itself through "works of art." This second category of the humanities is referred to as the **expressive arts**. We can further subdivide this category into the visual arts, the literary arts, and the performing arts. The visual arts comprise painting, sculpture, architecture—those art forms that are "plastic," or concrete. The literary arts include all the forms of creative writing, such as lyric poems, epic poems, fiction, and essays. The performing arts refer to those art forms that are experienced in the moment of performance, such as music, drama, and even films and opera. So again, as with the reflective arts, the label itself is rather self-explanatory; these are art forms that give explicit form to a set of values through a specific medium of expression.

All of this is summed up nicely by a famous modern sculpture, *The Thinker*, by Auguste Rodin (1840-1917). I like how this work of art illustrates everything we've just been defining; it's a depiction of a philosopher deep in thought—which makes me think of the reflective arts. But the work itself is an example of sculpture, which means that it is an "expressive" art object. And that sums up what the study of the humanities is all about. We reflect upon and try to understand our world, and then we seek to give expression to those ideas through the institutions of culture and the arts.

Why study the humanities?

On the foundation of that definition, I'd like us to consider briefly why it's important for us to study culture and its values. In one sense, I think we could stop right here and point to our answer. Our discussion of values should have already made the case as to why this is important. But I want to make this a little bit more structured and organize some thoughts under five main arguments, or five reasons for studying the humanities:

- the intellectual reason
- the cultural reason
- the academic reason
- the emotional reason
- the biblical reason

First, *the intellectual reason*. What do we mean by that? Well, this probably is the most compelling case we can make for the study of the humanities. I want to frame this particular argument around two or three great quotes from the past. One is from a Roman statesman who lived in the century before Christ. Another quote comes from an 18th-century German poet. And then the final quote will come from the pages of the New Testament.

The great Roman politician and orator, Cicero, made a compelling case for what we're studying—and he did so in a single powerful sentence:

> *"To be ignorant of what occurred before you were born is to remain always a child."*
>
> Cicero (106-43 BC)

Cicero has given us a very direct, in-your-face, rationale for the humanities. Back in Cicero's day they didn't speak of the discipline of the humanities; but he's talking about the same things that we are, and it will take a while to unpack his ideas. He's talking about the past, the study of culture and our understanding of the contexts of the past that create the situations of the present. He's saying, "If those things don't interest you, and if you don't think they are important, then plan on living the rest of your life like a child." Why? Because you won't have the qualities you'll need to navigate through the complexities of life unless you understand the complexities of the past. An understanding of the past provides a framework for the present; it's a tool, a resource that you can draw up on, as you go through life individually or as you go through life collectively as a society.

Cicero is speaking of children and growing up. I think of when my wife and I would take our children to school on the first day. That's always a fun, but also a bittersweet, experience for a parent. You take your youngest child to school and wonder where all the years are going. You also think of how you're entrusting your child to somebody else—to a teacher who will help further that process of training your child for living well in the world with knowledge and character. Certainly, this is what we desire for our children. We want them to grow up—to not remain children forever.

What is it that a child naturally lacks and is not well equipped to deal with? What are some of the things that Cicero might be thinking of? Let's list some qualities.

- A child is self-centered
- A child is naïve
- A child lacks perspective
- A child is dependent

Children come into the world thinking that the universe revolves around their diaper changes and feeding schedule. And then they wake up to the world around them and start to learn that they're part of a family. They have to compromise with the needs and desires of siblings and parents. Next, they go off to school and their world gets a little bit larger. Now they share the universe with 25 or 30 other kids their age. They've got to learn how to stand in line, raise their hand, and put their head quietly on their desk. They graduate out into the world—the world of neighborhoods, communities, and the entire world. Ultimately, they should learn that they are just one part of a vast human story that encompasses every person who has ever lived. In other words, history did not begin the year they were born.

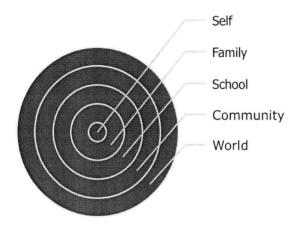

Self
Family
School
Community
World

Children are also naïve. They're gullible—and that's one of the things that most concerns a parent. Children have a natural innocence to them. You train your children not to believe everything they hear, and not to accept every offer that's made to them in life, because they can get into a lot of trouble if they don't know how to distinguish between truth and error, sincerity and false intention.

Let's consider a couple of examples of gullibility. These are pretty simple examples, but they drive home the point that we need to look at the world in a grown-up way. Our first example is a medieval wall painting from a little church in Austria. The painting dates back to the 14th century, but it was just uncovered at the end of the 20th century when art historians pulled the plaster off the wall and found what looks like a familiar cartoon character. It's easy to imagine a child looking at this painting and saying, "Wow, look at that! It's Mickey Mouse!"

But Mickey Mouse didn't exist in the 14th century. This is kind of an obvious example of how a knowledge of the past—along with a sophisticated grasp of the concepts of time and space—can keep one from looking at this painting like a child and saying, "Gee, I didn't know Mickey Mouse has been

around that long." Of course, we know that Mickey Mouse made his first appearance as "Steamboat Willie" in 1928; so this medieval picture must be depicting an entirely different creature.

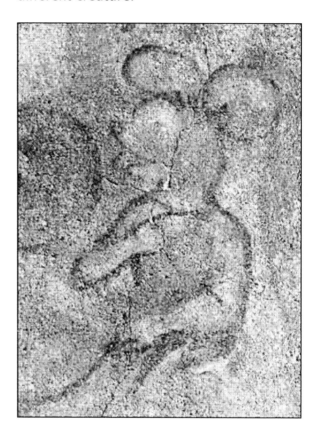

Let's consider another example. It's a painting that presents greater challenges, and it's raised the question in some people's minds of whether or not we can see the depiction of UFOs in Renaissance art. I'm referring to the painting "Madonna and Child with the Infant St. John" (late 15th century). As you look over the left shoulder of the Virgin Mary you see an unidentified flying object in the sky. It is, in that sense, a UFO. But is it an alien spaceship? That's the question that some people would pose.

When we examine a close-up of the section behind Mary's left shoulder, we see a man and his dog—and they are both peering up at the object in the sky. The man is shielding his eyes as he looks up; and the dog is rather interested in it too. The object itself seems to be radiating light. You can go on the Internet and find all kinds of websites that will cite this painting as prime evidence that Planet Earth has been visited many times over the centuries—probably starting from the time the pyramids were built in ancient Egypt (as the argument goes).

Well, how do you answer that? It may be reasonable for a child to believe this, since the child by nature is gullible and innocent. But how should an adult approach a claim like this? Cicero would remind us to look at the bigger picture and understand the history that lies behind what we see. And when we do that, when we start to study the Renaissance background of this painting, we suddenly find many examples of strange objects in the sky. Some depict men gazing upward. Some of them have dogs, some of them don't; but it doesn't really matter. They're looking intently at an object that has captured their attention. These are shepherds, and they're looking up at the glory of God descending in that moment when Christ came to earth, when "the Word was made flesh." It's a fairly easy task to document what's going on

here. This is a Renaissance way of showing the miracle of the Incarnation and the glory of God descending into the material realm. So what's my point? This is where the study of the past and the hard work of figuring things out can keep us from errors as we try to understand the nature of truth and the nature of the past.

Children also lack perspective. They lack the context necessary to understand what's happening moment by moment. We use the expression, "Don't cry over spilled milk," and we're consciously thinking of a child when we say that. That moment when the milk is spilled is the worst tragedy that has ever happened in the history of the world! And of course, we know that's not the case, but the child views it that way, because the child hasn't learned about the 20th century yet. There are a lot of things that we could cite very quickly that would probably be higher up on the scale of tragedy than that. As we grow up, we should be developing the ability to put the things that happen in life into a broader perspective. This is a powerful life tool, because it enables us to see the big picture and how we fit into it; we learn how not to overreact to adversity, how to scale our response appropriately to the situation.

A child is also dependent. As a parent, you want your child to develop the ability to be independent in the right ways, and to make good independent choices for himself or herself. This is part of being a healthy individual—one who is not completely dependent upon other people.

All of these observations take us into the heart of what Cicero must have had in mind. His argument is that the knowledge of the past really can help us to mature in such a way that we can face the complexities and challenges of life.

The second quote we're going to examine is very similar. It's also direct, even blunt, in its central argument. Johann Wolfgang von Goethe (1749-1832) was a German poet who is known best as the author of *Faust*. The story of Dr. Faust has been told since the Middle Ages, but Goethe gave the story its definitive telling. Dr. Faust was a college professor who knew a lot about books and abstract ideas, but hadn't experienced much of the world. Tired and bored of his world of ideas, Faust decided to sell his soul to the devil so that he could taste the full range of human experience from top to bottom, from good to bad. We should keep this story in mind as we look at Goethe's statement. The story of Faust forces us to think about the nature of experience in the world, what the function and purpose of that experience is, and whether life ultimately can be reduced to little more than a series of experiences lived out in the moment. Here's how Goethe framed the problem:

> *"Anyone who cannot give an account to oneself of the past 3000 years remains in darkness, without experience, living from day to day."*
>
> Goethe (1749-1832)

He's using a different metaphor, but it's the same idea that Cicero expressed. Goethe asks us to picture somebody who's in a dark tunnel, perhaps, fumbling his way along with only enough light to see the step right in front of him. He's essentially living in darkness. Now we would probably adjust Goethe's statement here and lengthen the timeframe from 3000 years to 5000. We have a larger historical framework now, due to all the archaeological discoveries of the last two centuries. But 3000 years or 5000 years—take your pick. What Goethe means is that we won't have the light we need to navigate into the future if we don't understand what lies behind us in the past.

I like how Goethe puts this. He says that we are really living "without experience." We're living day to day, moment by moment, driven by stimulus, impulse, and instinct. Think about it: If we reduce life to that, then we are reducing life to the level of how an animal lives. Goethe is challenging us to consider the very basis of our existence. Is my life really nothing more than going from one great experience to another, one thrill to another? This is a man who knew something about that idea, because he wrote the book, so to speak, on this very theme. That's what *Faust* is all about. And so Goethe is suggesting that this is not how life is to be lived—that *living only for experience is not really living at all*. You might think you're living a full life of experience, but it's really just a cruel illusion; you can't truly experience life, Goethe claims, when you only live for the moment.

The real depth of this quote lies in that phrase, "without experience." These words should speak to us directly, since we live in an age when people increasingly view life that way. Think, for example, of the popularity of extreme sports and the whole notion that life should be an uninterrupted thrill ride basically. I guess there are some limited rewards for bungee jumping, extreme skiing, rock climbing, and so on—if that's your sort of thing. But once the chemical composition in your bloodstream has been changed, what do you have to show for it? I mean, can you really reduce life to biological and chemical functions?

Certainly, it is the message of the Bible that our life *should* not—and *cannot*—be reduced to experience alone. God has created us for more than just the raw experience of this world. We are created to experience God fully. There is a spiritual dimension, a spiritual reality, to life; and if we don't have that, then we have nothing. I should point out that Goethe was no Christian. He is not arguing here from a biblical point of view.

But still, it made perfect sense to him that a life lived for momentary experience is shallow and incomplete, and that one needs something more than just the transitory nature of a chemical rush to make a good and meaningful life.

Let's look at one more quote to drive this point home. In addition to the Roman and the German poet, let's see what the apostle Paul had to say in Ephesians 4:14. In this passage Paul is describing the goal of maturing in Christ—growing up into "the fullness of the stature of Christ." Paul says that our goal should be that "we henceforth be no more children." I've often wondered if Paul knew Cicero's speech and was familiar with it. It's very possible because he was educated in the classical culture of his day and he may have been thinking of, and alluding to, what Cicero said; they both used the same metaphor of childhood. Paul wrote, "That we be not children, tossed all about, to and fro, carried about with every wind of doctrine." Here we have the idea of gullibility and innocence again. We must grow up, so that we won't be carried off "by the sleight of men, and cunning craftiness, whereby they lie in wait to deceive." What can we conclude, then? There is a very real intellectual component to our maturity in Christ. Yes, it is a spiritual work that God is doing in us through Christ; but maturity is meant to impact every part of who we are, including our minds, our intellect, our understanding of the world around us.

Very briefly, let's look at the other reasons why we should engage this course of study. There is *a cultural reason* as well. Now I don't want to make a lot out of this right now, because we'll have opportunities to analyze this more later. I'm really talking about the culture wars that polarize us and divide so much of western society today into competing camps of liberal and conservative, religious and secular. There is a real demographic divide in our nation between those who see us drifting away from traditional values and those who are promoting a progressive postmodern agenda. A significant part of that liberal agenda involves vilifying the West and the institutions associated with the western world, including Christianity.

So we will be looking fairly, but candidly, at the history of the West, at our institutions and traditions. We don't want to put blinders on and be ignorant of the truly regrettable things that have happened throughout our history. We'll examine those things. We'll look, for example, at the tragedy of the Crusades. There is nothing that can be defended in that, or in the debasement of the Christian message throughout the medieval period. All of those things are part of the history and culture of the West and should not be ignored. But I want us to look at our culture in its totality and to not be blind as well to the very good legacies of the past, the things we should strive to preserve as part of the Western tradition.

In recent decades there has been a trend among academic elites to tear down and denigrate the "traditional" values of the western world. This trend sometimes hides beneath some really good labels—ideas that are hard to argue with when taken at face value. For example, the words "pluralism," "multiculturalism," and "diversity," are often used as code words for a liberal critique of western values. The terms themselves are neutral, but they're often used as weapons against people of traditional values and orthodox Christian belief. In the name of multiculturalism we are told that all religious beliefs are equal. In the name of tolerance, we are told that we can't tolerate expressions of faith in the public arena. These ideas, and these words, are wielded as weapons in these culture wars. And so we need to be equipped to understand what's at stake and be able to participate in that larger debate within society.

The emphasis on diversity within western society is not all bad. Some good things have come about as a result of this focus on pluralism. We are, after all, a diverse and inclusive society built on democratic values and individual rights. But these concepts have also been misused and misapplied. The very foundations of our culture are under systematic attack. We see radical new interpretations of western history. For example, radical feminist theory essentially turns western history into the sad story of patriarchal oppression. The theoretical model known as "post-colonialism" translates western history into an unrelenting account of the oppression of minority peoples by non-Western cultures. Of course, there are some valid points to be drawn from these critiques of the West, since all of human history is filled with oppression and exploitation. But do we need to throw the proverbial baby out with the bathwater? Is there nothing good and redeeming about western culture? This is what I'm arguing. And that's why there is an important cultural rationale for what we're studying.

There is also *an academic reason* to study the humanities. The humanities is foundational to what a liberal arts education is all about. In the humanities we draw on many fields of study, many specific disciplines, as we seek to understand the values of culture. Certainly we draw primarily on history, philosophy, and the study of the various arts; but we also analyze anything that could be relevant to the task of understanding a given culture, including political theory, economic theory, and the social sciences. Culture is our focus, and everything that takes us in that direction is fair game. We can summarize the academic reason by noting that the essence of a liberal arts education—the goal of being well educated in every field—is inseparable from the spirit of the humanities. I would further argue that training in culture and values uniquely equips us to work "humanely" within all of those disciplines. After all, we want our scientists to think about *values* when they're splicing genes in the laboratory.

There is, furthermore, *an emotional reason* for studying culture. God made us to be creatures who both *think* and *feel*, and we shouldn't forget this important truth. What we're embarked on when studying culture is not just an intellectual activity, a means of developing our minds. Rather, we should also be developing our capacity to feel more deeply about the world. We should seek to experience the world in the right

ways that God intended, not in the wrong, self-serving ways that Dr. Faust was attempting.

Unfortunately, this is something that Christians easily misunderstand. It's not wrong to experience the world, provided we experience it to the glory of God. That's the key, the dividing point between two kinds of experience. I should ask myself, "Can I experience this thing, this activity, to the glory of God?" If I apply that standard consistently through all the choices I face, then I'm establishing my life on a firm, biblical foundation.

" What about the arts ? I need to learn MORE than just obedience! "

Yes, we are to feel the world, to experience it, to have a greater capacity to enjoy the world. This doesn't mean that we should become *sentimental* in our outlook, but rather that we should cultivate *sentiment*. What's the difference? Sentiment is usually described or defined as "feeling governed by thought." I imagine that we're all uncomfortable with people who are excessively emotional about everything. Something bad happens and they fall apart and become hysterical. Then something exciting happens, and they start screaming at the top of their lungs, running around and hugging everybody. It strikes us as immoderate, and maybe downright strange, to react that intensely to everything in life. We expect a person to go through life governing their feelings by thought and to bring some rational perspective to their experiences. The study of culture and the arts enables us to do that and to understand the complexities of experience more clearly.

There's a final reason for studying culture and values—*the biblical reason*. God created us in His image, and that's one of the greatest theological mysteries debated by theologians for centuries. What does that mean that God has created us in His image? We don't know exactly, but I think we can agree that one aspect of the *imago Dei* (the image of God) is our creative capacity, the ability to appreciate and experience the richness of the world. This biblical rationale really does legitimize what we're studying. If God has created us with this capacity, then we are meant to exercise it. Psalm 19 says that the heavens declare the glory of God. Clearly the Psalmist was contemplating the beauty of the natural world and he was marveling at the beauty of God's creation. Anything that can help us to understand, appreciate, and express the beauty of what God has made should be a good thing for us. As we look at art, we will be analyzing the principles of beauty. Our goal should be to try to understand those principles of beauty that God has coded into His creation; we should take these principles from creation and use them in the creation and interpretation of art.

The New Testament tells us that God has not just created the world around us but He wants to re-create us as well. Paul describes the Christian as a "new creation" (2 Corinthians 5:17)—a work of art meant to bring glory to God. Paul says we are God's workmanship created in Christ Jesus unto good works (Ephesians 2:10). God is described as an artist who is turning our lives into a masterpiece. Let's connect the dots. If we are made in God's image, then He has made us all to be "artists," so to speak. You might not look at yourself as an artist; but

each one of us gives expression to our creativity in different ways. And in large measure those are the kinds of issues we'll be studying together as we follow the story of western culture.

THE RISE OF CIVILIZATION

Chapter Objectives

- Distinguish between the concepts of culture and civilization.
- Explain the nature and role of technology in the rise of civilization.
- Understand how urbanization and agriculture reshaped human societies.

In this chapter we're going to focus on the rise of civilization; but before we do, we'll need to define very carefully how "culture" differs from "civilization." If we go back to the so-called "prehistoric" people in France and Spain who painted animal murals in caves, or the people who built Stonehenge in the British Isles, we are speaking of *cultures* but not *civilizations*. Whoever painted those remarkable images of animals in France and Spain—whatever those cultures were and however they defined themselves—we can be sure of one thing: *they were not a civilization*. And so right at the outset we've got to distinguish between two terms that we've already been using. So, what is culture? And what is civilization?

Culture is the most basic of these terms and refers to the *sum total of shared attributes and shared values that bind a people together*, such as a common language, common beliefs, a common history, and common institutions. So consider the most "primitive" tribe you can think of in the jungles of the Amazon, and you've got a cul-

ture—but you won't have a civilization. That raises the question again: What, then, is a civilization? We'll see, as we define it, that the notion of **civilization** implies *complexity*. This will be clear in what we see happening between 4000 and 3000 B.C., which is the period we'll focus on as we examine the rise of civilization in the ancient world.

What Is Civilization?

So what is this term? What does it mean? Let's look at the definition given by an American historian, Will Durant, who defined civilization as "social order promoting cultural creation." That definition doesn't take us very far because you've got to qualify what it means; you've got to add a lot of subpoints that clarify what kind of social order and what kind of cultural creation is being promoted. But already implicit in those few words we can see the idea of complexity. Also lurking behind that definition is the idea of progress, which is something clearly associated with complex civilizations.

Durant does go on to define more specifically what he's talking by listing four elements that give shape to civilization. We can add the word *complex* to each one of his statements—and you'll see why it's really necessary to do this.

First of all, Will Durant speaks of *economic provision*. As I said, we need to add the word "complex" to this. Why? Well, consider how those prehistoric tribes that painted the images of animals must have had a form of economic provision. They were hunters, and that's why they focused on animals in their cave paintings. But they didn't have a complex mode of economic provision, the kind you'd need if providing for a large population base in an urban center. We're going to see that urban living is one of the distinguishing marks of civilization; and the only way to feed all those people congregated tightly together is with a complex system of gathering, storing, and distributing food, which is a far more complex system than you find in a hunting and gathering society.

Secondly, according to Will Durant, a civilization also implies *a complex political organization*. Now, again, the most basic tribe you can think of has a political structure: there will be a tribal chief and village elders. But with civilization we're really speaking of the whole apparatus of bureaucracy—levels of government that are involved in managing the complexities of political, social, economic, and religious life within society. Ancient Egypt, for example, had a highly developed imperial bureaucracy that made that civilization hum along rather nicely for centuries.

Thirdly, Durant tells us that a civilization will have *a body of moral traditions*. He's really speaking here of the complexity of a legal system, such as the Code of Hammurabi, which is one of the earliest written legal codes from this ancient period. We could also cite the legal code that's part of the law in the Old Testament, the Mosaic Law. All of this reflects the general trend toward complexity, as more and more people are living in urban centers. There are many opportunities for all kinds of social interactions that invariably require legal rulings, judgments, and guidelines. These moral and legal traditions arise, therefore, out of necessity to enable this new urban life to be possible.

Finally, according to Will Durant, we see in addition to these other elements, *the pur-* *suit of knowledge and the arts*. This is where that idea of progress comes into focus as civilizations develop institutions that cultivate and preserve knowledge. These cultural products of civilization will be the focus of our study in the following chapters.

As we examine the rise of civilization, we'll be looking at two revolutions that occurred at the dawn of recorded history. (Keep in mind that we're defining "history" here as the threshold when written records begin to be kept in a systematic way.) These two revolutions are the Urban Revolution and the Agricultural Revolution. We don't know exactly when this process began, but we read about in the book of Genesis when it says that "So-and-So went out and built cities." This is referring, somewhat obliquely, to this process of urbanization that began to occur in Mesopotamia, in Egypt, and throughout the larger Mediterranean world.

Technology and the Urban Revolution

What historians call the **Urban Revolution** is when people began to congregate in communities along the banks of the Nile and along the banks of the Tigris and Euphrates rivers. A number of distinct technologies made urbanization possible, though it's very much a chicken and egg kind of question as to which came first. Do the technologies come first or does urbanization? They seem to have happened almost in tandem, out of necessity as people solved the problems that developed inevitably with new way of living.

We're going to focus on seven technologies that occurred during the fourth millennium B.C., but this is not an exhaustive list at all. Still, it will be a pretty good representative list. I won't be presenting these in any particular order of priority except that the last technology we'll look at is clearly the most significant of the lot.

One basic technology that emerged in this period was the manufacturing of bricks. Now that may not set us back on our heels and strike us as a very impressive technology. For us, "technology" is the latest digital gadget, something that fits in our pockets and connects us to the world. That's our frame of reference—and that limits our understanding considerably. I want us to see that technology of all periods really functions in much the same way. We can reduce all **technology** to a simple formula:

Technology is the manipulation of raw materials to produce some benefit.

Whether it's a digital gadget or a sun-dried brick, technology involves harnessing the powers of nature and using them to create some greater benefit. When you manufacture bricks, you're taking the abundant clay that you have along the banks of the river, pressing it into molds, and letting the sun bake it. You're taking natural resources and manipulating them to create something beneficial to society.

Consider what the manufacture of bricks can do for an ancient civilization. Suddenly, you're able to build massive government complexes, the palaces and temples that we associate with Nineveh and the other cities of Mesopotamia and Ancient Egypt.

Ancient cities even had multi-storied apartment buildings in cities such as Ur. Archaeologists have excavated these in great detail. In Ur, for example, we see how sophisticated the manipulation of raw materials was. The lower bricks in a wall— that is, the bricks near the foundation— were baked in an oven for strength; the bricks placed upon that foundation were simply sun-dried, which is not quite as durable. There's a basic economic principle at

work here as well. Sun-dried bricks are easier and more economical to mass-produce than oven-baked bricks. This is a simple example, but it points to the complex interplay of technology, social needs, and economics. We see rational problem-solving here as natural resources are taken and manipulated to solve real-world problems. This is the spirit of progress that lies at the heart of the civilizational ideal.

The second technology that we can associate with this period is pottery and the development of the potter's wheel. Once again, this is not a terribly impressive technology to us, perhaps; but it is something that enabled ancient civilizations to accomplish a lot of really important things. If you have pottery, then you can store and preserve things. You can store oil, spices, and other kinds of products; you can carry water along desert trade routes, and so forth. More importantly, pottery enables you to standardize things, making commercial activity between cultures easier and more accurate. So clearly this is a technology that is deeply integrated into the complex economic life of ancient civilizations.

We read a lot about pottery as a metaphor in the Old Testament, such as when God speaks through Isaiah and Jeremiah, saying to the nation Israel, "I am the potter, and you are the clay." This is a vivid metaphor, and we understand it when we read the verses; but we don't feel it the same way as ancient people would have understood the metaphor. Pottery was of such vital importance that this expression would have carried much greater force of meaning within that ancient culture.

Third, we see the development of wheeled transportation. We sometimes speak of the invention of the wheel as though it's just an expression. We say, for instance, "I don't want to have to reinvent the wheel." The very way we toss the expression around casually masks the fact that the wheel was something that had to be invented at some point. Think of it this way. The wheel is not a naturally occurring phenomenon. You don't go walking through the woods and discover a wheel and then figure out how to put it to use. It's a technology that was abstracted from pure thought, perhaps by analogy to the way trees were used as simple conveyor belts. Trees were cut down, turned into logs, and laid side-by-side. Put enough of these together, and you can push along heavy objects. Someone must have imagined the wheel from the circularity of those logs. Of course, this is just a theory; no one patented the invention. But once again, we can see how this technology would have served the larger needs of a complex urban civilization.

Speaking of transportation, the development of the sailing ship is our fourth technology. The sail illustrates the point of how brilliantly simple these technologies were. At the base of it, technology is just taking natural resources and learning how to harness their power. So, you put a sail on the ship and you are harnessing the power of the wind—which is technology, plain and simple.

Now imagine what this will bring about as people venture out into the wider world. They will be able to communicate across vast stretches of ocean and transport goods to and from remote places. People will migrate and come into contact with other people around the Mediterranean. Any period of migration leads inevitably to a rapid expansion of ideas. It's a kick-start for civilization, since people are exchanging ideas and comparing notes, so to speak. When cultures come into contact, it's like cross-

pollination. You introduce something new into another culture; but, in turn, you also find something in that other culture that you bring back home. This exchange leads to an explosion of culture and a rise in the development of new ideas.

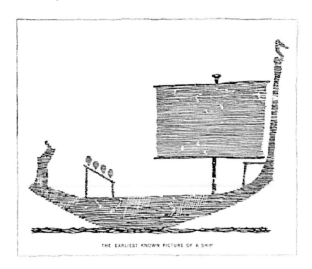

THE EARLIEST KNOWN PICTURE OF A SHIP

Fifth, we see another advance which we don't normally think of as a technology, and that's the domestication of animals. This, of course, is part of the larger agricultural revolution that we are going to look at in a moment. It's also something we read about and see alluded to in Genesis.

A sixth technology is the development of metal-working. Historians date vast periods of time in ancient cultures by reference to how natural substances were formed into tools and weapons. So historians speak of a Stone Age culture which is followed by a Bronze Age and an Iron Age. These are accurate terms that describe stages that every ancient culture invariably passed through. Whether you're talking about ancient China, the cultures of the New World, or sub-Saharan Africa, these are the stages that cultures pass through in a predictable fashion: first stone, then bronze, and finally iron. You can't leapfrog from stone to iron and bypass bronze altogether.

We get a hint of this in the Old Testament, where the Philistines are described as having more powerful weapons than the Israelites (1 Samuel 13:19-22). We now understand more fully what this means: the Philistines were more technologically advanced because they had passed from the Bronze Age to the Iron Age before Israel. Working with metal was the original arms race in the ancient world; those who worked with iron certainly were able to field the most powerful armies.

The seventh technology we're going to consider is the most important, and that is the development of writing. Like the wheel, writing is not a naturally occurring thing. Somebody had to come up with it, and in coming up with it people manipulate natural resources. You might take a piece of papyrus out of the swampy banks of the Nile and figure out how to turn that into a substance you can write on. And then you develop inks from other natural substances. But even before that you've got to have the abstract idea of what writing is—of putting symbols down so as to convey words and concepts to people who are not present or, for that matter, even born yet. Written messages can span vast stretches of time and space.

We take it for granted, but writing is a truly amazing invention. Just think about how someone can write a note, put it in a bottle, and throw it out in the ocean to be found sometimes many years later. It's an amazing thing that somebody can pluck that message out of the ocean and make contact with the mind of someone else they've never met—someone they only know through symbols on a piece of paper. That was the experience, of course, when archaeologists uncovered the libraries of ancient Nineveh in the nineteenth century and found vast quantities of cuneiform tablets. Once scholars were able to decode the script and the symbols, they began to enter into the intellectual and spiritual dimension of that ancient civilization. Only writing could make that possible.

Writing may be the most significant of all human inventions since it is really the basis of all other information technologies. It is the first of three great information revolutions, along with the invention of printing in the 15th century and the development of

digital technologies in our own lifetime. But the invention of writing is the foundation of all subsequent innovations in information. Writing transformed civilization; and we can predict, on the basis of what we see in history, that the revolutions and technologies that we're witnessing in information today will likewise have a profound and transforming impact on our own culture and on the very nature of human society itself.

When was writing developed? We don't know exactly, but scholars think that sometime close to the year 3200 B.C. writing began to emerge as a fully-fledged system. We also don't know exactly *where* writing was first developed, whether in Egypt or Mesopotamia; however, a consensus has formed among scholars that ancient Sumer in Mesopotamia was the likely cradle of writing and that the cuneiform script was was developed to meet the increasingly complex needs of commerce. Egyptian hieroglyphics probably developed shortly thereafter.

Hieroglyphics was the form of writing developed around 3200 B.C. in ancient Egypt. Scholars use the term **historical horizon** to describe the threshold we reach when writing was developed. The idea behind the term is that we're peering back through history towards the distant horizon, as far as we can see through a continuous written history that goes back to the time when the Egyptians started to tell their history of the dynasties around 3200 B.C. The pictograms that make up hieroglyphics stand for phonetic sounds. The story of how hieroglyphics was decoded is one of the great detective stories of modern archaeology—a story we'll take up in the next chapter when we look more closely at ancient Egypt.

Cuneiform was probably developed somewhat earlier than hieroglyphics. This form of writing emerged in the urban centers of Mesopotamia, along the banks of the Tigris and Euphrates rivers. Wedge-shaped markings were impressed upon the clay tablet while it was still wet. The tablets were then baked in an oven. These tablets have been found by the truckload in ancient Babylon, in ancient Nineveh, in ancient Ur, and the other urban sites of Mesopotamia. It took much of the 19th century for historians to figure out how to read cuneiform. Where would you begin to make sense of it? The markings look like what a bird would leave behind when running across wet clay! The decoding of cuneiform, like that of hieroglyphics, was another great intellectual detective story of the modern age. Our expanding knowledge of ancient history rests directly on these discoveries.

Tens of thousands of cuneiform tablets have been uncovered, though many more were destroyed in the careless early excavations of the 19th century. The first archaeologists were simply going for the gold, basically taking their pickaxes and just whacking through the ruins, shattering many tablets in the process. Still, many thousands have survived, though the vast majority (probably 90% of them) are records of routine, mundane business transactions. They record things like, "Tom sold Dick 10 bushels of barley and owes him three more at the next moon." But for the historian, ancient business transactions, legal documents and contracts, make for pretty exciting reading, since we can reconstruct the life of that society through the most mundane documents. One might have hoped for more historical records and great works of literature, though some of that has been found, too. In the next chapter we'll look at some of the Mesopotamian literature that was discovered that demonstrates some interesting parallels to the Old Testament.

The Agricultural Revolution

The new urban centers of Egypt and Mesopotamia were located along the fertile banks of great rivers, which reminds us that the urban revolution would not have been possible without the fundamental changes that agriculture brought about. Cities could not emerge without the means to feed a large, centralized, and growing population.

Agriculture radically affected the direction of human civilization in numerous ways, but I want to focus on two cultural byproducts: stability and "science."

First of all, agriculture produced stability within society. This is a logical inference that we can draw. If you're going to plant crops, then you'll likely stick around long enough to cultivate those crops, tend them, protect them, and then ultimately harvest them. By definition, agriculture presupposes that you'll put down both literal and figurative roots. A hunting and gathering people are going to be moving around based upon where the food supply is, the way migrating animals do. But if you start cultivating crops, you're going to become connected to the land in a territorial sense; your very identity will become connected to the land. The stability that comes from staying in one spot allows society to consolidate its resources, to grow and make progress.

The second byproduct is the more interesting one, I think: We can see a primitive form of scientific inquiry growing up out of the agricultural revolution. Of course, I'm not referring to science as we understand it today, with an emphasis on the empirical method of hypothesis and investigation. But nonetheless, we see that a rudimentary kind of science, based on observation and inquiry, does come about quite naturally when people begin to plant and harvest crops.

The process must have gone something like this. You're living along the banks of the Nile and you begin to notice year after year that the Nile is a very predictable thing. It floods, the water overruns the banks into the countryside, and then a little bit later in the year the water begins to recede once again and the water level goes down. Then you watch the next year and you see if the same thing happens; and when it does, you make another very important connection. You don't just look at what's happening on the ground, but you look up at the skies at the same time. You take note of how the constellations and planets are arranged. You write it down and then check it again next year. When the Nile floods again, you pull out your notes and you see that the night-sky looks the same as it did last year.

What are you doing? You're relating two natural phenomena; and that is what basic,

scientific observation is all about. On the basis of your observations and notes, you have now constructed an elementary calendar—another important early technology. Calendars were essentially planting and harvesting guides that correlated the earth and sky. We don't normally think of calendars as a means of predicting the future, but that's exactly what they are. You look at the calendar and you can predict when the leaves are going to fall, or when the buds are going to start pushing. In an ancient culture, this would be viewed as nothing less than magical. In ancient Babylon and Egypt the calendar-makers were the priests, because they were the ones who studied the zodiac. They were the ones who said it's time to plant; they were the keepers of that secret knowledge.

The fourth millennium B.C. was one of the greatest periods of human progress, spurred on by new technologies that rose out of the necessities of agriculture and urbanization. A futurist named Alvin Toffler gave us a nice way to put these transformations in the broader context of human history. In his book *The Third Wave* (1980), Toffler charted all of human history around three great transformations which he called "waves." He used the metaphor of a wave sweeping over the globe and transforming every aspect of human society in its wake.

The first of the waves that Toffler identified is what we've just been examining—the Agricultural Revolution. When this technology developed and spread, it certainly impacted every aspect of the political, social, economic, and religious life of early people. It dramatically changed the way people related to one another and how they related to the world. Most of human history has been lived under the agricultural wave.

What replaced agriculture as the economic basis of society? The Industrial Revolution, which spread outward from England in the 18th century, was the second wave that Toffler identifies. The process is continuing today as the remotest regions of the world are becoming industrialized. Once again, the basis of how people relate to the world and to one another was transformed by industrialization. Every institution of society was transformed on the basis of this new economic reality.

Alvin Toffler's point was to bring us up to the present. We're living now under the third great wave, the Information Revolution. I really like this way of classifying human history under three main categories. Of course, it involves an oversimplification; but there's much truth here as well. This framework of history can help us navigate through the present. We can infer from what we see in the past that what we are experiencing in our world today is just as cataclysmic, just as consequential as the development of agriculture thousands of years ago and the process of industrialization during the past two or three centuries. We know that the Information Revolution (the third wave) will have that same transforming effect. But since we are living through it, we can't necessarily gauge what the effects are going to be; nevertheless, we know that the way we relate to one another is changing in fundamental ways.

Look at the digital revolution and the way we communicate instantly now. Does that affect the way we interact and relate? Is this technology somehow altering the nature of our relationships? Absolutely. Think of the Internet. Does this global network affect the political realities of the world around us? Of course it does. The ability to get and exchange information is having a profound political effect. We can predict, then, that these new technologies will have a major effect upon the very shape of human society, though we can't be dogmatic as to what exactly that effect will be. Still, we can be confident that it will be as profound as the first two "waves."

All of this underscores once again the importance of looking at the past and studying its lessons. The past can give us a framework for understanding the present—for making sense of what we're experiencing right now as a culture and for navigating through the uncertain waters that lead into the future.

18

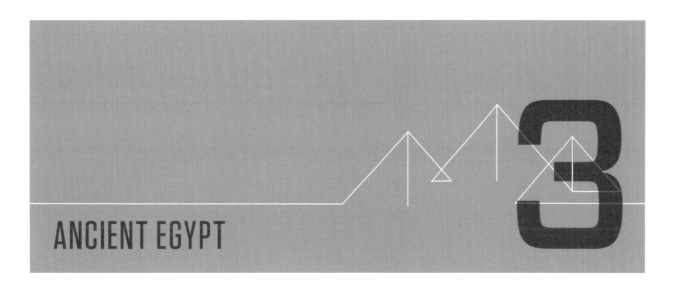

ANCIENT EGYPT

Chapter Objectives

- Describe how archaeology has reconstructed our knowledge of the past.
- Define the central value of ancient Egyptian culture.
- Analyze the principles that governed ancient Egyptian art.

We saw in the last chapter that the distinction between culture and civilization is significant. A level of sophistication is implied by the term civilization that involves complex social, political, and economic structures that you don't find in the concept of culture in and of itself. We also saw that certain technologies emerged in the fourth millennium B.C. that made life in urban centers possible. People began to settle down along the banks of the Nile in Egypt, along the banks of the Tigris and Euphrates in Mesopotamia; and with this urban and agricultural revolution, human history and human culture were transformed in some very dramatic ways. In this chapter we'll be looking at the fruit of this progress as we focus on two early civilizations. We'll look first at Sumer, which is the oldest civilization in Mesopotamia; we'll conclude by surveying the rich culture of ancient Egypt. These civilizations are interesting in and of themselves; but our main focus, as always, will be on the story of western culture. In the end, we'll be concerned with how these ancient civilizations provided a backdrop for the rise of the western world. Western culture drew from the deep wells of earlier civilizations—especially from Egypt; but western civilization also diverged in some very significant ways, as we'll see, from the values and beliefs of the ancient Egyptians.

Sumerian Civilization

We're going to be looking first at Sumer, the oldest civilization of Mesopotamia. This is the area of modern-day Iraq where two great rivers, the Tigris and the Euphrates, flow into the Persian Gulf. The word **Mesopotamia** means "the land between the rivers," referring to the rich, fertile soil between those two rivers where early agricultural settlements grew into powerful civilizations.

One of the most interesting things about ancient Sumer is that nobody even knew it existed until the nineteenth century; it had literally disappeared beneath the sands of modern-day Iraq. The great archaeological expeditions of the nineteenth century were focused on this area of ancient Babylon and Nineveh. Under the archaeologists spade, a whole civilization was uncovered that had been lost to history. The more scholars learned, the more they realized how complex that civilization really was. Scholars now recognize how much Sumer influenced the civilizations that rose up in its shadow. Doubtless, the invention of writing was the greatest legacy of ancient Sumer.

Once again, this enormous legacy was largely unknown until fairly recent times. Ironically, though, the Sumerians were there all along, right in front of us, even if they weren't recognized as such. Many Bible scholars believe that one obscure place-name in Genesis refers to Sumer. In Genesis 11:2, for example, we read about a place called "Shinar," which may be a reference to Sumer. It's interesting to note how this civilization, long covered by the sands of the desert, was still preserved as a historical record in the Old Testament. This makes a lot of sense, of course, since Abraham came out of this Mesopotamian world—though he would have lived many centuries after the first flowering of Sumerian culture. The pioneering archaeologists and historians who uncovered Sumer and began to reconstruct its distant history recognized that this culture formed the immediate backdrop to what we read about in the opening pages of the Bible. Genesis tells us that Abraham came from Ur of the Chaldees—and Ur is a Sumerian city.

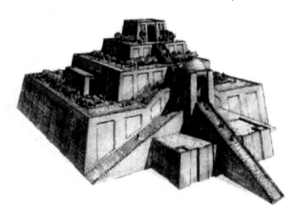

Much of the Sumerian literature that was discovered, decoded, and translated, provides direct backdrops and parallels to things that we read about in scripture. Among Sumerian poetry, for example, you can read an elegy that describes the destruction of Ur; scholars have noted how much it sounds like the book of Lamentations in the Bible, the elegy that Jeremiah wrote at a much later time about the fall of Jerusalem. And that suggests again that a common culture, a very ancient one, lies behind the literary traditions and styles we find in the Old Testament.

Sometimes the parallels are much more concrete and spectacular, such as the famous **ziggurats**, or temples, that once rose up from the fertile plains of Mesopotamia. The ruins of these can still be seen today in modern Iraq. Many biblical scholars believe that these ziggurats are described in Genesis 11, where we read about the Tower of Babel. Certainly Mesopotamia was an ancient center not only of idolatry but also of cultural sophistication and technological advancement.

Sumerian literature also relates stories that run parallel to what we read about in the Old Testament, such as the story of the creation of man, the Great Flood, and the long lives of the patriarchs in Genesis.

The most famous of all of the cuneiform tablets dug from the remains of these Mesopotamian cultures is known as the **Deluge Tablet**, because this tablet relates to us the Sumerian account of the Great Flood that we read about in Genesis. Biblical scholars disagree about the nature of the parallels and how exactly we should relate these to the Old Testament; but there is no doubt that there is a common culture between the Old Testament and Mesopotamia.

In this connection, we should take note of the single greatest work of literature that has been uncovered from this culture. We know it as the **Epic of Gilgamesh**. In this often moving story of a hero-king named

Gilgamesh, we read the Sumerian account of the Great Flood. In fact, the Deluge Tablet is a fragment from that very story. The Epic of Gilgamesh is recognized as the one of the oldest works of literature—and one of the greatest ever written about some of the central questions that man considers and contemplates as he looks at the world around him and reflects upon his own mortality.

Ancient Egyptian Civilization

We'll look a little more closely at our second example of early civilization, Egypt. We know much more about this culture, since it seems that people have always been fascinated by Egypt, from antiquity right down to the present. There's no forgetting the ancient Egyptians. They never disappeared beneath the sand; you can't overlook the pyramids on the horizon, or the Sphinx, or any of the other great monuments they left behind. Not to mention, who isn't fascinated by mummies? So, unlike to Sumerians, we have always known about ancient Egypt. But we have not always been able to read the hieroglyphic texts and inscriptions; once the secret of hieroglyphics was cracked, scholars were able to make great advances in our knowledge of the ancient world. Modern scholars have begun to realize how indebted western culture is to the civilization that emerged along the Nile. That's what we want to see as we focus our attention on Egypt.

We date the beginning of Egyptian history to this period that we have called the historical horizon, roughly the year 3200 B.C. This makes Egypt one of the oldest continuous civilizations in all of human history. What's significant about that 3200 B.C.? This was around the time writing was developed; but it's also the period of the **First Dynasty**—when the lower kingdom and the upper kingdom of Ancient Egypt were unified under a single ruler, a single Pharaoh.

The upper kingdom of Egypt is in the southern part, and the lower kingdom of Egypt is in the north, where the Nile feeds into the Mediterranean. It seems a little counterintuitive to place "Upper Egypt" in the south and "Lower Egypt" in the north. But these designations refer to the flow of the Nile. As you move up towards the source of the Nile, you are moving into Upper Egypt, even though you are going south. And then as you go down the Nile to where it empties into the Mediterranean, you are in Lower Egypt.

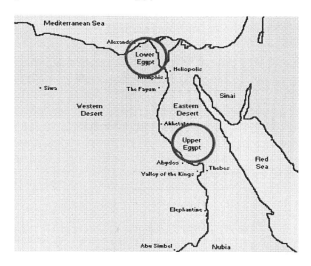

These were separate kingdoms in the fourth millennium B.C. and they were unified under Narmer, the first Pharaoh of the First Dynasty. One of the earliest and most significant artifacts from the earliest period of unified Egyptian history, the so-called **Narmer Palette**, commemorates this event. This clay tablet dates from around 3150 B.C. and is etched with images of conquest on front and back. It tells the story by depicting Narmer himself taking a club in his hand and bashing out the brains of his defeated enemy. Obviously, it's a very brutal projection of power that's depicted here—violent propaganda, which is something we often see in the official art of ancient empires.

We should notice how fully developed Egyptian styles and symbols already are at this early period of its history, as depicted on the Narmer Palette. The traditional representation of the Egyptian gods, for example, is already well established. This suggests a long prehistory of development before historical Egypt finally comes into focus around 3200 B.C. This imagery, which is so characteristic of ancient Egypt, would persist through its long history—for 3000 years, right up to the time of the "last of the Pharaohs," Cleopatra, in the generation before the birth of Christ.

Egyptian culture held together for so many centuries because it was organized around a "big idea"—a core set of values and beliefs. Before we look at the big idea that organized and animated Egyptian culture, we should consider briefly the sources of our knowledge. How do we know what we know about this ancient culture? One artifact, in particular, the Rosetta Stone, was the critical element in the painstaking process of deciphering the lost language of Egyptian hieroglyphics.

The **Rosetta Stone** is one of the prized possessions of the British Museum, and it was the key that enabled the code of hieroglyphics to be cracked. When Napoleon's army was in Egypt in the late 18th century, a French officer found a basalt stone embedded in the banks of the Nile. The stone ultimately made its way to the British Museum in London, and it took 23 years of

work before the inscriptions on the stone were ultimately deciphered. What's so special about the Rosetta Stone? If you look closely at the illustration, you can see that it is divided into three sections. That's because the stone is inscribed in three separate languages. Scholars recognized that the same text was written in three scripts; conveniently, one of those scripts was ancient Greek. Scholars have always known how to read Greek; but the knowledge of the other two languages—hieroglyphics (the priestly script of ancient Egypt) and demotic (the commercial script) had been lost in antiquity.

By using Greek as the key, these unreadable scripts were gradually decoded through trial and error. It took a very long time, but the hard work paid off and a lost treasure house of knowledge was opened up as a result. When scholars could finally read hieroglyphics, they could start making sense of everything that was inscribed on monuments and obelisks, on the walls of the tombs of the Pharaohs, and in papyrus manuscripts. Most of what we know about ancient Egypt is ultimately the product of this scholarly detective work.

The Quest for Permanence

A single big idea, one controlling value, seems to account for the uniqueness of ancient Egyptian culture. That idea, which is reflected in its traditions, institutions, art, and religion—can be described as *the quest for permanence*, the striving for the eternal, for the unchanging principle that governs the cosmos. Ancient Egyptians saw this principle reflected in the desert and the Nile, both of which seemed permanent and fixed; and they strove to mimic that permanence in their social, political, and artistic institutions. This idea must have occurred quite naturally to people living by the banks of the Nile. Every year the Nile floods and the waters recede—year after year, generation after generation, century after century. The Nile is so regular that you might begin to think that the whole world is like this—governed by unchanging laws and eternal principles. The desert, too, stretched for hundreds of miles at their backs—and the desert doesn't change very much either. Egyptian values may have emerged through their interaction with the environment around them. We'll never know, of course, but that's one theory at least. We do know, however, that this concept was very important to them and it was reflected in everything they did.

Let's consider three examples that illustrate this concept of a permanent, unchanging cosmic order. Consider first the most enduring architectural achievement of ancient Egypt, the pyramids. The oldest of these structures are nearly 5000 years old, built as early as 2800 B.C. An Arab proverb expresses their antiquity well: "Man fears Time, but Time fears the pyramids." It seems that the pyramids have always been there, and they're not going to disappear anytime soon.

Let's put their vast age in perspective. There was a Greek historian named He-rodotus, back in the Golden Age of ancient Greece 2500 years ago, who traveled around the known world and wrote a travelogue about what he saw. He went to Babylon and described the ziggurats and the other monuments that still survived. He traveled to ancient Egypt and wrote about the wonders along the Nile, such as the great pyramids at Giza. Herodotus was writing these things five centuries before Christ—and he describes the pyramids then as "ancient." They were as far removed from Herodotus as Herodotus is from us.

So, clearly, these ancient structures were built to last. This should tell us something. Obviously, they were built as a resting place for the Pharaohs for their eternal life in the afterworld. But more than that, they were built this way as a concrete expression of permanence and eternity. Even the geometric form of the pyramid suggests this. There is no more stable or permanent structure than a pyramid resting on a flat plane. Everything about these structures—their form and their function—expresses a *value*, which (in this case) is the idea that the cosmos is unchanging and eternal.

The most famous of the pyramids in Giza, Egypt is the one known as Cheops. This is the biggest, the most impressive, and the oldest, dating to as early as 2800 B.C. We don't know exactly how the structure was built and what technology was used; that's one of the great mysteries of the ancient world. At this time in their history, Egyptians hadn't developed the technology of the wheel, and yet they were building pyramids. All kinds of theories have been put forward—some good ones and a few really bad ones, like the claim that alien technology was responsible! Why do foolish ideas like this ever gain a hearing? Partly because modern people tend to undervalue the accomplishments of ancient civilizations; we think they could not possibly have done the things they did because they lived so far from our own time. We sit on our little perches and look down at these earlier civilizations and call them "primitive." And that's one of the reasons why I think these bogus ideas are given some currency. If we can't explain some accomplishment, then it must be the work of alien intelligence, right?

Well, not so fast. Obviously, the ancient Egyptians had the technology and mathematical skill to pull this off. They must have used various forms of pulleys and other devices to transfer weight. It took about twenty years to build a pyramid this size, so a Pharaoh would have to start building his tomb pretty early in his reign for it to be ready by his death. Some pyramids, in fact, were completed after the pharaoh's death and the body was then posthumously transported and reburied. It was so expensive and labor-intensive to build these, that pharaohs quit building pyramids very early in Egyptian history. Tombs were then built in underground chambers, such as the most famous one of all, the tomb of Tuthankhamun. It's ironic that what impresses tourists the most today—the great pyramids along the Nile—are not representative of the whole of Egyptian history, but just of the earliest period.

Cheops stood as the tallest man-made structure in the world until the nineteenth century—that is, until the rise of modern steel architecture such as the Eiffel Tower in Paris. And one more fact: Cheops is the only one of the so-called Seven Wonders of the Ancient World that is still standing. The Great Colossus of Rhodes, the Hanging Gardens of Babylon, the Great Lighthouse of Alexandria—all these were very impressive structures. But earthquakes and pillage have taken their toll. These are nothing but ruins now, even while Cheops continues to stand, having lost nothing more than a few feet off the top by erosion. It's worth repeating: *the pyramids were built to last*.

But we can turn to a second example to illustrate this Egyptian concept of permanence. What comes to mind most readily when we think of ancient Egypt? Mummies, probably. More than anything, this is what has captured the popular imagination. Every time the treasures of King Tut's Tomb go on international tour, people line up for several city blocks to get into the museum. The tomb of King Tutankhamun, discovered by Howard Carter in the 1920s, fired the imagination of the public—and Hollywood filmmakers as well. It was a cultural phenomenon, and it helped to spark a resurgence of interest in ancient Egypt. The discovery of King Tut's tomb was one of the great achievements of archaeology, and it remains the only time that an intact tomb of a pharaoh has been found. All the others had been opened and looted of their treasures in ancient times. When Howard Carter broke the seal on the door in 1922, he became the first person to step inside that tomb in nearly 3500 years. Everything was in the same pristine state as the day when Tutankhamun was buried around 1323 B.C. Even the flowers left on top of his sarcophagus were there—and the color of the dried flowers was still visible!

Mummification was an important practice, and it was not reserved just for Pharaohs. Anybody who could afford the process was mummified in death. And not just people, but animals were preserved as well. Cats, rats—pretty much anything that moved was a good candidate for mummification. The Egyptians perfected the science of preservation; they did such a good job that some of these mummies are extremely well preserved. Why this obsession with the highly complex process of preserving the body? Here, again, we see this central cultural value, the idea of permanence, lying behind the practice. They sought to usher the body into the afterlife, to prepare it for its journey down the River of the Dead, and preserve it for all eternity.

The mask of King Tut is a spectacular work of art, but also a reminder of the lavish attention which the Egyptians paid to the ceremonies of death and bodily preservation. A lot of effort and money were invested in artifacts like this, which should point us again to the concept of value. Where you see money spent, that's where you see value. And that's how we're going to approaching culture throughout the rest of this book, by following this simple logic—namely, to follow the money trail, as it were, in order to figure out what really drives a given culture. The wealth poured into King Tut's tomb (and all the other tombs that were looted in ancient times) demonstrates what the Egyptians valued.

We shouldn't fail to note just how opposite this concept is to what we read about in the Old Testament. We read, for example, in Psalm 49:17 or Ecclesiastes 5:15 that "we came into this world with nothing, and we're going to leave this world with nothing." The reason why that is stated with such emphasis in the Old Testament is because most of the pagan religions among the nations surrounding Israel asserted that you could take it all with you when you died. That's why the tombs of the pharaohs were loaded up with so much loot. King Tut was a fairly minor pharaoh, and yet the wealth of his tomb was utterly amazing. All the things that King Tut would need in the afterlife were there, overlaid with gold. Of course, he would need to sit down; so he had a golden chair. He would need servants; so there were little statues that were supposed to come to life magically and wait upon his every need. So, when scripture says emphatically that you can't take it with you, we need to read that statement against the background of the value system of ancient civilizations.

Our third example of this central value is more abstract. We see the idea of permanence in the art—the paintings and sculptures—of ancient Egypt. In fact, we believe that personal images were painted on the walls of tombs and that the likeness of a Pharaoh was included on his sarcophagus for one simple reason: to preserve that person's identity for the afterlife. The Egyptian word for sculptor literally means "one who preserves," and so their art really functioned as part of their overall religious beliefs and practices. As we look a little more closely at the Egyptian practice of art, we're going to examine two works, a painting and a sculpture.

First, let's examine the "Painting of a Pond," which is a wall painting from a tomb in Thebes. (See Color Illustration A.) This painting dates from around 1400 B.C., which is roughly 50 years or so before the birth of King Tut. As we analyze this work of art, let's try to see what's distinctively Egyptian about it. Let's see what we can learn about the Egyptian mind as we try to make sense of why they painted the world around them in such a "peculiar" way.

The painting simply depicts a pond in the middle of a garden. In the water we see ducks and fish; all around the rectangular pond are garden trees and shrubs. What strikes us as particularly unusual when we first look at this painting? It looks flat and two-dimensional to us. But there's more that's strange as well, at least from our point of view. Let's analyze the painting by focusing on its sense of perspective. Perspective is an important concept in art, and we'll have occasion to come back to it later. **Perspective** simply means the angle from which you see something. From our modern western point of view, the perspective in this Egyptian painting is altogether wrong. We expect a painting to show us a single perspective, the one angle from which the painter is seeing the world.

When I look at a landscape by van Gogh, I expect to see exactly what the painter was looking at when he set up his easel in the open air. I expect to stand, figuratively speaking, where he was standing and to look through his eyes at that landscape in the south of France. Ancient Egyptian art doesn't meet those expectations we have. It gives us multiple perspectives. How so? Well, consider the perspective from which we're looking at the pond itself. We're looking *down* at it from an aerial perspective—as though it's a sunken pond and we're standing next to it, looking down at its rectangular shape. But how are we looking at the fish? We're looking at them from the *side*, unless these are dead fish floating on their side on top of the pond (which we can be pretty sure is not the case). We're looking at fish the way you see them through the glass of an aquarium. This is multiple perspective, because we're simultaneously looking down at the pond and sideways at the fish. The perspective seems all wrong to us. It's illogical. We can't look at the world from multiple perspectives simultaneously, since we have only one pair of eyes.

Now either the ancient Egyptians were completely unsophisticated and incompetent in their approach to art because they hadn't yet figured these things out, or they knew full well what they were doing and chose to paint this way for reasons that made good sense to them. What's the best answer? You should be able to see where I'm going with this. It's never a good starting point to assume that other cultures do things differently because they are "unso-

phisticated" or "childlike" in their view of the world. Presumably, any culture that could build pyramids that we still can't explain would have been able to draw like Michelangelo if they had wanted to. The key here is that *they didn't want to*. The Egyptians took a different approach to art because they were expressing different values. We shouldn't expect that *our* way of doing art is binding on anyone else. Egyptian art, like the art of every culture, operates according to its own laws of order and perspective, because the art is expressing values unique to that culture.

So why did the Egyptians opt for multiple perspective? How does this express their value system? Scholars believe that Egyptian painters and sculptors were trying to depict objects from their most characteristic angle—that is, from the angle we "see" things mentally, in our mind's eye. Of course, that just begs another question: Why are they doing that? Trust me, we'll try to pull that together and connect the dots in just a second; but, first, let's think a little bit more about what it means to paint an object from its most characteristic angle. Imagine that I had asked you to take out a piece of paper—before we ever discussed Egyptian art—and said, "Draw a fish for me in thirty seconds or less." What would you do? Once you got over your bewilderment at my question, you would probably draw a fish the way the Egyptians did—from the side. You'd draw a fish that looked something like this (though yours probably wouldn't have as goofy an expression as mine does):

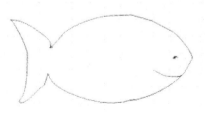

You'd draw it like this because that's the most characteristic way we "see" a fish in our mind when we think. In fact, I *know* you would draw it this way, because I have performed this little experiment in class before. And guess what? I ended up with a hundred or so Egyptian fish! Nobody drew a fish the way it would look if you looked down at it, or looked at it straight ahead or from behind. Of course, you'll always get somebody who's creative or eccentric—somebody who tries to subvert the assignment by drawing a crazy cartoon fish with bulging eyes; but then the exception just proves the rule. If you have to draw a fish out of your mind, then you'll draw one like the Egyptians did. When you reach into the back of your mental filing system and pull up the file labeled "Fish," this is what you see. And then you would draw that fish, the mental fish, from its most characteristic angle—as *a symbol of the idea of a fish*.

That's fine and good, but we still haven't answered the question of why they're doing this. Why is it that they painted and sculpted things from the most characteristic angle? Well, that question leads us to the heart of the matter. Scholars have offered a convincing interpretation of this—namely, that Egyptian art is all about *painting what the mind knows, not what the eye sees*. When I say "fish," you pull up a mental idea and then you put that down on paper as a symbol of something that is permanent, unchanging, and eternal. So, once again, why does the Egyptian artist do this? Because this approach to art is consistent with his view of the world; it's consistent with his value system. The Egyptians believed in the eternal principle of the universe, the unchanging order of things, and they strove after that central value in everything they did. They are depicting the unchanging form of things—the eternal form of a fish, if you will. It's the mental construct of that object that Egyptian art is giving us. Suddenly, when looked at this way, Egyptian art looks a whole lot more sophisticated than we first thought. It doesn't matter to the Egyptian that the painting is not "realistic," that you don't see fish like this when standing over a pond looking down. That's

completely irrelevant to what the Egyptian artist is trying to do. He is creating a collage, so to speak, of abstract mental concepts that are eternally existing.

As we turn our attention to the human form, we'll see this same concept on display. So, let's look at our second example of Egyptian art, the portrait of Hesire, which dates from a much earlier period, roughly 2700 B.C. (See the illustration below.) This portrait demonstrates the characteristic Egyptian style of depicting the human body. It appears contorted and unnatural to us. The shoulders are turned to the front; the legs are turned sideways; and all four limbs are visible in profile. The head, too, is shown in profile with one eye looking outward. If you try to stand this way, you'll find it quite uncomfortable. Did people walk around ancient Thebes like this? No, of course not. So why is the body depicted is such an unrealistic way? Were they unsophisticated in their style of art? Again, this is never a very good answer when analyzing different cultures. We must assume that the Egyptians knew what they were doing and did it deliberately.

Clearly, they were not trying to depict the world as they saw it. Instead, they were depicting the human body in the same way the painter showed us the pond—as a composite of different elements imagined from their characteristic angles. What is the characteristic way of thinking of the upper body? What is the characteristic angle of the feet, of the limbs? These are shown in their fully articulated forms. The head is in profile because this, to the ancient observer, was the most characteristic way to imagine the head. The body is fully represented with all its parts functioning, because this is how you wanted to go into the afterlife. The Egyptian artist would never "hide" an arm or leg behind the body, even though the eye may see it that way from the side. If art is a preservative, then you wouldn't want to send somebody into the afterlife like that—with one arm or one leg. You want to enter the afterlife with two legs, two arms, with the body fully formed, and that's why we see every characteristic element of the body. The only exception we see here is the single eye, as it must have seemed too strange even to the ancient Egyptians to depict two eyes on the side of the head!

We might disagree with the ancient Egyptians as to whether or not the head in profile is the most characteristic angle of the head. If I were to ask you to draw a *head*, you would probably draw a *face*. In the modern age we've become very much oriented towards thinking of the face as equivalent to one's identity. But the ancient Egyptians would have seen the profile as the distinctive way to think of a head. The portrait of Hesire, then, is really a composite construction; it's not meant to be viewed as a realistic rendering of the human form, and so it's unfair and unhistorical to analyze it on those terms. Rather, the portrait must be viewed as a symbolic image that preserves for the afterlife.

The term **frontality** is used to describe this Egyptian style of depicting the human body. This refers to the way the human body is given a frontal orientation—the way the shoulders are squared and the torso is *fronted*. A complex **canon** of rules governed every aspect of this style. Artists didn't make the rules up for themselves, but followed ancient codes and guidelines based on elaborate ratios. The young art student would have learned the proper ratio of the upper body to the lower, of the head to the trunk, and the ratio of the limbs. All this was governed by fixed rules; the canon was immutable and unchanging—just the way the ancient Egyptians understood the cosmos to be. This is why we see relatively little change in the style of Egyptian art over the many centuries of its history.

I have presented the consensus view of scholars, which is our best guess in explaining all the data. This interpretation of Egyptian art is not a blind guess, however; it's consistent with the larger pattern of Egyptian culture. They built structures that have lasted for thousands of years. They preserved bodies with elaborate care. It stands to reason, then, that their art as well would reflect the idea of an eternal, unchanging, moral structure of the cosmos. It's worth emphasizing again that this is what we do when we study a culture: We look at all the information we have and then try to identify the underlying patterns, the systems of belief, the *values*, that make sense of it all.

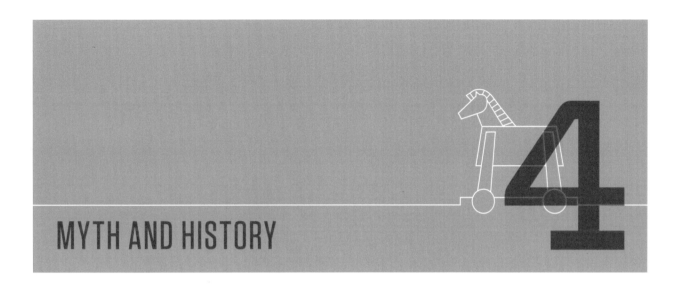

MYTH AND HISTORY

Chapter Objectives

- Explain how the Minoans and Mycenaeans relate to western civilization.
- Defend the proposition that myths often contain historical truth.
- Describe how cultures define themselves through myths and epics.

In the last chapter we looked at two ancient civilizations—Sumer and Egypt. Once scholars figured out how to read cuneiform and hieroglyphics, our knowledge of these two civilizations increased tremendously. Sumer was essentially rediscovered in the nineteenth century; but Egypt has always been there in our memory and imagination. It's been impossible to forget Egypt, given the scale of its monuments and the incredible continuity of its civilization—all the way from 3000 B.C. down to the time of Christ.

So we focused our attention on Egypt with two things primarily in mind. First, we were interested in the connections between ancient Egypt and the rise of western civilization. This point was only hinted at in the last chapter; but it will be developed more fully as we examine the rise of ancient Greece. We're going to find that when the Greeks began to build, they looked to Egyptian techniques as their model; when they developed their own traditions of art, they initially followed the techniques and styles

of the cultural superpower of the Mediterranean, which was Egypt.

There's a second reason why we focused on Egypt—and that's because Egypt illustrates very clearly what we do when we study a culture. We look at the artifacts, we look at their institutions, and we try to figure out what the common denominator is. We try to put our finger on the values that lie at the base of the culture and all it produces. We discovered that the quest for permanence, the belief in an eternal cosmic structure, held their world together. Their political and social structures, no less than their ways of painting and sculpting, reflected this core set of values and beliefs.

In this chapter, we're going to be looking at two more ancient civilizations that will bring us to the very doorstep of western culture. We'll be looking first at the culture of a seafaring people called the Minoans who were centered on the island of Crete. Then we'll transfer our attention to the culture of the Mycenaeans who were centered on the mainland of Europe, the area of the Aegean. This is the same region where ancient Greek culture would emerge—the place we traditionally call "the cradle of western civilization." You'll notice a recurring theme as we examine these two pre-western cultures—namely, the curious relationship between myth and history. Scholars believe that myths often contain a kernel of history; and once you peel away the fantastic details about monsters and giants and so on, then you'll find that something historical must have motivated that myth in the first place. Myths and stories, then, become one more "artifact" that we can analyze when reconstructing the values of a culture. We'll be looking back, through the mists of myth and lore, just as the ancient Greeks themselves did when they remembered the people who came before them.

Minoan Civilization

The Minoans were a seafaring people centered on the island of Crete, in the middle of the Mediterranean, sometime between 2600-1100 B.C. Of course, these are very rounded dates; you know we're working with phony figures when the dates are that nicely rounded and they all end in zeros. But that's as precise as we can be.

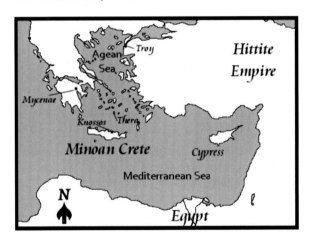

Notice that our dates have them surviving down to 1100 B.C. That's a little bit misleading, though, since a great catastrophe in the 17th century B.C. nearly wiped them completely off the map. (But more about that shortly.)

Nineteenth-century archaeologists managed to bring the Minoans back into the light, much as they had with the Mesopotamians and Egyptians. The palace at Knossos in Crete was one of the great excavations that yielded curious and sensational discoveries during that "golden age" of archaeology in the late 19th and early 20th centuries.

When this citadel was excavated, a multi-level palace was revealed—an enormous structure with royal chambers decorated with colorful wall paintings.

The palace even had a "basement" that was an intricate, honeycomb of storage rooms that Sir Arthur Evans, the British archaeologist, immediately associated with Greek mythology. As he excavated the site, Evans remembered the story of how ships would appear on the horizon in Greece, and youth would be carried away into slavery to be sacrificed to a half-man and half-bull monster called the **Minotaur**. This creature roamed in the lower depths of a structure known as the **labyrinth**. Modern scholarship has shown over and over again that myths often contain some kernel of historical truth; and this story, too, as fantastic as it is, no doubt records distantly recalled memories that the Greeks had of the Minoans.

Let's try to fit this together. We can be sure that there was never a bull-like monster living in this structure; but we do know, based upon the archeological evidence of sculpture and wall paintings, that the Minoans seemed to worship the image of the bull. And so that's an interesting correlation right there—a detail that's verified or validated by the myth. We also know that youth were taken into slavery from the Aegean islands of Greece; furthermore, this complex structure that looks like a maze is hard to ignore. And so, even in a story like this, there can be real historical information that's verifiable through excavation. This means that we can throw myth into the mix when we look at the ancient past and try to reconstruct scientifically what happened in an ancient culture.

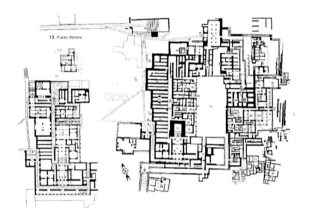

The ancient Greeks remembered the Minoans; they continued telling these stories long after the Minoans had passed off the scene. The Greeks remembered the wealth and power of this civilization, and so they told stories about one of the island's legendary rulers, King Midas with his so-called golden touch. We still speak today of having "the Midas touch." Once again, the myth records something that is historical—namely, the wealth and prestige of the Minoan civilization.

Now we said that the Minoans were a seafaring culture and we said also that the last centuries of their rule were just a faint reflection of their glory days. What happened to them? Scholars believe, and we now have good evidence to support this view, that the height of their civilization came to a cataclysmic end in the late 17th century B.C., even though Minoan culture might

have straggled on for a few more centuries. Scholars are even more precise than this, claiming that it was probably around the year 1628 B.C. when the Minoan civilization was largely destroyed. Now how can we conclude that? There are no written records of what happened to the Minoans, no eyewitness accounts of the events of 1628 B.C. And yet we are fairly confident of the details, which makes this another one of those remarkable historical detective stories. Different converging lines of evidence have led us to a point where we know more, in a sense, about what happened to the Minoans than the ancient Greeks probably did—even though they lived much closer to the Minoans than we do.

Let's put the pieces together. We're all familiar with the story that Plato first told in the fourth century B.C. The great philosopher told of a civilization, a city named Atlantis, that was cataclysmically submerged beneath water. Ever since Plato related that myth, people have wondered whether there might have been such a place. Could there possibly be any historical truth lurking behind the obviously fantastic story? Scholars today are pretty sure that there is something historical there—not the way Disney has portrayed it, of course, and not even the way Plato recounted the details over two thousand years ago—but historical truth, nonetheless.

Marine archaeologists discovered around the islands of Crete that there are submerged portions of cities beneath the waterline; obviously, these ruins were submerged in some great catastrophe. These are not whole cities like Atlantis; but nonetheless the ruins point to a great natural disaster in which human settlements were washed under by the waves.

The final piece of scientific evidence has to do with the volcano known as Akrotiri, about 100 miles north of Crete. If you look at an aerial shot of the island, you'll see that the volcano itself is now a blown-out crater that was filled in by the Mediterranean. The eruption is believed to have been one of the most destructive of all volcanic disasters in history. The great eruption of Krakatoa in the Pacific in the nineteenth century would have been on a similar scale. That explosion was heard two thousand miles away—and Akrotiri is believed by some to be as much as two times more powerful than Krakatoa. So clearly this was a major event that would have created enormous tidal waves. It would have swept out across the Mediterranean, devastated all of the low-lying areas, not just in Crete, but probably throughout the coastline of the entire Mediterranean world.

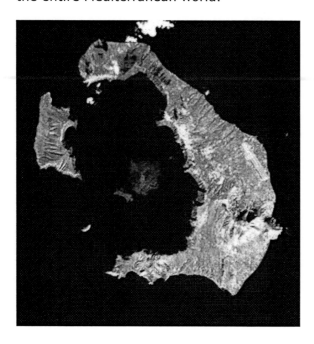

How can we date this eruption so precisely to around 1628 B.C.? There are no eyewitness accounts and no historical records of the event. This makes sense, of course, given the radical discontinuity that a violent event of this magnitude would produce. But we do have a record of a different sort. Far away in Greenland, scientists have drilled down into the ice cap, taken out a plug of ice, and subjected it to laboratory analysis. A layer of volcanic ash has been found in the ice plug, and this ash can be dated by laboratory methods to around 1628 B.C. Detailed analysis of tree rings from North America and pine cones from northern Europe also confirm this time frame. This scientific evidence converged with the mythical and historical evidence and leads us to conclude that 1628 B.C. was the probable

time when this happened—with catastrophic consequences for Minoan civilization.

It's amazing to think that we can take all of these disparate pieces of evidence, mythology, marine archeology, migratory patterns, scientific evidence—and create from this an explanatory framework that takes us beyond what even ancient people who lived much closer to this time would have known. So, although I will continue to emphasize that we must be humble when we talk about the past and recognize the limits of our knowledge and the thresholds beyond which we can never penetrate, I will also emphasize that we have new methods at our disposal today that have led to incredible breakthroughs in our understanding. The story of Akrotiri is one of the truly remarkable examples of this fact.

As a side note, some biblical scholars believe that the people we know from the Old Testament as the Philistines were refugees from this catastrophe. We know that the Philistines were a seafaring people who were technologically advanced. We know they settled along the coast of Canaan, modern Israel. We know as well that they were a non-Semitic people; that is, they were not related to the Canaanites, to the Israelites, or to the other Semitic peoples of that region. They were, in fact, ethnically related to European people groups. And so it's a very plausible hypothesis that some of these refugees migrated after this catastrophe and became the people we know as the Philistines.

Mycenaean Civilization

We're going to journey now from Crete to the European mainland as we discuss one more pre-western civilization, the Mycenaeans. We're now at the threshold of the ancient Greeks; in fact, the Mycenaeans were ethnically related to the later Greeks who gave us Homer, Socrates, and Alexander the Great. They spoke a Greek dialect, and so, in every respect, they were Greek people. So why don't we just call the Mycenaeans "Greeks"? Because they were a distinct civilization from the later Greeks, the classical Greeks, who emerged a few centuries later—and we don't want to confuse the two. But, as we'll see shortly, the classical Greeks remembered their distant "cousins" in the stories, legends, and myths they told.

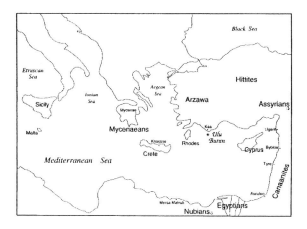

Mycenaean civilization flourished between 1600 and 1000 B.C. on the Aegean islands and the Greek mainland, in the same area where the ancient Greeks took up residence and where modern Greece is today. It's interesting to note that we see the Mycenaeans emerging around the time when the Akrotiri disaster occurred. When you see conjunctions like that in history, you can logically assume there must be some connection. Certainly, the natural disaster would have cleared out coastal settlements, and new settlers would have moved in and built on the ruins of whoever preceded them. This pattern is repeated constantly in history.

Let's look first of all at the archaeological remains. The so-called **Lion Gate** from the citadel of the kings is the most famous monument from ancient Mycenae., the capital or royal center. Mycenae was not really a *city*, however, as you and I understand the word, but more like a citadel or fortification. The Lion Gate is marked by a simplicity of design; it's not as impressive as the Egyptian Pyramids or some of the other architectural wonders that we'll be examining. But it has a simple elegance to it. The lion, of course, is an ancient symbol of royalty; so clearly this must have been the palace of the kings. Note as well the

simple design of the entrance: two vertical slabs of stone with a horizontal slab placed on top. That's what we define in prehistoric times as a "dolmen" and that's exactly where this design ultimately comes from. There's a basic continuity here with remote ancient cultures that will be carried right through the architecture of the classical Greeks and Romans.

The Mycenaeans are very obscure people to us; we know even less about them than we know about the Minoans. But we do know one thing very clearly—and that is that *the Mycenaeans were a Greek people*, which means they were ethnically related to the people who emerged several hundred years later whom we call "the Greeks." The problem is we don't know the nature of that cultural continuity. We don't know the precise family relationship between the Mycenaeans and the Greeks; but nobody doubts that there was a family relationship.

The linguistic evidence points clearly to this relationship; but another reason can be found in the stories, legends, and myths that the Greeks told centuries later, long after the Mycenaeans were a distant memory. The Greeks remembered these people, along with the Minoans, and they told stories about them. In fact, these stories formed the basis of their own national mythology as they told the story of a great battle that we know as the Trojan War. This story would become the central Greek epic as it was retold in the *Iliad* of Homer and the follow-up epic known as the *Odyssey*.

In nineteenth-century Germany, a little boy named Heinrich Schliemann grew up learning these stories, as every little boy getting a good classical education back then did. Schliemann was fascinated by these tales of adventure and heroic deeds, and he wondered if they could possibly be true. Perhaps Homer's epic was more than just a story; perhaps it was based on some real events that took place in the remote mists of antiquity.

As a little boy Schliemann decided that he was going to find out for sure—when he grew up. And so little Heinrich grew up to become one of the founders of the new science of archaeology. Schliemann was a pioneer in the methods of excavation, so we shouldn't fault him too much for his highly destructive methods. The first archaeologists were learning how to do it by trial and error. They didn't excavate a site the same way as we do today, meticulously sifting out the earth, section by section, and documenting everything they find, no matter how insignificant it may seem to be. Instead, they took pick axes and shovels to the site and broke through the ruins with little documentation or preservation. They were looking for gold and monumental art; anything else was bound for for the refuse heap. When Schliemann excavated Troy, for example, he cut a big gash across the site—known as Schliemann's Trench—and irrepa-

rable damage was done in the process.

Eventually archaeologists did develop thorough methods of analysis. Nowadays, ancient settlements are analyzed layer by layer. Sites like Troy, Jericho, or Megiddo were occupied continuously for thousands of years. Each settlement left its own layer of debris, one on top of the other, to be sifted, sorted, and dated. The time periods can be determined by the pottery shards and the other remains found in a given level of settlement. Each level of settlement, typically, will be divided by a thin layer of carbon—which means, of course, that the settlement had been burned to ash. It's a pretty bleak history that extends sometimes through twenty or more settlements, indicating recurring patterns of settlement, invasion, destruction, and resettlement. The ruins of Troy contain many distinct layers of settlement. Unfortunately, Schliemann assumed wrongly that the earliest layer of debris would be Homer's Troy. We now know that he smashed his way right through the very thing he was seeking to discover, and he destroyed precious evidence in the process.

So does the *Iliad* contain some actual historical truth? Yes, it's been pretty definitively demonstrated that there was a great battle fought between the Mycenaeans and the Trojans during the 13th century B.C. Was the battle started over a beautiful woman named Helen? Certainly not. And did it end with a great wooden horse? No—those are the fantastic details that legend provides. But strip away the romantic details, and the very fact of a battle fought between these two cultures is something that legend does bear historical witness to. Once again, it's fascinating to see how the historian and archaeologist can take a myth or legend, and take scientific evidence of various sorts, and put the whole package together when reconstructing the past. We can conclude, then, that the Homeric poems, the *Iliad* and *Odyssey*, constitute a distant memory by the ancient Greeks of the glorious past of their predecessors, the Mycenaeans.

What happened to the Mycenaeans? Again, we don't know. Perhaps they were the victims of a natural catastrophe such as the Minoans faced. Perhaps their land was invaded, or perhaps they suffered a calamitous plague. Scholars have theories, of course, but nothing is known for sure. What we do know is that when the Mycenaean civilization fell, the Greek-speaking people of the Aegean entered a period of several hundred years known as the "Greek Dark Ages." We have little hard evidence to work with when trying to reconstruct this "dark" period. We'd like to know more, however, since this was the period that gave rise to the ancient Greeks, the classical Greeks as they would be called—the civilization that gave us the achievements of Athens and the conquests of Alexander.

So everything we've discussed so far—the rise of civilization, the cultures of Sumer, Egypt, Crete, and Mycenae—all of this has been a long drum-roll before our main subject appears. Emerging out of the shadow of these earlier civilizations, the ancient Greeks will emerge. And their culture, radiating out from the Aegean Sea, was destined to become the cradle of the western world.

The Indo-Europeans

Where did the Greeks come from? And who were they, exactly? You can look at the things they wrote down about themselves, and you're not going to find a lot of answers to those questions. Why? Because the Greeks didn't really know much about their ancient history. This is one of those areas where we might be able to say, in a very qualified way, that we know a few things about their own history that the Greeks didn't know themselves. In reconstructing their ancient history, I will be presenting the consensus view that has emerged over the last couple of hundred years of research.

We can say with confidence that the Greeks are descended from a tribe that lived somewhere in Central Europe around 3000 B.C. So we can actually trace their history— and the whole history of western culture— back 5000 years. Scholars call this tribe the **Indo-Europeans**, which is just a scholars' term; we have no idea what they called themselves. It's a made-up term to describe the geographic region over which they ultimately spread—westward throughout Europe and eastward to India.

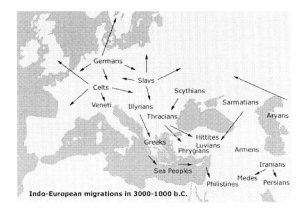

Indo-European migrations in 3000-1000 b.C.

At one time, the Indo-European tribe was a single group of people speaking a single language with a single set of religious beliefs and cultural practices. But as that tribe grew and expanded, the way an extended family will do, various branches began to migrate away. Think about how cousins might keep in touch for a while until eventually, over the generations, they lose all contact and forget where they came from and who they are related to. This is how the Indo-European tribe began to split into separate family groups that migrated out from their original homeland. Over time, their customs and languages changed.

One group—or "cousins," as I am calling them—migrated as far west as they could go. They ended up in the British Isles, and we know these as the ancestors of the Celtic peoples. Another group migrated towards northern Europe and became the ancestors of the Germanic peoples—the Angles and Saxons and all the other tribes that later became the English, Germans, Dutch, and Scandinavians. Others stayed pretty much in central Europe and became the ancestors of the Slavic peoples—ethnic Russians, Poles, Serbs, and Czechs. Another branch migrated south into the Italian peninsula; and when we first begin to see them around the eighth century B.C., we recognize them as Romans. Another group migrated down into the Aegean, sometime before 1000 B.C., and these people were the Greeks. Others migrated to the area of modern Iran, and these people became the ancient Persians. That means that Iranians today, who are the descendants of the Persians, are more closely related to European peoples than they are to any of the people around them in the Middle East. There are many other examples we could cite, among them the ancient Hittites whom we read about in the Old Testament. This civilization was rediscovered through recent archaeological work. Another group migrated as far east as the Indian subcontinent and became the ancestors of a large portion of the modern Indian population.

We know that all these people have a common ancestry. How do we know this? Not from any written historical records, since the Indo-Europeans were a pre-literate people. Not from the excavation of any of their cities, since they were not a civilization and built no cities. So how can we be absolutely sure about the conclusions that I have presented? The answer is found in *language*. In the late 18th century, scholars began to study and compare the languages of these disparate people groups—both in their ancient and modern forms—all the way from Europe to India. These languages are all related in ways that you can demonstrate conclusively; and so based upon this linguistic evidence, the kinship of all these people groups has been conclusively proven.

This is why we can say that the Greeks were Indo-European—which is something the Greeks themselves didn't know. Nor did the Romans know their ancient lineage, and this leads to some interesting observations. When the Romans led their armies against the Picts and Celts in the British Isles, they looked at these people as the lowest form of barbarians. The Celts would paint their naked bodies blue and run screaming at the Roman armies—and I imagine the Romans would have been horrified to realize these people were distant cousins! And the same is true of the Germanic tribes that the Romans faced on the battlefield. The Greeks and Romans referred to these people as *barbarians*, and they had no idea that they had all descended from a common ancestry.

The Greek Epics

When we see the Greeks emerging out of that catastrophic "dark age" around 1000 B.C., we see them embarking on a very normal process that every people, every nation, every tribe goes through early in its history. They looked in the mirror, so to speak, and they asked, "Who are we? And how are we different from those people over there?" These are the same questions we ask in the humanities about culture: Where did we come from? Who are we? What are our values? What's our history? What do we stand for? What do we call ourselves? The Greeks went through this process, and they came out on the other side calling themselves **Hellenes**. We don't know what that means, but that's what they called themselves. They called their country **Hellas**. (We use the words "Greek" and "Greece," but those are the Latin terms; that's what the Romans called them, and those are the terms that have stuck.)

As I said, this process of developing a national identity is something that occurs in the history of every civilization, every nation, and every people group. We should note that the questions that emerge in the early stage of a culture's history are very much like the questions the late adolescent and young adult ask as well. As you journey into young adulthood, you're trying to figure out who you are. Certainly, you're related to your family on the one hand; but you're also different and distinct as well. You want to "discover yourself" and find out who you are as a unique individual. What are *your* values? What do *you* believe? This is a process of self-discovery and identity formation as you stand in front of the mirror and try to understand yourself. Cultures are simply reflecting on a big scale what each of us as individuals experience naturally in life.

How does a culture answer those questions? Well, initially, they answer them by telling stories—or *myths*—about themselves. The word "myth," as used in this sense, doesn't mean "stories that aren't true." Rather, a **myth** is a meaningful story that answers the most basic questions of life and meaning: *Who are we? Where did we come from? What do we believe?* The grand national myths that answer these questions are called epics. We've already identified the two great epics that the Greeks recounted, the *Iliad* and *Odyssey*. But now let's consider what those epics do for a culture. What purpose did they serve for the ancient Greeks? Let's start by defining what an **epic** is and how these great stories of heroes provided answers to the basic questions of values that people ask early in their history.

An epic is a long narrative poem that recounts the deeds of a hero and illustrates the main virtues and values of its society.

As we watch an epic hero like Odysseus facing challenges, we learn what it really means to be Greek. We see embodied in Odysseus the main values of his society. So if you are a little boy growing up in ancient Greece, you learn this story as part of your cultural training; it's one of the ways you learn how to model your behavior according to what is expected of you within society. You would want to cultivate the same val ues of rationality and ingenuity that we see in a figure like Odysseus.

Notice the process: the part stands for the whole. One hero represents the whole nation, such that if you want to know what it is to be Greek, you look at Odysseus. If you want to know what it means to be an Anglo-Saxon around the year 1000, you look at Beowulf. If you want to know what it means to be a Mesopotamian, you look at Gilgamesh. If you want to know what it means to be a Roman, you look at Aeneas, the hero of Virgil's great epic *Aeneid*. Every culture produces sweeping stories that give answers to questions about values and identity. Scholars have even claimed that modern cultures such as the United States, which obviously doesn't have an ancient history of the type we're discussing, nonetheless follows this natural process. The early history of America can be understood as a search for the unifying story that tells us who we are. Some have even suggested that a great novel like *Moby Dick* functions like an epic, giving expression to the American character and the individualism that we see in ourselves. Others suggest that the semi-mythical stories of the western frontier are an expression of our national character and values.

Clearly, this is a natural and universal process. We could even say it's one of the immutable laws of civilization—that we create our identity out of the stuff of the past, and that "myth" and "history" are deeply intertwined in our cultural imagination.

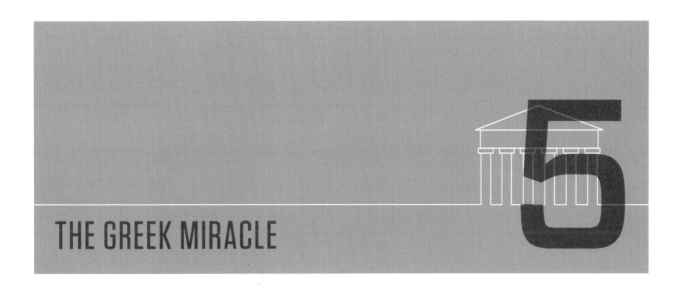

THE GREEK MIRACLE

Chapter Objectives

- Defend the idea that ancient Greek culture was remarkable and unique.
- Describe how a culture begins to form and express its own identity.
- Chart the broad divisions of ancient Greek history.

The ancient people we know as the Greeks emerged sometime about 1000 B.C. following the collapse of the Mycenaean civilization. We don't know exactly what happened to the Mycenaeans, but take your pick among the following choices: natural disaster, military invasion, plague or famine. Those are the usual suspects when ancient civilizations fall. When the dust settled from whatever catastrophe befell the Mycenaeans, we see a new branch of the Greek family moving into the Aegean. These Greeks will be the ones who give us Homer, Socrates, and Alexander the Great. They will become the "classical Greeks." Understanding the relationship between the classical Greeks and the earlier Mycenaeans clarifies for us why the Greeks told stories about the Mycenaeans—the stories, most notably, of the Trojan War.

The Achievements of the Greeks

What do we see in ancient Greek culture that warrants the kind of attention we're going to pay to them? Here are two answers to that question: *their achievements were wide-ranging and long-lasting*—which is a way of describing both the breadth of what they did and the length of their influence.

First of all, *their achievements were wide-ranging*. They were good at everything they did, which is a remarkable thing. How many cultures can you say that about? How many individuals can you describe that way? Think of how humbling it is when you run into somebody who speaks several languages, who plays a few musical instruments, is good at math and sports, and is good-looking and popular as well. The Greeks were like that; they seemed to have the whole package of talents. They became the gold standard of cultural achievement, not just in the ancient world, but for centuries to come. Let's consider some of those areas in which they excelled by listing the names of some famous Greeks.

Myron, Praxiteles, Ezekias, and Ictinos. These names are probably not very well known to most people; but we'll be looking at the works they produced. These names represent the world of the arts—painting, sculpture, and architecture. The Greek achievement in the visual arts was considerable; they "invented" western art and established styles and norms that we still follow today. We'll look closely at the way they sculpted the human form and the way they painted on vases and urns. We'll look at the great architectural achievements of the Parthenon. We'll see how Greek art became the standard of excellence which subsequent cultures, starting with the Romans, looked back at with admiration and envy. But most importantly, we'll see that these styles of art reflected the values of a culture that was pervasively humanistic.

Socrates, Plato, Aristotle, and Pythagoras. We're on much more familiar ground here. The philosophical achievement of the Greeks was considerable, and we'll be focusing a good deal of attention in the next chapter on this remarkable aspect of the Greek legacy. We'll look at what the Greeks believed and consider how they arrived at the doctrines they hammered out about the nature of reality.

Euclid and Archimedes. These names draw our attention to science, mathematics, engineering, and technology. The important contributions that the Greeks made in these areas formed the foundation of science and mathematics well into the Middle Ages.

Solon, Pericles, and Alexander. Once again, these are some familiar names—especially the last one. The world of politics and military affairs comes to mind. Solon and Pericles were great rulers in Athens. Alexander, of course, the greatest ruler of all ancient Greek history and one of history's most successful conquerors. We need to remember that the Greek achievement wasn't limited to purely intellectual activity. In fact, the Greeks recognized no clear division (as we do) between reflection and action. One of the keys to their genius, I believe, was that they understood that good thinking was the flip side of good acting. Alexander was trained in philosophy by Aristotle before he went out and conquered the world. For the Greeks, this made perfect sense to bring thought and action together in the real world.

Sophocles, Sappho, and Aeschylus. These names take us into the world of the literary arts—poetry and drama. We'll look more

closely in a later chapter at how the Greeks sketched a sophisticated view of man's position in the cosmos in their drama. Their achievement in tragedy has been particularly influential throughout the western tradition.

Let's reflect on this achievement a little more. I've used five different categories to highlight what they did—from the arts to the sciences—as a way of emphasizing the breadth of their accomplishment. But there's something misleading about how I've presented this; I've used the filter of the modern university, with its separate disciplines and specializations. As modern people, we tend to view knowledge in a fragmented way—and this would have puzzled the Greeks very much. We often overlook the rich interconnectedness of diverse branches of knowledge; in fact, one of the great tragedies of modern life and modern philosophy is that knowledge has become fragmented. It was a feature of the Greek mind, however, and an element of their genius, that they believed in the unification of knowledge. They would not have viewed these areas of achievement as distinct and separate bodies of knowledge at all. It was the most natural thing for them to see a connection between philosophy, say, and what you did in the political arena. Why? Quite simply because, for the Greeks, if your philosophy was true, then it should impact every aspect of life.

That's one of the reasons why the figure of Alexander is so interesting. As we already noted, Alexander is best known to us as a great conqueror and a great military figure; but he was trained as a philosopher by none other than Aristotle, the greatest philosopher of his age. Consider how we generally divide life into the world of thought and the world of action. The Greeks didn't see these as distinct and separate. The one was just the opposite side of the same coin for the ancient Greeks; that is, if you think clearly about the world then you should act clearly within the world. We'll analyze this quality more closely when we look at their philosophy; I believe this is one of the greatest accomplishments of the Greeks.

We today who live in a highly fragmented world could learn much from the ancient Greeks on this point.

The Greeks were also *long-lasting in their achievements*. We still talk about them, not because they were some brilliant flash in the pan, impressing people for a short time before fizzing out. No, we still talk about them simply because they are such a marvel. We could even describe them—less charitably, perhaps—as a "freak of nature." They were so out of the mainstream, so far from the ordinary and average, in the same the way that incredibly brilliant people are.

Take philosophy as one example. Today, philosophers still go back to the basic questions and answers that the Greeks hammered out—questions about the nature of reality (metaphysics), the nature of truth and knowledge (epistemology), and the nature of what is good and just (ethics). It's not an exaggeration to say that no new questions have been found, or that any new answers have been produced, since the time of the great Greek philosophers. Of course, there's much detail and nuance that the history of philosophy has brought to the basic philosophical questions; but the broad outlines were set in place by the Greeks, and philosophers essentially go back over the same territory and prioritize things in different ways. One philosopher at the beginning of the twentieth century, Alfred Whitehead, summarized this conclusion when he stated that all western philosophy is a footnote to Plato. Plato laid out the agenda, and then everybody, from Aristotle on, responded to it.

Another example of the lasting influence of the Greeks is how they defined a sense of style and beauty based upon principles of order and structure. Greek art and architecture gave concrete expression to these principles, and they still act as a point of reference in the West when we describe something as beautiful or structured and orderly. Here's one simple example. Just drive through Main Street, USA (at least in the South) and look at the architecture of the Court House or the First Baptist Church.

You'll be looking at what's called "Greek Revival Architecture." The English poet, Shelley (1792-1822), summed up this long-lasting influence when he said that, "We are all Greeks." They're in our bloodstream—they're part of our cultural DNA. From art to politics, from mathematics to philosophy, the Greeks are part of who we are and how we think about the world today.

Scholars used to speak of the **Greek Miracle** as a way of expressing how remarkable and dynamic their accomplishments were in the context of the ancient world. The term has fallen out of vogue in recent decades, due in large part to the increasingly negative critique of the western tradition within academic circles. The multicultural agenda has sought to minimize the uniqueness of the Greeks and relativize their achievements. But it remains a point worth defending that the Greeks were a remarkable civilization—and we can't just pretend, for political reasons, that this isn't so. Think of the Egyptians, by way of contrast. Of course, there is much that's remarkable about this culture that built pyramids and perfected the science of mummification. But it's a very different culture from the Greeks; Egyptian culture was relatively static by comparison, and emphasized an unchanging structure and order. The Greeks were very dynamic—constantly changing, innovating, trying to make things new and refine our understanding of the world. Right there, in that dynamic instinct, we see the engine of the western world—that quality of progress, innovation, and the mastery of knowledge. That's one of the greatest legacies of the ancient Greeks, and I would argue it still defines to a great extent what the western world is today.

What is so "miraculous" about the Greeks? We've already seen some of the answers to that question in the vast diversity of what they accomplished; but let's move from the concrete to the abstract—to some Greek ideas that continue to occupy central places in western thought. One of those concepts, for example, is *freedom*. Of course, the Greeks defined it differently from us. Their concept of political freedom did not extend to slaves and women. And yet we do rightly look back at them and see a culture that was beginning to experiment with notions of representative government—government by "the many" as opposed to the authoritarian form which was the norm in ancient civilizations.

Another remarkable concept among the Greeks is *individuality*. We take this idea for granted today; we see ourselves first and foremost as individuals—not as members of a family, a clan, or a tribe. But most people, living at most times in human history, have not thought of themselves that way. Why and how the idea emerged among the Greeks is not clear to us. By way of contrast, we can be sure the ancient Egyptians didn't see themselves that way at all. They wouldn't have understood what we meant by the concept of an individual. They must have seen themselves as part of a great system, a cog in a big machine with the Pharaoh at the top and a whole bureaucracy beneath him. They would have seen themselves as a part of a system.

But the Greeks began to explore the idea of what it means to think of yourself primarily as an individual—to be a unique center of consciousness, creativity, experience, and rational thought. This is a powerful, transforming concept, and it's obviously inseparable from the very idea, not to mention the institutions, of democracy. You cannot have any real semblance of democracy without a fully developed notion of individuality. Otherwise, what is it that the individual is going to contribute, if not a unique perspective on matters of debate? It is the democratic ideal, if not always its reality in practice, that we carry our unique perspectives and values into the voting booth, not our affiliation with a tribe or family. Again, we speak of the Greek Miracle for good reason, since this idea is the rare exception in ancient cultures.

A third Greek concept that we still value today is *rationalism*—the belief that human reason can guide us to a true understanding of the world. The Greeks believed in the power of rational thought to find answers to the central questions of life. We'll be exploring the power of this idea in greater detail when we look at the philosophical legacy of the Greeks.

A fourth and final concept—though this is by no means a comprehensive list—is the idea of *beauty*. We've already alluded to the fact that Greek ideas about beauty have cast a long shadow over the western world. We'll explore this legacy in greater detail as we examine the development of Greek art and architecture. In particular, we'll see that the Greeks pegged their notions of beauty to the concept of the human form.

Let's turn now to another question. We've been discussing our modern appraisal of the Greeks as we look back at them from a great distance. But how did the Greeks see themselves? Those two perspectives are not always the same—how other people see you and how you see yourself. In this case, however, there's a remarkable correspondence between how we see the Greeks and what they saw when they looked in the mirror. Obviously, they knew they were pretty remarkable and they didn't hesitate to pat themselves on the back about it. Perhaps the best example we could cite is a famous speech, the so-called "Funeral Oration," given in Athens during the fifth century B.C. by Pericles. The speech is recorded by the Greek historian Thucydides.

Pericles was a great Athenian statesmen during the 5th century B.C.—that Golden Age of ancient Greek culture. He led Athens during a particularly trying time in the life of the city of Athens, when Athens was locked in a life-and-death struggle with its fellow city-state Sparta. Athens would go on to lose that war against Sparta, and it had tragic consequences for Athens. After a particularly devastating loss on the battlefield, Pericles delivered his famous funeral oration, much as we expect the President today to speak to the nation during a moment of great crisis.

This is the same kind of situation, a moment of crisis, when Pericles was addressing his fellow countrymen. These are always very revealing moments, as when President Bush spoke to the nation after say 9/11, or Abraham Lincoln at Gettysburg. If this sort of speech is going to be effective, then it must harmonize with the character and the values of who we are as a people; the speech must call us to face this challenge by drawing on our greatest virtues. So that's why speeches like this, given at significant moments, become telling documents that express how people see themselves. We previously saw that epics reveal the national character of a people; high, ceremonial speeches given at moments of great crisis do as well.

Let's look at the Funeral Oration to learn more about how the Greeks viewed themselves. Towards the end of the speech Pericles says: "To sum up, I say that Athens is the school of Hellas." We've already seen that Hellas is how the Greeks described their land. Pericles goes on to say that "the individual Athenian in his own person, seems to have the power of adapting himself to the most varied forms of action with the utmost versatility and grace. And we

shall assuredly not be without witness," Pericles says. "There are mighty monuments of our power which will make us the wonder of this and of succeeding ages."

This is definitely a very self-confident statement that Pericles makes. There is nothing humble at all about his assessment of who the Athenians were. He describes Athens as the school of Hellas. Among all the city states of ancient Greece, Athens was the trendsetter. Paraphrasing Pericles, we might say: "If you want to know what it means to be a Greek, then you've got to come to Athens, because we're teaching all of Greece what that means." Pericles was boasting—but he was also telling the truth. Consider that we'll be focusing on the culture of Athens—not Sparta, Corinth, Ephesus, or any of the dozens of other Greek city-states scattered around the Aegean and Asia Minor. There was much more to "Greece" than just Athens; but Athens at its height was the cultural stand-out, the smartest kid in the class, the jewel in the crown of the Greek world.

What is it that Pericles sees in his own people that's so great? We'll notice that Pericles identifies some of the same qualities we've already pointed out. He mentions, for example, the quality of individuality. "The *individual* Athenian *in his own person*," is how Pericles puts it. He is emphasizing that the power of Athens doesn't derive from the collective. It doesn't come from the State. It doesn't depend upon military power alone. What makes Athens great is the genius and initiative of its individual citizens. This is why we can look back at Athens and link specific achievements with individual names. We can say things like, "Ictinos is the architect who made this," or, "Ezekias is the painter who painted that vase," or "Aeschylus is the author of this tragedy." We can say these things because the Greeks valued their own individuality. We generally can't identify as readily the individuals who produced the works of other early civilizations. We look at their works of art and we don't know who created them. The artists were anonymous figures in the great bureaucratic machine. So Pericles is paying tribute to this remarkable quality of individuality.

Secondly, Pericles identifies the quality of flexibility, adaptability, or versatility. The individual Athenian has "the power of adapting himself to the most varied forms of action with the utmost versatility and grace." Pericles is saying: *Whatever you throw at us, we can handle it. We'll figure it out.* The epic hero Odysseus embodies this quality in abundance. As he makes his journey back from Troy, trying to reach his wife Penelope who has been waiting for him all those years, he has to go through many challenges. He has to fight Cyclops. He has to deal with the Sirens and all the other tests and traps along the way; and what we see in Odysseus as he faces those challenges is the adaptability, versatility, and flexibility of a character who figures out how to solve problems. Odysseus commits his rational mind to the task of getting out of one tough scrape after another until he finally reaches home. That's the very ingenuity that the Greeks saw in themselves.

Pericles identifies something else in the Athenian character. He says, "We will assuredly not be without witnesses. There are mighty monuments of our power which will make us the wonder of this and succeeding ages." I guess the word "legacy" would be the easiest way to summarize that. They believed that they were building something that was going to last. And he was absolutely right. Here we are today looking back at the ancient Greeks, still talking about them, looking at the monuments that they made, and wondering about them. So Pericles pretty much got it right. This is the modern appraisal of the ancient Greeks; but it is also how the Greeks saw themselves.

How do we account for the Greek Miracle? There's no simple answer, but let me sketch the broad outlines of two possible ways to approach this question.

- a materialistic explanation
- a metaphysical explanation

First, we can answer the question of why the Greeks are unique by reference to their environment. This is the materialist answer—one that emphasizes material conditions. This was the approach we took to the ancient Egyptians when we wondered if they might have derived the idea of an unchanging moral structure to the universe by looking at the Nile and desert—two permanent features of their landscape. This idea is attractive, but I'd only want to carry it so far. We're much more than the product of our environment—unless you're a Darwinian who believes we're nothing but the product of the material forces of biology, chemistry, and physics. But as a Christian, I don't accept that materialist definition of human life at all; and so any answer that emphasizes a purely environmental cause can only be, at best, a partial explanation.

How would a materialist try to explain the Greek Miracle? The answer would go something like this. *They lived in a mountainous, rocky area of the world where it's tough to scrape out a living; so, they had to rely on wit, ingenuity, rational problem-solving— the very things we see in a figure like Odysseus. Their distinctive qualities were arrived at out of necessity, conditioned by their environment.* Scholars in the late nineteenth and early twentieth century were quite serious in trying to account for the ancient Greeks this way. But the argument is deeply flawed. It fails to take into account why people groups in far more difficult circumstances around the world have not likewise been motivated toward the same achievements that we find in ancient Greece. There's something arbitrary and selective about the explanation—and that is its fatal flaw.

There's a better way, I think, to account for the Greeks—and that's to look beyond the material to something that is essentially theological. This is the "metaphysical" explanation, because it looks beyond the physical world for an answer. I believe that the way people view God—or, in the case of the Greeks—the way they view the gods— will impact the way they live and what they value. The one will be a mirror reflection of the other. The Greeks believed in a pantheon of deities. They held to a fatalistic way of looking at the gods, seeing them as capricious and unpredictable. And since you can never know what the gods are up to, the best thing that you can do is to try to steer clear of them and rely upon yourself. This fatalistic view was so deeply rooted in the Greek way of thinking that it motivated them, paradoxically, to accomplish great things. In a sense they were just turning their backs on the gods—leaving them up on Mount Olympus and not wanting to have anything to do with them. And so they relied on themselves. This turn away from the gods represents the beginning of humanism as a philosophy in the western tradition. What the Greeks accomplished was no thanks to Zeus. They continued to pay tribute to the gods, to build them temples (perhaps to keep them out of their hair, so to speak); but over time, the Greeks became more and more reliant upon themselves. This tendency, I would argue, was built into the Greek idea of fatalism. We'll discuss this more in the next chapter as a backdrop to the rise of philosophy in ancient Greece.

The Historical Framework

Let's look more closely at that dangerous and unpredictable world, as the ancient Greeks saw it, and how they responded to it through some pretty amazing achievements. We'll start by placing the Greeks in their historical context, defining the three main periods of Greek history and culture.

- Early Greece
- Classical Greece
- Hellenistic Greece

You can see from the outline that it's neatly divided into thirds. This very fact should give you pause to question the method, to be a little suspicious of it, to ask whether this is not just a kind of scholarly creation and a kind of fiction. So even before we go through this outline, I want to undercut its credibility and remind us that there's always something artificial about what we do with the past. We look back and divide

things up into logical units of analysis as best we can. We use the term **periodization** to describe what we do when we label the past. For example, we divide all of western history into three broad categories—the ancient world, medieval world, and the modern world (which is the broad outline we're following in this book). Historians, in particular, have a special fondness for sets of three. As we look at the past, we're always looking for patterns; we look for breakage points, patterns of continuity and discontinuity, and then we divide things up, label them, and ascribe dates to them that are neatly divisible by 100. What we're doing is trying to find patterns that make sense; these periods aren't arbitrary in the sense that we are at least lumping things together according to common characteristics. But my point is that *we* do the classification, and this is the reflective aspect of history that we discussed in the first chapter. So, although our labeling system is artificial, we trust that it's not entirely arbitrary; and even more than that, I hope it's pretty accurate as well.

A simple logic underlies our labeling of the past into thirds. It seems natural to us—because that's how life is divided up. As we pass through the cycle of life, we go from youth to maturity to old age. And so we project that pattern onto the story of cultures. Bringing this little digression back to our subject, we'll see that this tripartite outline of Greek history is very helpful as a tool for understanding the progression of the Greeks from the earliest period to full maturity and then decline. As we follow their history, keep that in mind that early Greece is like the adolescence of Greek civilization. The second period is equivalent to their maturity and middle age. An individual expects to be at his peak of performance, at least in his career and professional life, during his middle years—and this was certainly true of Greek civilization. We'll see, finally, that Hellenistic Greece corresponds to the later years of an individual's life.

We're going to subdivide each one of these periods further into several sub-categories; and so, with this in mind, let's go ahead and jump right into the beginning, with early Greece. The dates for this period are traditionally given as about 1000 to 480 B.C. You'll recall that this is around the time when Mycenaean civilization collapsed. We don't know natural disaster or invasion that brought them to an end; but we do see in this period, in the centuries following the Mycenaeans, that another civilization—the Greeks—gradually began to appear on the historical radar screen.

We can subdivide the early Greek period, first, into a period we call the "Greek Dark Ages" which runs from 1100 to 800 B.C. That term, *Dark Age*, is something of a misnomer; and even as I use that term here; I'm not speaking of the Dark Ages in the centuries following the fall of Rome. **Dark Age** is a generic term we use for any period where there is a radical break with the past, where the continuous flow of culture is interrupted, and where knowledge is lost. Cultural memory is carried over, of course, from one period to the next, even after great catastrophe; but that knowledge will often take the form of myth and legend. We saw that this was the case with how the Greeks remembered the great war fought between Troy and Mycenae. Perhaps the term Dark Ages, though, is best understood as a description not of the people living back then—since they didn't have the sense that they were wandering around in the dark. Rather, the term describes us as well. As we look back at that period, it's like looking down a dark corridor. We can't see things very clearly, because *we* are in the dark. We lack light—the information and data, the archeological evidence and literary remains, all those things that would help bring that period to light for us. Instead, we have very little to go on when we reconstruct the framework of this period.

We do know, however, that this was the time when the ancient Greeks made that fateful transition that we talked about before—the transition from bronze to iron, a great technological leap within every early civilization. We know as well that this is the time when they began to experiment with their own styles of arts; the few remains

that we have are labeled by art historians as the **geometric style** of art. One of the best preserved examples of this style can be seen in the British Museum, the so-called **Dipylon Vase** (c. 800 B.C.). It was excavated from an ancient cemetery outside Athens and stands nearly three feet tall. Let's take a couple of minutes to analyze some of the qualities of this vase, since our analysis will become a reference point for us later when we discuss the development of Greek art. We'll use this vase as a touchstone against which to compare their later achievements as we look back and see where they came from and where they ultimately ended up.

The style is called *geometric*, as you can logically infer, from the patterned repetition of geometric forms and motifs that comprise the overall design. It's very decorative and quite abstract. We see checkerboard patterns, swirling shapes, cross-stitching forms—all sorts of repetitive motifs that are drawn from the broader cultural styles of Mediterranean art in this period. We find these same motifs in Mycenaean, Minoan, and Egyptian art as well. In fact, some of these interlocking forms are still used today as decorative motifs. Many of the elements that make up the decorative arts have an ancient lineage behind them; they go all the way back to ancient Egypt, in some cases, and have been continuously used over the past several thousand years.

The other thing to note about this style, in addition to its clearly geometric nature, is the way human beings are depicted. The human form itself is represented as an abstract composite of geometric forms and shapes. An inverted triangle represents the upper portion of the body. The head is a circle. The arms form a rectangle over the head. In other words, this is not at all a natural, realistic depiction of the human form; instead, the human form has been translated into a highly stylized abstraction—part of the overall geometric design. This is an important point to take note of, because we're going to see Greek artists move light years beyond this starting point in their development of the human form.

Simply the human form in the vase with one of the masterpieces of classical Greek art—the *Discus-Thrower* by Myron which was sculpted about four hundred years later (c. 450 B.C.). Look at the muscle structure that you see in the athlete. This is so realistic in giving a sense of movement, the sense of energy and dynamism. We'll talk much more about the development of this

style; but clearly, Greek art had a long way to go to get from the geometric style to this fully realized image of the human form. If we can explain how the Greeks got from A to B—from the geometric form to the athletic form—then we will have cracked the riddle of the Greeks.

What can we conclude? Obviously, whatever it was that made the Greeks who they would become at their height—whatever concept transformed their culture—has not yet emerged during this earliest period of their history. The conditions have not yet fallen into place to make the Greeks what they would become. They don't yet see themselves as fully realized individuals. The human form on the geometric vase tells us this, since the body is depicted simply as part the geometric landscape. At this point, the Greeks are still heavily dependent on the larger Mediterranean culture.

The Greek Dark Ages was also when the Homeric epics were composed. Sometimes this period is referred to as "the Heroic Age"—since people were looking back at an earlier time when "men were men and giants roamed the earth," so to speak. This early period of Greece was the mythological age, that period in a culture's history when its values and identity come together in the raw material that gives us epics. For the Greeks, this formative process would produce the *Iliad* and *Odyssey*.

Now, as we move out of this roughly 300 year period of Greek history, the picture becomes a little clearer. The archaeological evidence starts to accumulate. We're able, therefore, to say more and to say it more definitively about the periods that follow. The second subcategory of early Greek history takes us from about 800 to 600 B.C. and is known as the Age of Colonization.

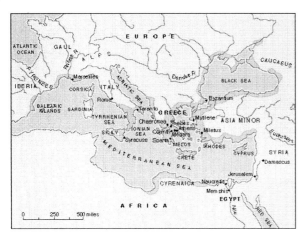

The Greeks began moving out into the larger world after they consolidated their position in the Aegean. The Greek city states were emerging, and now they were looking out on the horizon for more places to colonize with more cities. Periods of colonization are always highly productive times in the life of any culture. We talked a little bit about this when we considered the invention of the sailing ship and how that enabled people to migrate across vast stretches of sea. Any time of migration or colonization involves a process whereby one culture comes into direct contact with another. Two things inevitably happen: people kill each other and they transfer knowledge and cultural information. Cross-pollination of ideas and technology occurs, which, in turn, leads to even more cultural progress.

Where did the Greeks colonize? The Aegean was the epicenter of Greek civilization; and from this base, they began to move out toward the east, all the way into the Black Sea. They colonized the coastline of this rather remote and mountainous area. The area furthest west was like the "wild, wild east" in the Greek mythic imagination. This is the frontier region that provided the setting for some well-known adventure stories: Jason and the Argonauts and Jason and the Golden Fleece.

The Greeks also settled all the way down around the coastline of Asia Minor, even settling further inland (though they remained a largely coastal people). This would be the region where the apostle Paul would evangelize so extensively in his missionary journeys—places like Ephesus and Philippi. These were all originally Greek city-state, founded during this time period.

The Greeks settled widely throughout the Mediterranean, including the coast of North Africa. They settled Sicily and southern Italy. When the Romans were still a minor tribe, not even able to govern themselves, the Greeks were busily putting down roots in the neighborhood. This will be significant for the early history of Rome; we'll see that the Romans were in close contact with the Greeks and learned much from their culture firsthand.

Greek cities were established as far west as southern France and Spain; for example, the port city of Marseilles, France began as a Greek city state back in the eighth century B.C. Greek adventure stories tell of how Greek sailors navigated out through the Strait of Gibraltar into the Atlantic and explored as far north as the British Isles. So they were very active during this period of time. And they were laying the foundation for what we will see later—several hundred years down the road—when Greek culture would permeate the social, political, and cultural fabric of the ancient world. All of this migration and colonization is important for understanding the New Testament period as well, as we will see in a later chapter.

The third subdivision of early Greek history runs from 600 to 480 B.C. We call this the Archaic Period. During this period the Greeks emerged as a civilization fully aware of its own achievements. This is the period when permanent architecture began to be built. Before this time, the Greeks had built temples out of timber and other perishable materials; now they started to build temples out of marble. One of the earliest examples is the Temple of Apollo in Corinth, which dates from around 540 B.C. We can imagine the temple still fully formed and in use when Paul was there during his missionary journeys. Not much has survived—just a few columns which are not very well preserved.

We also see the emergence of a new type of sculpture during the Archaic Period known as the kouros form. This term doesn't refer to a single sculpture; it's not the title of a specific work of art. Rather, "kouros" refers to a generic type of sculpture of which there are many examples. A **kouros** is a statue of a standing male nude servant. Why are Greek statues depicted this way? Why are they nude? That's an unavoidable subject when discussing Greek art—so let's get it out of the way right now. Interestingly, the ancient Greeks made statues of both male (kouros) and female (kore) servants. The female servant is al-

ways clothed, but the male servant is always nude. There is nothing prurient or pornographic about this artistic nudity for the Greeks; rather, it has to do with one of their central values—humanism. They considered man to be to be "the measure of all things," as one of their philosophers put it. Man is the standard and the ideal against which they understood all reality; and that's why the human form, and specifically the male form, became such a significant vehicle for expressing Greek ideals.

We're not going to take the time right now to analyze the kouros form, since we'll be doing that in detail in the next chapter. But as a starting point, we can note once again how far removed the kouros is from the geometric style—but, also, how far the Greeks have yet to go to reach the fully realized athletic forms of the classical period.

As we leave the Archaic Period, we are moving out of that 500 or 600 years that historians describe as "early" Greek history. As we enter the second period—Classical Greece, from 479 to 323 B.C.—consider the analogy of a life cycle again. This second period corresponds to maturity, adulthood, and middle age. During this period, the Greeks were at their peak performance. They reached the greatest level of cultural achievement. We still use the word "classic"

to convey that sense. Think of how you might describe something as a classic game, or a classic remark, or a classic moment. What do we mean when we use that word? We mean that X was the most exciting game, the standard by which we can judge all others; Y is the most important moment; Z is the wittiest remark. These things we call "classic" are *in a class by themselves*. They are the gold standard—and that's the same way we use that term when referring to the Classical Age of ancient Greece. Most of the great accomplishments that we are going to be looking at in the next few chapters—achievements in sculpture, architecture, philosophy, and literature—most of these will date from this highly productive period.

Historians typically subdivide Classical Greece into two shorter periods. The first of these, from 479 to 404 B.C., is known by several different terms. It's called the Age of Pericles, which refers to the great statesmen who ruled Athens during the fifth century B.C.; but it's also called the Golden Age of ancient Greece. Notice how the dates get much more specific the further we go into Greek history. The dates 479 and 404 B.C. refer to pivotal events, two wars that shaped the world of Athens in the fifth century. The first date, 479 B.C., marks the end of the Persian War; the second date, 404, marks the end of the Peloponnesian War.

In 479 B.C., in one of the most remarkable military campaigns ever recorded, the Greeks managed to turn back the advancing Persian army under Xerxes, the king of the Persians. Xerxes had conquered so much territory, and his Persian Empire was so great, that he was looking for new places to go. He looked west, saw the Greeks, and decided to take his army into Europe. Back then, wars were fought over long stretches of time—sometimes decades. If you lost a battle, you might bide your time, raise and army, and then strike again when the time was right. People had long memories. This was the case with the Persian War. The Persians had already invaded the Greek mainland, and the Greeks knew they were

coming back. The culminating battles were fought in 480 and 479, when Xerxes brought an army estimated at nearly a million men toward Greece. The number is probably exaggerated; but it would have been an enormous army nonetheless, and the Greeks were vastly outnumbered. In addition, the Persians brought hundreds of ships.

How big was the Greek army? They had about 50,000 troops, and so this was a David-and-Goliath confrontation. Though outnumbered 20 to 1, the Greeks managed to defeat the Persians and turn them back. The Persians would never again threaten Europe. You can see why the Greeks looked back at this as a pivotal event in their history—one they looked back at with great pride, and one that tells us much about who they were as a people. So, how did the Greeks do it? After their first encounter with the Persians, a Greek statesman named Themistocles stood up in the assembly and said to his fellow Athenians, "We've got to have a plan, since the Persians will be coming back." Themistocles went on to argue that the Greeks needed to build a navy—something they had never had. These ships would be, as he called it, their "wooden wall" of defense.

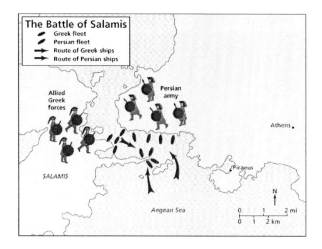

So that's what the Greeks did. They built a few hundred ships, and they were ready when Xerxes came knocking a second time. The Spartans were great warriors, and they fought heroically; but the Spartans couldn't hold back the Persian advance. So the final

50

plan, the final strategy, was to concentrate the Greek ships in one sheltered harbor, the Bay of Salamis. It looked like a crazy thing to do; in fact, when the Persians sent their spies out and saw what they had done, they thought the Greeks were sitting ducks. To use another metaphor, they thought it would be like shooting fish in a barrel.

Of course, this is exactly what the Greeks wanted the Persians to think. They were just waiting for them. The Persians fell for it, and directed their entire navy into the bay in an attempt to destroy the Greeks completely. The Greek navy was outnumbered maybe three to one, but they had built smaller vessels which could maneuver easily. The Persians had huge transport ships that were slow and couldn't turn around very easily. The Greeks were able to swoop in next to them and engage in hit-and-run tactics. Naval warfare in the ancient world was pretty interesting—involving, as it did, propelling objects at close range, such as flaming missiles or even clay pots filled with poisonous snakes. You can imagine the chaos on the enemy decks when those pots cracked open! Xerxes was sitting on the shore on his golden throne—ready to watch another glorious victory for Persia. Instead, he saw his entire navy go down in flames. With his navy gone, and lacking any troop support for supplies, he was forced to withdraw the Persian army. This is considered one of the greatest victories in military history. We can look back and wonder what western history would look like if the Persians had prevailed. Would there even be a "western" culture to talk about? Probably not.

The Greeks looked back at this as a red-letter date—one that stamped their identity on the world. They were a rational, problem-solving, freedom-loving people. These are the attributes they valued in their mythologies and legends; it's what they project onto a figure like Odysseus. How, after all, does Odysseus get from Troy back to his home in Ithaca? He has to navigate through all the tests and trials; he has to use his wits in overcoming the Cyclops and

avoiding the Sirens. He does this in typical Greek fashion—by his wit, by his cleverness, by his wiliness. And that's what we mean when we point to epic poems as evidence of the deepest things a culture values.

What about the other date—404 B.C.—that bookends this period? The Peloponnesian War was a devastating civil war fought between Athens and Sparta. It, too, had a profound impact upon Greek culture. We'll look at this a little more when we examine the career of Socrates. This period—between the Persian and Peloponnesian Wars—was truly a Golden Age, a time when many of the major Greek achievements of architecture, drama, and sculpture were produced.

The second subdivision of classical Greek history is the Late Classical Period which runs from 404 to 323 B.C.—that is, from the end of the Peloponnesian War to the death of Alexander the Great. Philosophy flourished during this time. Socrates died around the beginning of the period (399 B.C.), and the careers of Plato and Aristotle span the fourth century. The Greek Empire would rise during this time through the careers of Philip of Macedon and his son, Alexander the Great.

When Alexander died in 323, the Greek Empire broke up quickly; but the culture that Alexander spread throughout the known world remained. The language, the philosophy, the styles of art—all those things continued to exert influence

51

throughout the world in the final period of ancient Greek history, Hellenistic Greece. This period is dated from the death of Alexander in 323 to the conquest of Greece by Rome in 146 B.C. After the Roman conquest, Greece would be a province of the Roman Republic, and then later, the Roman Empire. The implications of this are profound, because Rome didn't destroy Greece. Rome absorbed it whole, swallowing it whole like a boa constrictor does, digesting it and using it. We know so much about Greece in part because the Romans preserved Greek culture and transmitted it as part of our common heritage. The Greek language continued to be the language of culture, learning, and philosophy in the ancient world. This is why we see the New Testament written in Greek, not Latin. Greek is a remarkably rich and complex language and was well suited, then, to the rich and complex theological ideas laid out in Paul's letters to the early churches.

We describe this process whereby Greek culture spread throughout the known world with the word **hellenization**. We use the word to speak of Greek influence much in the same way we describe American influence today with the word "Americanization." In the twentieth century the United States spread pop culture, fast food, Coca-Cola and Facebook throughout the world. Two thousand years ago, the Greeks were spreading art and philosophy. That's why we call it the "Greek Miracle."

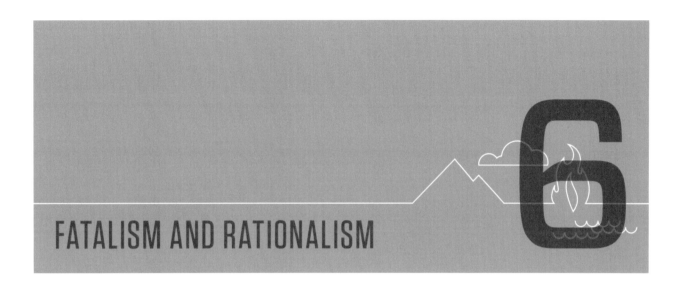

FATALISM AND RATIONALISM

Chapter Objectives

- Summarize the fatalistic theology of the ancient Greeks.
- Explain how the Greeks viewed philosophy differently from us today.
- Identify the prime philosophical question and the only two answers.

In this chapter, we're going to examine the most enduring, and arguably the most significant, legacy of the ancient Greeks—philosophy. And we'll be looking at this legacy against the backdrop of the Greek fatalistic worldview. The Greek view of the gods should be central to our understanding of their values and achievements. As we go through this chapter, we'll see that the ancient Greek view of man's position in the cosmos is remarkably similar to the secular humanistic view that prevails today in the western world. We'll first look at four extracts of Greek poetry by way of trying to form a picture of who the gods were in the Greek imagination. Then we'll build on that to see how the Greeks responded. I'll argue that the whole edifice of philosophical thought can be viewed as an eloquent response to this fatalistic outlook on life.

Fatalism

Let's start with a passage from Homer's *Iliad.* It's a passage where he digresses a lit-

tle bit, as he often does. These digressions can seem tedious to the modern reader; but they are usually very revealing sections. They give us a little window onto the Greek mind. Homer is speaking of the gods, and this is what he says:

Such is the way the gods spun life for unfortunate mortals, that we live in unhappiness, but the gods themselves have no sorrows.

Right here we see that Greek theology is based on a fundamental injustice: the gods are living in luxury on Mount Olympus while we're struggling in misery to survive.

Homer goes on to say:

There are two urns that stand on the door-sill of Zeus. They are unlike for the gifts they bestow: an urn of evils, an urn of blessings. If Zeus who delights in thunder mingles these and bestows them on man, he shifts, and moves now in evil, again in good fortune. But when Zeus bestows from the urn of sorrows, he makes a failure of man, and evil hunger drives him over the shining earth, and he wanders respected neither of gods nor mortals.

The idea here is that you can't predict Zeus's mood on any given day. If he gets up on the wrong side of the bed, he might decide to take the vase labeled "curses" and pour it down on you or your city, or maybe even on the whole world if he's in a really bad mood. Or if he's in a good mood, he'll take the urn of blessings and pour that down on you. You can't predict; there doesn't seem to be any rhyme or reason to the things that happen. The best you can do is try to get out of Zeus's way and live your life as best you can. What a bleak way to view the gods! If you view God as vengeful, if you view God as unpredictable, then would you really want to have a personal relationship with Zeus? You can see why the Greeks didn't want that. This provides important context for our understanding of what the apostle Paul would later write to Greek Christians. Paul was evangelizing people who had this view of the gods, and so he emphasized over and over again that God is personal and loving, and that God has revealed these qualities to us in Jesus Christ. This was a revolutionary idea to people who believed that the gods were as distant and malevolent as Homer has described.

Let's look now at some short lyric poems, fragments from the eighth century B.C. The titles have been given to them by translators. The first one is "Friends Lost at Sea." Once again, we're looking for the Greek theology—the Greek way of looking at their world and the gods.

If you would irritate wound, Perikles, no man in our city will enjoy the festivities.

You've got two individuals here. One is mourning the loss of a mutual friend who died at sea. The other one is saying, *Get over it. Let's go on with living. There is a party here in the city and you're ruining all the fun right now. So nobody in the city will enjoy the festivities, if you keep crying about what happened.* It's a very blunt statement about grief. The poem continues:

These men were washed under by the thudding
*   sea waves*
and the hearts in our chest are swollen with pain.
Yet against this incurable misery, the gods
give us the harsh medicine of endurance.
Sorrows come and go, friend, and now they strike us
and we look with horror on the bleeding sores,
yet tomorrow others will mourn the dead. I tell you,
hold back your feminine tears and endure.

What's the point here? You can't look to the gods for comfort. You can't look to them for anything but the harsh medicine of endurance. Picture a father and his little boy as

you're walking through the park. You see the scene and you immediately recognize what's happening. Obviously, the little boy has had a birthday and has received his first bike and dad is helping him learn how to ride it in the park. The little boy does what all of us did when we learned how to ride a bike: he falls down and scrapes himself up. Now as you are watching this scene, imagine that the father walks over to the little boy, looks down at him and says, "Get up, brush yourself off, stop crying like a baby, get back on the bike, and do it right this time." If you saw that, you would obviously think that this was the worst father ever; you'd be expecting him to give his son a hug and some encouragement, instead of the harsh criticism. This is a good picture of how the Greeks saw the gods. All they give you is the harsh medicine of endurance—just enough to get back on the bike and try it again.

Now think of how the apostle framed the gospel to Greek-speaking people. In 2 Corinthians 1:3-4, we read a very telling passage where Paul emphasizes that the true God is a "God of all comfort."

Blessed be the God and Father of our Lord Jesus Christ, the Father of mercies and God of all comfort, who comforts us in all our tribulation, that we may be able to comfort those who are in any trouble, with the comfort with which we ourselves are comforted by God.

Paul mentions the word "comfort" so many times that it's obvious Paul is trying to make a point to these Greeks. God isn't like Zeus. He is not one who just gives us the harsh medicine of endurance, but He is one who has revealed Himself in Christ as a God of love, a God of mercy, a God of grace, a God that we can turn to in times of need. So, again, our knowledge of the Greek background to the New Testament really opens up the meaning.

Let's turn to another poem from the eighth century B.C., titled "Providence" by its translator.

Let the gods take care of everything. Many times
they resurrect a man whom disaster left lying
face down in the black earth. Many times they topple

a man and pin him, back to the soil, though he
was solid on his feet. A multitude of evils
descends on him, as he wanders hungry and mad.

In other words, you can't predict what's going to happen. You might be walking along whistling—everything seems fine—and all of a sudden you get slammed from behind. That's how the gods treat you. Or they might see you lying face down—out for the count—and they decide on a whim to resuscitate you and give you a second chance. Life is capricious, unpredictable, and fatalistic. So, how do you respond to a world like that? The last poem we're going to look at, "Moderation," shows us how the Greeks responded in an essentially humanistic way.

O my soul, my soul—you were mutilated helplessly
by this blade of sorrow. Yet rise and bare your chest,
face those who would attack you, be strong, give no
*   ground.*
And if you defeat them, do not brag like a loud-mouth,
nor if they beat you, run home and lie down to cry.
Keep some measure in your joy—or in your sadness
*   during*
crisis, so you will understand man's up-and-down life.

How do you respond to an unpredictable cosmos governed by fatalistic forces? By trying to control the little you can—your own heart and mind. You live a moderate life. That's the whole point of the well known myth of Icarus. Daedalus and his son Icarus were prisoners on the island of Crete. They made wings out of feathers and wax. Before they flew off to freedom, Daedalus instructed his son: "Don't fly too high to the sun, since it will melt the wax and your wings will collapse. Don't fly too low to the waves, since the waves will lap up and pull you down." And then Daedalus concludes with a simple piece of advice: "Take the middle course." What did Icarus do? He disregarded his father's advice and flew too close to the sun. The wax melted, his wings fell apart, and he crashed tragically into the ocean.

Why tell a story like this that's so obviously fantastic, improbable, and historically untrue? Remember that myths are always told to make a point. The whole point of the myth of Icarus is to emphasize moderation, which is one of the central values of classi-

cal Greek culture. Certainly, the Greeks believed that the cosmos is a rational place and that the human mind can tap into that order. But they also believed in gods who were capricious and fickle—gods who changed their mind one day to the next. Moderation in all things was the only rational response. The Greek poet wrote, "Keep some measure in your joy." That's the key. You should respond to success and adversity in the same way—moderately—since you know your fortunes will turn around in time. We shouldn't swing wildly from one extreme to the other. Consider the kind of people we usually admire. We admire those who can "keep it together," people who face difficulties with steadiness and resolve. It concerns us when people respond at the extremes of their emotional range. It's not moderate to swing from wild excitement to deep despair all the time. We place value on moderation—and this is a good classical idea.

So, once again, how might the Greeks respond to the capriciousness of the gods? There are only two possible responses. You can give up and resign yourself to fate. Or you can decide to exercise control over your mind, your heart, your attitudes. You can't control the gods. You can't control nature or the cosmos. You can't control how other people treat you or react to you. But you *can* control the little universe that is yourself. I can control the interior life of *my* reactions and *my* attitudes. The ancient philosophers placed great stock in this ideal of moderation, of controlling oneself in the midst of an unpredictable and uncontrollable world. It is a rather noble philosophy, and there are lots of good things to commend it to us—unless you turn it into a creed of self-sufficiency. Of course, that's exactly what happened, and that's the legacy of Greek humanism.

As we move into the Roman period, we'll see that the Romans too were very fond of this idea. They turned self-discipline into a whole philosophy that we know as Stoicism, which has its roots in Greek thought. The New Testament addresses these philosophies of self-reliance. Furthermore, the New

Testament endorses the idea that it's good to be temperate and moderate in all things; but, ultimately, we need to know where our strength comes from to live this self-controlled lives in an unpredictable world that we don't fully understand. That power doesn't come from us, but from the indwelling power of Christ.

The Rationalistic Response

As the Greeks turned inward toward themselves, they began to understand that reason could be a powerful tool for finding answers within the world. We'll see that the greatest expression of reason for the Greeks was philosophical analysis. Before we get to that, however, we'll need to define some important terms. What is rationalism? And what is philosophy?

The Greeks saw themselves as a rational, philosophical people. That's how they would describe themselves to you and me today. So what do we mean when we say that the Greeks were rational? What does it mean that they placed a high value on the rational faculty of thought, logic, and human intelligence? Let's define **rationalism** and then analyze its implications.

Rationalism is the belief that human reason—not experience, revelation, or authority—is the ultimate source of knowledge about the world.

Rationalism is a theory of knowledge, and it's important to understand both what it is and what it's not. The key word here is "primary." If you are a rationalist, you believe that *reason and logic are the foundation upon which all truth rests*. Reason is the standard. When a rationalist says, "This is true," he means that it conforms to rational analysis. The matter comes down to what is foundational—to what constitutes ultimate Truth. Does this definition of rationalism mean that one who believes in divine revelation must not believe that we know things through reason or experience? Not at all. The question again is what is *primary*; what forms the standard, the foundation, the ultimate source of truth. The Christian is claiming that reason, experience, and authority are not the primary

basis of truth, but rather secondary sources of truth. Ultimate truth has been revealed by God—through creation, through scripture, and through Jesus Christ who declared, "I am the way, the truth, and the life" (John 14:6).

The rationalist, though says that there's no such thing as spiritual revelation. What we know about the world we know through human reason. By contrast with the rationalist, the empiricist would claim that what we know comes through experience, through our five senses. Now again, just to emphasize the point, the issue at stake here is what is the most fundamental basis of truth. What's the bedrock on which human knowledge about the world ultimately rests? For the Christian, we say that it's what God has revealed to us about Himself. For the secular materialist today, who doesn't believe in God, knowledge and truth are achieved through the rational methods of scientific inquiry. So, a lot is at stake in our understanding of what truth is, what knowledge is, and how we know what we know about the world. The Greeks started with the human condition and the human faculty of reason. One of the early Greek philosophers, Protagoras, famously said that "Man is the measure of all things." You start with man and then you use him as a measuring-stick for truth—an idea which Leonardo da Vinci expressed in his famous sketch known as the Vitruvian Man.

We already noted in passing how similar the Greek emphasis on rationalism is to modern scientific thought. Secular thinking today has staked out an extremely arrogant position—namely, that the human mind can solve and figure out all the mysteries of life with God completely absent from the equation. This arrogance stands in stark contrast to the biblical perspective, eloquently stated in a prayer by David. In Psalm 39:4-5, David takes the question of truth in the opposite direction—away from man and toward our Creator. "Lord, help me to know my end," he prayed, "and the measure of my days." Note that phrase, *the measure of my days*. It sounds a lot like Protagoras, but with an entirely different emphasis—

one that is God-oriented, not man-oriented. David goes on to say that our days are just a "handbreadth." That's how short our lives are—just a blip on the scale of eternity. And then David concludes by saying, "Truly, man at his best state is altogether vanity." The very best that man can accomplish is nothing when scaled against the glory and the majesty of a sovereign God.

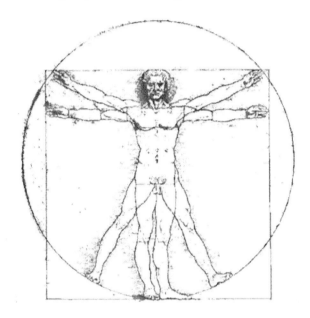

Scripture presents the exact opposite of the humanistic formula. Man measures all things, according to Protagoras and the claims of modern science. Scripture says, however, that man is only properly measured by God. Man is not a measuring stick, but the one who is measured by his Creator. What is it we find in scripture when we're measured by the glory of God? We find that we fall short (Romans 3:23). This truth should prompt in us an attitude of humility. We need to approach the study of culture this way, because we're going to see some pretty amazing things that ancient man and modern man has accomplished. We've spoken of the Greek miracle and we'll examine their truly impressive achievements in the area of Greek philosophy. They put their finger on a lot of truth through the power of human thought and rational inquiry. Later on, when we examine the Renaissance, we'll marvel at the great artistic achievements of Michelangelo, da Vinci, and others. Later on still, we'll dis-

cuss the great scientific advances of the modern age. These are all formidable achievements. But David reminds us that man at his best state—be that the ancient Greeks, the Renaissance, or modern science—is altogether vanity.

The Philosophical Tradition

It is in their philosophical traditions that the Greeks gave the fullest expression to their rationalistic impulses. So let's turn to that now and define what philosophy meant to the ancient Greeks. **Philosophy** itself is a Greek compound word, meaning "the love of wisdom." Right here we could stop and note how impressive this concept is. It's a remarkable thing that the Greeks, in describing themselves as a philosophical people, chose not to define themselves by the love of money, the love of experience or pleasure, the love of power—or even the love of knowledge. Consider knowledge, for example. Knowledge is a good thing, but the Greeks went well beyond that. Knowledge can be transferred in data bytes, downloaded through a USB cable. But wisdom is acquired only through living. Our culture today doesn't look at philosophy this way; we don't value it. Most people would see it as a waste of time—the ultimate "ivory tower" activity, completely divorced from the realities of life. The Greeks would have been puzzled by our view. Philosophy was the most essential thing for them. What could be more important than trying to understand what the world is, who we are, and how we relate to the world? The Greeks would have said, "How can you live your life well if you don't have answers to those questions?" The concept of living a good life is a rich, classical idea, and it was the ultimate objective of Greek philosophy.

I've already mentioned that the Greeks saw themselves as a philosophical people. Philosophy was something of a cultural fixation—at least for the Athenians. It's worth looking at this idea a little more closely and seeing just how deeply invested they were in philosophical inquiry. Let me give two examples to illustrate this point. The first is a biblical example from Acts 17. The second will be taken from Greek history.

The apostle Paul, as recorded in Acts 17, found himself in Athens for a few days. It was like an unscheduled layover for him as he waited for his colleagues to join up with him on one of his missionary journeys. What did Paul do? Paul disputed with the Jews in the synagogue and he debated in the marketplace and presented the claims of Christ. Paul always followed the same pattern; he engaged his countrymen in the synagogue and then he went to the marketplace to preach to the Gentiles. Note that the term "marketplace" in the Greek is agora—an important place in every Greek city. The **agora**, the marketplace, was the center of commercial, intellectual, and political activity. It's where you went to buy bread or fish; but it's also where you went if you wanted to debate the burning issues of the day. That is such an incongruous concept to us, to think that the center of commerce, buying and selling, could be the same place where philosophy was debated. Imagine trying to discuss philosophy in the aisles at Wal-Mart! This picture doesn't compute for us, but it helps to emphasize how different the Greek estimation of philosophy was. Philosophy for us belongs in a proverbial ivory tower. But philosophy for the Greeks belonged right in the very center of everyday life with the smell of fish all around. Philosophy was not some arcane, obscure thing that didn't relate to life; rather, the most essential thing you could do was to consider questions about the nature of the world, the nature of human experience, how we relate to the world, how to live a good life, and how to create a just society. How else can you live, the Greeks would say, if you don't deal with those questions first?

So, Paul knew where to go; he knew what the drill was. He was confronted by the local philosophers, the Epicureans and Stoics, and they engaged him in debate (Acts 17:18-20). At this point in the story, I like what the writer, Luke, tells us. He gives us a little extra information to explain the behavior of the Greeks; and in so doing he shows us what the reputation of the Greeks

was in the ancient world. Luke tells us that "the Athenians spent their time in nothing else but to tell and hear some new thing" (Acts 17:20). This was common knowledge in the ancient world; and we can almost see Luke rolling his eyes as he writes this. "There they go again. Typical Greeks!" It's not an especially flattering portrait; but it does emphasize how closely associated the Greeks were with philosophical inquiry.

Another example of this Greek obsession with philosophy comes from the life of one of their most eccentric philosophers, Diogenes. Without a doubt he is the most colorful of all of the Greek philosophers, and the fact that he was tolerated at all within Athenian society speaks volumes about how they esteemed the philosophical life. I'm going to take a little bit of time to tell the story of Diogenes, a little of his background, and then bring the story to the end of his life and his very famous encounter with Alexander the Great. The payoff is worth it, I think, as we'll be able to grasp more fully how important philosophy was within Greek culture.

As a young man Diogenes grew up in Asia Minor, in the city of Sinope, where his father worked in the imperial mint making the gold and the silver coins of the empire. But Diogenes' father was also an embezzler who was skimming off the gold and silver, adding in base metals, and pocketing the difference. When his crime was discovered, the whole family, including Diogenes, were sent into exile. This was the worst fate that could befall you as a Greek—since the Greeks saw themselves as belonging to a city, a **polis**. We get our words "citizen" and "political" from these two words. So if you are exiled from your polis, you didn't really belong anywhere. And that is how young Diogenes began his life.

But things went from bad to worse. As a young man, Diogenes was captured by pirates in the Mediterranean, which was a very common danger in the ancient world. He found himself in shackles in a Greek slave market, where the wealthy merchants came to check out the new inventory of slaves. You might think this would be a good time to keep your mouth shut if you were standing in his spot. But Diogenes spoke up. He looked at the men who were looking at him; and then he pointed to one of them and said, "That man right there, sell me to him. It looks like he needs a *master*." The man was very impressed with the boldness of Diogenes. He was obviously a self-confident, well-educated young man. And so the rich man bought Diogenes on the spot and took him into his home as the live-in tutor for his children—which, for an educated servant, was really the best you could hope for in the ancient world.

Diogenes was able to pursue a life of philosophy and he eventually earned his freedom, becoming one of the most famous philosophers of his day in the fourth century B.C. He was a fixture in the agora of Athens. He never lived in a home during most of his life—at least until he became a very old man. Diogenes seemed always to remember his days of poverty and exile by showing contempt for material things. He would pull stunts like walking around the streets of Athens with a lantern in the broad light of day shouting, "Hurry, hurry! Follow me in the darkness! I will show you the way." Imagine how strange that sounded in the full sunlight; but it was a parable, and he was challenging the Athenians to confront his philosophy and the pursuit of truth.

Diogenes founded a school of philosophy known as the Cynics, which is the origin of our modern word. The word in Greek means "little dogs." Imagine that you're walking down the sidewalk and a little dog is yipping at your heels; that's the role Diogenes saw for himself and his philosophy. He wanted to be the cynic, the little dog, who exposed the foolishness and wrongheadedness of the rich and powerful. It's truly amazing that he was tolerated at all in Athenian society. But, again, the point in telling the story of Diogenes' life is that we learn something about Athenian culture—something about the great value they placed on philosophy and people like Diogenes who pursued the philosophical life.

Diogenes said a number of things that are still quoted today. Recalling his life of exile, he said, "I am a citizen of the cosmos." And he coined a word, *cosmopolitan*, to express that idea. He also said—and you will recognize a variation of the quote—that "the agora, the marketplace, is the root of all evil." Several centuries later a young man named Soul would grow up in Tarsus, a city that had a school of Cynic philosophy, and he would go on to write in one of his epistles that "the love of money is the root of all evil." That's an interesting little echo of Greek philosophy in the New Testament.

Let's fast-forward to the end of Diogenes' life. He had lived a long and full life, up into his eighties. Alexander the Great was now ruling Greece. Finally, after years of sleeping in a barrel, Diogenes decided to move into his own home, and so he settled in the Greek capital of Corinth. Alexander was a thirty-year-old man, returning from one of his great conquests in the east. Everybody in Corinth who was somebody came running out to meet him, falling over themselves to be seen by Alexander, and throwing flowers down before him. Alexander looked out at the poets, playwrights, and politicians and had one question: "Where is Diogenes?" The one man whose respect he most wanted, whose approval he most sought, was this eccentric old gadfly who pulled these kinds of stunts and who had nothing in his life but philosophy.

Alexander's men told him that Diogenes was probably back at his house, and so Alexander said, "Take me to him." When they arrived, they found the old philosopher stretched out in front of his house, sunning himself. It's one of the most interesting encounters in history. A young man and an old man; a world conqueror and a man who had lived most of his life on the street. Alexander walked up to him, looked down, and said condescendingly: "Diogenes, I have just brought the Greek army back from another great victory for Greece. Is there anything I can do for you?" Diogenes leaned up on an elbow and said, "Well, you could step aside a little bit. You're blocking the sun."

Alexander turned and walked away. His men looked at him with a puzzled expression on their faces and said, "Alexander, why didn't you just give us the word and we would have struck him dead on the spot for his disrespect?" But Alexander said something that has long puzzled historians. He said, "No, if I could not be Alexander, I would be Diogenes." What did he mean by that? Perhaps he meant that if he couldn't have the world, he'd like to have something of greater value—what Diogenes had, his self-respect, his sense of identity. Greek philosophy was all about striving to know oneself, to understand the mystery of what it means to be human being in this world. Diogenes had that quality, and Alexander recognized and admired it. This was a quality, as Alexander acknowledged, that you can't put a price tag on. Can you imagine any other ancient ruler, Xerxes or Nebuchadnezzar, saying what Alexander did? But Alexander was a Greek—and he was trained in philosophy.

The Pre-Socratic Philosophers

We're going to turn now to the beginnings of ancient Greek philosophy. We'll first examine the so-called pre-Socratic philosophers, which simply refers to the philosophers who came before Socrates. Then we'll turn our attention to the three great philosophers—the triumvirate, if you will, of Socrates, Plato, and Aristotle. We'll see that if

we understand these pre-Socratic philosophers and how they were trying to figure out the world, then we'll pretty much understand the rest of the story of philosophy in many ways.

Philosophy as a method of inquiry had its origin in the Archaic Period—not in Athens, but in the Greek settlements of Asia Minor (the area of modern Turkey). Two different schools of philosophers emerged, and both of these camps or schools were trying to answer the same basic questions. They were simply going about it in different ways. These two schools of pre-Socratic philosophy were the materialists and secondly the idealists.

First, the **materialists**. They were concerned with the origins and the nature of material reality. They were focusing their attention on the physical world that we know and experience through the senses; they were trying to find the basis of reality in material things. The earliest of these philosophers speculated that there were four basic building blocks of all material reality: earth, wind, water, and fire. With a little more thought, they came to realize that this didn't make much sense, especially when you start combining those elements and canceling them out. But we should note that they were trying to inquire rationally, philosophically; they were laying out theories and putting them to the test.

Materialist philosophers then moved on to speculate in a much more impressive way about the nature of material reality. Some argued that all things that we see, everything that makes up the material world, is composed of invisible and indivisible particles that they called *atomos*. We derive our word *atom*, of course, from that Greek word. So 2500 years before the development of modern physics, the ancient Greeks were already analyzing the physical structure of the universe and doing that through the power of rational thought!

The second group of philosophers were the **idealists**. They too were inquiring into the nature of the world, but they were approaching it from the other end of the telescope so to speak. They were looking at the rational design of the big picture, the universe as a whole. They were searching for what we might call the "cosmic blueprint." Think for a moment of Newton or Einstein or the British physicist Stephen Hawking. What these physicists have pursued is the cosmic blueprint, the central idea that can explain all physical laws—gravity, electromagnetism, atomic theory—in one grand equation that you could write on the chalkboard. Like these modern physicists, the idealists were searching for a "theory of everything"—the principle behind the rational construction of reality. This is why mathematics factored so prominently in their theories. Pythagoras, for example, was a prominent idealist philosopher, and he was looking for the mathematical harmony underlying cosmic reality. The idealists were asking the same questions as the materialists; but they weren't looking at physical, material things for the answer. Instead, they were looking beyond the material world to some kind of unseen, transcendent, rational structure, plan, or design. Materialists focused on what is visible, while the idealists focused on the invisible; materialists looked at the material world, while the idealists were looking beyond what is physical to a transcendent reality.

Let me emphasize the point again, since it is of vital importance. Both materialists and idealists began by asking one fundamental question which acts like a common denominator in philosophy: *Where do you locate the essence of reality?* This is the prime philosophical question that sets the whole process of inquiry in motion. All answers flow from that question. I would even say that it's the first order of business in philosophy, since you really can't talk about anything else until you have a framework of assumptions that you're going to operate under. Furthermore, I would argue that at the base of it there are only two possible answers to that question. The materialist says that you can locate reality within the nature of matter itself—in what you see in the here and now. That is, if you want to understand what really is, then you've got to understand matter. The idealist counters by claiming that we must locate the essence (that is, the ultimate expression of) reality beyond the physical realm in some *ideal* realm. This ideal realm cannot be seen or approached through our senses; it's transcendent. We could call it "the mind of God," if you will—but it's beyond the physical limitations of time and space.

Those are the two possible answers. Notice how these remain the only two answers today to the question, "What's real?" A secularist today who doesn't believe in God would answer by saying, "What you see is what you get. This world must be understood as the product of physical laws and nothing else." Human life is thus reduced to biological and chemical (that is, material) causes. The scientific materialist today asserts that science will uncover and explain every mystery—the mystery of life, the mystery of consciousness, the origins and nature of physical reality. The materialist today believes that you locate reality in what you can see and study with science and that we don't need to assume a transcendent realm to answer anything at all.

By contrast, the person of faith answers that fundamental question by locating the essence of reality beyond this world, in the realm of a Creator who stands outside time and space. All that we see is dependent upon, and ultimately derived from, this ideal realm. The Christian, for example, responds to the secular materialist, by arguing that the essence of reality resides in God Himself, who is the one from which all things flow and who is not just the Creator, but the sustainer of all physical reality. Apart from God, this world could not even exist. That's the idealist answer, and that's how the Christian worldview fits into the debate. It's easy to see why the early Church Fathers found so much in Plato that they agreed with, since Plato was the greatest of the idealist philosophers. Early Christian theologians recognized that Plato was putting his finger on some great truths when he argued for an ideal realm lying beyond this material world.

Socrates

Let's turn now to the three great philosophers in ancient Greece: Socrates, Plato, and Aristotle. Socrates is probably the prototype of all philosophers. If you were to ask a hundred people on the street to name a philosopher, I'm pretty sure Socrates would rank near the top of your survey. Socrates took philosophy very seriously. It was important enough to live for—but it was also to die for. And, in fact, Socrates both lived and died for philosophy.

Socrates lived during the Golden Age of Athenian culture, from about 470 to 399 B.C. As a side note, it's interesting to see how long these Greek philosophers lived. In the ancient world, where you were considered old when you reached your forties, these men lived typically into their seventies or beyond. So that's one good thing we can probably say about Greek philosophy! It seemed to have a salutary effect on the philosophers themselves. They lived good and full lives. Socrates would have lived even longer, had he not made so many enemies in Athens. As a serious man, he didn't like what he saw around him among the professional philosophers of his day. There was a group of professional philosophers that Socrates had nothing but contempt for. We know them as the **sophists**, and they practiced what we refer to as sophistry. Socrates rejected all that the sophists represented, all that they practiced and believed. They were philosophers, but they were philosophers for pay; they were taking what Socrates saw as the great and noble pursuit of wisdom and were basically selling it to the rich families of Athens. They were making careers of out of their philosophy by training the rich youth of Athens in how to get ahead and be successful in life through the techniques of philosophy. They were teaching how to use logic and reason and all those things that philosophy concerns itself with not to pursue truth, but to win friends and influence people, to be successful in politics and commerce. This was, in Socrates' view, a prostitution of philosophy and deserved nothing but his contempt. It was inevitable that Socrates would make a lot of enemies, since these sophists were well connected to the powerful families of Athens.

Socrates also lived at a time when Athens fell into misfortune at the end of the Peloponnesian War. Athens had lost the devastating civil war to Sparta, and Socrates got caught up in the ugly politics of that military defeat. Ultimately, having made so many enemies, he became a convenient scapegoat for all the problems that Athens was facing. He was accused, tried, convicted, and ultimately executed on two charges. Socrates was accused of blaspheming the city gods. Everybody knew that it was a bogus charge. They had to dust off the old law books to charge him with that. No sophisticated Athenian believed literally in the gods at this time. That was something the country folk might still have believed—the fables of the gods and the goddesses. Sure, the Athenians still built their temples, and the gods were part of the rituals of civic life; but literally believing all those old stories was quite another thing. Philosophy had begun to replace the old cultic gods; philosophy was the religion of Socrates.

The second charge is more problematic and a little more difficult to understand, namely that he corrupted the youth of Athens. We don't fully know what was meant by that, but there are some good theories and some things that we can plausibly reconstruct based on the context and politics of the time. I'm going to give you the political interpretation. Imagine the whole picture, once again. Athens had just lost to Sparta. The city had been locked in a life-and-death struggle for survival. It had been vitally important for Athens to raise armies of young men who were willing to go out on the battlefield and die if necessary, facing the fiercest Greek warriors, the Spartans. Now add to this picture an old man named Socrates, wandering the marketplace of Athens, teaching young people to think for themselves, question authority, and not believe something just because somebody says so. You can see why he would be seen as a particularly dangerous and vulnerable individual and why he would be a convenient scapegoat for the problems that had fallen upon Athens.

It also seems clear from the record that Socrates' enemies didn't necessary want him to die. They just wanted to get rid of him. There is some evidence that the city elders would have turned their backs, left the door open, and let Socrates exile himself from Athens. But Socrates refused this. Exile was the worst fate for a Greek. It would have been the denial of everything he had taught and lived for. As a philosopher, he believed in the rule of law. He believed in the process, and he basically said, "You've tried me, convicted me, and now the sentence must be carried out." His death would be his final object lesson, his final lesson in what was worth living for and dying for.

In the late eighteenth century, a great French painter, Jacques-Louis David, interpreted Socrates' final moments. (See Color Illustration B.) Of course, the picture has no historical authority at all, but it's based loosely on Plato's descriptions. The painting is best understood as an eloquent interpretation of Socrates' life and death, painted at a time (around the French Revolution) when David wanted to remind his own countrymen of the high demands of an honorable life. We see Socrates sitting on his couch, teaching his disciples right to the end as he reaches out to take the hemlock poison. The sentence was self-execution. With his other hand, he's gesturing—pointing up as if to say to his grieving disciples that we must look beyond the material to the ideal. There's more at stake, Socrates seems to be saying, than the here and now. Socrates was an idealist; he believed that there was a realm of absolutes that transcended the physical world. Notice the figure seated at the end of the couch with his back turned to Socrates. This is Plato, the greatest of Socrates' students. Plato can't even bear to watch the scene. But notice what's at his feet—the scrolls, which he will pick up, presumably, and carry down that corridor on the left to you and me. That's what Plato did; he wrote down his master's teaching and even described this scene for us. What we know of Socrates we know largely through the writings of his student Plato.

What do we remember Socrates for? Not his writing certainly, since he didn't write anything down. Apart from his heroic death, we probably remember him best for his teaching method which we call the **Socratic Method**. Socrates would teach by asking questions and the teaching would advance through questions and answers. Sometimes we mistakenly think that the Socratic Method is just asking questions—any questions. But the type of question is of utmost importance. I could ask you what the capital of United States is, and you could answer, "Washington, D.C.," but we've not engaged in the Socratic Method. We are just engaged in rote questions and answers that require very little thought. The difference is between a "closed question" (with a single, simple answer) and "open questions" (which are highly complex and nuanced). Socrates would begin by asking something like, "What is truth?" You can't just pull up a 3×5 index card and give a quick memorized answer to that question. What you'll need to do is slow down, look carefully at the question, formulate the grounds upon which you're going to answer the question, define your terms, and then proceed methodically from that foundation. Socrates will guide you as he fine-tunes your thinking with questions along the way.

The student is really teaching himself as he looks inside to formulate answers in response to those questions. It is a directed process of self-discovery. The student can look back at the end of the lesson and see that he has largely been self-taught; the teacher has wisely guided the student with very precise questions. This wasn't an arbitrary pedagogical choice for Socrates; the method itself reveals much about the Greek view of philosophy. There's a familiar Greek quote that reads simply, "Know thyself." That idea lies at the heart of how Socrates taught, since the most basic starting place for truth (for the Greek, at least) was self-knowledge. The Greeks would be so bold even to say that self-knowledge, self-discovery is the beginning of wisdom. So that's why Socrates asks questions, to force the student to look inward and pull answers out of himself. Doing philosophy well is a function of truly knowing yourself.

Let's critique this. I've said that there is a lot that we can be challenged by and a lot that we can learn from the ancient Greeks in their emphasis on absolute values and their striving for things that are permanent, not temporary. But they were also wrong about a lot of things; that is, they pursued these good goals through wrong means. As we noted, self-knowledge for the Greeks was the beginning of wisdom. But what does scripture identify as the beginning of wisdom? We find out in the book of Proverbs: "The beginning of wisdom is the fear of the Lord." Notice how radically different those two assumptions are. For the Greek, wisdom is located inside ourselves, since (to quote Protagoras again) man is the measure of all things. Scripture tells us that we're not going to get very far doing that because man doesn't measure anything by himself; rather, man is measured by the glory of God. The beginning of wisdom is not ourselves because we're fallen and corrupt; we're under the condemnation of sin and death. What do we find when we look inside our heart? Jeremiah tells us: "The heart is deceitful above all things, and desperately wicked. Who can know it?" (Jeremiah 17:9). The Bible denies that we can even know our own hearts! That's a very different perspective from ancient Greek philosophy. Scripture affirms that wisdom begins outside ourselves, in a right understanding of who God is. There's a universe of difference between these two perspectives on truth and wisdom—between Greek theology and biblical theology.

We also remember Socrates for some of the things he said that Plato wrote down. I think the greatest quote from Socrates is something he said before he drank the hemlock poison: "The unexamined life is not worth living." There's a library of wisdom in that simple statement. Socrates is challenging us to consider what kind of life we'd live if we never reflected upon what we're doing, how we're living, what our goals are. Socrates is tapping into a deeply classical idea that life ultimately acquires meaning as we understand ourselves and how we fit into the cosmos.

Plato

Plato, as we've noted, was the greatest of Socrates' students. He lived roughly from 428 to 347 B.C. He would have been about a 30-year-old man when his teacher died. Our knowledge of Socrates rests primarily on what Plato wrote down in philosophical works known as **Dialogues**. As dialogues, these works are written like plays in which characters are speaking. Socrates is one of the leading characters in these little philosophical dramas. Plato is considered not just a great philosopher, but one of the greatest literary figures in the western tradition; these works are remarkable literary achievements, quite apart from their profound philosophical content. The fact that Socrates is a character in Plato's literary works, however, has raised the question in the minds of some scholars of whether or not we can trust what Plato says about Socrates. Is Plato faithfully representing his teacher? Or is he dramatizing him in a way that is fictional? It's a scholar's debate—and we'll never really know the answer. Most scholars, however, are comfortable with the view that Plato has given us a more or less faithful portrait of Socrates. It seems apparent that Socrates was an idealist, as was Plato.

Plato is best known for one over-arching philosophical idea, sometimes called the "doctrine of ideal forms." This would be his greatest contribution to western philosophy; in fact, I would argue that this is the single greatest philosophical idea in the whole history of western philosophy. This is essentially what Whitehead meant when he said that all western philosophy is a footnote to Plato. In other words, philosophers are forced to accept, rejected, or modify what Plato said about reality—but they have to deal with him.

So, let's define Plato's big idea. We've already noted that Plato was an idealist. Now, if you're an idealist, and you believe that there is an ideal realm that transcends this realm of material reality, then you have a problem on your hands. You have to explain two things, two worlds. You see, the materialist only has to explain what is material. The idealist has to explain both the material and the ideal—and then explain what the relationship is between them. Plato's doctrine seeks to do this. If there is an invisible realm, and if we live in a visible world of material experience, then how do we connect these two things. How are they related? As we look at Plato's answer, keep in mind that it will sound, at first, a little crazy to us. We need to look beyond the counterintuitive claims, the things that easily correspond to what common sense tells us, and try to see what's ultimately at stake in this debate. So, let's roll up our sleeves and dig into Plato's big idea.

According to Plato, what we see in the material world around us is really just a copy or shadow of the real thing which exists in the ideal realm. Sometimes that ideal realm is referred to metaphorically as the mind of God, though that's not Plato's term for it or even what Plato was intending. Everything around us that looks so real and so solid is really just an imperfect reflection, a shadow, of what is essential and real. Consider the chair that's holding you up. You don't doubt for a minute that it's real and firm and solid. Plato would say, just to make his point, that you're really sitting on seats that are shadows or copies of some ideal chair that exists in an ideal realm—the perfect *idea* and *form* of a chair, if you will.

This is the point where Plato seems to lose us. He seems to be fulfilling our worst stereotype of the philosopher as one who plays word games and mind games, who talks about irrelevancies. This all seems very disconnected from everyday life. But I think we can illustrate what Plato was talking about by using the ordinary example of language. How we use words takes us a little closer into Plato's idea. Consider how remarkable it is that we understand each other when we use words. But of course we don't understand each other perfectly. Words can bring ambiguities because we live in an imperfect world. If I were to use the word "dog" in a sentence, you understand what I am saying because you have an image in your mind that you pull up. Maybe you're seeing a German Shepherd while I'm imagining in my mind a Chihuahua—entirely different dogs. But both of those dogs are copies of some concept of "dogness" that transcends the actual physical thing itself. That's what Plato was grappling with and what he was trying to understand—namely, the nature of, and relationship between, the visible with invisible realms of reality.

Plato engages this idea most fully in his longest work, *The Republic*. It's a huge work, extending a few hundred pages in translation. The work is essentially a political treatise, in which Plato was speculating on what a perfect society would look like. Who would be qualified to rule others? Plato argued that philosophers were qualified, since they are the ones who spend their time trying to look beyond these shadows and reflections and peer into the ideal realms of truth, justice, and beauty—the very things you need if you're going to rule your fellow man. In other words—and this is very important—Plato is trying to see the practical implications of this philosophy. If X is true about the world, then how should we live our lives and how should we structure society so that it can be true and just? Once again, we see the deeply practical nature of Greek philosophy. It's not some abstract pie-in-the-sky activity. It should impact the way we actually live.

The way Plato understands physical reality is expressed most fully in the well-known **Allegory of the Cave**, sometimes called "The Parable of the Cave" or "The Story of the Cave." Think of it as a chapter in *The Republic*. And it's the one chapter that provides the skeleton key to the rest of his philosophy. Plato deploys a vivid metaphor as he asks us to imagine a cave, a dark cave, in which all humanity is imprisoned, shackled at the wrists, ankles, and necks. We can't turn around; we can't get up and leave. We're just sitting there staring straight ahead. It's a very bleak picture of human existence. We're bound in a dark cave and we're able to look in only one direction. (That's is a pretty good picture of our fixation on modern media and entertainment, by the way.)

Behind us, further down the cave is a fire. That fire is burning and casting light in our direction. Between the fire and the back of our heads is a wall; and across the top of that wall objects are being carried back and forth, creating a shadow show on the wall in front of us. We can't see the real objects behind our heads; all we can see are the flickering shadows that are cast on the wall. This is the human predicament, according to Plato. The shackles on our wrists and legs represent the limitation of our senses. We see and touch and hear the world—and it's so real to us that we think that's all there is. But we have no idea that there is an ultimate, ideal reality upon which all the things we experience ultimately depend. Plato believed that philosophy was the only way one could ever free oneself and see beyond the material realm. Only through philosophy can we peer into the realm of absolute truth, absolute justice, absolute beauty—the absolute forms that give reality to the material world we're living in. That's why philosophers are uniquely qualified, he thought, to rule other men.

Interestingly, we find faint echoes of Plato's idealism in the New Testament.

While we look not at the things which are seen, but at the things which are not seen: for the things which are seen are temporal; but the things which are not seen are eternal. (2 Corinthians 4:18 KJV)

They serve at a sanctuary that is a copy and shadow of what is in heaven. (Hebrews 8:5a NIV)

It's interesting to note as well that modern science has given us a new twist on what Plato was talking about. A contemporary physicist named Gerald Schroeder, in a book called *The Hidden Face of God* (2002), asks us to think of the following example. He writes:

[S]olid matter, the floor upon which we stand and the foundation that bears the weight of a skyscraper, is actually empty space....The solidity of iron is actually 99.9999999999999 percent startlingly vacuous space made to feel solid by ethereal fields of force having no material reality at all (p. 4).

The world seems so solid to us—but it's something of an illusion. We can be deluded into thinking that this is all that's real because the world is so immediate and "solid" to us. But modern science tells us instead that the things we think are most solid are actually quite the opposite; they are an elaborate Wizard-of-Oz illusion. Schroeder asks us to imagine scaling an atom to a manageable, visible size. Scale up the nucleus of the atom to 4 inches. How far away would the electrons be that are orbiting the center? They would be four miles away from that four-inch nucleus—and what's in between, as Schroeder says, is basically emptiness. Now certainly there are subatomic particles that can be mathematically demonstrated; but these don't alter the point. The most solid thing we can imagine—iron, for instance—is essentially empty space. So, in other words, Plato was right after all.

Aristotle

Finally, let's turn to Aristotle and discuss how Plato's great student came along after him and disagreed with Plato about the nature of reality. Socrates and Plato were idealists, but Aristotle was a materialist. This is how Aristotle would answer that prime philosophical question about reality. *The essence or reality of a thing resides within the thing itself.* What does that mean? Remember that Plato, as an idealist, believed in an ideal reality beyond ourselves. Aristotle, as a materialist, is saying that we can locate the essence of a thing within the thing itself. Let's put it in philosophical terms in a way that kind of sounds ridiculous. Aristotle would say that the chair you're sitting on is every bit of a chair in itself—because *it has the essence of chairness within it.* Plato would say, "No, it's a chair because it depends ultimately upon some ideal concept in a transcendent realm—a realm which gave rise to, and continues to sustain, all that is material."

This is not just a word game. The question comes down again to where we locate reality. It's really the essential question you could possibly ask. The question brings us back to whether there is a God and whether He has created all things. Is there something or someone greater than the physical stuff that makes up our material world? Aristotle is not denying the existence of God; in fact, he spoke about a Prime Mover who started the whole causal chain to begin with. But Aristotle is the father of modern materialism in a sense, because he is claiming that reality is understood by its own material makeup, by reference to itself. A modern scientific materialist would say that the world around you is all that is—that there is nothing that cannot be understood in material terms. You understand the nature of the world as you study it scientifically, not by reference to some concept like "God." So, again, what's at stake is not word games, but essential disagreements about the most important questions of life.

And so we can see that Plato and Aristotle stand at the threshold of western thought as representing two different ways of answering that basic question. Raphael depicted the central disagreement well in his great Renaissance painting, "The School of Athens" (c. 1510). Two figures stand in the middle of that painting, debating philosophy with one another. The older man is pointing up, while the younger man next to him is holding his hand downward. Plato, of course, is pointing up to the ideal realm, while Aristotle is defending materialism. It's as though Raphael is depicting how their very gestures would answer the question, "Where do you locate the essence of reality?"

THE HUMANISTIC IDEAL

Chapter Objectives

- Correct some of the misconceptions we have about ancient Greek art.
- Express how Greek art illustrates the ideas of rationalism and humanism.
- Analyze the masterpiece of Greek architecture, the Parthenon.

In this chapter we'll be turning our attention to another notable achievements of ancient Greek culture: the visual arts and architecture. We're going to see that the same humanistic ideal that anchored their philosophical inquiry is eloquently expressed in the way they sculpted the human form and designed their great temples.

Here's how I want to proceed. First, as we analyze their art, I want us to consider what our knowledge rests upon. How do we know what we know about Greek art? How did the information get into textbooks in the first place? This isn't just a trivial question. We're not following a rabbit trail. This is one of the most important questions we must remember as we study culture. What does our knowledge rest on? How sure are we of our conclusions? I can guarantee that we'll discover some interesting things as we apply this question to Greek art.

I want you to realize that the things we're studying are the direct product of scholarly investigation and debate. There are certain things that can be viewed as settled knowledge about the past; but there is much we are still learning and much we'll never fully understand about the past. Studying history and culture is a dynamic process. Too often, I think we consider that history is just a collection of things that are known about the past, things that historians have written down—as if all we have to do is open the book, memorize some facts, and you'll understand the past. The reality is that confronting the past is a dynamic process; our knowledge changes with each new discovery, technique, or method of interpretation. We often need to clarify, refine, and sometimes even reverse our view of things we once took for granted. So this is an important question to ask: How do we know what we know about this subject? We're going to see that our knowledge of Greek art has always been restricted by a lot of misconceptions; and this illustrates, once again, the difficulty that we face when we try to understand the past.

After this introduction, we'll move on to look at the development of ancient Greek art and architecture. We'll see that the Greeks single-handedly "invented" western art. And we're going to claim that they did this two ways:

- they moved toward naturalism
- they developed realistic perspective

A Question about Method

But first of all, a question about method. Since we're going to be reaching some conclusions about Greek art, it's reasonable for us to ask, "How do we know about this subject?" What is the basis of our knowledge?" These questions gain urgency when we recognize some fundamental misconceptions we have about Greek art. Go to any museum and you'll find those misconceptions reinforced; as you walk through the ancient art galleries of, say, the Metropolitan Museum in New York, you're going to see a lot of marble statues on display. You might easily form the impression that the ancient Greeks valued sculpting in polished marble. You might even assume that marble represents their highest form of sculptural art. An ancient Greek would be surprised by that, because marble didn't represent the highest achievement of Greek art to them, even though over 90% of what we have on display in museums today are Greek marble statues. In reality, they didn't value marble nearly as much as they valued sculpting in bronze. They would have filled out a museum with bronze statues as the highest achievement of what they could accomplish.

Why is it, then, that we have so many marble statues in our museums and so few bronze statues? Why not just stock up our museums with more bronze so that they're more representative? The last thing we want is people leaving a museum with misconceptions. Michelangelo lived with the same misconception five hundred years ago. He thought of polished marble when he thought of classical Greek art. He thought that was the highest classical expression of the human form, which is why he sculpted that way in imitation. Think of his great statue, *David*, as one famous example. But the Greeks preferred sculpting in bronze, and marble was a less valued medium. Even then, however, they painted their marble statues and decorated them with accessories—something that definitely doesn't come across when you walk through a museum. So, in other words, we have many misconceptions. Here's the problem we face: *We can only display in a museum what has survived*. That's pretty obvious—but it explains why we have so much marble and so little bronze. It explains why we have a distorted view of ancient Greek art. You can recycle bronze much more easily than you can recycle marble. You can take a bronze statue and melt it down and turn that metal into other things like coins to pay the army with or weapons or tools. And this is exactly what happened over the centuries to many of the greatest bronze masterpieces. Most of the bronze statues that would have adorned the main squares of the Greek city states or the imperial palaces of the Roman emperors have long since disappeared. Most of the bronze statues that we do have today were pulled out of the ocean from ancient shipwrecks.

Let's pursue this question of knowledge a little more. How do we know the little that we do know about Greek art? One of main sources of knowledge, interestingly, is Roman art. The Romans admired Greek culture and reproduced their bronze statues in marble copies. When we discuss Myron's "Discobolus" (the "Discus Thrower"), we'll note that the object we're looking at is technically not a Greek statue at all; rather, it's a Roman marble copy of a Greek bronze original. Nearly five hundred years separate the lost original from the Roman copy. And yet the Romans made such faithful reproductions that we speak of the marble copy as a "Greek statue."

What the statues we have in museums? Where did they come from? Many were found the old-fashioned way: archaeologists dug them out of the ground. Statues have been found in the remains of old temples, imperial palaces, and sometimes even quarries. Some statues were sculpted on site and then discarded once a flaw was found in the marble. One particularly fruitful area of excavation was the Acropolis—the great temple site overlooking Athens. Some of the most famous surviving Greek statues were found there, including the "Calf-Bearer" and the "Kritios Boy." We need to remember that the objects we see in museums didn't come from a mail order catalogue. Somebody dug them out of the ground, dusted them off, reassembled missing heads, and labeled them for public display.

Archaeologists have been unearthing artifacts for the past two hundred years; and every year new discoveries are made. Perhaps the greatest frontier for archaeology, however, lies underwater. A wealth of ancient artifacts awaits discovery in the waters of the Aegean, Mediterranean, and the Black Sea. Scholars estimate that as many as 10-15% of all ships in the ancient world never reached their destination. The same technology that Robert Ballard used to explore the Titanic in the 1980s is now being used to discover ancient shipwrecks throughout the Mediterranean world. Each year our knowledge expands with every new discovery.

One of the best preserved bronze Greek statues ever found was located underwater by a Belgian scuba diver in 1996 off the coast of Croatia. So just when we think that everything has been discovered, a treasure like this comes to light. This reminds us again of how dynamic our study of the past is and why we have to revise our textbooks constantly. National Geographic spearheaded a recovery team that identified the underwater remains found by the scuba diver as a Roman ship. Part of the ancient cargo, a bronze statue, was found half-buried in sand; it's a nearly perfect example of a type of Greek statue called an **apoxyomenos**, which is a life-size statue of an athlete. The Greeks idealized the athlete as a prime example of the active, autonomous individual.

New laboratory techniques allow us to learn more from ancient objects than ever before. Once in the laboratory, the statue found off Croatia was photographed thousands of times so that a virtual, digital copy could be analyzed within a computer environment. The computer age has revolutionized the way we engage the past with new techniques and resources. Other clues came from the physical object itself. Bronze statues are hollow because they're cast from a mold; in the hollow leg of the statue researchers found the remains of a mouse's nest. They could determine from the position of the nest that the statue obviously was transported on its side in the ship. They were also able to date the material that they found to around the first century of the Christian era, during the Roman period. We know from the style of the statue that it must have been made in Greece in the fourth century B.C., and yet the evidence shows that it was being transported about 400 years later. From this information we can reconstruct something of its history. Many Greek statues like this one were taken from their original Greek locations in the Roman period to decorate Roman palaces, villas, and temples. This one obviously never made it to its final destination.

So, who knows what remains to be found? Let me tell you about my dream discovery—the one I hope I read about someday. At the end of the Roman Empire, Rome was sacked by the Vandals who sailed from North Africa in 455 A.D. For several days they pillaged all the treasures from Rome, including its great collection of art. Rome had looted all of the treasures of the ancient world, and now the Vandals were taking all of that loot and shipping it back to North Africa. Over twenty ships were loaded up; all the statues were placed in one ship. Every ship made it back to North Africa, except for the one that contained all of the statues taken out of the temples of Rome. The ship is still lying somewhere on the bottom of the Mediterranean Sea, waiting to be discovered. If it were ever found, who knows how it would change what we thought we knew about ancient Greek art and ancient Roman art. Textbooks would have to be rewritten!

So there is much yet to be discovered. Our knowledge of the past is an ongoing, dynamic process of fine-tuning what we know.

But it's an important challenge, and an important process, because the goal is truth. The truth about the past, not some myth about the past, is what is at stake. As we turn our attention now to the development of Greek art, we'll try to be true to the evidence. But keep in mind everything we've been considering about the sources of our knowledge. Test every generalization in light of the evidence.

The Move toward Naturalism

As we look at the artistic legacy of the ancient Greeks, we're going to focus on two main developments that we can trace in the surviving record of artifacts. The first of these is what I call *the move towards naturalism*. When we first see Greek art emerging, it's not very natural at all. It's pretty lifeless, pretty dull; the human form is expressionless and abstract. The art is static. In other words, early Greek art looks rather Egyptian. Consider the qualities that we associate with Egyptian art—the static quality, the expressionless forms and unchanging styles. All of this describes the earliest Greek art. The Greeks "learned" how to paint, sculpt, and build from the Egyptians—the cultural superpower of the Mediterranean world. The influence is clearly seen in vases produced in the geometric style.

You would not, for a minute, describe the human form depicted on a geometric vase, such as the Dipylon Vase, as lifelike, realistic, or natural. It's abstract and stylized. There is nothing natural about it. This is the beginning point of Greek art. So how do we get from this to the "Discus-Thrower"? That's the mystery that scholarship tries to explain. What I'm calling "the move toward naturalism" is an attempt to describe what is happening as we go from abstract human forms to athletic, muscular, and lifelike human forms that are natural.

The Egyptian style—or, in a broader sense, the Mediterranean style—is evident in Greek sculpture as well, as illustrated by the kouros statues produced in the late Archaic period from around 600 to 525 B.C. You would not describe these statues as natural or lifelike. It doesn't look as though the statue is about to break out in conversation with you. There is an expressionless quality to it. There is a rigidness in the form, and that's for good reason. It is imitative of the Egyptian style. When you put a Greek kouros side-by-side with an Egyptian statue, you see the obvious similarities.

It's not coincidental; the one form is done in imitation of the other. Let's isolate what those characteristics are. First, the rigidity of the form can be seen in the clenched fists of the statue. What happens when you clench a fist? It defines the muscle structure and emphasizes the rigidity of the form. Secondly, we see the expressionless face in both statues—and we're focus on the story of that face in Greek art shortly. About the only thing that's a little bit lifelike at all is the slight shifting of weight that we see in the left foot. Interestingly, it's always the left foot that's moving in ancient art. That's never been satisfactorily explained. Why the left foot and not the right foot? Even Michelangelo, when he imitated the ancient style, picked up on that convention; for him, the left foot became the center of movement and activity. This little mystery about the left foot underscores again that we often reach thresholds to our explanations. We can observe these things; but we can't always explain or interpret what we're observing.

Let's see how the Greeks began to experiment with the "dead" Egyptian forms that they started with. They must have become tired or bored very quickly of sculpting the same way. It might have been acceptable for the Egyptians to sculpt and paint the same way in 1000 B.C. that they did in 2000 and 3000 B.C. But that's not the Greek mindset. The Greeks were constantly changing and trying to make things new. That means we can actually date their art decade by decade, not century by century or millennium by millennium, because that's how rapidly the art was changing in style. As we move beyond the Greeks, we'll see that this remains one of the enduring qualities of western culture. We continue to be a rapidly changing culture, and that's one of the legacies of the ancient Greeks.

We can imagine some Greek artist, we don't know who, getting bored of making the same kouros sculptures, year in and year out, and wondering one day in his studio what a statue would look like if he put a smile on its face. Somebody had to think that thought, because all of a sudden, starting in the late Archaic period, we see kouros statues that are smiling and even grinning. We don't know who started the trend, but art historians have named it the **Archaic smile**, after the period when it first appeared. These smiles are almost as enigmatic as the Mona Lisa's expression. Why are they smiling? Most likely, it's a simple case of trying to make the statue more natural by defining the structure of the face. The sculptors seem to be trying to make these statues come alive—in a way that's reminiscent of the Pygmalion myth, as though a fully human form is beginning to emerge from the marble.

Of course, they didn't perfect this naturalism right from the start. The Greek artists were experimenting, and some of their earliest examples, from around 530 B.C., are rather pathetic. The expression isn't natural at all; it's more like a goofy grin. But they kept working with it, through of experimentation and innovation. They didn't settle for what was done in the last decade or previous generation; they wanted to do it better. This represents a very different way of looking at the world, motivated by a different set of values, than we saw with the Egyptians.

A rare and famous bronze statue, the "Charioteer of Delphi," shows how much progress the Greeks had made by around 475 B.C. The expression is more relaxed, more natural—detached, but not in a lifeless way. Another 150 years of artistic development and we'll end up with the far more expressive portraits of Alexander the Great. These portraits are much more natural and lifelike, even if they don't exactly reproduce the features of Alexander's face. The Greeks always idealized their portraits, making them all look like Greek gods. Nevertheless, we see the move toward naturalism here, as evident in the furrowed brows. Imagine how it would be to conquer the whole world and have all that responsibility on your shoulders. That's what the artist seems to be trying to capture—the lifelike image of Alexander as a living, breathing human being.

Realistic Perspective

We can identify a second tendency in the progression of Greek art, namely *the development of realistic perspective*. When we analyzed Egyptian art, we defined perspective as the angle from which something is seen. We noted that the Egyptians painted art from multiple perspectives, according to the characteristic angle of the thing they were painting. That's why we see the pond depicted from the top and the fish depicted from the side. This mixing of perspectives is disorienting to us; we expect a landscape, for example, to reproduce the vision of the artist. Why? Because we've inherited the Greek way of looking at the world through art. They rejected the multiple perspective of Egyptian art and began to paint what the eye sees, not what the mind knows.

This principle of multiple perspective is reflected in the Egyptian style of frontality, in which every element of the human body is depicted according to its most characteristic angle. The Greeks imitated this as well in their vase painting, showing the limbs and head in profile. But just as with sculptural art, we see the Greeks moving toward a new style, a distinctively Greek style in how they painted. In a vase painting known as "The Warrior's Leave-Taking," we begin to see a very subtle, but profound, shift underway. This painting captures a moment, a snapshot that documents the beginnings of western art. I would say that the whole story of the development of Greek art can be told through the two feet of this warrior.

We see the young man getting ready to head out to the battlefield and saying goodbye to his mother and father. We also see how Egyptian this all looks—at least at first glance. The young man's head is shown in profile, the torso is seen from the front, and all four limbs are visible. But then you see something very interesting that's happening with his feet. The warrior has what we could call an "Egyptian foot" and a "Greek foot." What I'm calling the Egyptian foot is the one seen from its most characteristic angle; what I'm calling the Greek foot is the one that shows realistic perspective, the one that shows how a foot actually looks when you look at it straight ahead. You see the five toes and the foot is compressed. An Egyptian might look at that and say, "No, we can't send someone like this into the afterlife with a deformed foot!" Art for the Egyptians was all about preserving one's identify for the afterlife. But the Greek artist isn't thinking like that. For him art is a way of understanding the world. He is a rationalist, and he is using his art as a philosopher would—to try to understand the world better. He wants to paint what the eye sees. This left foot, then, documents the shift from an Egyptian to a Greek way of thinking about art—and, by extension, thinking about the world.

The left foot of the warrior illustrates an optical phenomenon called **foreshortening**. This term describes the way an object appears shorter and more compressed than it actually is when seen from a certain angle. We see and experience the world this way every day as we look at things from different vantage points. This painting, then, is moving toward the kind of realistic perspective we experience naturally. Here's an example. Imagine that a person who is six feet tall is stretched out in a couch. If you look at that couch from the long side, you'll see all six feet of that person's stature; but if you stand at the head or foot of the couch, you'll see that the person's form is compressed, or foreshortened. We know intuitively what's going on; we know that the person hasn't suddenly gotten shorter. This is just how the eye sees it—and that's exactly what the rationalistic Greek mind is seeking to express in the visual arts.

Myron's *Discobolus*

Let's sum up what we've been analyzing by looking at one of the greatest of all Greek statues, "Discobolus" (the Discus-Thrower) by Myron. We have been tracing the development of naturalism and realistic perspective, all of which culminate in the masterpieces of the classical age. Statues of athletes were staples of Greek art; they idealized the athletic form, which they saw as the epitome of the active man. Myron's statue was produced in the classical period, the Age of Pericles, right around 450 B.C., and it represents a summation of the humanistic ideal in ancient Greek culture.

The British art historian, E. H. Gombrich, offers some brilliant insights into this mas-

terpiece. His analysis lays out clearly why Myron's work was both a representation of all that is Greek and, at the same time, a work of stunning originality.

The attitude looks so convincing that modern athletes have taken it for a model and have tried to learn from it the exact Greek style of throwing the discus.

Gombrich is pointing out that when the Olympic games were reintroduced in the 1890s, nobody knew how to throw a discus. Nobody had thrown one for several millennia, and so athletes were trying to figure out how to do it by looking at this ancient statue. Gombrich cautions us against thinking of the statue that way.

But this has proved less easy than they had hoped. They had forgotten that Myron's statue is not a 'still' from a sport's reel but a Greek work of art. In fact if we look at it more carefully we shall find that Myron has achieved his astonishing effect of movement mainly through a new adaptation of very ancient artistic models.

In this analysis, Gombrich has given us a textbook definition of genius in art. We have trivialized the notion of genius in the modern age, as if it's all about producing something completely new—something that nobody has ever seen before, such that there's nothing to compare it with. The work of genius (for us) is supposed to be a work that comes from nothing, *ex nihilo*. We equate genius with complete originality. But as Gombrich reminds us, *true genius lies in working within a tradition and transforming it from the inside out*. The element of genius is seen when an artist is able to take an old outworn tradition and breathe new life into it, such that we look at something familiar through unfamiliar eyes. That's what Gombrich means with the phrase, "a new adaptation of very ancient artistic models." What exactly is he talking about here? Let's keep reading.

Standing in front of the statue and thinking only of its outlines we become suddenly aware of its relation to the tradition of Egyptian art.

This is a brilliant observation. Gombrich is saying that you can look at that statue, which is so breathtakingly original, and you can see the ancient and outworn tradition of Egyptian frontality still within it! The torso is fronted, the head and limbs are in profile. It's Egyptian frontality, but with a Greek twist—a literal twist here since the body is in movement. Gombrich is emphasizing that this stature is a subtle reinterpretation of the old form; Myron must have realized, as a flash of genius, that he could take the old form and make it completely new. He takes the old form, and he pours the new dynamism of Greek art into it.

Like the Egyptian painters, Myron has given us the trunk in front view, the legs and arms in side view, like them he has composed his picture of a man's body out of the most characteristic views of its parts.

Again, that's genius at work. Whether you're talking about Michelangelo or Mozart, Shakespeare or Plato—the same principle holds true. These great artists and thinkers took old forms and put them to new uses. They are doing what Jesus spoke of in that memorable phrase: *pouring new wine into old wineskins*.

Let's come back to our initial question. Why does it matter to try to figure these things out? What difference does it make it we truly understand an ancient piece of art on its own terms? Why isn't it just fine for us to live with our misconceptions about the past? Does it really matter if we think of polished marble, and not bronze, as the highest expression of Greek art?

Yes, these question do matter. The past is worth studying with care, because of the many ways the past can be misused. Some of these ways are even pernicious and evil. There's no more sobering example of this than how the Nazis reinterpreted the past—including the whole legacy of ancient Greece. Hitler could reinterpret the "Discus-Thrower" as a testimony to racial superiority, as a cultural vindication of his perverse political aims.

You might say, "But it's really trivial to know that the Greeks admired bronze and not marble." But where do we draw the line? How many benign and trivial details does it take before we have a badly distorted picture of the past that might justify all

sorts of wrongs? The study of the past really does matter, because so much that happens in the present depends upon it.

Greek Temple Architecture

Let's turn now to the subject of ancient Greek architecture. We'll continue in the same vein, focusing on the development of the styles and how this helps us to understand the Greek mind a little better. We are, after all, trying to understand the Greek worldview by analyzing the things they made. We are trying to identify the common denominator that holds all these things together. We're operating on the assumption that we can "read" the Greek mind by looking at the way they sculpted statues, how they asked questions philosophically about the world, even by how they built temples to their gods. As we go through some of the technical details of this subject, keep your eye open for those common qualities that we've already identified in the ancient Greeks. Let's see what else we can discover about their humanism and rationalism.

We have already learned—from their philosophy and works of art—that the Greeks were motivated by one central preoccupation. We can describe this as *an obsession with refining the image of the human form*. The Greeks didn't refine the human form only through a chisel; they did it through the hard work of philosophy as well. We should recall again that quote of Protagoras that we keep coming back to:

"Man is the measure of all things." We should also recall how Socrates taught that knowing oneself is the beginning of wisdom and knowledge about the world. The Greek idea was that if you understand the human condition, then you are able to project that knowledge outward onto the cosmos. It shouldn't surprise us, then, that the Greeks looked at their temples much the same way. When you and I look at a Greek temple, we see all the elements arranged geometrically. We see lots of columns and the triangular form that rests upon the columns. We don't see anything there that reflects the human image. But the Greeks surely did.

Everything they looked at, everything they considered, everything they made, came back to that reference point of self—that desire to understand the individual's position within the world. Here's what one architectural historian, Norberg-Schulz, has said about this.

[I]t was the human aspect that the Greeks took as their point of departure, making the trabeated structure an expression of the living forces of carrying and being carried. Accordingly, the Greek temple appears as a muscular body, as a truly organic form, which concretizes life as action in space and time.

Now did they actually look at their temples and "see" them that way? I don't think that's what Norberg-Schulz is literally saying; but at some level this interpretation is almost certainly correct. If the human form was central to the ancient Greeks, as we've seen it to be, then we should expect to find this central value lying behind their architecture as well. Why? Because cultures, like people, are consistent. In everything they did, the Greeks were trying to express the wonder and mystery of being an active human force within the world. I especially like how Norberg-Schultz has described the Greek temple as a muscular body, a dynamic form illustrating the active principle "of carrying and being carried." We are going to see that the columns were structured almost like biceps that are holding up the enormous weight of the temple. The notion that it's a dynamic form that "concretizes life as action and space in time" could be a description, not of a Greek temple, but rather of "The Discus Thrower." The whole point behind Myron's statue is to explore the human form as a dynamic center of energy and action in space and time. This humanistic ideal is one of the common denominators linking together everything that the Greeks did.

Here's how we'll proceed. First, we'll define the general style of Greek temple architecture. Next, we'll sketch the layout of the temples by focusing on how the floorplans developed and became more complex. Following this, we'll look more closely at some of the technical aspects of the exterior style of a Greek temple. Finally, we'll sum up what we've learned as we examine the greatest of all Greek temples, the Parthenon. Once again, the payoff for all this detail should be a little clearer picture of the Greek mind.

Greek temples are an example of **post-and-lintel** architecture. This term refers to two elements that make up the overall design. Greek temples, then, can be thought of as a binary structure, divided into a vertical and horizontal section. The "post" (or vertical section) is composed of the columns; the "lintel" (or horizontal section) is made up of the triangular pediment that rests upon those columns. We can trace an ancient lineage behind the Greek temple that goes all the way back into prehistoric times. The dolmen structure in prehistoric times provides the basic kernel of the idea—a couple slabs of stone with a horizontal slab resting on top. In the Mycenae-an period, recall this same combination of vertical and horizontal elements in the Lion Gate of the Great Citadel of Mycenae. This is the lineage that came through ancient Egypt, through the cultures of the Mediter-ranean, and ultimately to the Greeks. I am emphasizing the background to this post-and-lintel style not just to demonstrate the connectedness of these early cultures; I also want to draw out an important contrast that we'll be discussing in a later chapter. We'll see that though the Romans built this way too, they also developed an entirely different concept of architecture. The Ro-mans developed the technology of the arch and would build the arch into everything they constructed. So later on as we talk about the Romans, we'll contrast their method of building with the Greek style.

So we've traced an ancient lineage for the Greek style; but let's also extend this style beyond the Greeks, down to our own time. Since this was the classical style of archi-tecture, we'll see the form revived and imi-tated during the Italian Renaissance. Archi-tects who were looking for new ways to build were inspired by the classical world and went back to the Greco-Roman models. Palladio, for example, was an Italian archi-tect in the late sixteenth century who built villas in the classical style. A couple of cen-turies after this we see another revival of classical style—the neoclassical period; this is when Thomas Jefferson built Monticello in the Greco-Roman style. I'm emphasizing here the continuity that we see—going all the way back into ancient times. It's a con-tinuity that lies beneath much of our archi-tectural legacy today, specifically in gov-ernment buildings and church buildings that reflect the ancient classical forms.

Let's turn our attention to how the Greek temple floor plan developed through four successive stages. Then we'll come back to the façade and analyze the overall structure of the temple in a little bit greater detail. The first stage in the development of the floor plan is very basic, more like a simple shrine. Notice the terms that describe the key elements of the structure. The word

naos means "room" in Greek, and this is where the cultic statue would be located—the god or goddess to whom the shrine was dedicated and before which sacrifices would be made. Leading into the room is a porch, called a *pronaos*. Notice that the columns don't yet make up a very significant part of the overall design in this earliest period.

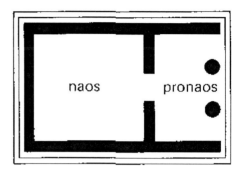

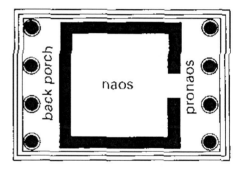

Now notice what happens as we go from the first to the second floor plan. We see something that's typically Greek in this de-velopment. We can imagine Greeks walking around the first structure, looking at the design and saying, "There's something not quite right about it; it's not balanced." As rational people, the Greeks were always looking for order and balance in the world; so it shouldn't surprise us that they would make the structure symmetrical by adding a back porch. Notice as well that the col-umns are becoming a more dominant part of the overall design.

As we move from the second to the third floor plan, we see a fully realized Greek temple with columns extending all the way around the perimeter of the design. In the center, we still have the basic core of the design; but now we have a superstructure over the whole thing—a roof that's supported by columns that run the entire perimeter of the structure. This is called a **peripteral** temple—named for the columns that run around the perimeter or periphery of the structure. The columns stand on an elevated platform with steps leading up on all sides. The best known example of a peripteral temple from ancient Greece is the Parthenon, which we'll be analyzing shortly.

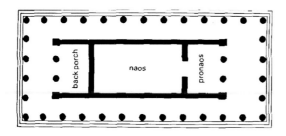

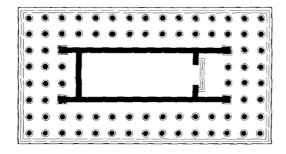

In the final stage of temple design we go from a single row of columns to a double row. This is known as a **dipteral** temple ("di" being the same root word that gives us the word "double"). By doubling the columns, you're essentially doubling the cost of the building. It was extremely expensive to sculpt these things—to create the ornate capitals that were at the top of each one of the columns. That's why we see these temples primarily in the very wealthy city states of Asia Minor. The best known dipteral temple is found in the remains of Ephesus, a city that's important in the New Testament. These cities obviously are projecting a sense of wealth through this design, since everything we make, everything we build, is a reflection (or projection) or our values.

Let's focusing our attention now on the façade of the structure. This is how we think

of a Greek temple—as seen from the exterior. As we analyze the façade, we'll be focusing on the three different styles of building these temples what are referred to as the three **orders** of temple architecture. These orders, or styles, developed chronologically in ancient Greek culture and expressed different values to the Greek.

- Doric
- Ionic
- Corinthian

The Doric order (see A below) emerged in the late Archaic period and seemed to symbolize strength, simplicity, and stability to the Greeks. We see this quality in the thickness and plainness of the columns.

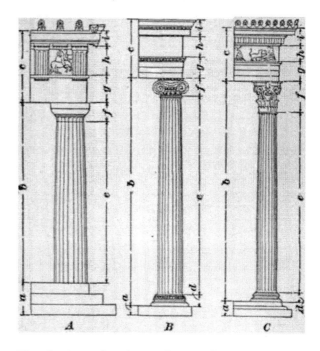

The Ionic order (see B) was developed during the classical age, the fifth century B.C., and projected the qualities of refinement and elegance associated with that Golden Age of Greek culture. Finally, the Corinthian order (see C) emerged in the late classical period and became the standard style of the Hellenistic age. In the intricacy of its design it represented the wealth of imperial Greece. The very complexity of the sculpture is a projection of wealth—the same way luxury items function today (like a Lexus car or a Rolex watch). In order to sculpt each one of those Corinthian columns, you would have to employ a lot of very skilled artisans. The columns don't fall off an assembly line stamped "Made in China."

Every nook and cranny of the Greek temple had a technical name. We'll analyze just a few of the key elements that make up the binary structure of the design. Let's start by looking at the column. This part, of course, is the vertical element (the "post"). We can subdivide the column into three main parts.

- base
- shaft
- capital

The base is seen in the Ionic and Corinthian order; strictly speaking, the Doric doesn't have a separate base where the column meets the foundation. The second element is the main part of the column, the shaft. Up and down the length of the shaft, ridges were sculpted into the surface of the column, known as **flutes**. Think again of the manpower required to sculpt these columns individually, according to precise measurements, and then translate those hours into a budget item. All these elements add up to create a very expensive building to construct. The third element is the **capital**, which refers to the headstone which connects the vertical and horizontal elements of the temple. The capital is the most significant element in the design, since this is the easiest way to identify what order a temple is.

The Doric capital, as illustrated in the Parthenon, is best described as a simple stone slab—very utilitarian, functional, with nothing ornate and elaborate about it. There's no excessive projection of wealth, just the sense of simplicity and strength. The Ionic capital has been described variously as looking like a ram's horns or a scroll. The overall design is elegantly simple and balanced, which made it a good reflection of what the Greeks saw in themselves during the classical period. Finally, the Corinthian capital. You can see how this is far more intricate and ornate than the two previous

orders, an excessive style that speaks of the wealth of imperial Greece. What is being depicted in the capital? This is the leaf of the acanthus, an indigenous plant in the southern Mediterranean.

Resting on the columns is the horizontal element of the temple, known as the **entablature**. The entablature itself is broken down into several further categories—for example, the architrave, frieze, and the cornice. Notice the frieze, in particular. This is a very significant part of the entablature, since this is where you would see relief sculptures around the length of the temple. These exterior sculptures were an important part of the Parthenon's design. On all four sides were elaborate depictions of the gods and the heroes of ancient Greece.

Most of the remaining sculptures were forcibly removed from the Parthenon by Lord Elgin, a British officer stationed in Greece in the early nineteenth century. They are now found in the British Museum, to the consternation of the Greek government. Ancient writers described the relief sculptures on the Parthenon as being among the greatest of all Greek art.

Speaking of the Parthenon: let's focus a little more closely now on this primary example of Greek temple architecture. This greatest of all Greek temples was built in the old Doric order, even though it was built in the middle of the classical age when the Ionic style was coming into vogue. Why did they opt for this older style? It was probably for political reasons, as if to say, "Look, we are still here; we survived the Persians." The strength, solidity, and stability of the Greek nation is what they were trying to convey. So that's why they opted for the Doric order, as opposed to the trendier new form that was being developed in other temples of the time.

If you were to make a list of the ten greatest buildings in the history of the world, the Parthenon would be on your list. And the reasons for that are many. It's a beautiful building, to be sure, and we're going to note some of the technical achievements that are pretty amazing. But the rich history of the Parthenon also sets it apart in a class by itself. It was built during Greece's Golden Age (during the middle of the fifth century B.C.) and it was intended as a "thank you gift" to Athena, the patron goddess of Athens. The Greeks were expressing thanks for her help in saving them from the Persians in 479 B.C.

The temple stood fairly well preserved for 2500 years. We can imagine the apostle Paul standing near this site when he debated the Greek philosophers (Acts 17). The Parthenon was the most important structure on the Acropolis overlooking Athens; but it was just one temple among a whole complex of temples and shrines. For most of its history, down into the early modern period, the Parthenon was remarkably well preserved. This is because it was transformed in the early Christian era into a Catholic church; and then, after the Turkish conquest of Greece, it was converted into a mosque. In fact, it would have looked today much like it did in the apostle Paul's day if not for what happened about three hundred years ago.

In the late seventeenth century, the Turks and the Venetians were locked in a bitter battle and Athens was the focus of much of their conflict. When the Turks held the region, they made the fateful decision to turn one of the great artifacts of western civilization, the Parthenon, into an ammunitions depot. The Venetians were out in the harbor, lobbing missiles at the Turks, and one of them landed in the middle of the Parthenon. You can imagine what happened next; it was like an explosion in a fireworks factory. The inside of the building was basically blown out, and what we see today are the remains. Up into early modern times, local residents helped themselves to the ancient marble and used it for private building material. We're fortunate that the Parthenon is still standing at all after all this abuse.

Clearly, the Parthenon has a great history behind it. But why does the building itself stand apart when compared with other Greek temples? What makes it unique as an architectural masterpiece? The Parthenon has some unique design features that place it in a class by itself. Yes, the same post-and-lintel architecture is here—but it's executed with a twist. The architects brought some subtle adjustments to the overall design. As we analyze what they did, I want us once again to see the Greek mind at work. This is what we're trying to understand as we study our way through the western story: how do these cultural artifacts take us into the value system, the beliefs, the worldview, of the cultures that produced them? We're going to see that the architects tweaked the design; they modified the structure in certain ways that are not even entirely perceptible to the human eye. This obviously begs the question, "Why did they do this?"

The architects made three adjustments, or refinements, to the Parthenon. The first refinement was in the horizontal plane. This means that *on all four sides of the structure there is a slight upward curvature in all the horizontal planes* from the base through the entablature. There is a curvature, a swelling upward in the middle of the horizontal line at the base of the temple (on all four sides) and the entablature (on all four sides). You could stand in front of the Parthenon and look at it all day without "seeing" this. The adjustment is very slight—but it's measurable. Modern scholarship has demonstrated that it's a built-in design feature.

Now, how do we know that this is not just the result of the earth settling through seismic activity after 2500 years? How do we know that it was designed that way? Very simply, because it's measurable, precise, and repeated through all the horizontal planes on all four sides. It couldn't be the product of coincidence. This leads to an important point that I'll mention in passing here because it's just too good an analogy to ignore. It's interesting to note that scholars today will take out their intricate measuring devices and show the regularity and the design in this particular structure and infer, logically, that it must have been designed this way with purpose and intelligence. And then they will turn to the fields of biology and chemistry and astronomy—where we also find complex design which is

measurable and repeatable, but infinitely far more complex than the Parthenon—and they'll declare it to be the product of chance and accident. There is a profound philosophical disconnect between those two ways of thinking about the world.

There is a second adjustment and refinement that the architects brought into the Parthenon, and that is *a tapering in the columns*. The eye can see this adjustment: the columns have a slight swelling about two-thirds of the way up. They bulge like biceps holding up tremendous weight. The temple is like an organic, dynamic form—an active agent in the world. Once again, we see the human principle so typical of Greek culture.

Finally, in addition to the horizontal plane and the tapering of the columns, we see that *the angle at which the columns are set* is also slightly adjusted. That means that none of the columns is strictly vertical; they all lean inward slightly. Once again, this is something you wouldn't see if you stood there and looked for it; but in a strange way, you would be conscious of it nonetheless. You can't quite put your finger on it, but you are aware that the Parthenon doesn't look like any other Greek temple. It looks more natural, more lifelike. You would expect the columns to stand at exact right angles to the entablature and the base. In fact, the columns on all four sides lean inward slightly, imperceptibly, towards the center.

What is the reason for these very minute adjustments? They are based on precise measurements and you can't even consciously see them; so what's the point? As I noted, you *are* aware of them at an unconscious level. That's what makes the Parthenon seem different. The architects built a complex optical illusion into the design. One historian has described it this way:

Any simple post and lintel structure made out of many identical repeated units is in danger of looking lifeless and mechanical. Many buildings that imitate the Parthenon do. The architectural refinements are meant to counteract this. They modify just those parts of the temple that otherwise would look most severe and rigid: the straight lines and right angles.

The Romans never quite figured out the secret, which is why their temples always looked boxy, even though they were trying to imitate the Greeks. As you stand in front of the Parthenon, you're not consciously aware of the precise details; but you know that this doesn't look like other temples. It has a natural feel to it, because the severe angles have been softened a bit. What does this tell us about the Greeks? It tells us once again that they were using the faculty of reason to manipulate the world of experience. We see the rational, scientific impulse at wprl again—just as we saw it in Greek vase painting.

As impressive as the building is in its design, consider what was on the inside. In the *naos*, the central room, stood a huge statue of Athena. The original has not survived; but we have many small Roman copies, made in marble, that give us an approximation of what it looked like. These are poor substitutes for the original, however. The original statue stood forty feet tall—absolutely enormous and imposing. You can imagine just how impressive it would have been to go into the *naos* and see this statue in the dark interior, lit only by torchlight. A reflecting pool stretched out in front of the statue.

Let me describe this statue just to give you a little sense of how impressive it must have been. The underlying structure was carved out of wood, which was then cov-

ered with gold from top to bottom, except for the areas of exposed flesh (arms, neck, face) which were sculpted out of ivory. The breastplate, shield, and headdress were studded with precious stones and jewels. Forty feet of gold, ivory, and precious stones. As you can imagine, the statue of Athena cost more than the rest of the temple put together. The Greeks realized how close to annihilation they had come when the Persians had invaded, and so they spared no expense in thanking Athena.

The statue didn't have a chance to survive the invasions and political turmoil of the centuries. It was probably still there when the apostle Paul was in Athens. But sometime during the early Christian era, when idols were being destroyed, Athena must have been removed and melted down. Who are the architectures responsible for this incredible building? Let's give credit where credit is due. The architects were two men, Ictinos and Callicrates. This was the leading architectural firm in Athens during the Golden Age. They constructed many other buildings, but the Parthenon was their single greatest accomplishment—a masterpiece of the humanistic ideal.

THE GREEK SENSE OF TRAGEDY

Chapter Objectives

- Explain how comedy and tragedy originated among the ancient Greeks.
- Defend the idea that ancient Greek drama expressed a philosophy of life.
- Summarize Aristotle's six characteristics of tragedy.

We have been developing our understanding of the ancient Greeks by analyzing the things they produced—their philosophy, art, and architecture. Under each of these categories we have focused on the origin and development of Greek ideas. We have traced that development and then analyzed more closely one particular work of art that summarizes this development. In this chapter we'll examine the performing arts in ancient Athens, in particular their notions of comedy and tragedy. Then we'll look more closely at what is arguably the greatest, or at least the most famous, of all ancient Greek tragedies, *Oedipus Rex* by Sophocles. Finally, we'll look at Aristotle's brilliant analysis of the philosophy behind Greek tragedy. Once again, it will be the underlying values of rationalism and humanism that we'll be exposing throughout this chaper—just as when we examined philosophy, art, and architecture. The ancient Greeks have already shown themselves to be a pretty remarkable people, originating ideas, concepts, and values that have endured throughout the story of western cul-

ture. The origins and development of comedy and tragedy in ancient Athens will give us one more opportunity to engage this rich legacy of ideas.

Perhaps the two masks of comedy and tragedy come to mind when we think of Greek drama. The one mask has an upturned mouth used by actors in comedy; the other has a down-turned mouth, signifying tragedy. These masks represent the two branches of drama that originated in Athens. Indeed, Greek drama marks the beginning point for the dramatic arts in western culture—right down to what we experience when we go to the movie theatre or turn on the television or go to the theatre and watch a play.

Drama was nonetheless very different for the ancient Greeks than it is for today's audiences. In a lot of ways, it would be hard for us to sit through an ancient Greek production. They were very stagy, prosaic and speechy—that it is to say, they were highly choreographed productions. Not a lot of action occurs on stage. You watch people standing around talking about things, delivering very long speeches for which we nowadays would have little patience. And yet the play, the plot itself, might be about all kinds of major events; you just don't see them happening. You only see messengers who come on stage and deliver long-winded speeches about things that are happening off-stage. Murders, conspiracies, political struggles and all kinds of great issues are discussed and form the basis of the plot; but there is little action—and this, interestingly, reflects that Greek orientation toward philosophical thought. The ancient Greeks were much more excited about listening to people discuss weighty issues and the philosophical implications of those events than we would be.

Another thing that we would find off-putting nowadays is the ancient Greek **chorus**. At the side or corner of the stage you'd see a group of men standing in long robes, chanting in unison at various points throughout the play. For the Greeks they were the omniscient voice of fate, commenting on the hero's actions, commenting on what had just happened, or preparing the audience for what was about to happen. This was a very different way of looking at drama from what we expect from a play or a TV show.

And yet all this represents the origins of western drama.

So how did these two art forms of comedy and drama emerge? What were the conditions that gave rise to them? And how do we explain what they meant originally, in that early culture? Scholars believe that comedy and tragedy had their origins in religious ritual, in the annual fall festivals. For example at harvest time, there was the celebration of the god Dionysus—the god of wine, harvest, and intoxication. He can be thought of as the Greek "party god." In this sense, he was the antithesis of everything that the Greeks usually saw themselves to be—that is, rationalists, people who lived moderate lives controlled by thought. At this one time of the year during the festival, however, they let loose. It is believed that both comedy and tragedy had their origin in these ancient Dionysian festivals.

Greek Comedy

Let's focus first of all on comedy. An important clue to the origin of comedy can be found in the typical comic plot. In classical Greek comedy, *the comic plot portrays the integration of the hero back into society.* Obviously, that presupposes that the hero is on the edge of falling outside society. Consider some examples of great comic actors in the modern age. Whether we think of a classic clown like Charlie Chaplin, or more recent comic actors, one of the things we always find to be true about comic figures is that they are *eccentric* in some way. They are oddball characters—not your average, typical, normal individual. This is the quality that makes us laugh at them.

That sense of eccentricity is the kernel of the idea as we look at the Greek comic character. Imagine society as a circle, and imagine the comic figure as somebody who is on the edge of that circle, needing to be brought back into it—to be brought back into the normal ebb and flow of social life. The word "eccentric" draws our attention to this, as it literally means "away from the center." This is true of all comic characters—they are misfits in society. Why would it be necessary to domesticate the eccentric figure and draw him back into society? To answer this we need to look at the philosophy that lies behind Greek comedy. We'll see that it really is not just a form of low entertainment; rather, for the Greeks, even comedy is a way of philosophizing about the world.

Let's approach this with a completely different example—one drawn from nature. You may have seen nature documentaries about East Africa and the migration of the wildebeest, those enormous herds that fill the plains of Kenya. And then you see cheetahs and lions lurking on the edges of that herd, looking for the straggler. Those ones are always vulnerable. It's believed that this is the idea behind Greek comedy as well. There's something dangerous about being on the edges of society. You are vulnerable and, as a comic figure, you are a threat and a danger to society itself. In what sense? In ancient cultures, the idea of survival was of utmost importance. Of course, it's an important concept to any culture; but in a modern society we are somewhat immunized from the constant sense of threat that ancient cultures experienced. Survival was a pressing very much on their mind.

The preoccupation in prehistoric cultures with hunting and fertility clearly exemplified this. The values of ancient civilizations, too, were bound up with these values. So if you are going to be a society that perpetuates itself and survives, you cannot be a society of eccentric misfits. Instead, great emphasis will be placed on uniformity and con-

formity to the social norm. Scholars believe that this social ideal lies behind the comic figure as a misfit; society has to grab hold of this individual and bring him or her back into the norms of society—since survival itself is at stake.

How, then, is the comic figure to be fully integrated back into society? The ending of the comedy gives us the clue. A classical Greek comedy typically ends with the wedding of the hero, a big marriage ceremony. Why? Because this oddball character is now fully integrated into the life-cycle of that society, and marriage is the institution that seals the deal, so to speak. That's why at the end of every Charlie Chaplin film, he gets the girl and settles down as a normal family man.

But this matrimonial element is not something we commonly associate with comedy today. Comedy for us is, simply, what makes us laugh. If it doesn't make us laugh, then it's not a comedy. The Greeks wouldn't understand that idea because they approached everything as philosophy. Comedy for them was a way of looking at the world, at society, and at man's position within society; comedy was a way to reflect upon the greatest questions and values. Greek comedy can thus be viewed as a kind of philosophy. By comparison with the Greeks, we have a relatively impoverished view of comedy. Interestingly, Shakespeare's comedies really nailed the formula, and his comedies are, in that sense, quite "Greek." In the fifth act of Shakespeare's

87

comedies, there is a big wedding ceremony and all of the subplots and the major plot are all brought together: the servants get married and the aristocrats get married, because it's all about integration and social stability. It's all about making everything balanced once again after the chaos of the comic plot.

Scholars believe that the origins of Greek comedy lie in the ancient fertility rights that formed the foundation of much of the Dionysian festival. Fertility rites involve the celebration of all that marriage represents to society—and that's why marriage is the capstone event of the comedy. The values of procreation and the survival of the tribe are in a sense commemorated in that story pattern and ritualistic celebration.

Greek Tragedy

What about tragedy? The classical Greek tragic plot takes us in the opposite direction. Where comedy gives us the integration of the hero into society, *tragedy gives us the alienation of the hero from society*. The prepositions are very significant here: integration *into* and alienation *from* or *out of*. As with comedy, we can draw the tragic plot with a circle with the circle representing society. The tragic hero begins in the center of society; but by the end of the play, the hero is expelled and completely alienated from society. Typically, the tragic hero is a figure of noble birth—a king, for example. No one could be more central to the life of that society than to be, say, Oedipus the King. By the end of the play, however, Oedipus is blinded and expelled from the city gates. That's the movement that we see in tragedy. Why is that? And how does the tragic plot typically end?

The typical ending for a tragic plot involves the death of the hero, which is, of course, the ultimate alienation from society. The hero has become a kind of scapegoat or a victim, a sacrifice for the larger community. Oedipus dies so that the penalty and punishment for some crime could be lifted from the city. This takes us into the theology that lies behind the Greek notions of trage-dy. Let's consider the greatest of all Greek tragedies, the story that Sophocles told of *Oedipus Rex*. A lot of us are familiar with the basic plot which has filtered down to us through Freud's theory of human development. The Oedipal complex, as he termed his theory of psychological development, is based upon this myth of Oedipus.

Here's the basic story. When baby Oedipus was born, the oracle spoke a prophecy that Oedipus would grow up eventually to kill his father, the king, and marry his mother, the queen. Naturally, his parents were deeply worried upon hearing such a dreadful prophecy. His parents therefore decided to place baby Oedipus into the hands of a servant and have him taken out into the wilderness to be abandoned. This horrible practice, known as "exposing" infants, was commonly practiced in the ancient world. Unwanted newborns were exposed to the elements and wild animals as a form of infanticide. This practice was found in nearly all ancient western cultures until it was abolished with the emergence of Christianity within the Roman Empire. So that was what happened to little Oedipus early in life. But a shepherd came along and heard his cries and took pity on him, rescued him, raised him—and Oedipus grew up to fulfill the prophecy of the gods that he would murder his father and marry his mother.

When the play opens, Oedipus is the king of the city, and the city had fallen on bad times. The gods were judging the city for his crime against fate, for his attempt (whether he knew it or not) to circumvent and frustrate the prophecy of the gods. Ultimately, the identity of Oedipus was found out and he had to pay the penalty for that. It doesn't sound fair at all to us, but Oedipus takes that penalty and becomes the sacrifice for the larger community; he bears that penalty, and then the guilt and the punishment is relieved from the larger community. That's the doctrine of sacrificial atonement—the kernel of it—right there in Greek mythology five centuries before Christ. This is interesting because it suggests that the Greeks were already thinking about sin and guilt before Paul ever preached to them; they were reflecting on the need for a sacrifice to be made, for somebody to pay the penalty for that guilt. This helps us to understand why Greek-speaking people were so receptive to the gospel when the apostle Paul traveled through their cities and preached. They were already programmed to hear Paul's message because of the ideas that ran deep within their own cultural experience.

We'll examine the nature of tragedy more closely in a moment, but first consider this question. As you think of comedy and tragedy in philosophical terms, one showing integration and the other alienation, which do you think more accurately describes the overall structure of the Bible? Taking the Bible as a totality, an overall message, and a single package, would you describe it as a tragedy or a comedy? The answers "neither" and "both" won't work, since the way a story ends is the definite answer to what kind of story it is. So, what do you see when you look at the end of the story—the final chapters of Revelation? We see the so-called "Marriage Feast of the Lamb." How interesting that the Bible ends with a marriage feast—a beautiful symbol that God's eternal purpose is being completed as we are fully integrated back into His perfect will. Certainly, there are elements of both tragedy and comedy throughout the biblical narrative; and if you focus only on one part—say, the death of Christ—then you'll see tragic elements to be sure. But that's not the end of the story. You've got to see the culminating point. We read in scripture that "God was in Christ reconciling the world to Himself" (2 Corinthians 5:19). That's the ultimate goal—the integration of all things back into God's eternal plan. We're not used to thinking of the Bible as "the greatest comedy ever told." Yet the Greeks would surely understand that description, because comedy for them was a way of understanding the world.

Aristotle's Definition of Tragedy

Let's look now at the brilliant analysis of tragedy given to us by Aristotle. Once again, we're going to see some interesting

biblical parallels. Aristotle was a brilliant man who wrote on many different topics—from biology to literature. In his book *Poetics*, Aristotle was dealing with the nature of tragedy and he focused in particular on the story of *Oedipus Rex* for his primary example. Aristotle believed that if you understood this tragedy, *Oedipus Rex*, then you'd understand the essential nature of what makes something tragic. Aristotle listed six characteristics of tragedy that you have to take as a self-contained package. There is a logical line of argumentation that goes from one to six. You can't rearrange these.

Let's first notice how Aristotle was thinking philosophically as he proceeded in his analysis. His stated goal is to try to understand the essence of tragedy; in order to do this he takes a particular tragedy and tries to find the essence of tragedy within that play. Think back, briefly, to how Plato might have described the chair you are sitting on right now as being a copy or shadow of an ideal chair. Aristotle would reply, "No, it is fully real in and of itself, because it has the essence of chairness within it." That is how Aristotle reasoned as a materialist; and that's what he's doing with tragedy as well. He is saying that *Oedipus Rex* is a tragedy because it has the essential characteristics of tragedy within it.

The first quality of tragedy, according to Aristotle, is that *the tragic hero must be of noble birth and of exceptional character*. He can't be just anybody. It's not John Q. Public we are talking about here. He's got to be somebody who in some way or other stands above and beyond everybody else. Typically, the hero will be a king or a nobleman. This is true for Shakespeare's tragic heroes as well. Just think of King Lear, Macbeth, Hamlet, and Othello. Notice, too, as well that the individual has to be of exceptional character. You can't be a tyrant and be a tragic figure. Why is this first point critical to a tragedy? There's a simple logic to it. The greater the height, the farther one falls, and the greater is the tragedy. If you fall off the first rung of ladder, nobody is going to rush up to you and tell you to lie down and stay immobilized until they can get paramedics there. After all, you only fell a few inches.; it's no great tragedy. But if you are at the top of that ladder, up on the third floor of a building, and you fell from that great height, your fall could be tragic; the consequences would be much more severe. That's the simple spatial logic that governs this idea. Similarly, the tragic hero has to be morally good, since this makes his loss to the world all the more poignant.

Aristotle's second point builds on that. *Although the tragic hero is good and exceptional, the hero has a tragic flaw*. This is best described as a character defect or a weakness. The Greek word for this is **hamartia**, which is the word that the apostle Paul uses in the New Testament when he is describing sin. It may be the same Greek word, but Aristotle isn't talking about sin, but rather a character defect. It's best understood as a point of vulnerability, a point of weakness. Consider, for example, how an airplane can fail structurally if one small part weakens and goes bad. For example, if a weakening in the tailfin, the vertical stabilizer of an aircraft, can lead to catastrophic failure. That's the kind of thing Aristotle is describing—a defect in personality or character that will be the undoing of the hero.

For Oedipus, the fatal flaw is his pride, his **hubris**. This is the Greek word that Aristotle uses to describe an overweening, all-consuming pride. It's a word that we still use today when the word "pride" just doesn't suffice. When you need something stronger, then *hubris* is the word we choose to describe a blinding pride. Oedipus can't see clearly because this *hubris* has taken over and controlled his life. Oedipus is living in defiance of the gods and the prophecies spoken at his birth. Recall Shakespeare's tragic heroes. They are great and noble figures, with many excellent qualities, and yet they all have some character flaw. Think of the indecision of Hamlet, or the jealousy and rage of Othello. As with comedy, the Shakespearian example very closely follows the Greek model.

Third, because of this defect, this tragic flaw, *the hero is partly responsible for his own downfall*. This is a very important element to understand, since we don't use the word "tragic" today in the same way as the Greeks. We describe a lot of things as tragic that would make the Greeks shake their heads in puzzlement. Let's say somebody goes out driving and dies unexpectedly in a traffic accident. On a human level, that accident appears random and arbitrary—which is why we call it an "accident" in the first place. We would probably describe what happened as "tragic." But a Greek would say (without meaning to sound insensitive), "What's tragic about that?" You see, it can't be an accident if its tragic; *there has to be some element of personal culpability* in order for there to be tragedy in the Greek sense.

Of course, we can tweak that traffic example to turn it into a Greek tragedy. Let's say the weather is bad and there has been a major ice storm. Tom wants to get in the car and drive from Point A to Point B, but everybody tells them, "No, you can't make it. It's a mountain pass and it's icy and dangerous." But Tom, in his pride, says, "I'm the best driver in the world. I can make it. I probably won't even have to slow down to do it!" So, he gets in his car and, blinded by pride, he drives off a cliff and dies. Now the Greek would say, "That's more like it! That's closer to what a tragedy is all about." For the Greek, if it were just a random occurrence, then that was just life. And life, as we've seen, is governed by fate. But when you lead yourself to destruction by the choices you make, then that is the essence of tragedy.

Aristotle's fourth point is that *the gods punish the hero more severely than he deserves*. That sounds like the Greek gods that we have come to know. When they see you falling, they give you a stiff push from behind. The gods were fickle and even vengeful at times. There was no grace and no mercy. We look at what happened to Oedipus Rex, and we say, "Wait a minute, that wasn't fair! The gods seemed to be enjoying this too much! Why didn't they reach down and deliver him from his ignorance? Presumably, he didn't know he was killing his father or marrying his mother, or he wouldn't have done those things!" So we wonder, where were the gods in all of this? Why were they so unjust? Why did they exact so much punishment on him for what happened when he was only partially responsible?

Notice how different this view of the gods is from the biblical view of God in the Bible. God does not punish anyone more severely than he deserves—or God wouldn't be just. And right there we see that important dividing line again between the false religion of the Greeks and what God reveals of Himself in scripture. In fact, it's the doctrine of grace and mercy that tells us that God does not punish us to the extent that we deserve. This would have been an alien concept to the ancient Greeks. How welcome that idea must have been when the apostle Paul preached the grace of God to them!

Aristotle's fifth point is that *the fall of the hero is not a complete loss; he gains some insight along the way*. He learns something from his experience. Of the six points, this is the one point that is the hardest for us to understand as modern people. Oedipus, right in the center of society, is respected by everybody; he is the king. Then the next day everything is going wrong and he is exposed as the man who killed his father and married his mother. He is blinded and expelled from the city. The Greeks look at that and say, "Hey, but it's not a complete loss! He learned something along the way." That strikes us hard to swallow. What could you possibly learn that would make that experience worth the tragedy? Our modern point of view says as much about us as it does about the Greeks. Once again, I would argue that our view is much more shallow. The Greeks saw Oedipus gaining something of inestimable value, even as he fell from favor to disfavor. Oedipus, and all tragic figures like him, capture a little insight into fate, into the mysteries of human existence and the workings of the gods. Maybe it's just a momentary glimpse that he gains, but he learns a little bit more about the most profound things of life. He knows more about himself, too.

So, what does this tell us about the Greeks? It tells us that they placed a high price tag on knowledge. This is central to their philosophy; that's what they were pursuing. The reason this fifth point is so strange to us is because we, as modern people, don't value these things as highly as the Greeks did. For them, the deepest knowledge of life was something worth dying for. That's a sobering thought for us to consider. I believe the apostle Paul understood what the Greeks were talking about. We can read his autobiography in Philippians 3:4-8 as a Greek tragedy. Paul was writing to a Greek audience, telling his own life story and translating it in Greek terms as a tragedy. Paul describes how he was respected early in his life. "I was a Jew's Jew," he says. "I was of the tribe of Benjamin, a Pharisee, zealous for the law, right in the center of the esteem and respect of my countrymen." Then he goes on to say that these things were once of utmost importance to him. He says, "I now count all that as loss, as dung." Loss in comparison with what? With the knowledge of Christ. In other words, Paul said, "I lost all of that. I had to lose all of that stuff that was so important, just as Oedipus lost it, so that I could gain the knowledge of Christ." And how does he gain the knowledge of Christ? By dying. By dying to himself. Just as in a Greek tragedy, knowledge comes through death. Paul gained the knowledge of Christ by dying to himself. It is deeply challenging for us to approach the New Testament like this from a modern perspective. We forced to admit how little we understand what Paul is talking about in a passage like this. We capture little of the full weight and the power of what he is communicating—that is, until we look at it the way his Greek audience would have understood his words.

There's a sixth point that Aristotle makes: *By vicariously identifying with the hero, the audience experiences catharsis*. Aristotle uses this term, **catharsis**, to describe how the audience identifies with the tragic hero. What do we get out of a play when we are watching it? We "bond," so to speak, with the hero—and this identification with him makes us feel better in the end. Catharsis means "purging." The word literally means "laxative"—and it suggests in a rather vivid way how you are purged of all the pent-up negative feelings you might have going into the theatre. You're now able, Aristotle said, to re-enter society as a healthy, productive citizen. Aristotle is giving a psychological explanation of sorts; but it's also deeply theological in its picture of identification.

We've all had this experience: we go to see a movie that's action-packed from beginning to end and we walk out of the theater feeling drained. That's what Aristotle was talking about. We have identified with the hero and all he experienced, so that we don't have to experience it ourselves. We're purged of all those negative feelings. As we watch the play, we see Oedipus suffer in our place. We're able to walk away feeling relieved. In the play, Oedipus suffers in our place, so that we can walk away relieved. Once again, we see how closely this mirrors the doctrine of sacrificial atonement—the principle of one dying for many. Paul preached the gospel to Greeks who understood this concept. He presented Christ as the one who suffered for the many so that the punishment would be lifted from us all.

Which characters in the Bible seem most closely to illustrate the tragic formula? Which are tragic figures in various ways? Samson is the best example. He's an exceptional character who has tragic flaws—wine, women, and song. Because of that, he is responsible for his own downfall by giving into the seductions of Delilah. But what about Aristotle's fourth point? Does God punish Samson more severely than he deserved? You've got to put the brakes on whenever you apply that fourth point to a biblical example, because that is not the God of the Bible. God does not punish anyone more severely than he deserves. Nevertheless, in the end, Samson gained some insight through his fall; he recognized what the true source of his strength was and he called upon God one last time.

Job was a tragic figure in many ways; and his story probably illustrates Aristotle's fifth point as well as any other biblical example.

In the last chapters of the book of Job, we see the insight that he gained from suffering—insight into the very nature of God. God asked Job many questions that he couldn't answer, by way of emphasizing man's need to trust in God's sovereignty even when we don't understand what's happening around us.

David, too, is tragic in many ways. We can add Saul to this list as well, though Saul didn't learn anything in the end. Moses is an interesting tragic figure, and the best biblical example, perhaps, of Aristotle's fourth point. Of course, God doesn't punish anyone more severely than he deserves; but it does seem to us, on a human level, that Moses was severely punished for his disobedience in striking the rock. There are many more examples that we could cite, not just in scripture, but also as we look at popular culture. We talk about the rise and fall of political figures. People are fixated on celebrities who fall from public favor. The way we look at these events, and the way we tell the story of their lives, follows the pattern of Greek tragedy.

There is something essential here that Aristotle has put his finger on. He is really pointing to the tragedy of sin. The original tragedy is the story of Adam; and so all of these stories, all of these accounts, all of these biblical figures, are simply *re-enactments of the original tragedy*. We come back to this, and the ancient Greeks came back to this, because it says something essentially true about human nature.

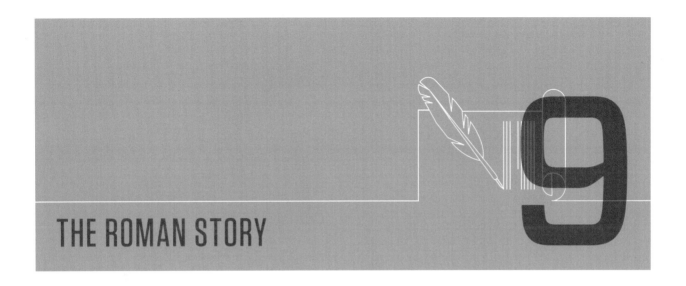

THE ROMAN STORY

Chapter Objectives

- Defend the idea that the story of Rome follows the pattern of a life-story.
- Chart the key events in Rome's rise to imperial power.
- Analyze the changes in Roman culture as Rome declined and fell.

We have been tracing the beginnings of western civilization back to the ancient Greeks. Now, we'll continue the story of western culture into the Roman period, emphasizing the continuity between these two great cultures. The Romans are a fascinating people, and they're a little more familiar to us for a couple of reasons. First, the Roman Empire forms the cultural backdrop to the period of the New Testament. Second, the movies that Hollywood has made about the ancient world have typically been about Rome, not Greece. Just think of *Ben Hur* and *Gladiator*. There have been some recent films about ancient Greece, but that's rather unusual for Hollywood.

We still use a number of expressions today to talk about Rome and the Romans, and that's further evidence of their lasting importance. When we say, "All roads lead to Rome," that expression recalls the power and central position of Rome in the ancient world and its lasting legacy. When we say, "When in Rome, do as the Romans," we're recalling how Rome set the standard for

culture and civilization. When we say, "Rome wasn't built in a day," we recall the long history that made Rome was it was—a history we'll be recounting in this chapter.

So, there's a lot of truth in these expressions. But we also have a lot of popular misconceptions about the Romans. For example, we often think of the debauchery and the immorality of Roman culture. As we think of Rome and its emperors, the picture of Nero or Caligula might come to mind as typical examples. Yet for most of its history, Roman culture valued self-sacrifice, self-discipline, and the values and virtues of responsibility and submission to authority. These kinds of values are very important if you are going to build an empire and maintain it for hundreds of years. You are not going to be successful in building an empire if you are just debauched and immoral in everything that you do. But the Romans did have strong values and even virtues over much of their history. We also think of the brutality of their military machine and their conquest of other nations. But as we are going to see, the Romans seldom destroyed their enemies. In fact, their tendency and their instinct was to preserve, not to destroy. The Roman instinct for preservation was one of their greatest qualities.

We think of Rome as the gold standard among the ancient empires. What we often forget, however, is just how humble their origins actually were. So who were the Romans? They originated from the Indo-European people who, as we've already seen, were thought by scholars to have lived about 5000 years ago in Central Europe. Different groups and people descended from the Indo-European tribe: the Celts, Germans, Slavs, Persians, and many others. The Greeks and Romans, too, were descended from this tribe. The Romans migrated down into the Italian Peninsula at some distant period; and then, when we see them in the first millennium before Christ, emerging as a distinct people with a distinct language, they obviously thought of themselves as a unique people no longer connected to this Indo-European tribe.

We see them first emerging in history around the same time that the Greeks emerged from their own "dark ages." At this point, however, there was nothing about the Romans that would make them stand out. They were quite modest in their origins. They lived in thatched-roof huts about the eighth century B.C. and they weren't even independent or self-governing. In fact, they were under the control of a people known as the Etruscans, a powerful group of people living in Italy. The Romans were just a minor tribe under Etruscan control.

Let's look at seven dates that, taken together, present to us the story of the Roman people. These seven dates will chart their rise from a humble beginning; their achievement of power in the Mediterranean world; and their gradual decline and fall. It's a narrative that sounds like the story of a life: birth and adolescence, followed by maturity, the gradual decline of old age, and then eventually death. This particular life cycle spans the 1000-year history of the Roman people in the ancient world. To talk meaningfully about the Romans, we've got to have a benchmark, a historical framework, what I'm calling "the Roman timeline." These are some of the "red letter" dates of their history, and they'll help us understand where they came from, what they believed, and how they saw themselves in the world. In other words, these dates will help us tell one of history's most amazing stories—the story of Rome.

753 B.C.

The first and the last of these dates are very problematic. The first date, 753 B.C., because is a legendary date; and historians continue to debate the significance of what occurred in A.D. 476.

When the Romans themselves would tell the story of where they came from, they went back to 753 B.C. That's what they would point to. For them, that was "Year Number One," just as we date our calendar from the birth of Christ. What happened on 753 has very little historical credibility; but the date does document a historical reality nonetheless. It's around the eighth century that we see the Romans first appearing on the historical landscape.

The story that the Romans told about this date focuses on twin brothers, Romulus and Remus. These brothers, abandoned in the wild, were raised by a she-wolf and grew up to found the city of Rome. It's not a very flattering way to tell the story of where you came from, and yet the Romans never hesitated to depict the story of Romulus and Remus in their art. In a famous statue that stood for centuries in the center of Rome, we see little Romulus and Remus, latched on the underside of the she-wolf. We think of the Romans as a very proud people; and at the height of their empire, in the first couple of centuries of the Christian era, they were the great superpower in the world. Why would anyone that powerful and proud want to point back to this story? The story affirmed the greatness of their achievement. It's as though they were saying, "Look at how far we have come! Look at how far we had to come!" It is essentially the story of a self-made man. Through their own effort, their own ingenuity, and their own struggle, they had achieved great things; furthermore, they saw themselves as divinely favored by the gods in that process. This is a story of pride, of humanism, once again—in many ways the same kind of pride that we identified in the Greeks, who were similarly very proud of where they had come from and the great accomplishments of their own civilization.

510 B.C.

The second date in our Roman timeline is the first one that is a truly historical date: 510 B.C., when the Romans became independent. Up to that point, they were under the control of the Etruscans. Now they expelled the Etruscans from their little town of Rome. It wasn't much of a town. It certainly was not yet the great center of the Roman Empire; it was just a small village. But the Romans began to assert self-control and self-governance over their lives. They established a republic much in the way that the Greek city states were governed. For the next five hundred years Rome would be a republic, although as we are going to see that it began acting a lot like an empire early in its history.

The Romans got that first taste of freedom in 510 B.C. and they never looked back. We can trace their history over the next 300 years as one of a gradual assertion of control, first over Italy, extending their control from North to South, and then moving farther out into the Mediterranean world. And as they did that, they came into contact with the other great powers of that time—starting with the Etruscans in the north and the Greeks in the south. (See Color Illustration C for a map.) They also came into violent contact with the other great Mediterranean power known as Carthage in North Africa. Carthage, located in modern Tunisia, was a great naval power, with military and commercial interests throughout the Mediterranean.

Carthage's greatest general was a man named Hannibal. He is considered one of the greatest of all military geniuses. In fact, in the great wars that Carthage fought with Rome, Hannibal took elephants from North Africa across the Mediterranean in order to invade Italy from the north, across the Alps. This must be the most outrageous military plan ever concocted, and it almost worked. The Romans came very close to losing to the Carthaginians, just as the Greeks had narrowly escaped the Persians. Just imagine how different western history (world history, really) would be if those battles had turned out differently! These wars that Rome fought with Carthage occurred in the third and second centuries before Christ. They were called the Punic Wars and they came to an end in 146 B.C.

146 B.C.

With the end of the Punic Wars, Rome was unchallenged in the Mediterranean. Rome had conquered two cities in 146 B.C. at the end of the Punic Wars—and how they handled them differently tells us much about the Romans. The first city was Carthage in North Africa, which was the capital of the empire that had threatened Rome for so long. The Romans marched in and destroyed the city completely, top to bottom. Then they sowed salt into the ground. As if that wasn't enough, they brought their prophets out to speak curses on anybody who would ever dare to rebuild Carthage. That was not the normal Roman way of conquering an enemy. You had to push them and push them over a long period of time before they would bring down that degree of vengeance upon you.

The Roman instinct was to preserve, and we see that in the treatment of the second city the Romans conquered in 146 B.C. When they seized Corinth, Greece, they treated it very differently from Carthage. The destruction of Carthage was the culmination of a long history of confrontation; the last thing the Romans wanted was for Carthage to rise again and threaten them in the centuries to come. Corinth, on the other hand, was the capital of Greece during the hellenistic period, and the Romans admired the achievements of ancient Greece. They loved its architecture and art; they loved its philosophy and rich literary language. So, being in love with Greek culture as they were, the Romans preserved Corinth and all its institutions. That, more than anything, is why 146 B.C. is such an important date in the history of western civilization. It's a date that speaks of continuity. When we talk of classical civilization, we call it **Greco-Roman civilization**—using a hyphen to emphasize the continuity. Though they were very different people in character and values, the Romans preserved, cultivated, imitated, and transmitted Greek culture down through the ages all the way down to you and me today.

From the Punic Wars onward, Rome began acting very much like an empire. It was a republic governed by senators in Rome; but it was behaving in the world with imperial intentions. It had a large standing army now and powerful generals, like Julius Caesar, commanding those armies. So in the first century B.C., we are going to see that Rome is no longer manageable or governable as a republic. It's becoming more like an empire.

27 B.C.

The senators back at Rome were fearful that Julius Caesar was becoming a dictator, and they were fearful that he would come back to Rome to assert his control over the entire Roman military machine and replace them, the senators. So on the "Ides of March," March 15, 44 B.C., on the floor of the senate, Julius Caesar was assassinated. There is a lot of mystery surrounding the causes and the motivations behind the assassination; but we know that Rome was plunged into a civil war that lasted for fifteen years. Two factions struggled for control of Rome's destiny; one was led by a man named Octavian, the adopted nephew of Julius Caesar. The other faction was led by a man named Mark Antony. Then across the Mediterranean, in Egypt, the last of the pharaohs, Cleopatra, was playing one side against the other. She threw her weight behind one and then allied herself with the other. In the end, she supported Mark Antony, and that was a bad decision, because he was defeated by Octavian in the naval battle at Actium in 31 B.C.

In 27 B.C. Octavian proclaimed himself the first emperor of Rome and took the name Caesar Augustus. We therefore date the beginning of the Roman Empire with this very important pivotal point in Roman history. Of course, we read in scripture that it's under the reign of Caesar Augustus that Jesus was born. So it's a pivotal time in history for many reasons.

The apostle Paul wrote "that when the fullness of the time was come, God sent forth His son" (Galatians 3:3). Paul is specifically referring to the fulfillment of Old Testament prophecies, but there's another way we can read this phrase. It was the fullness of time in a historical and cultural sense as well. All the political instability was behind Rome when Jesus was born. For the next two centuries, Rome would be at the height of its power and the Mediterranean world would largely be at peace. It was the perfect time for Christianity to arise.

From 27 B.C. to A.D. 180, we enter a period known as the "Roman peace." We use the Latin phrase, **Pax Romana**, to describe this time when Rome was at its height, unchallenged in its rule, and when many of its greatest accomplishments were achieved.

This was the time God chose for Christ to be born and for the church to emerge within the Roman Empire. The gospel was able to spread throughout the Roman Empire during this time of relative peace, and all of the institutions of imperial Rome facilitated the spread of Christianity—without intending to do so. Most of the great achievements of Roman culture and architecture, such as the Colosseum, were built during this time of the Roman Peace. Many of the greatest Roman emperors ruled during this time as well. We should add, of course, that a few of the worst Roman emperors like Nero and Caligula were also in this period. But never saw greater emperors than the line of leaders produced in the second century: Trajan, Hadrian, and Marcus Aurelius.

180 A.D.

Marcus Aurelius was the emperor with whose death we date the end of the period of the Pax Romana in A.D. 180. He was a great military emperor, but he was also a philosopher. After Marcus Aurelius died, the wheels of the empire began to come off. It took a long time for Rome to fall, several hundred years to be exact; but most historians date the beginning of the end of the Roman Empire from the death of Marcus Aurelius. A series of very bad emperors followed his reign. Rome was Rome overextended and gradually it began to decline and fall, even as Christianity continued to grow within its boundaries.

313 A.D.

One of the last great rulers of Rome was Constantine the Great, the first Christian emperor. Constantine converted in A.D. 312, and by 313 he had legalized Christianity with the **Edict of Milan**, also known as the "Edict of Toleration." Within another generation, Christianity would become the official state religion of Rome.

The years leading up to Constantine had seen some of the most intense prosecutions of Christians. Now all that was over, and Christianity was becoming the most powerful institution in the empire. So that's why A.D. 313 is a pivotal point in Roman history. This is a date we're going to come back to in a later chapter, as it will help us explain many of the changes brought about with the rise of Christianity within the Roman Empire. The nature of the church before Constantine was very different from the political institution it would become after his influential rule. We'll also see that early Christian art, first produced in the catacombs of Rome during times of persecution, would change considerably after Christianity was legalized. The once persecuted Church would slowly begin to acquire the imperial trappings of the empire.

476 A.D.

The last two centuries of Roman imperial history make for a pretty sad story. It's a story of barbarian invasions and a shrinking Roman military. And that's how we reach the end of the line in A.D. 476—the date traditionally cited by historians as "the fall of the Roman Empire." In this year, the last Roman emperor was deposed and replaced by a Germanic chieftain, one of the members of the tribes that were afflicting the Roman Empire in its final centuries.

The last emperor of Rome was a man named Romulus Augustulus. He was named after the legendary founder of Rome, one of the twin brothers we encountered back in 753 B.C. The young emperor's second name was really a nickname, Augustulus, which means "Little Augustus." The nickname was doubtless meant to be a mocking term; the emperor was probably about eighteen years old and didn't have any real, tangible power. He was little more than a figurehead. The Roman and German soldiers called him "Little Augustus" as a way, perhaps, of demeaning his authority. Historians have long noted the ironic name of this last of the Roman emperors—his name recalling both the founder of Rome, Romulus, and the first Roman emperor, Augustus.

So the last Roman-born emperor was deposed; but in many ways, Rome and its institutions just continued on. Nothing cataclysmic happened in A.D. 476. The city of Rome wasn't destroyed and obliterated. It continued on. Roman institutions and the Roman language, Latin, continued on; the Roman legal system and political institutions continued on. In fact, the Roman senate continued meeting right through the next couple of centuries as though nothing had happened!

Historians rightly debate whether or not Rome ever "fell" or whether it just morphed into something different over time. We'll come back to this question later; specifically, we'll ask why a powerful and long-lasting empire like Rome could ultimately reach such an anti-climactic end. That is one of the greatest of all historical problems. There are scores of answers to the question, "Why did Rome fall?" Military answers, political answers, economic answers, and social answers. We will try to sort these out and evaluate them. In the end, we won't answer the question in any definitive way. But the compelling nature of the story of Rome demands that we at least try.

98

THE ROMAN CHARACTER

Chapter Objectives

- Clarify the positive way that Romans viewed imperialism.
- Illustrate the Roman spirit of electicism through key examples.
- Describe how Roman practicality motivated their major building projects.

As we've already seen, Roman history speaks volumes about who the Romans were. They were a very impressive people—a culture worth getting to know and understand. When you meet somebody new, you start to form an impression. You try to figure out what kind of person they are. We're doing that right now as we "meet" the Romans. Since we can't sit down with the entire Roman Empire and ask its inhabitants these questions, all we can do is look at the things they left behind—their ideas, accomplishments, monuments, and works of art. With these resources in hand, we try to create what we hope is a fair and accurate picture of who these people were.

We began the story of the Romans the same way we did with the Greeks—with the simple observation that they were an Indo-European people. But what kind of people were they? What was their value system? (Keep in mind that this is what we're trying to figure out as we study culture.) In this

chapter, we'll identify three qualities that shaped the Romans worldview:

- Imperialism
- Eclecticism
- Practicality

These words represent value statements; they take us into the Roman mind, into what the Romans saw, so to speak, when they looked in the mirror. These words tell us what the Romans saw when they looked out at the world around them. We'll be defining each of these terms carefully; and then we'll contrast each quality with Greek culture (emphasizing differences) and compare each to American culture (emphasizing similarities). This pattern of comparison and contrast will enable us to place Roman culture in relief and see its qualities more clearly.

Roman Imperialism

First of all, the Romans were imperialists. I list that as the first quality because it's where the Romans would themselves start if telling you about themselves. What do we mean when we say that the Romans were imperialistic? What would the Romans themselves mean by that? Today, the word isn't intended as a compliment. In political discourse the word is used frequently by left-wing ideologues who would characterize American foreign policy, for example, as "imperialistic." The term captures the belief in the superiority of one's own culture and then the belief that one should even take and impose that culture and its values on other people, even by force, if necessary. Certainly, the Romans would endorse that definition of what imperialism is, and they wouldn't be offended at all by the label. If you were to face a Roman eye-to-eye, and wag your finger at him and say, "You are an imperialist," you might mean to criticize him; but he wouldn't be offended. He'd probably say, "Well, thank you for noticing, thank you very much"—because that's the quality they saw in themselves and the one they wished to project to the larger world.

In fact, the Roman concept of imperialism went even further. They didn't just think their culture was superior and that they had a right to impose it on other people. The Romans also believed that they were a people of destiny—that they had been given a unique mission in the world. This belief would become the defining value of Roman civilization. They committed themselves to fulfilling that mission, establishing the Roman way of life and enforcing the Roman rule of law throughout the known world. Their national stories were bound up in that mythology and projected a message of divinely sanctioned destiny. One of the clearest examples of that is the great literary epic that captures this aspect of the Roman character. It's a story told by Virgil, a Roman poet living in the generation before Christ. Virgil wrote *The Aeneid*, the story of Aeneas, the mythical founder of the republic who was a man marked out by the gods for that destiny and mission; the gods favor Aeneas as he pursues that destiny and faces various challenges. What we see in Aeneas is the history of Rome herself. The Romans saw themselves in his life, and in the destiny that he had been called to.

We believe that Virgil wrote his epic around 31 B.C. If we place this event on the Roman timeline, we can understand the significance of the poem in relation to what was happening historically and politically. Octavian has just emerged victorious after years of civil war. It's apparent that Octavian is the one who is going now to lead Rome—and Virgil is writing his poem for the new leader. So the poem can be read not just as a great work of literature but also as a very skillfully written work of propaganda. Virgil's poem affirms two things. In telling the story of Aeneas, the poem affirms the right of the Romans to rule the world. But there's a more narrow focus as well, a more immediate political message that Virgil is selling: *not only is Rome chosen to rule the world, but this man, Augustus, is chosen to rule Rome*. Most scholars therefore read Virgil's *Aeneid* as conveying political messages of imperialism, divine right, and destiny.

Let's contrast this idea with how the Greeks looked at the world, and then we will compare it to American values as well. The Greeks were very different from the Romans; you couldn't describe them as imperialistic. Sure, under Alexander the Great they had marched their armies all the way to Afghanistan and created a great empire.

But the empire fell apart as soon as Alexander died. It fell apart because the Greeks weren't natural empire-builders; they weren't talented imperialists. They could conquer other people, but they couldn't rule them. And the reason for this, as best we can determine, is that they didn't have the same political concept of "empire" that the Romans did. The Greeks thought of their citizenship in very local and individual terms. Everything for them was a matter of individuality and a matter of community. Each Greek described himself first and foremost by his home city—not as a Greek, but as an Athenian, Spartan, Corinthian, or Ephesian. The message of Pericles' "Funeral Oration" is that the power of the Greeks didn't rise from their collective power as a nation, but out of individual genius and the local community in which they lived.

The Greeks could set aside their differences and band together when they had to—such as when a million-man army was marching from Persia. But that was the exception for the Greeks. After they defeated the Persians, they quickly disbanded that alliance of convenience, and they went back to thinking in very local and individualistic terms.

How does American culture compare? We can see some interesting points of similarity between American and Roman values—as long as we focus on that aspect of imperialism that concerns living out one's destiny. A sense of destiny describes the nature of American culture and American history. This is the self-concept that Americans have always had of ourselves—whether we think of John Winthrop four hundred years ago, describing his vision of a "city on the hill," or how Ronald Reagan famously used that phrase and tapped into its vision in his political speeches. This concept was even described as "manifest destiny" in nineteenth-century America: the right to conquer the continent, to civilize it and spread American democracy and white picket fences from coast to coast. I don't intend to gloss over the fact that a lot of wrong things, such as the treatment of native Americans, were justified in the name of destiny. The point

to be emphasized, though, is this positive quality of seeing oneself as a people of destiny who have a mission in the world. And this has always characterized the way we see ourselves within our culture and how we have chosen to operate within the world. These are controversial ideas; but it does seem evident that the American self-image finds a striking parallel in the Roman experience. And this is just one of several parallels we'll observe.

The triumphal arches that the Romans built are eloquent expressions of this concept. More than anything else, the structure of the **triumphal arch** gave expression to this self-concept of "Who we are in the world and what we are trying to do." These structures embody what the Romans were constantly trying to remind the world—both friend and foe—about themselves.

"Triumph" is a Roman word. We use the word as a synonym for "victory," but in the Latin language the word referred specifical-

101

ly to a military parade. When the Romans brought their victorious army back from battle, the general led a parade with all the spoils of victory and the captured prisoners. They were led down the city street, right through the center of the triumphal arch. As a monument, this is the only "function" that the arches performed. The only thing you can do with the triumphal arch is to march through the middle of it. The whole point of the triumphal arch, as with Virgil's *Aeneid*, was to make a propaganda statement about the divine right of Rome.

The Arch of Titus featured in one of the most famous of all triumphal parades, in the aftermath of the Jewish War and the destruction of Jerusalem in A.D. 70. In the illustration above you can see some of the images on the side of the Arch of Titus. They commemorate the artifacts captured from Herod's Temple in Jerusalem and carried in that triumphal parade.

Triumphal arches help us imagine what we mean by Roman imperialism, because they bring a very physical, concrete quality to the idea. The meaning of these arches was widely understood all the way down to the modern period; so it's no surprise that a couple of modern European conquerors who saw themselves as Roman emperors either built or planned to build triumphal arches as a way of confirming who they saw themselves to be. Napoleon understood what a triumphal arch was all about. He saw himself as a Roman emperor, so he needed a triumphal arch, of course; and you can still see the Arc de Triomphe in Paris today. The second European conqueror never actually got around to building his arch, but we

have his blueprints. We know how it would have looked, standing in the center of Berlin. I am referring, of course, to Adolf Hitler, who also saw himself as a kind of Roman emperor. When Hitler spoke of the thousand-year reign of the Third Reich, where did he come up with that figure? He got it from the history and the thousand-year rule of Rome.

One story about Hitler and the Arc de Triomphe illustrates how the triumphal arch symbolizes the concept of Roman power. In 1942 Hitler's army captured Paris. Hitler saw this victory as the ultimate payback for the German humiliation in World War I. So he staged a good old-fashioned Roman triumphal parade and took his army and tanks in tight formation right down the streets of the Champs Élysées in Paris— right through Napoleon's arch. He understood the symbolism and was making the very same point that the Romans had made two thousand years before.

Roman Eclecticism

A second characteristic of the Romans is that they were an eclectic people. When we use the term "eclectic," we are referring to something that's made up of, or combined from, a variety of different sources. You mix and match different things that don't normally belong with each other. If you decorate your living room in an eclectic style, as opposed to choosing one dominant stylistic pattern, then you might have a Persian rug on the floor; you might have a piece of early American furniture; you might have, depending on your budget, a Ming Chinese vase on a side table. On the wall, you might have an avant-garde, early modern abstract print. In other words, you combine things that belong to different periods, cultures, and styles that you wouldn't ordinarily see together. But if you like the diversity of all those different cultures, you might decorate in that kind of an eclectic way. This is very much the way Romans viewed the world. Yes, they very comfortable and confident about who they were, but they liked different things as well. We will see that this is true of their religious beliefs and practices, as well as their philosophies. This principle is also true of their art and their architecture.

The Greeks were very different. They were all about consistency and order. If you picked a style, then you would stick with that style and see it through to the end. You don't mix and match. This is one thing a Greek architect would never do. He would never say, "You know, I want to build a temple that's predominantly Ionic, but I would like to bring a couple of Doric flourishes into it and maybe a touch or two of the Corinthian style." A Greek architect would be striving after what is ideal, what is pure and consistent in form. That's the way they constantly approached every task in life.

Americans, on the other hand, can readily identify with Roman eclecticism. We have a diverse and eclectic culture. We can see this in some of the most trivial ways—such as fast food. Drive down the main drag of any American town and you will see a diversity of options. Do you want Chinese takeout? Do you want Italian? Do you want Japanese takeout? You can increasingly choose all kinds of options, because that's who we are. We like that kind of diversity. The melting pot idea is a very descriptive metaphor of how we've absorbed different cultures and made them our own, much as the Romans had done.

Let's look at two examples of this eclecticism in the architecture of the Romans: the Colosseum and the Pantheon. The Colosseum looks like a perfectly orderly and simple structure and is very consistent in its pattern and use of repetition. So, what looks eclectic about that? You really have to get much closer to the structure itself to see.

The arch was a hallmark of Roman engineering and they incorporated these into everything they built. On both sides of every arch in the Colosseum are Greek columns. The Romans loved Greek culture, so they're building these Greek elements into what they design. But the interesting thing about these Greek columns is that on each of the three stories, the Greek columns are different. On the bottom level, the columns are Doric. On the second level, they are Ionic. On the third level, as you could guess, they're Corinthian.

Imagine an Athenian visitor in the second century A.D. coming to Rome and looking at this from his Greek point of view. It would simply appall him. It would look all wrong, because a Greek wouldn't build that way. If you decide to build an Ionic temple, the whole thing should be Ionic. Every aspect of the design is governed by one set of blueprints that make up what the Ionic form is. And the Roman would be puzzled by that. "Why wouldn't you mix styles?" he'd say. "If you like all three orders, why not put them together?" To the Roman that was the most logical thing to do. It's kind of like the example we used of mixing and matching when you design a living room in an eclectic style. If you like it all, then employ it all.

The Pantheon is another example of Roman eclecticism. This Roman temple was built in the early second century A.D. for the worship of the "many gods." It looks like a Greek temple from the front; but this form is combined with a distinctively Roman dome—a combination of styles that fits the eclectic tastes of Roman culture.

Roman Practicality

Let's consider the final element of the Roman character. It's a personality trait that follows logically from the things that we have already said about the Romans. The Romans were a deeply practical people. They had their feet firmly planted in the world. They were materialists, which you would have to be if you were an empire builder. Rather than sitting around thinking about abstract ideas of truth, beauty and justice the way Greeks philosophers did, the Romans were concerned with *this world, this time, this place.*

If you're going to build an empire, you should already have a plan for how you're going to govern and maintain it. It's one thing to be able to conquer; but it's quite another thing to be able to rule and govern. The Romans would always point to their imperial governance as one of the keys to understanding who they were. The fact that they did develop an effective political and legal infrastructure within their cities to make imperial life possible and extend it over the centuries supports this contention. The Romans were ideally suited to this by their temperament since they thought in terms of solutions; they thought in practical terms about what works. If there was a better way of doing something, they were going to find it. These were people who developed civil engineering in the modern sense. Roman cities were complex engineering feats with underground sewage systems and running water, including hot water, piped into their buildings. They had amazing cisterns that would pump the water into various parts of the city. They were brilliant engineers, constantly trying to figure out better ways of accomplishing things.

Once again, let's contrast the Romans with the Greeks and then compare the Roman values with American culture. We acknowledged that the Greeks could conquer; Alexander the Great proved that beyond dispute. But the Greeks couldn't govern other people well; they couldn't manage a vast empire. This doesn't mean, of course, that the Greeks were impractical people. They didn't have their heads up in the clouds thinking about philosophy all the time, such that they couldn't even see a huge army bearing down on them from Persia. They were able to live in the real world in very practical ways, figure things out and solve problems. That's certainly what the Persian experience teaches us. That's also the message they conveyed through a mythological figure such as Odysseus, who is able to figure out how to get home to Ithaca and solve a myriad of problems along the way. But for Greeks, practicality is always an expression of their philosophy; it's the bodily form, so to speak, of their rationalism. The Romans, though, never made the philosophical connection between thought and action as clearly as the Greeks did. The difference is really a matter of priority; that is, one could say that the Romans solved problems first and then thought about the implications later, while the Greeks thought long and hard about an issue and then applied their thought to the real world.

Let's say that the Greeks were thinkers, for the sake of argument, which I think is pretty well borne out by their history of accomplishments. What then does that make the Romans? Doers. So we have thinkers and doers, and we often divide people in this way. There are people who like to sit around and think about problems, and there are those who like to roll up their sleeves and do something about it. Again, however, there is a great deal of simplification here, because you have to do both (think and act) in order to be successful. It can be pretty dangerous just to jump into a problem and start trying to fix it without thinking about what you are doing. Finding the balance is really the key. What I am emphasizing here are the respective priorities of these different cultures. The difference has to do with which foot you lead with—thought or action.

What about American culture? Are we like the Greeks who would think first and act second? Or are we like the Romans who would act and only think later if they got around to it? I think it's pretty clear. We sympathize more with that "can do" practicality of the Roman mind. This practicality is evident in our character right from the beginning of our history—and for good reason. Just as the Romans had to be practical people if they were going to build an empire, we can similarly claim that the pioneering experience of our early history inculcated values of practicality in our national character. If you imagine being in Jamestown during that first winter in the early seventeenth century, you are unlikely to be spending valuable time debating Plato and Aristotle with your fellow colonist. You would be building a fort, gathering firewood, establishing a food supply for the winter, and trying to establish friendly contact with the neighboring tribes—all practical things. Similarly, frontier life during the westward migrations of the nineteenth century required that practical matters of survival were going to motivate you. Little time would be devoted to reflection and philosophy when pure action was required.

We don't have a lot of patience for people who just think about things, and that's why we have a hard time understanding the Greek love of philosophy. Within American culture, we tend to caricature philosophers as irrelevant people who sit up in ivory towers. I think it's to our detriment that we don't understand the world the way the Greeks did, in terms of the real world implications of philosophical thinking. Nevertheless, the fact that we do so underscores our own orientation toward what is practical. We are inventive and entrepreneurial, and these qualities express our practicality in a way that the Romans would understand. If there is a better way to build a mousetrap, we are going to try to figure that out, just as the ancient Romans would have.

So let's look at some of the major Roman building projects that suggest their practicality to us. The Roman **aqueducts**, for example, were one of the preeminent expressions of their engineering genius. Their great cities needed a reliable water supply, and this is one of ways in which they provided for that, bringing water overland from great distances. The water would flow as far as thirty or forty miles from the source to the city itself. These aqueducts were so expertly engineered that, over the course of a mile or so, the grade descends only a matter of inches. This was done in order that the water not cascade down the aqueduct, but rather flow in a fairly stable and steady rate until it ultimately reached the cistern in the city.

And those cisterns, too, were pretty amazing works of engineering; they had pumps that would direct the water into the major districts of the city, depending on how high the water level was. If there was plenty of water, then it would flow into all of the districts; and if it was low, it would be rationed and pump only into the governmental and administrative districts. The Romans also had indoor plumbing in their major buildings and flowing hot water indoors.

Thus, a lot of the things we take for granted in the modern urban world were familiar to the Romans. They developed all of the infrastructure that we think of when we consider our cities today. That's why civil engineering can be traced back directly to ancient Rome.

A second and very different type of structure that the Romans built in most of their major cities were large public buildings known as **basilicas**. The ruins pictured above are from the most famous remains of one of these structures, the Basilica of Constantine. One can get a sense of the scale of it just by looking at the tourist in the foreground. These were impressive buildings with domed roofs and they functioned like a civic center in the heart of a Roman city. It was a multipurpose building: it was a gathering place and inside you would be likely to find all kinds of rooms and meeting

places, sometimes even indoors spas, boutiques where you could shop, and places where you could conduct business. It was a very modern sort of building, and it played a central practical role in the life of a Roman city. This example once again emphasizes the practical way these buildings were used to make all the business, political, and social activities function more easily within the Roman city. Later on, during the Catholic Middle Ages, architects would fine inspiration in these Roman basilicas—using them as a model for the great cathedrals of Europe.

Another very famous example of Roman engineering is the highway system. We talked about some of the expressions that we associate with ancient Rome today, such as, "All roads lead to Rome." Well, that expression itself causes us to think about their highways that spanned from north to south and east to west, all the way from the British Isles through North Africa and modern Israel, crisscrossing thousands and thousands of miles. This artery of roads obviously made the transportation of the Roman legions and the defense of the Roman Empire possible; but it also facilitated commerce, travel, and all the other practical considerations of the complex imperial system of Rome.

One of the most famous stretches of that highway system was known in Roman times as the Via Appia, or the Appian Way in English. It is a beautiful stretch that leads out of the south of Rome, in an area where the Roman upper classes had their villas. Other well-preserved parts of the old Roman highway system can be seen in the deserts of Libya and modern Israel. It's interesting to note that the very extensive Roman highway system in Europe has largely disappeared, except that the routes themselves still exist as the foundation of modern autobahns today, which, in some cases, were built directly over these Roman highways.

Here is an interesting analogy to think about. In the 1950s, under President Eisenhower, the U.S. interstate system was proposed and funded by Congress. It took many decades to complete. The case that was made for the American interstate system was basically the same case that the Romans would have made for their highway. You and I may think that the interstate system exists to get us from one place to another very quickly on vacation; but the case was originally made that this was going to be an integral part of our civil defense at the height of the Cold War—a way to connect the continent from coast to coast. Both the ancient and modern highway systems arose from the need to transport men and material very effectively.

Let's look at another type of structure that the Romans built in their cities: public baths. The largest of these were in Rome, such as the spectacular Baths of Caracalla (early third century) which are now just ruins. Every major provincial Roman city had public baths, including the smaller cities and towns. Taking baths was considered

essential to a civilized urban-dwelling Roman. Inside these baths, you would find hot and cold spas, separated such that the women would bathe together and the men would bathe together. That was the extent of privacy, however, as these were very "public" baths in every sense of the word. Bathing was one of the rights of Roman citizens, and these were places to go and visit with people and transact business in an informal setting. The best preserved of all of the public baths we have today is found far from Rome—in Bath, England.

This reminds us again that wherever the Romans traveled, they took their values with them—even to the rocky outpost of Petra, overlooking the Dead Sea (pictured below with its heating system beneath the floor).

These public baths, like almost all Roman structures, were decorated with mosaics and other pictures. Some of these mosaics have survived, and they give us insight into

107

the way Romans actually used these facilities. It's amazing to reflect on how contemporary these typical Romans look as they engage in physical and recreational sports. This reminds us again that if we go back two thousand years, we'd find that Romans living in their cities were very much like people living in modern cities today, with all of the infrastructure and amenities of modern life. In that sense, then, not a lot has changed.

THE ROMAN ACHIEVEMENT

Chapter Objectives

- Summarize how Rome adapted and extended the Greek cultural influence.
- Describe how Rome expressed her materialistic values through its art.
- Explain how Roman philosophy reflected their character.

We've looked at the Roman character—the values of imperialism, eclecticism, and practicality that defined their culture. We're going to turn now to the things they produced as an expression of these values. First, we're going to look at the unique contributions which the Romans made to western art; then we'll turn our attention to the achievement of the Romans as engineers. Finally, we'll consider one aspect of their intellectual life—the philosophical systems of Epicureanism and Stoicism.

The Romans as Artists

When we think of ancient art, we automatically think of the Greeks. They were the masters and they taught the Romans in many ways; but there were three areas of art that the Romans uniquely developed.

- Portraiture art
- Narrative art
- Landscape art

We'll look at these one by one as we con-

tinue to define who the Romans were as a culture. We'll see that Roman art expresses a materialistic perspective on the world.

Portraiture Art

Portraiture is clearly the one area in which the Romans excelled. When you look at a Roman portrait, you are looking at something that is almost photorealistic in appearance. If, for example, you were to run into this man pictured below, you would recognize him as Cicero; that's precisely how he looked.

The bust is as good as a photograph of him, and that's truly a remarkable thing. The Greeks never attempted this kind of realism in their art. As natural as their art became, as lifelike and full of energy, they never took it to that next stage of making it look *just like the person himself*. I don't think this is the case because they couldn't do this. With all that they were able to accomplish, the Greeks could have done so if they had wanted to. It's just that their artistic goals lay in a different direction.

Let's see if we can draw out the difference between the Greeks and the Romans in this field a little more clearly. What I want to draw out is the contrast between how literal and lifelike the Roman portraits were and how idealized and fundamentally generic the Greek portraits were. I will do this by contrasting a style that I call *universal* with a style that is *particular*. The Greek style can be characterized as universal; it's attempting to achieve universal, general and ideal qualities. They are striving for the ideal of male beauty, for example, not the exact form of the actual Alexander the Great.

When you look at the portrait of Alexander the Great (see illustration below), you are not seeing him as he was and as he lived and breathed and conquered; you are not seeing him as he walked around the city of Corinth. You are looking at an idealized portrait that looks something like a Greek god.

But when you look at the particular style of the Romans (as in the portrait of Julius Caesar above, right), you get something quite specific. You are looking at a highly *particularized* portrait of a *particular* man, who had a *particular* shape to his nose and a *particular* shape to his overall face, and so on. That's what the Romans are trying to give you: not some generalized, idealized or universal form—as with Alexander the Great pressed into a generic form—but rather the true appearance of Julius Caesar.

It's a very different way of looking at the world and then producing art as a reflection of that. I think you can see how the Greek approach is much more philosophical. It reflects the striving for ideals in the way the Greeks worked. The Roman approach is much more material, much more practical. The Romans just considered what Julius Caesar looked like. Their sculpting in this manner is a very clear expression of their character, and they brought it to such a high level of excellence that you can be sure that these are, as I have described them, photographic likenesses of the individual that we are looking at.

In order to illustrate this point, let's consider some actual Roman portraits. Consider the portrait of one of Rome's great emperors, Trajan of the 2nd century (illustrated above). As one can see, this can by no means be considered a "glamour shot." This is clearly not intended to be an idealized portrait of the Roman conception of beauty. From the profile, we see the big Roman nose that Trajan has, and his ears seem a little too large for his face. I believe that Trajan would have been very flattered by this portrait. He would not have looked at it and said to the sculptor, "Take it back and make me look better." In fact, he would have been flattered, because it was an exact representation of who he was. That's what he expected, and that's what he got.

Let's look at a second example—a portrait of Hadrian (illustrated above), who was known as a great general and a great military emperor. He is remembered for the wall in northern England that bears his name, Hadrian's Wall. Notice how different these portraits are from one another. When you look at a whole bunch of Greeks statues, in contrast, they all start to blend together. They all look very much alike. And for a good reason: the Greeks are striving for the generic, universal form of beauty. The Roman portraits are all very distinctive, as is the one of Marcus Aurelius, another of the great emperors (illustrated below). He died in 180, and we date the end of the Pax Romana with his death. He was a philosopher emperor, as we'll note a little later in this chapter, and this is why he styled himself with the full beard—a very un-Roman style.

The remarkable thing about Roman portraits is how lifelike they are, and we found in this, once again, an important point of distinction between the Romans and the Greeks. The Greeks, being a philosophical people, tended to look towards the abstract idealized form of a thing rather than really caring what Alexander the Great looked like in real life; they pictured him almost symbolically as a representation of the male ideal. The Romans, in contrast, considered these questions from a completely different point of view. They were very practical peo-

ple and for them, when you made a portrait, the most practical thing to do was to make that portrait look like the person you were representing.

We should also note that portraiture was for the Romans an expression of their religious values. They did, after all, worship their ancestors; Romans would carry busts of their ancestors in funeral processions (see illustration below). At a later stage in Rome's history, Romans worshipped and burned incense before the images of the Roman Emperors. It makes sense, if you are going to do that, to want to know what the person that you are worshipping looks like. If you are going to pray to your great-grandfather, then it would make sense to have an exact representation of how he looked, or whichever emperor happened to be in power at the time.

Therefore, the bottom line is that the way they sculpted reflects their values, their personality, and the way they looked at the world. We are going to see that this is also the case in the second and third contributions to Western art that we trace back to the Romans—their sense of narrative and their development of landscape art.

Narrative Art

The second Roman contribution to western art is their development of a narrative sense in art. By the word "narrative" we mean relating to stories or having the quality of stories. Romans liked to tell you what happened in their art, especially if it was a depiction of a historical event such as, for example, a Roman military victory. They want to show you what happened, just like you are looking at a news reel, say, of that particular event.

This is very different from the way the Greeks sculpted. When you look at the sculptures on the exterior of the Parthenon, the great Greek temple of the gods and heroes and the various mythological events associated with them (see below), one feels no sense of drama in them. There is no sense of an event as it might have happened, but it is rather a symbolic representation. There is nothing about it that is real

and dramatic in the sense of the way we would tell a story in the real world.

Roman art, though, has dramatic power. Furthermore, it's factual and it's rooted in the real world. We can trace this tendency in Roman art back to the second century B.C. When Roman generals coming back from the Punic Wars returned to Rome and led triumphal parades, one of the things they carried with them—right through the streets of Rome—were big posters that depicted what happened in the victorious military campaign.

One can see why a Roman general would have an interest in this, as it would be a way of inflating his reputation. In a larger sense, however, it also served the propaganda interests of the Roman Republic and later the Roman Empire by declaring the might of the state. In other words, the Romans painted in this narrative style for a reason: they told stories about themselves—which was, after all, their favorite subject—and reinforced that message of who they were in the world. Hence, the narrative quality of their art had a deeply practical dimension, one that served the imperialistic goals of the Romans. It can be seen that their art is an expression, once again, of their values and character traits.

Let's look at the most famous example of this kind of narrative art that functioned as a form of political propaganda—**Trajan's Column**. It's one of the best preserved of all Roman monuments. You can still see it today, and, although it's now topped by a very different statue than it was in ancient times, it's essentially intact. It's called Trajan's Column, because what it commemorates are the military victories of Emperor Trajan as he led the Roman armies in military battles in the East. And so it presents a highly detailed narrating of the different stages of that campaign.

Trajan's Column dates from the early second century, roughly around 113 A.D. As you go around it in a circular motion, from the base to the top of the column, what you see (as the close-up shows) are over 200 yards of continuous narrative art. These are depictions of around 2500 separate events. You start from the base, and it's like reading a comic strip or a graphic novel. In fact, one art historian has called it a "petrified comic strip." It's also like reading a history book. It's really an amazing document, a history book in stone, and it's very typically Roman in the sense of wanting to tell you what happened, just like the Roman generals who carried posters in their triumphal parades. Trajan's Column commemorates for posterity his military victories. In ancient times, administrative buildings surrounded this particular square, so you could actually go up to a balcony on the second or third floor and get a closer look at the

upper portions of the column, and thus "read" it in its totality.

This particular style or technique, this narrative quality in Roman art, is called the **continuous style** by art historians. The term is pretty self-explanatory, referring simply to the fact that the Romans developed a style of depicting an event continuously. This technique starts with event A, and leads logically to event B, all the way through the story, showing you the events in a continuous form. It's kind of a like a film strip: if you hold a film strip up and look at the different frames, you see the continuous representation of an event, and that's what we get in Trajan's Column.

This contribution is something we see enduring in western art for a thousand years after the Romans have passed off the scene. For example, we can see this technique in the painting dated to around 1425 by an Italian Renaissance painter, Masaccio, called *The Tribute Money*. (See Color Illustration D.) Masaccio depicts the scene in which Jesus is confronted by the scribes and the Pharisees and is asked whether a good Jew should give tribute to Caesar. We see this in the middle of the painting. The disciples surround Jesus, who is standing in the center. The man with his back turned to us, without a halo over his head, is the tax collector. On the left side of the painting we see Peter, who has been sent by Jesus on an errand. What is he doing? He gets a fish out of the lake and takes a coin out of the fish's mouth. On the extreme right of the painting we see Peter giving that coin to the tax collector, the same tax collector we identified in the center. This can be a very confusing painting to make sense of if you don't realize that it's painted in the "continuous style" that was first developed by the Romans over a thousand years earlier. Masaccio gives us three separate events; but they are not in chronological sequence, because they start in the middle, then go to the left, and then to the right. But nonetheless we have a series of three separate events narrated in one painting, and you need to know how to read it. The point that's been illustrated here is that this contribution to Western art is something that was in usage for a thousand years after Rome had passed off the scene.

Landscape Art

The same is the case with the third Roman contribution to Western art, namely, the development of landscape. When we speak about landscape in Roman art, we are referring to the natural setting, often what's in the background of a painting. You might have the action in the foreground, but in the background you have mountains, rivers, trees, and whatever constitutes the material, physical, natural background of that event. The Greeks didn't paint that way—they couldn't care less what was in the background. They were just interested in the symbolic meaning of something, seen in isolation by itself.

For the Romans—being, again, a practical, materialistic people—it was the most natural thing in the world when painting an event to include what was present in the surrounding world. You and I take that for granted: when we look at a painting, we expect to see various things in the background that fill out the scene and make it natural, since that's how things appear in the real world. The Romans, though, were the first to apply that commonsense way of depicting the world around them.

Let's consider a couple of examples of this. This style can be seen in the few examples of Roman wall paintings that have survived from the villa of Livia, the wife of Caesar Augustus. These wall paintings—that in-

clude garden scenes with flowers and birds—date from around 20 B.C. The Romans valued these aspects of the material world. The very fact that they have taken the trouble to paint this, though, is what is significant, because they are opening their eyes to the natural world around them. The Greeks, again, didn't do that.

Other wall paintings survive from Pompeii, such as the depiction of a scene from Homer's *Odyssey* (above). Obviously, there are events happening in the foreground; but notice the trees, rocks and mountains in the background. This is a very typically Roman way to paint the world around you, and this technique carries on through the rest of the history of western art.

This style is known to us basically from the paintings that survived in Pompeii, the city that was destroyed catastrophically in 79 A.D. when Mount Vesuvius erupted. The volcanic ash preserved the city like a time capsule. Much of what we know about everyday life in ancient Roman times is based upon the detailed excavations of this city. The wall paintings have been preserved, the statues have been preserved, and even the bread that was in the oven at the time the volcano erupted was fossilized and preserved. Much of what we know about Roman art also comes from the examples that have been found in the city of Pompeii.

Summarizing Roman Art

Let's summarize the things that we have said as we have looked first at portraiture art, secondly at narrative, and finally at landscape. What are the common denominators among these? What do they tell us about the Roman mind? They tell us once again how materialistic the Romans were, and what I mean by that is that they are focused on the real, material world. It is important to keep in mind that they're empire builders: this is where their treasure is, this is where their heart is—on the "real world." They paint that way—they paint the way a person *really* looks, they paint the *real* world of nature around them, and they paint the way a story is to be told *realistically*, since this world for them is where the action is. The Romans were also practical, and this is evident, too, in the way they painted and sculpted. We could describe them as down to earth or rooted in this world. As we turn to Roman architecture, let's not forget that we're trying to understand the Roman mind and the Roman character by looking at what they made.

The Romans as Engineers

We're going to look next at the Roman achievement in architecture. Here again, we gain some clear insight into who the Romans were in the decisions they made about how to construct buildings. The chief contribution of the Romans to western architecture is the arch. In fact, the word "architecture" is a Latin compound word that literally means, "the technology of the arch." We use the word here in the more general sense, but it originally had direct application to Roman architecture, because everything the Romans built used the arch.

They didn't invent the arch, however. The Greeks knew about it, too, but they weren't terribly impressed by it. The Greeks were perfectly content building in the post-and-lintel style which made possible everything they wanted to do in architecture. But the Romans found great potential in the arch to build in a distinctively Roman way. Being empire builders and world conquerors, they needed an architecture that was up to the task of expressing the grandeur and glory of who they were. They needed to build bigger, taller, more spacious edifices than the Greeks had ever contemplated. You couldn't do that in the post-and-lintel style; but you could do it with the arch.

Think about the Parthenon. How tall a temple could you build in the Greek style? Think of all that tonnage pressing straight down on those columns. It would buckle and collapse if you tried to put a second floor on the Parthenon. The genius of the arch is how it handles all that weight. The arch works by distributing weight equally down the sides. It takes that weight and it diffuses it and distributes it. Then, if you take an arch and extend it through 360 degrees, you have a dome.

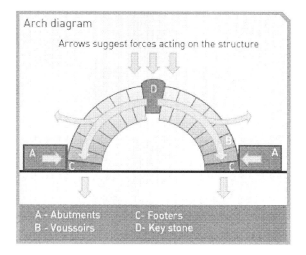

Arch diagram

Arrows suggest forces acting on the structure

A - Abutments   C- Footers
B - Voussoirs   D- Key stone

And so, in Roman architecture, we see arches and domes and very spacious, impressive structures, which, from their point of view, were appropriate to who they were as world conquerors. Every significant Roman architectural monument uses the arch. Let's look at some examples.

First of all, we see the arch in a type of Roman building that could be described as a forerunner to the modern sports arena, the Colosseum. The arch is a central design element in the structure.

Second, another kind of building that was important to Roman civic life was the basilica. These large buildings were the centers of law and commerce, and so they were built to accommodate a lot of people. Incidentally, basilicas were used as the model when Christian churches began to be built in the late Roman period. We can thus trace the lineage of the later medieval cathedrals all the way back to the Roman basilica.

A third type of Roman structure that used the arch was the aqueduct, a structure that carried water into the cities.

The fourth example is what I would describe somewhat misleadingly as the only "non-practical" structures that the Romans built—the triumphal arch. They did use them, of course, but only in a ceremonial, monumental way. The use of the arch in this structure should be especially noticed, since the triumphal arch is the most important type of Roman monument. When the Romans designed their most characteristic monument, one that spoke of who they were in the world, they chose a triumphal arch. It's not a triumphal square, or a triumphal triangle, or a triumphal cube, or some other structure; it's a triumphal arch. It is the arch that the Romans recognized as distinctively Roman, speaking to their engineering genius and their practicality in the world. Thus, they elevated this engineering form as a monument to who they were as a people in the world.

Finally, we see that Rome's most famous building, the Pantheon, also employs the arch as a very important design element. Like the Greek Parthenon, the Pantheon is a temple. But unlike the Parthenon, which was dedicated to one goddess, the Roman Pantheon is dedicated to the worship of the many gods, which is what the word "pantheon" means. So, as you look at the interior of the building, you notice that all around the circumference are found little niches, little shrines, each one of which would have a separate statue to a different god or goddess. It's kind of a one-stop religious center. Whoever your god of choice was, you could go to the Pantheon, the temple of the many gods, and there burn incense and pray to that particular deity.

What quality in the Roman mind, in the Roman personality, does that speak to? Their *eclecticism*. They worshipped many gods. They absorbed many different things from different cultures. They were very diverse in their taste, and religion was no exception. We've already looked at how their architecture was eclectic in the way they built the Colosseum, for example; but their practices were eclectic as well. Paul noticed this when he was in Athens, which was then under Roman control. In Acts 17, Paul jokingly refers to the fact that they have many altars to all these gods, and they even have an altar to the unknown God. This was the Roman practice of the spirit of eclecticism.

One more thing to note about this is that when this temple was converted to a Catholic church in the late Roman period, it was a fairly easy transformation. If you look at the interior (see illustration below), you've got these little niches of gods and goddesses. When the practice of the veneration of the saints began in early Catholicism, all they had to do was to yank out statues of the gods and goddesses and replace them with the statues of the various saints. Romans who were in the habit of coming to

116

the Pantheon to pray to their favorite god or goddess could now come to this church and pray to their favorite saint. Later, as we look at the rise of Christianity, we'll see that the church began to be corrupted like this by Roman practices and Roman ideas.

The Pantheon is the oldest continuously used religious building in the West, having started off as a pagan temple and then converted to a Catholic church. One more interesting fact has to do with the big opening in the top of the dome. They didn't run out of building material and decide just to round it off. It was designed that way and the term for that opening at the top is **oculus**, the Latin word for eye. Symbolically, it is meant to reflect the point of contact between the divine and the human realms. It's an eye opening up onto the sky, symbolizing that when you come into that temple, this is the place where you make contact with the gods, where the divine and the human realms interface.

The other thing to note is that from the front the Pantheon looks a lot like a Greek temple, and then you see this big thing bulging out behind. Here we have Roman eclecticism all over again. They integrated a Greek façade with a Roman dome. A Greek would look at that and think the architecture was horrible with its mixing and matching of styles and so on. But for a Roman, that's just what they did; it's that sense of eclecticism again. Notice as well that this is the form of architecture that gets revived in the neo-classical period in the eighteenth century by architects like Thomas Jefferson. This is what Jefferson's house, Monticello, looks like. It's the same kind of a pattern—the Greek façade in the front, the Roman dome behind.

So once again, as we look at Roman architecture and focus on the most famous Roman building, the Pantheon, we see distinctively Roman qualities in their use of the arch. We see their practicality, their imperialism expressed in grand building projects, and their sense of eclecticism in worshiping the many gods and eclectically designing a building like the Pantheon.

The Romans as Philosophers

As we turn our attention now to Roman philosophy, the last aspect of Roman civilization we're going to discuss, let's keep looking for evidence of what the Romans thought and believed, and what their values were. The main thing we want to keep in mind is the question of what's uniquely Roman about their schools of philosophy. We've left Roman philosophy to the end for a very good reason: it's not the first thing you think about when you think of the Romans. With the Greeks, it was the first thing we considered, and we're reversing that because obviously the emphasis is different with the Romans. As we noted before, the Romans are "doers," while the Greeks were "thinkers."

But that doesn't mean that the Romans didn't think or didn't cultivate schools of philosophy. We're going to identify two, the Epicureans and the Stoics. Both of these have their roots in hellenisic Greece. Both of them, incidentally, are mentioned in Acts 17, a passage I keep coming back to that describes when Paul was in Athens. Acts 17 mentions both of these philosophies by name. We are going to find out that the epicureans and stoics had very different worldviews and they debated their differences vigorously.

Epicureanism

Let's begin with the Epicureans. We trace epicureanism back to Greek philosophy, specifically the philosopher Epicurus, who argued that the chief goal of man was the pursuit of pleasure and the avoidance of pain. Epicurus and his followers were materialists. They believed that the material world and human experience within the material world is all that is real. When you die, that's it; there's nothing else. There is no afterlife for the epicureans. They believed that this world is all there is.

If asked that old question, "Where do you locate the essence of reality?" the epicureans, like the materialists, would say, "Right here, in human experience in this realm." Hence, it's perfectly logical, if you believe that to be the case, to try to get as much pleasure and to avoid as much pain in the few years that you have—that is, to "eat, drink and be merry, for tomorrow you die." That's the epicurean philosophy.

Now it's important to note, though, that Epicurus did not teach that you should give your life over to libertinism or hedonism. In fact, what Epicurus argued, in typical classical fashion, is that you should pursue pleasure *with moderation*. Think of the logic of it: You're hungry and you walk into the kitchen. You see a freshly baked chocolate cake sitting on the counter. It looks and smells really good. It can be pretty tempting. So you decide you're going to take a piece of that cake—and it tastes great. It's very pleasurable, so much so that you decide you're going to have a second piece. Probably the second piece is still going to taste pretty good. But consider what would happen if you ate a third and fourth piece and then decided to simply finish off the whole cake. You know exactly what's going to happen. Pleasure is going to turn into pain; enjoyment is going to turn into the exact opposite. You're probably going to

end up in the bathroom, vomiting it all up, because it's not going to be pleasurable if you indulge in too much. Any pleasure taken to an extreme can become painful. Epicurus argued this very simple point. Hence, you seek to pursue pleasure with moderation and you avoid pain.

I mention this because we sometimes caricature them as hedonists. We picture a fat Roman emperor reclining on a couch with grapes over his head and a chalice of wine in the other hand; but that's not what epicureanism is about. Certainly, there was an indulgence in luxury and pleasure in Roman culture; but the true epicurean did not follow that kind of an ethic and certainly did not espouse that philosophy of life.

Stoicism

Where the epicureans did not believe in an afterlife, the stoics believed in a divine principle, a moral structure to the universe. They believed that the purpose of humankind is to harmonize your life with that larger moral structure of the universe. In order to do this, they emphasized self-discipline and self-control. Stoicism has its roots in Greek philosophy, specifically the philosopher Zeno and later Roman philosophers such as Epictetus.

But why self-discipline and self-control? This is how a stoic philosopher would argue it: *As an individual you can't control fate, you can't control the world, you can't control other people; but you can control yourself.* You can control yourself; and, according to a stoic, you can do so by your own efforts. If you're self-disciplined enough and exercise enough self-control over the passions of your flesh, then you can do it. It's a self-help philosophy. The stoics believed that if you could carve out a little point of stability in a world of otherwise fatalistic forces, then you could live a good life by doing and following what is right.

As you can see, this is pretty different from epicureanism, which says there is nothing greater than yourself to live for. Stoicism says, by contrast, that there are greater things than yourself to live for, and that it's good to live a moral life, to be in harmony with the moral purpose of the universe. This philosophy is best expressed in the little book written by the Roman emperor Marcus Aurelius, the *Meditations*, which is acknowledged as the greatest work of stoic philosophy. (Remember that Marcus Aurelius was the last of the great Roman emperors who ruled during the Pax Romana. He died in 180 A.D.)

The greatest expression of Roman epicureanism was a philosophical poem, *On the Nature of Things*, written by the poet Lucretius in the 1st century B.C. One of the really interesting thing to note is that Lucretius lays out in this work the basic elements of evolutionary theory, nearly two thousand years before Darwin. Consider why this akes sense. The epicureans were materialists. They believed that this world is all that is that we are defined by material and natural forces. It makes sense, if you're an epicurean, to view the world that way and to look for purely naturalistic explanations for reality. Evolutionary theory, then, was definitely not new in the 19th century when Charles Darwin put forward his theory of natural selection. We can really it all the way back to ancient philosophy.

Epicureanism did not assume an afterlife, while stoicism did. Epicureanism emphasized pleasure, while stoicism emphasized self-discipline and responsibility in the world. What is the biblical response to these philosophies? If these are the prevailing philosophies of the world when the apostle Paul was evangelizing in the Greek cities and in the Roman Empire and writing his letters to the early churches, it seems reasonable that we might see some response to these philosophies in what he wrote.

The Biblical Response

We do indeed find responses to these prevailing philosophies of epicureanism and stoicism in Paul's writings. I would argue that perhaps the clearest response to epicureanism in the New Testament is found in 1 Corinthians 10:31, where Paul writes,

"Whether therefore you eat or drink, or whatever you do, do all to the glory of God." Epicureans were all about "eating and drinking and being merry, for tomorrow we die." That is, they advocated eating and drinking to the satisfaction of one's flesh, eating and drinking as an end in itself. Paul takes those two things, eating and drinking, as his example, since they are the most material things you can imagine. God created them to be pleasurable, and Paul doesn't reject the fact that they're pleasurable. Instead, he says that we should take these things and make them acts of worship to God. Do them not for yourself, not for the lusts of your flesh, as an epicurean would, in order to get as much pleasure as possible. Rather, we should recognize that "the earth is full of the goodness of the Lord" (Psalm 3:5) and that God has given us all good things to enjoy (1 Timothy 6:17). These things are to be enjoyed not as an end in themselves but rather to the glory of the one who made them, the one who is the author of every good and perfect gift. This is a radical way of looking at the world, or it would certainly have been so in the first century in the epicurean climate of the Roman Empire. Paul is calling the church to recognize that we have been called out from the world. We are to live differently from the world—to enjoy the things that God has given us, but to enjoy them while acknowledging the origin of every good thing.

What about Stoicism? The Stoic philosopher says "You can do it." It's like a self-help philosophy. You can create a good and orderly life through your own efforts, through self-discipline and a sense of responsibility. You can do that yourself through your own strength. It doesn't matter what circumstance you're in, it doesn't matter if it's good times or bad times. The stoic philosopher says you can be a stable point of self-discipline and responsibility within the chaotic cosmos. Paul responds to the stoic philosophy in a well-known passage, Philippians 4:11-13. Using the language of stoicism, Paul says, "Not that I speak in respect of want, for I have learned in whatsoever state I am, therewith to be content." He goes on to say: "I know both how to be abased, and I know how to abound: everywhere and in all things I am instructed both to be full and to be hungry, both to abound and to suffer need." Just like a Stoic philosopher, he says that it doesn't matter what the circumstances are, you can be content in that.

A stoic philosopher would agree with that, but it's at this point that Paul parts company with the stoics. Notice what he says. What is the source of the strength? What enables you to do that? Is it like Marcus Aurelius said in his *Meditations*, that you can do it by yourself? Paul rejects this attitude. He claims that the only way I can live out that stoic ideal is through the life of Christ living within me. "I can do all things through Christ. He alone strengthens me."

This is again a radical and revolutionary take on the philosophy that was current in Paul's day, and I think it remains a very relevant challenge to you and me. We, too, live in a world that is governed by epicurean and stoic philosophies. Epicureanism is alive and well today in the view that you should go out and live your life seeking as much pleasure as you can—because that's all that there is to life, according to the materialists. On the other hand, there are others who view life like the stoics and tell us that we can live a life of discipline; we can do it on our own, through our own effort. Both of these are worldly philosophies that Paul directly challenged by saying that we can only live through the power of Christ as we live to the glory of God. That's what we, as Christians, have been called to do.

THE RISE OF CHRISTIANITY

12

Chapter Objectives

- Describe why Christianity survived and flourished within the Roman Empire.
- Summarize how early Christians expressed the theme of persecution.
- Explain why the image of Christ changed radically in early Christian art.

As we've already noted, the rise of Christianity occurred in the early Roman Empire. It began with the birth of Christ and under the reign of Caesar Augustus, and then we see the rapid founding of the church in the decades that followed. In a very real sense the story of the rise of Christianity is inseparable from the story of the Roman Empire, and that's one of the key things that I want us to keep in mind as we look at early Christianity and study it as a culture.

We need to consider the rise of Christianity against the backdrop of Rome and the things that we've said about Rome. We spoke about the materialism of Rome, the fact that, as empire builders, they were very much focused on this world and the values of this world, and that this was where their treasure was. These are the values that we very clearly identified with the Roman Empire in the way they sculpted, painted, and built the great buildings that filled their capital and the other great provincial cities of the Roman Empire.

It is important to keep those values in mind as we look at the message of Christ and the early church, and as we evaluate the nature of the church and the values of the early Christians. It will help us to understand more clearly the two cultures that we're talking about, Rome and the early church. Keep in mind the perspective we're going to bring to this subject: *we're going to analyze early Christianity as a distinct culture*.

That is, we'll be applying the very same methods of analysis that we've applied to Egypt, Greece and Rome. This is probably an unfamiliar way of thinking about the topic, but it's an approach that will draw out the story of the church very clearly. This approach will also present us with some intriguing facts that we'll have to wrestle with; more than anything, we'll be challenged as we look at the way early Christians gave expression to their values within the alien culture of the Roman Empire.

As we noted, it was in the fullness of time, as Paul says in Galatians 4:4, that Jesus was born. That's such a rich phrase because it obviously suggests the fulfillment of all the prophecies of the Old Testament, from Genesis 3:15 through the prophets. It also suggests, I believe, the broader historical sense that this was time God chose through His sovereignty for Christ to enter into the world. It was the time when the gospel would take root within the Roman Empire—for all the reasons we've talked about, such as that Rome was at peace and Rome was the only superpower in the Mediterranean world. The Roman highway system and political and legal systems provided the environment and the atmosphere within which Christianity took root, grew and flourished, even during times of great persecution.

The Emergence of Christianity

Why did Christianity grow so rapidly within the Roman Empire? We've already noted that there were many religions to choose from along with many philosophies of life. We've noted that the Romans were a people of eclectic tastes. They tolerated many forms of religious practice, as is clearly indicated to us in Acts 17, where we read of the apostle Paul debating the philosophers on Mars Hill. Why is it that one out of a number of small mystery cults—as most Romans of the first century viewed Christianity—flourished? You wouldn't have necessarily marked it out as anything different from the general mix of what a Roman citizen could select from if he chose to pursue a religious life; and so there was nothing that initially appeared to threaten the Roman Empire about this minority religion that began to filter into the Roman capital from the east.

It was only later, as Christianity grew and flourished and as Christians gave expression to its values in their lives, that the differences became unavoidably clear to the Roman authorities. It was then that Christians began to be seen as a threat by the Romans and were persecuted. The persecution of the church was not something that occurred consistently from the first through the fifth centuries. Rather, there were sporadic periods of very intense persecution. Nonetheless, Christianity was severely persecuted as we know. All this changed in the early fourth century, when the first Christian emperor Constantine took power and legalized the practice of Christianity within the Roman Empire in 313 A.D.

Within a generation Christianity would become the official religion of Rome, and paganism would then be persecuted and ulti-

mately stamped out of Roman institutions. We need to look at how it is that Christianity arose from this minority status, when nobody would have taken much note of it, to the point where it ultimately became the official religion of the Roman Empire. After that, we will also consider how, when Rome passed off the scene at the end of the fifth century, the church would continue on as the Roman Catholic Church, becoming the dominant institution of western culture in the middle ages. Interestingly, the story of the church patterns the rise of the Romans themselves, but for very different reasons (that is, not through military conquest). I'm not sure the Romans ever had time to really absorb the irony of that; but there is a beautiful irony to this changing of the guard between the Romans and the Christians in the first four centuries of the Christian era.

Why did Christianity grow so rapidly within the Roman Empire? Of course, as a Christian I go to the Bible for the ultimate answer to that question; the book of Acts records the rapid spread of the gospel within the Roman Empire. Acts gives us two reasons for the phenomenon. The first is the witness to the resurrection, which is one of the great themes of Acts. As Jesus himself says, in Acts 1:8, "You will be witnesses." They were witnesses of the resurrection, and that's repeated over and over, beginning with Peter's great speech on the day of Pentecost (Acts 2), where he gives testimony to the event that validates who Jesus is and the claim that he has on our lives. The second reason that Acts gives us is the power of the Holy Spirit. That's the Biblical answer that I affirm as a Christian.

As a Christian scholar, however, I look at the history of the church as a *historical* phenomenon as well, as something that did in fact occur within time and space, within historical contexts, and which has to be understood historically as well as theologically and biblically. The point is not to give priority to these historical explanations; but I certainly believe we can discuss this as a historical issue just as we talked about the rise of the Greeks and the rise of the Romans within historical contexts.

For the historical answer, I would turn to a British historian who has given us a very succinct and brilliant analysis of the rise of Christianity within the Roman Empire. His name is E. R. Dodds, and his work was presented a generation ago in a book called *Pagan and Christian in an Age of Anxiety*, published in 1965. E. R. Dodds offers one of the best secular, historical explanations of the rise of Christianity. I'd like to use his three-part formula to explain this, because he's not writing from a Christian, but rather a self-acknowledged agnostic, point of view. He is not, therefore, pushing a "Christian agenda" in what he says.

Interestingly, we're going to find out that Dodds put his finger pretty accurately on three main reasons that correspond largely with what scripture has to say about the unique features of Christianity and the message of the gospel. The first value of the early church that E.R. Dodds identifies that helps to explain the rise of Christianity is what he calls *the exclusiveness of the Christian faith*. Dodds writes the following:

The religious tolerance which was the normal Greek and Roman practice had resulted by accumulation in a bewildering mass of alternatives. There were too many cults, too many mysteries, too many philosophies of life to choose from: you could pile one religious insurance on another, yet not feel safe.

Rome was an eclectic, "tolerant" society—at least in the context of the ancient world. You could worship Isis or Mithras or Christ. You could worship Yahweh, if you were a Jew in the Roman capital, or you could choose a more philosophical approach to life such as stoicism or epicureanism. All of these possibilities were open to you. The passage in Acts 17, which mentions the many altars to all the gods, clearly expresses that a pervasive religious anxiety was motivating factor in all that diversity. As Paul notes, there was also an altar to the "unknown God." There is a sense of not wanting to offend anyone that you might have left out. And so, what do you choose? Who do you worship? This is the problem if you live in the hellenistic and Roman periods. Dodds continues:

Christianity made a clean sweep. It lifted the burden of

freedom from the shoulders of the individual. One choice, one irrevocable choice, and the road to salvation was clear.

This is his secular way of approaching the issue; but if we translate that into biblical terms, we see that Dodds is very accurately describing the message of the gospel. It's exclusive. Jesus himself said in John 14:6, "I am the way, the truth and the life. No one comes to the Father except by me." This is the message that the apostles gave us as well as they he began to preach the gospel in the days after Pentecost. In Acts 4:12 Peter preached that "There is no other name given under heaven whereby we must be saved." It's an exclusive message.

And so, if you're hearing that as a Roman and you're kind of bewildered by all of the options—Who will you worship? What way will you live your life? What philosophy will you pursue?—the message of the gospel is clear: "Sweep all of that aside; there's only one way to God." There is only one revealed "way" to God, and that is the Son of God, Jesus Christ. Thus, Dodds very accurately identifies the key value within the Christian message, something that marked Christians within the Roman Empire as people to keep your eyes on. The Romans could tolerate many faiths, as long as people also worshiped Caesar on the side. The Roman attitude would be, "Go ahead, worship Christ, but burn incense to Caesar." The Romans couldn't tolerate the exclusive worship of Christ.

This establishes an interesting analogy with our own day. In this "tolerant" multicultural society that we live in, the one thing that cannot be tolerated from a secular and a humanistic point of view is anyone who dares to make the claim that there is salvation exclusively in Jesus Christ. That's the one thing that gets everybody's feathers most ruffled in our society. If we think about that by analogy with the Romans, who were also a tolerant, eclectic people, we see that the gospel causes offense today, just as it offended back then. Nothing really has changed.

Second, Dodds draws attention to *the inclu-*

siveness of the Christianity. This might strike us as internally contradictory. How can it be both exclusive and inclusive? Dodds gets out of that apparent contradiction by saying that the message of the gospel was inclusive for all. All could receive salvation in Christ. Or, as Dodds puts it:

Christianity was open to all. In principle, it made no social distinctions; it accepted the manual worker, the slave, the outcast, and the ex-criminal.

He does argue, however, that later on it did develop a very strong hierarchical quality as the church developed into the medieval Catholic church. Certainly, though, in the early centuries, we see that Christianity was very much as Dodds describes it. In the pages of the New Testament we read rebukes for giving preference to people on the basis of social position. There is never any place for that in the church. As James says in his epistle, it's wrong to give precedence to the rich man with a big fat ring on his finger when he comes into church; it's wrong to usher him down front, fuss over him, and give him the honored position in the front row. James said that's not what the church is all about. Or as Paul said, "In Christ, there is neither Jew nor Greek, neither male or female, neither bond nor free" (Galatians 3:28). This is beautifully illustrated in the letter that Paul wrote to Philemon—the short personal letter consisting of only 25 verses, in which Paul asks Philemon to receive back his runaway slave Onesimus. Paul writes: "Onesimus ran away from you and he did you wrong, but he came to know Christ. I'm now sending him back to you not as your runaway slave, but as your brother in Christ." We should note how radical that idea is within the Roman Empire, given the practice of slavery. We see that Christianity directly challenges social distinctions and says that in Christ there is neither bond nor free. And so the inclusiveness of Christianity was a liberating message within a Roman context, just as it should be a liberating message within a world today that has just as many social divisions as that of the Romans two thousand years ago.

Third, Dodds argues that it was *the other-*

worldliness of Christianity that contributed to its success. Again, we're talking about the value system of the early Christians considered as a culture. The other-worldliness of Christianity directly challenged—note this well—the *materialism* of the Romans. Here's what Dodds says:

[I]n a period when earthly life was increasingly devalued and guilt-feelings were widely prevalent, Christianity held out to the disinherited the conditional promise of a better inheritance in another world.

The Romans were all about *this world now*. *This* was the empire they were building; *this* was the kingdom that occupied their energy and attention. Jesus said, "Follow me and you're really following after the kingdom of God," the kingdom of heaven. And so the message of the gospel challenged the worldliness of the Roman Empire, just as the gospel two thousand years later challenges the materialism of our own world today.

What has changed in two millennia? In terms of values, very little has changed. We live in a world system that's still under the condemnation of sin and death and is still organized around these false values of humanism and materialism. For me, as a Christian scholar, one of the great benefits and virtues of the study of the past is that we can see the false values of our own day more clearly when we look at the values of the Romans. We can always see faults in other people much more easily than we can see in ourselves. We can see the faults and the limitations of the Romans as we look back at them from the vantage point of two thousand years; we can see how materialistic they were in pursuing their own worldly possessions and power. But if we use that observation as a mirror to reflect upon our own culture now, then we'll be challenged by the reflection we see. And that's what I'm going to be stressing in the pages that follow—that we should be challenged by the values we identify in the first Christians.

The Beginnings of Christian Art

With that as a backdrop to the values of the early Christians and how diametrically opposite those values were to those the Roman Empire, let's begin looking at their art. As we do that, I want to put us on notice that the early art of the Christians looks like amateur art to us. By this I mean that the quality of the art that we're going to be examining takes a real dive as we go from the Greeks and the Romans to the early Christians. This art wasn't made by professional artists, but by humble people living out their faith within the world and feeling the need to give expression to their faith. They did this through the things they wrote and the images they etched into the walls and ceilings of the catacombs. In so doing, they were producing art as a beautiful and eloquent expression of their faith; still, it's not "high art" of the kind produced by Michelangelo or the classical Greek sculptors. This art is going to look pretty basic and simple to us, but let's not make the mistake of thinking that it is unsophisticated just because it's crudely produced. The art of every culture is equally sophisticated in its purpose and function, even if it is of unequal quality and craftsmanship. We'll see that earliest Christian art is not equal in quality to what the Greeks and Romans produced; but it is equally "sophisticated" because it does what art always does: *it gives expression to values*.

Let's look at some of the earliest artifacts we can identify from the catacombs. Not even the earliest art from the Christian period comes remotely close to the apostolic age. We don't have any artifacts about which we can say, "This is a first century Christian work of art." None exist. Presumably the Christians did not produce art in that period of the New Testament. It's only as we enter into the second century, and much more in the third century, that we begin to see art in the Roman catacombs.

And so, keep that in mind as we look at the first two examples. These are usually described as medallions or jewel-like objects. It's important to remember that these objects were small works of art, and that, as personal objects, they would have given expression to the beliefs and values of their owner.

Now, as we look at the first one of these, one of the things we're going to note is that there is no story being told here in the sense that the Romans told stories with their art. All we have in this medallion is a collection of symbols, objects, and images that have to be read for their symbolic meaning theologically. And that's the way I want us to proceed. Let's identify the objects, the images that we see and then the motifs that we find in these medallions, and then let's identify the theological meaning that the early Christians attributed to these objects.

The most dominant image that you see in this first medallion (above) is the image of the boat or a ship. This is one of the very pervasive images that we find in this earliest period of Christian art. The ship or the boat is invariably present in both early Christian writings and art. When you see a boat or ship in art of this context, it is symbolizing the church.

What else do you see? Note the fish in the foreground. Here again, the images are not very skillfully drawn or chiseled in this particular medallion. The fish look like torpedoes in front of the boat, but we can identify them clearly as that ubiquitous image of the fish that we associate with the early church. Now, the boat, as we said, was a very common symbol in early Christian art, but it largely fell out of usage in Christian art completely. The fish and the cross are the two images from the earliest periods of Christian art that continue to this day to be universally recognized as symbols of the Christian faith.

What did the fish represent? Why was it that it was such an important symbol to the early Christians? Well, if you have ever heard the nonsense that it was some kind of a secret symbol or code, used to identify Christians in a period of persecution, then you can put that out of your mind. It's a very romantic story, and it sounds good, but it doesn't have any historical credibility whatsoever. Everybody knew what the fish represented: it was a symbol of the Christian faith. To the best of our knowledge, the fish held such a unique position in early Christian art because it had mystical significance. The symbol of the fish and the Greek word for fish itself seemed to contain the very mystery of the gospel, the person and work of Jesus Christ. And so, that's why I say that it really contained a kind of mystical quality to it. What am I talking about here? The Greek word for fish is **ichthus**, and the early Christians saw that word as an acrostic that, in the Greek, spells out the phrase, "Jesus Christ, Son of God, Savior." Obviously, when you think of the fish, you think of what Jesus said: "I will make you fishers of men." This probably factored into it as well. But more importantly, in the word itself, you get the whole story of who Christ is—his person and work as the Son of God, the Savior of the world. That's the best explanation I think that has ever been offered for why the fish was such a uniquely pervasive symbol in the early church.

Let's note some other features of this medallion. We see the very artificial symbol of the cross balanced on the ship. This is a Greek cross, as it's usually called, having all sides equal. It is one of several different styles of the cross that developed in early Christianity, among which are the Byzantine cross, the Crucifix form that became the standard Catholic symbol, and the Celtic cross that prevailed in the British Isles. Notice, as well, that the mast is literally depicted as a mast, but you can also see the cross in it. This is meant, I believe, to suggest that the cross is centrally located within the church itself, within the ship. I love the beautiful, simple symbolism of that. Right in the center of the church is the cross! The church is to be defined by, and around, the most significant element in the gospel.

What repetitive patterns can we identify in this medallion? What things just seem to get repeated over and over again? What abstract idea gets repeated? We see the number three. We see it in the number of oars and the number of planks on the side of the ship. We see three heads along the side of the ship and three drapes on the mast. The number three is clearly dominant in this overall design. When we see the number three we obviously think of the doctrine of the Trinity. Now, I'm not suggesting here that these shapes, these round forms here are to be literally equated with God the Father, God the Son, and God the Holy Spirit. Rather, it's the fact that the number three is repeated here that suggests that doctrinal truth. Importantly, we are here not seeing a story being depicted, but doctrinal ideas and beliefs. We don't see, for example, Jesus on the Sea of Galilee. We see a collection of symbols put together—fish, ship, cross, and the number three—that function together almost like a systematic theology of the early church. The art declares: "This is what we believe; these are the truths that we affirm and the values we accept as a community."

Let's look at the second medallion (below) a little bit more quickly. There aren't as many elements to note here. The letters make up the Latinized form of the Greek word ichthus. The expression means something like "belonging to the ichthus," which is another way of saying, "The owner of this object is a Christian." We can recognize a couple of figures, such as the large tuna-like fish at the bottom of the illustration, which again expresses the familiar symbol of the ichthus. What else do we see? What's the dominant image in the center that defines the rest of this form? It appears to represent the form of a cross, but it is not literally a cross that's being depicted. It also looks like a scale—like a balance for weighing things. I can categorically say, however, that this is not a balance for one simple reason. We never see scales or a balance represented in early Christian art.

By contrast, from the very early period of Islamic art we see all kinds of balances and scales. Why is that? Think again of values and consider the theological significance of that. Weighing the good and the bad is not something that has anything to do with the gospel. We don't stand in front of God and hear him say, "Let's weigh the good things in your life and let's weigh the bad, and we'll see how you come out." That's what Islam teaches, which is why you see that value expressed in the image of the balance. But the message of the gospel is the message of grace; this rules out the balance as a possible symbol. (The balance also appears widely in ancient Egyptian art, as a way of symbolizing how our deeds are weighed in the afterlife.)

What else could this image possibly be? It's

an anchor. It may not look like an anchor to you and me, but we have examples of Roman anchors and so this identification is fairly certain. The image was another common symbol in early Christian art, and it's even identified as such in the New Testament where Jesus is described as the anchor of our soul. The image also conveys that sense of anchoring the ship in the harbor, the sense of safety and security in the midst of the storms and persecutions of life. This is a very common, pervasive, and rich symbol.

Let's look now at our first example of a catacomb painting, a ceiling painting. It's not very elaborate, and it's perhaps not very impressive as a work of art. You have to imagine yourself standing in a little niche where the early Christians buried their dead and looking up at this ceiling and seeing this decoration in that catacomb crypt.

This is what you see as you look up. I just want us to briefly identify the several key elements of this particular form and things that we haven't seen yet, but that will be important for our understanding of the development of Christian art.

Right in the center of that ceiling painting you see a figure standing in a very classical pose. There is that shifting of the weight that we associated with Greco-Roman art. It shouldn't surprise us, because these are Christian artists who live in Roman cities where they see Greek and Roman art all around them. When they produce art, they're going to draw the human figure the way they see it represented in the world around them. This figure that we see standing like a classical statue in the center of the painting is Jesus, depicted as the Good Shepherd. In the early church, there was considerable disagreement, theologically speaking, about what Jesus must have looked like. Some argued that he was the paragon of humanity; others argued, on the basis of Isaiah 53:2, that he looked like an ordinary human being and nothing would have distinguished him physically. Significantly, when Jesus was first depicted in Christian art, no attempt was made to represent him literally. Instead, he's shown as a symbol. We see that this figure has an animal, probably a lamb or a sheep, draped around his neck. This is the first way, the first manner or mode in which early Christians depicted Jesus Christ. He was not depicted in historical terms; he was not depicted as a teacher. Nor was he shown on the cross in that traditional Roman Catholic depiction of Christ. None of those are the earliest ways that Christ was depicted. The first way that he was depicted is highly significant. We've been talking about symbols of ships, of anchors, and fish and so on. Christ himself is depicted as a symbol, and the symbol is that of the Good Shepherd.

The role that Jesus himself describes for himself in John 10 is as follows: "I am the Good Shepherd, you are the sheep." This is a very important point. There's a humility to that role that is so appropriate to the description that we have of Christ, one who humbled himself from the glory of heaven, and took upon himself, as it says in Philippians 2, the image of man, the form of man, becoming obedient to death, even the death of the cross. The story of the incarnation is a story of the humility of Christ in that sense, and there's nothing more humble than the role of a shepherd. Shepherds were not widely respected people in the ancient world. They were viewed—to put it bluntly and in a way that draws upon our worst stereotypes—in the way that gypsies are viewed. They were not viewed the way

we depict them on Christmas cards. They didn't have social prestige and social position. In that sense, it's all the more remarkable that Jesus identified himself that way. Obviously, there's another tradition of David as a shepherd king that is much more ennobling, but within the social context of the ancient world, shepherds occupied the lowest position on the social scale.

So this image of one who lays down his life for the sheep is appropriate for Jesus in that great role of humility that defined his ministry and death on the cross. It's interesting to note as well that the early Christians came from the lowest social classes of the Roman Empire—slaves and servants. How did they see Christ? How did they identify with Christ? They identified with him in his humility, and that's something I think we need to see and be challenged by. As Jesus said, "The son of man came not to be served, but to serve" (Mark 10:45). That's the sacrificial service that Jesus modeled by washing the disciples' feet (John 13). In following him, we are to be like servants, humbly serving one another.

Below the feet of the Good Shepherd you see what I think we can safely say is a dove. At the top of that scene we see a human face. What are we looking at here? It's a female face, and we've got to be careful when we interpret things like this. We tend to bring our expectations to what we see. When we see a bird in the context of Christian art, we think of a dove; that might lead us to think of the Holy Spirit, who is often symbolized by the dove. When we combine this with the image of Jesus as the Good Shepherd, we're getting close to having the whole Trinity here! That might lead us to see this face at the top as God the Father—except that it's a female face. We might then adjust very quickly, and predictably, by identifying the face as representing Mary. Wrong again. We don't see the Virgin Mary until a little bit later when she begins to be venerated in the Catholic tradition, so we can rule that out. The female face we see is, in fact, a symbolic representation of the soul of man, referred to in Latin as **alma**. The alma is depicted as a female form, because the word *alma* is a feminine noun in the Latin language; and so, the spirit of man is personified as a female figure. Remember, this painting is taken from a burial place, and the very thing that the early Christians are thinking about is the hope of eternal life. We need to read these and understand these paintings in the context within which they were used. So, even as these Christians are mourning the loss of their loved one, they're thinking of the fact that their soul has departed to heaven, into the promise of eternal life, and that's what's been affirmed by this image. We're going to see that the doctrine of the resurrection is one of the great themes of the Christian message that is repeated over and over again in early catacomb art.

We haven't discussed the vines yet, but all that vegetation that we see in the painting is the same imagery you'd see in Pompey in a pagan context representing Dionysian fertility rights. It certainly doesn't represent that here. Instead, what we have here is a Christian artist taking pagan motifs that they would have seen in Roman art around them and reinterpreting them. They're giving new meaning to pagan motifs in light of Christianity. We can see here that the vines would have had a symbolic meaning of Christ as the true vine (John 15). We'll find more examples of early Christians taking images and motifs from pagan Roman art and reinterpreting them through the message of the gospel, as we see being done here. This is a very important principle, and it's one we can learn from and reflect upon today. As we look at early Christian art, we will see how the early Christians tried to live within an alien culture, how they tried to be, as Jesus said, "In the world, but not of the world."

Persecution and Deliverance

Let's continue to approach the emergence of Christian art by looking at how they struggled with the challenge of being in the world but not of the world. Certainly, their belief system was diametrically opposed to the materialism of the ancient Romans, and we're going to see how that conflict played out in early Christian art. Before we go any further, let's consider four generalizations about early Christian art that will help us make sense of what we're looking at.

First, *the early history of the church (and its art) must be understood against the backdrop of the history of the Roman Empire*. The two will be tracking side-by-side as we'll see, and this has profound implications for how we understand the art of the early Christians.

Second, *the earliest Christian art is very simple in its form*. It's not very skillful in its form, as we've seen, but it is certainly no less sophisticated in its function than the art of any other culture. Certainly by comparison to the imperial art of Rome or the highest achievements of Greek art, it doesn't rank well in terms of its craftsmanship and skill. But it is no less an eloquent expression of the values of the people who produced it.

Third, I mentioned that we need to keep in mind as well that *the earliest Christian art is at least a century and a half after the New Testament period*. By this time, the church had become less Jewish and more Roman and that will be reflected clearly in the cultural products of early Christianity.

Fourth, we've already seen that *the earliest Christian art is strictly symbolic*. It doesn't tell stories the way the Romans did. It will do that in time. But initially the art is simply a collection of motifs and images that have symbolic meaning which must be decoded by reference to Christian doctrine and theological concepts. These doctrines are symbolized by images such as the fish, ship, cross, and anchor. Even the image of Christ as the Good Shepherd is a purely symbolic way to represent who he is.

Now, we are going to begin to see examples of stories told in the art of the catacombs which date from the early third century. When the early Christians began to paint biblical stories, they turned to Old Testament stories exclusively for their subjects. One theme dominated early

Christian art and determined which stories from the Old Testament they chose to depict. Of the hundreds of stories in the Old Testament that you could paint on the walls of the catacombs, they kept coming back to a handful of stories. There's got to be a reason for that. Why would you keep returning to the same subjects? It's because those stories conveyed a simple but powerful message—the dominant theme of early Christian catacomb art: *persecution and deliverance*.

This theme captured the reality of their lives as early Christians. They were persecuted in this world but held to the promise of deliverance in Christ. If art conveys values, if art is an expression of how we see ourselves in the world around us, then this is a beautiful example of how art functions. Three examples of the depiction of this theme are:

- The Fiery Furnace
- Moses Parting the Red Sea
- Jonah and the Great Fish

These catacomb paintings are reproduced as Color Illustrations E, F, and G. As you examine these paintings, look for the following interesting details.

Notice, for example, how the depiction of Shadrach, Meshach, and Abednego is lacking one figure—the fourth figure "like the son of God" (Daniel 3:25). That figure has often been understood as a pre-incarnate appearance of Christ. Instead, we see a bird in the center of the painting. I would argue that this is the mythological bird, the phoenix, which rises from its own ashes every thousand years. In the early church, the phoenix was a symbol of the resurrection. Once again, we see in this painting the theme of persecution and deliverance.

The most curious aspect of "Moses Parting the Red Sea" is the way Moses is depicted. He looks like a young Roman general—not the old patriarch of Exodus. Even more interesting than that is the swastika on the lower hem of his toga! Though the swastika was adopted by the Nazis many centuries later, we need to try to set that unpleasant fact aside as we look at this. The swastika is an ancient symbol; in the early church it was used as one of the symbols of the cross. Moses is being "branded" by this cross symbol as a prefiguration of Christ. Just as Moses delivered the Children of Israel from Egypt, so will Christ lead us to deliverance from sin.

The painting of Jonah is the most complex of these works. In the center of the painting we see Jesus as the Good Shepherd. On all four sides of the painting, we see episodes in the story of Jonah. We see Jonah being thrown out of the ship. Notice, in particular, that the "great fish" is depicted as a sea monster. We also see Jonah being spit out of the creature onto dry land. Finally, we see him reclining in the shade of the plant that God provided for him. The story of Jonah was the most widely represented, the most popular, story in early Christian art. This is probably because of how well it captured the essence of that theme— persecution and deliverance.

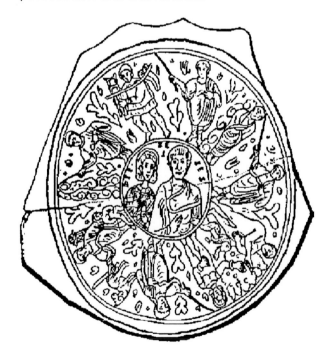

Physical artifacts from the catacombs also document the beliefs and values of the early church. For example, pieces of glassrk illustrated with biblical stories have been excavated from the plastered walls of these early burial places. One example is the so-called "Wedding Dish" (probably dating from the late third century A.D.). It depicts a Christian couple in the center, surrounded by scenes drawn from the Old and New Testaments. The figure holding a rod in his hand sometimes represents Christ (as Good Shepherd), and sometimes Moses (with Aaron's rod). The depiction of the fall of man—Adam and Eve in the Garden of Eden—is particularly noteworthy. We see in this simple representation a pattern for how the biblical account would be depicted throughout the history of Christian art.

Post-Constantine Christian Art

The church underwent a significant transformation in the period following Constantine's reign. When Constantine legalized Christianity in 313 A.D., the systematic persecution of Christians came to an end. This would have a profound impact upon the art as well. Many of the earlier themes and subjects would continue on for centuries in the art of the church; but the art began to change in important ways. The image of Christ went from Good Shepherd to universal ruler, the **Pantocrater** ("universal ruler"), seated at the right hand of God. When the church was a persecuted minority faith, with its adherents drawn largely from the lower classes of society, Christ was depicted in all his humility. But once emperors began identifying themselves as Christians, we see Christ being depicted as an emperor. Once again, we see that the art reflects the values "on the ground," so to speak.

The singular masterpiece of this post-Constantine period of Christian art is a **sarcophagus**, a burial box (pictured above; also see Color Illustration H). This one is known as the Sarcophagus of Junius Bassus, a man who was an important Roman official around the middle of the fourth century. The sarcophagus shows the wealth and power of its owner; but it also documents the changes that are underway in the relationship between the church and empire during this time.

Here's what the ten panels of the sarcophagus depict, from left to right.

Upper Level

- The sacrifice of Isaac
- The arrest of Peter
- Christ enthroned in heaven
- The arrest of Jesus
- The scene before Pilate

Lower Level

- The sufferings of Job
- The fall of man (Adam and Eve)
- The triumphal entry
- Daniel in the lion's den
- The arrest of Paul

Note as well how Christ (in the upper central panel) is depicted as a young emperor. (See detail below.) He is flanked on his right hand by Peter, and on his left by Paul—two pillars of the church. They are holding scrolls in their hands that represent the New Testament. Christ's foot is resting upon the head of a pagan Roman god—the sky-god Caelus (also known as Atlas). This god certainly also represents Satan. The depiction here is doctrinally and politically complex. Christ is shown as triumphant over Satan in fulfillment of the first Messianic prophecy of the Bible, Genesis 3:15. But there's a political message as well. The church has triumphed over Roman paganism. That's the over-arching message of the Sarcophagus of Junius Bassus.

Many of sthe earlier biblical subjects, seen first in the catacombs, are still being depicted in this work; but it's clear that the status of Christianity has fundamentally changed within the Roman Empire; and that change is documented in the way Christ is depicted on the sarcophagus in imperial terms.

Most of the early Christian art that we've examined is of not the highest quality when you set it side by side with the classical achievements in art. But the sarcophagus of Junius Bassus is quite different; here the difference lies not only in the fact that we have a very rich and highly complex statement of doctrinal ideas, but also in the social status of the individual buried in that box. With money and power now allied with the church, the quality of the art would improve significantly.

Let's look at one final work of early Christian art—an ivory door from a Roman church (dating perhaps from the late fifth century). In six panels we see six miracles from the ministry of Jesus. We also note something different here: the emergence of the halo in Christian art. Where did it come from? Pagan Roman emperors were depicted in Roman art as radiating divine glory from their person; after the Christianization of the empire, this quality was transferred to the image of Christ in art. Initially, a halo is seen only around Christ's head; later, in the Middle Ages, the halo would be extended to the apostles, the saints of the church, and the Virgin Mary.

Conclusion

Early Christianity arose in the Roman Empire as a distinct culture, with a distinct set of values. Where Rome was materialistic, Christianity was calling people to look beyond this world to the promise of eternal life. Despite intense persecution, the early Christians held on to the hope of deliverance. They gave expression to their faith in the objects they made and the paintings they produced in their burial chambers, the catacombs, beneath the city of Rome.

In the early fourth century, Constantine legalized Christianity. During the course of that century, Christianity went from being a persecuted minority faith to the official religion of the Roman Empire. The status of the church changed radically, and Christian art was transformed by the new political realities. Christ was no longer depicted as a humble shepherd; now he was a ruling emperor, seated in heaven. The church was well on its way to becoming the dominant, shaping institution that it would remain for the next thousand years in western culture.

FROM EMPIRE TO CHURCH

13

Chapter Objectives

- List eleven answers historians have given for the fall of Rome.
- Explain how the medieval church emerged from the Roman period.
- Identify three important Church Fathers during this transitional time.

We now turn our attention to the fall of the Roman Empire and the end of the ancient world. After this, we are going to be turning to the period known as the Middle Ages. Thus, we are now in a pivotal point in western history. It's a very difficult period in many ways to understand and reduce to simple terms—but we'll do our best.

This is a difficult period to understand because we are really ushering out one great period of history and ushering in another. We should, therefore, tackle the question of how the ancient world becomes the medieval world, or (as we'll see later) how the medieval world turns into the modern world. It looks easy on paper—when you look back from the vantage point of several centuries and all the interpretations are laid out for you in a textbook. But if you think about it, it's a very difficult challenge to account for historically.

Think of it this way: People didn't go to bed one night in the ancient world and wake up the next morning and look at the newspa-

per and say, "Oh, we're in the medieval world now!" It doesn't happen that way. We make it look like a simple process, as I said, because we slice up periods and put labels on them. But the reality is that these kinds of changes occur over vast periods of time. The people living through these periods may recognize that "the times they are a-changin'" (as Bob Dylan put it); they may recognize that some sort of transition is underway. But they can't necessarily see it clearly when they're living in the midst of it.

What I'm describing here is historical and cultural change on a big scale. I'm not talking about the day-to-day kinds of changes, the things we read about in newspaper headlines. I'm talking about big change, such as going from the ancient world to the medieval world, or going from medieval world to the modern world. This is, as I said, something that occurs over a very long period of time, and it's a very complex phenomenon. It's important to keep this clearly in mind as we talk about the issues before us. This is really the central issue that I want us to try to grapple with in this chapter.

Let's simplify the matter. Imagine that we have a piece of graph paper in front of us and we are going to draw two trend lines on this sheet of paper to illustrate the two main things that are occurring during this transitional period from the ancient world to the medieval world.

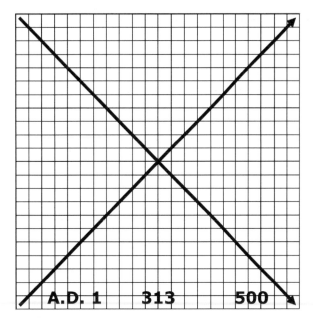

There are two institutions that experience very different destinies during this period of time. One of them we can represent as a trend line going precipitously from the upper-left to the bottom-right. So, obviously, the fortunes of one institution are steeply on the decline in this period. But there is another institution which is sharply on the rise, represented as a trend line from the lower-left to the upper-right. One institution is on the rise while another is on the decline.

What are these two trends that define the shift from the ancient to medieval world? One is the rise of the medieval church. Clearly, the fortunes of the church have improved markedly in this period of time, as we have seen. What is the great institution that's on the decline? The Roman Empire. So you have the empire that's declining and the church that's increasing in power. If you want to give numerical values to our improvised graph, we can put the years down as AD 1 and AD 500. Over the course of this five hundred years we see the beginning of the empire and its steady decline to its eventual fall around 476. Over the same period, we see the birth of Christ, the beginning of the church, and its growth to dominance. The lines describing these two trends cross at a certain point. The most logical point at which to plot this moment

would be at about 313 A.D. when Constantine came on the scene, was dramatically converted, and then legalized Christianity within the Roman Empire. From this point on, there was no turning back; Christianity would become the official state religion of Rome. When Rome collapsed and fell off the scene, the Roman Catholic Church would became the dominant institution that shaped the Middle Ages.

This graph, then, represents the large-scale changes that tell the story of this period—how the ancient world gradually gave way to the medieval world, how one dominant institution (the Roman Empire) was gradually replaced by another (the Roman church). I would describe this as a "changing of the guard" between empire and church. Looking at the Middle Ages and particularly at medieval Christianity, we are going to see that the story is not entirely a pretty one. In fact, a lot of ugly things happened as a result of the politicization of the church as it began to act more and more like the empire it replaced. The church began to act like a political bureaucracy, and the practice and the doctrine of the church became corrupted. Whenever the church becomes a political institution, it becomes corrupt by definition, and its doctrine and its practice will be adversely affected. This is the framework I want us to keep in mind as we discuss, first of all, the collapse of the Roman Empire in late antiquity. So, let's start with the negative trend line.

The Fall of Rome

We're going to survey very quickly eleven explanations that historians have given for the fall of Rome. They really cover the whole range of possibilities. Still, this is not at all a comprehensive list; rather, this is meant to give you an introduction to some of the dominant explanations that have been offered.

A popular explanation in conservative Christian quarters, which I have heard as a sermon illustration many times, is that Rome was undone by immorality. The argument is that Rome was corrupted by moral license and luxury. The prevailing ethic of the late empire was that you did whatever you wanted to, and that wealth and laziness, combined with immoral values, contributed to the decline of the stoic virtues and the sense of Roman discipline.

That is certainly part of the equation, but it's much more complex than that. If you want to account for the fall of the Roman Empire on the basis of just moral issues, then you are going to have to explain why Rome stuck around as long as it did. Rome was always immoral, and it always tolerated a whole range of immoral acts throughout its history; therefore, this alone doesn't account for why Rome fell when it fell. This is hence a caution against the overly simplistic claim that Rome fell because it was immoral. That is obviously ultimately the explanation for why all human societies and empires collapse—because of their sinful nature—but it doesn't account for the specifics of why Rome fell when it did.

Second, there is a so-called Christian, or more accurately "Augustinian," answer. Augustine, in the *City of God*, said that Rome fell because it had to make way for the City of God that was to be established on earth. We now know, however, that Augustine, despite his impressive contributions to biblical interpretation, was wrong on that count. His eschatology was off, but this was nonetheless the interpretation he gave as he was struggling to understand the historical phenomenon that was playing out during his lifetime.

Third, we see that historians of the eighteenth century gave what is known as the rationalist answer for the fall of Rome. The historian Edward Gibbon, who wrote *The Decline and Fall of the Roman Empire*, is the best-known exponent of this view. (See portrait below.) Gibbon's belief was similar to that of the pagans back in Augustine's day, who claimed that the church was to blame because the people's allegiance had changed. Christians no longer cared whether Rome lived or not, or survived another day, because, after all, their citizenship was in heaven. Personally, I think there is some

credibility to this argument, in that Christians did in fact turn their allegiance to the church and certainly to the values of their faith, and away from the political and materialistic values that had held up the Roman Empire.

A fourth explanation that has been offered is called the political answer. There are many variations of this; some would say that the concentration of power in the office of Caesar corrupted Rome, such that Rome could no longer effectively be governed. The loss of public spirit and the failure of civilian control of the army meant that powerful generals would rise up in the provinces and, like Julius Caesar way back in Rome's history, march their armies to Rome and seize power. This was sufficiently destabilizing to the Roman Empire to cause it to collapse. Furthermore, the state had become unwieldy. It could no longer govern itself and therefore collapsed for political reasons. This is certainly part of the reason, but by no means the full story. Notice how we're finding that that's the case as we go through each one of these. There is some truth in each answer, but none comes close to telling the whole story.

Fifth, the social answer is espoused by historians who emphasize that there was a fundamental war of the classes in Roman society. This was caused by the injustice of slavery on which Roman society was based, where a majority of those living in the Roman Empire were not free. History tells us that any society structured like that will collapse, and that certainly was the case with the Roman Empire.

Sixth, some historians emphasize economic reasons for Rome's collapse, such as stagnation in trade that led to less wealth. There was also low productivity at the end of the Roman Empire for various reasons, along with a scarcity of gold and silver. Less economic activity means less wealth. When dire economic conditions prevail, you can't pay the army; and if you can't pay the army, then it's not going to fight to defend Rome. It's easy to see the interconnectedness of all these ideas. In other words, Rome is collapsing in every way possible.

A seventh explanation that has been offered is the physical or environmental answer, which considers the long-term effects of, say, the depletion of top soil, deforestation, climatic change, and drought. These are very contemporary ways of looking at Rome's fall. We have more of an appreciation today of the environmental consequences of certain actions than they did in the Roman Empire. If you keep planting in the same field, century after century, you know you are going to have a decrease in crop yields and you are not going to be able to feed the Roman population. This is all going to have a very destabilizing impact on Roman society, which in turn is going to have political consequences.

Related to this is the eighth answer, the so-called pathological explanation for the fall of Rome. According to this view, pathogens like the plague and malaria might have destabilized Roman society. Some contemporary historians have even looked at the role of lead poisoning in the collapse of Rome. The Romans had indoor plumbing and the pipes that brought the water into their city, into their buildings and so on, were made out of lead. They also cooked in lead pots. We know today, of course, that lead doesn't combine well with brain cells. Could this be the reason why Rome fell—because of lead poisoning? Certainly not. Perhaps it was a contributing factor, however, as part of the overall equation.

The ninth explanation represents an outdated and even repugnant view known as the genetic answer. It is associated with German historians of the nineteenth century, when German scholars began toying with the idea of a "master race" and "pure" ethnic lines and so on, which would ultimately result in the tragedy of the rise of Nazi philosophy in the twentieth century. This strand of German pseudo-scholarship argued that there was a breakdown of what they called the purity of the old Roman stock in the late Roman Empire through intermarriage, such that people basically no longer cared anymore whether Rome survived or not since their bloodlines had been compromised. I think we can put that one aside by placing it within its own troubled context of racist ideology; but I mention it simply as a curiosity of historical explanations for why Rome fell, much as we did with Augustine's outdated explanation.

The cyclical answer, our tenth explanation, also comes from the dustbin of nineteenth-century Germany historiography. It's a curious explanation that doesn't really explain anything at all. Basically, the cyclical answer tells us that Rome fell because Rome was an empire—and that's what empires do as part of their "life cycle." Empires have an origin; they mature, reach their strength, and then they decline and collapse. As you can see, that doesn't take you very far by the way of explaining the specifics of why Rome collapsed.

Finally, our eleventh answer looks at Rome's military situation. This explanation claims that Rome couldn't any longer defend itself from the barbarian tribes that were invading the Empire. This explanation is best seen as the proverbial straw that broke the camel's back. Rome had been weakened socially, politically, economically, and in other ways such that the empire was no longer strong enough to withstand invasion.

So, then, why did Rome fall? We don't know exactly. The best answer is to say some combination of all of these factors. A more important issue, to my mind, is: *What does the fall of Rome illustrate to us?* The fall of the Roman Empire illustrates the classic example of what we call a historical problem. When we use the phrase **historical problem** we mean *a set of historical circumstances so complex that it defies easy explanation*. An easy explanation is exactly what you and I want; but that's exactly what we *can't* get when we talk about a historical problem such as why Rome fell.

Are we ever going to explain why Rome fell? No, there is not a chance that we'll ever arrive at a comprehensive, final answer. And once again that suggests to us the important principle of how we need to approach the complexity of the past. It should remind us of the limits of our knowledge, and it should reinforce once again this attitude of humility that we need to bring to these incredibly complex problems when we study the past. We need to recognize what we can claim and what we can only guess at; we need to remember that some explanations are better than others, but that we are never going to get the full picture—certainly not in this world, and not in this lifetime with the limited resources we have.

The Rise of the Church

We're going to turn now to the second trend line. We are going to try to account for the fact that the church became the dominant institution in that 1000-year period that we are going to be talking about, from roughly 500 to 1500. As we try to explain the rise of the Church, we'll look first at *three great figures* who contributed to the church's growth. Second, we'll look at *three historical factors* that enabled the church to replace the Roman Empire in the early Middle Ages.

I want us first of all to look at some of the towering figures in this period of late antiquity. We call them Church Fathers. I want us to look at three of them in particular who were instrumental in establishing the practice, beliefs, and doctrine of the early church at this period of time: Augustine, Ambrose, and Jerome. I am guessing that Augustine is the best known name on this list, and for good reason. We are going to find out that he was, without doubt, the most influential church figure of this age.

It's very important to understand that these were men who saw the fall of Rome all around them. Augustine lived from 354 to 430, Ambrose from 339 to 397, and Jerome from roughly 342 to 420. They saw what was happening in the world around them. Rome's power as a political institution was diminishing and these men were part of that important process of change whereby the church established itself as the dominant institution of this age.

You should note as well that these three men knew each other. They lived in different parts of the Roman Empire—Augustine in North Africa, Ambrose in northern Italy, Jerome in Palestine—but they corresponded with one another. We have some of the letters that they wrote. Of course, these are very different from how you and I would correspond today. We sit down to type and send off an email that's almost instantly received on the other side of the world. But back then, it would take them several weeks for a letter to travel from one part of the Roman Empire to the other. Nevertheless, they did correspond about the big issues of the day, political and theological.

Augustine was without a doubt the most important of this group of early church fathers. He was born in the Roman province of North Africa, but he traveled to Italy, which was still the center of the Roman Empire; he came under the ministry of Ambrose, the second man on our list, and he was baptized by Ambrose in the city of Milan in northern Italy.

Augustine has the reputation of being the greatest theologian in church history—at least outside the pages of the New Testament. When you think of all the great theologians—John Calvin, Martin Luther, and so on—Augustine towers above them in his influence, the greatness of his conception of biblical teaching, and the original nature of his thinking. He was certainly a great thinker and a great theological mind; but he was also a brilliant apologist. He defended the faith during a time when Christianity, though already the official state religion, was still under attack by pagan philosophers and pagan politicians. These pagans looked at the shrinking power of Rome and the collapse of the Empire and blamed the Church for it. Augustine decided that this allegation required a response, which he gave in his treatise known as the *City of God*, a sweeping look at history and biblical teaching on eschatology.

In this book Augustine he defends the faith against those who charged that Christianity was to blame for the collapse of Rome. He turned the tables and claimed that Roman paganism had done a pretty good job of ruining Rome on its own. He further argued that the Roman Empire had to fall in order that the "City of God" (i.e., Christ's reign on earth) could be established in its place. Augustine was an amillennialist; he believed that the Kingdom of God would be established in our time in this world system and that God's kingdom would be ushered in as a historical reality.

Another one of the great works that Augus-

tine wrote is his spiritual autobiography, known as *Confessions*. It's a beautiful work, and one that's worth reading today. Christians can still benefit from reading this because Augustine lays out the story of his coming to faith in Christ and his personal struggles with the flesh and the world. The book is called *Confessions* because that is what he is doing in it: baring his soul and placing it all out there for us to read and to be challenged by as we look at one of the great figures of church history and how he himself struggled with temptation. It's certainly the greatest spiritual autobiography, and Augustine established a literary tradition that runs all the way down to the twentieth century. One example of this tradition is the great autobiography that C. S. Lewis wrote, *Surprised by Joy*. C. S. Lewis's autobiography is very consciously written in the Augustinian mold. Lewis tells the story of his own coming to faith in Christ and his struggles with doubt and so on. We look back to Augustine as the one who first established that type of autobiography.

Ambrose is the second figure that I want us to consider. He was born into one of the great ruling families of Rome that traced its lineage back to the republican days before Caesar Augustus. He served the church as Bishop of Milan, one of the great cities in the late Roman Empire. Just as it is in Italy today, Milan was arguably the cultural and economic capital even as Rome was the political capital. Ambrose is an important figure for his work in organizing the church's teaching and practice. For example, he formulated principles of biblical interpretation. He didn't have as original a mind as Augustine, but he had a knack for organization. He took the church traditions and the practice of hermeneutics (how you interpret scripture) and he organized these, establishing when it's appropriate to interpret the Bible allegorically or to use a typological approach to understand the meaning or significance of a passage. Again, he didn't originate these principles, but simply organized them and systematized the way the Bible would be interpreted throughout the Middle Ages.

Ambrose also brought his organizational ability to the practice of the church and he was involved in developing church **liturgy**. When you read scripture, when you deliver the sermon, when you stand up and sing a hymn—all of these aspects of church liturgy are things that he developed and systematized. It can be seen that he was therefore very important in establishing the highly ritualized mode of the service that would become the standard in the medieval Catholic Church. He also wrote church hymns, some of which are still used in translation in some churches today.

The third figure is Jerome. He lived from around 342 to 420, was born into a Christian family, and was educated in Rome. He thus received the best classical education one could get in the late Roman Empire as he studied the Latin and Greek languages. This gave him the credentials he needed to make his great contribution to the early church. The contribution that we associate with Jerome is that he single-handedly translated the entire Bible into Latin.

Consider just how monumental an accomplishment that was. Today, when translations are made, they are made by a committee of people, a committee of scholars, each one of who has his or her own individual specialization—Hebrew, Greek, Aramaic, maybe focusing on a particular part of the Bible as their specialization. What's amazing again to keep in mind is that Jerome translated this by himself. He was a committee of one, and his translation is still considered one of the greatest and most accurate translations of the Bible. Why did he do this? What was the passion and the burden on his heart that led him to tackle this great challenge?

Well, what was the language of the late Roman Empire? Latin, and the Bible was not written in Latin. It was written in Greek, Hebrew, and portions were written in Aramaic. Jerome wanted to bring the Bible into the language of everyday Romans, the language of the street, the language spoken in the fish market. The great irony of this is that the Catholic Church in the Middle Ages

took his translation and made it the official version of the Catholic Church, which it continued to be well into the twentieth century long after ordinary people stopped speaking Latin. Imagine that you are a medieval Frenchman in the thirteenth century and you go to church and hear the parish priest delivering the homily or celebrating mass. The priest will be reciting from the Bible, but he will be speaking Latin. You won't have a clue what he's saying. This became the practice for hundreds of years in the Catholic Church, which is exactly the opposite of what Jerome had wanted.

That was one of the big issues in the Reformation: to bring the Bible back into the language that ordinary people like you and me actually speak. So, during the Reformation, we see Martin Luther translating the Bible into German. We see the King James Version of the Bible at the end of the period of the Reformation striving to accomplish, once again, what Jerome wanted to do—bring the Bible into the language of the people. We see the same thing with the ongoing translations into contemporary English. We call Jerome's translation of the Bible the **Vulgate**. This word comes from the same root as the English word "vulgar." The meaning of vulgar in this sense is "common," as in "the common language."

Each one of these church figures had a different set of gifts that they gave to the church, but each one was important in contributing to the rise of the church in the late Roman period. Let's now look more specifically, now, at three historical factors behind the rise of early medieval Catholicism. I want us to consider once again the question of why and how. We know that Rome was on the decline, but how is it that this institution, the church, was positioned so well to become the dominant institution in the Middle Ages? I am going to give you three quick answers.

The first of these relates to the way the church inherited the influence and structure of the Roman Empire—what I call the "imperial connection" of the Church. The "changing of the guard" between empire and church meant that the church began to acquire the trappings of old imperial Rome—and this legitimized the Church. Constantine, of course, had played a crucial role in bringing church and state together. Geographical factors came into play. Rome was the center of political power, so it logically became the center of religious power as well. It's not a coincidence that we call it the *Roman* Catholic Church, just as it's not a coincidence that the Pope has his headquarters in the Vatican, in Rome. As this changing of the guard occurred, the church gradually became the mirror reflection of the Roman Empire by adopting the imperial structure of Rome. The Catholic Church to this day is a rigidly hierarchical structure. At the top of that hierarchy is a Pope who looks very much like an emperor. He wears imperial clothing, he has a scepter-like object in his hand, he has a crown-like object (a mitre) on his head, and he has a big imperial ring on his hand. Where did all these trappings of imperial power come from? Certainly not from the New Testament! They came from the period of time when the church adopted the structure, the style, and even the hierarchy of the Roman Empire. Just as the Roman Empire had governors stationed in the provinces, the Catholic Church has its cardinals.

None of this is a coincidental development, but rather a logical transference of power from one to the other. We need to always keep this in mind as we look at the nature of the early medieval Catholic Church, because this is when errors begin to creep into the church. The church begins to become corrupt in its teaching and practice, because it's becoming more and more of a political and economic institution.

Second, medieval Catholicism emerged as the dominant institution in the West as the office of the pope centralized its power and authority. We see two figures in particular in the late ancient world and early Middle Ages who are influential in this process. The first of these so-called early popes was Leo. His name means "lion." He was a courageous figure and thus appropriately named. He was the Bishop of Rome (they weren't

called popes at this time), and his reign was from 440 to 461, right at the end of the Roman Empire. During this period, Attila the Hun was threatening the Roman Empire and invaded Italy. Leo left the city of Rome and went out and met Attila the Hun face-to-face in one of the most remarkable encounters in all history. Leo must have been a pretty impressive man, because he convinced Attila to turn away and not to destroy Rome. What do you think that did for his reputation? It spiked up pretty considerably, enhancing the prestige of his office, Bishop of Rome; this event, therefore, contributed to the rise of what would ultimately be recognized as the office of Pope.

The second thing Leo did that was very important was that he consolidated his authority over the church. He was the first Bishop of Rome to specifically lay claim to what we call Petrine authority. This is the authority given to Peter. The Catholic church teaches that when Jesus turned to Peter and said, "You are Peter; and upon this rock, I will build My Church," that Jesus was establishing an office that carries down to the latest Pope in Rome. Of course, Protestants have a very different interpretation of what Jesus was actually saying to Peter, but this teaching began to be developed as a way of enforcing the authority of the Bishop of Rome, and Leo was very instrumental in developing that doctrine.

The second figure who was very influential in the rise to power of the papacy was a man named Gregory who lived a century and a half after Leo. He was Bishop of Rome from 590 to 604. In fact, he was the first bishop formally to be given the title Pope, which is a variant of the Latin word for "father."

We know him as Gregory the Great. Consider, for a moment, how something has really gone wrong with the church when its leaders are given the epithet "the great." We think of military leaders such as Alexander the Great bearing that title, but certainly not church leaders. For one thing, it indicates how far the church had come from that image of service that Christ illustrated in his life.

Gregory was a talented administrator and he tirelessly promoted the interests of the church. He is best remembered for his work on church music. We all know what Gregorian chants are. He didn't write these, but he organized them and his name became attached to them from that point as as "Gregorian chants." Gregory's contribution to the church was very much that of an activist pope who promoted missionary activity throughout the former Roman Empire and especially into northern Europe.

The third reason is a negative way of explaining the rise of the medieval Catholic Church. By this I'm referring to a growing threat from outside Europe that we know as the rise of Islam. As you know, there is nothing like a good threat from the outside to pull people together. Families illustrate this well. Families can really fight and squabble among themselves, and even have knock-down, drag-out fights sometimes; but the minute somebody from outside that family challenges them, they'll close ranks pretty fast. The same thing is true in the case of medieval Europe, and it's a good way to understand the process we're discussing. There was a lot of division in early medieval culture, but the minute Mohammad appeared on the scene in the early seventh century and, in the century following his death, Islam spread rapidly across all the areas around Europe. Christendom was, in a sense, surrounded by this rising militaristic power to the south and east. Medieval Europe rallied around the church and they put aside a lot of differences. The church's power grew in response to this, because they were the dominant institution, and they were perceived as the ones who could organize the response to Islam.

We date the origin of Islam from the so-called flight, the **hegira**, into exile of Mohammad in 622; and in the century that followed, Islam spread remarkably quickly across North Africa, ultimately establishing a foothold in Europe itself.

Spain was a Muslim-ruled country for several centuries in the Middle Ages, and this long influence left its mark on the architecture, art, music, and language of Spain. Hence, Europe was directly and immediately threatened by Islam, and we can't fully understand the dynamics of medieval culture without recognizing that Christianity and Islam were at odds, very directly and in a military sense, during this period. Ultimately, this conflict would culminate in the tragedy of the Crusades at the end of the Middle Ages—and we'll turn to that part of the story in a later chapter.

THE EARLY MEDIEVAL SYNTHESIS 14

Chapter Objectives

- Identify the three cultures that are synthesized in the early Middle Ages.
- Describe how Charlemagne embodies this process of cultural synthesis.
- Summarize the important role of manuscripts in the Middle Ages.

In the last chapter we were examining a period of great transition and cultural change. How do we account for the differences between the ancient world and the medieval world? How do we get from the one period to the other after the chaos of the fall of Rome? In history, as in nature, chaos is not something that lasts very long, and things will adjust and balance. Equilibrium will once again be reestablished. It's interesting to note that history seems to follow that same natural formula that we recognize in the world around us—chaos moving toward equilibrium.

Great cultural change always comes out of chaos and social turmoil. This is true for the period we're examining; but it's going to be true as well when we get to the end of the Middle Ages. We'll see profound change brought about in the aftermath of destabilizing events like the Crusades and catastrophes like the Black Death. Looking further back, we see that the ancient Greeks emerged out of the chaotic period that brought the Mycenaean civilization to an end. Looking ahead to our own time, we may well be going through a similar time right now in light of the chaotic and transforming events of the twentieth century.

After a profound period of chaos, something like the fall of Rome, a culture enters a period of adjustment—a period when the dust settles, so to speak, and new directions are charted. We'll be analyzing this kind of period as we turn now to the early Middle Ages. We'll use one key term to describe the cultural adjustment that we can identify in this period—and that word is *synthesis.* Different cultural elements—values and institutions—will come together to synthesize something completely new, and the "something new" that's being created here is obviously medieval culture.

Now there are three distinct backgrounds that are being synthesized in the early Middle Ages. Most significantly there is the Christian background with the church, as we've noted, being the dominant institution. There was also the heritage left over from the fall of the Roman Empire in the form of political and legal institutions. The Roman language, Latin, would also continue through the Middle Ages to be a kind of a living language among scholars, a language of knowledge and literature. Much of classical culture survived the fall of Rome, and it's part of the mix of what's going on in the early Middle Ages.

There's also a third element added to the mix—something we haven't seen yet: the influx of Germanic and Celtic tribes into the British Isles. These pagan people are going to be Christianized during this period of time, but they bring with them their pagan ideas and values. We can use Beowulf as a cultural reference for these people. These were a pre-Christianized people who were bound together by tribal allegiances and believed very much in loyalty, honor, and ties of kinship; their social and political structures were based on these values. They were polytheistic, as the ancient Greeks and Romans were. In some trivial ways we can even see to this day the survival of some of these pagan ideas in western culture in something as simple as the names of the days of the week. Other examples of this influence are the common gesture of knocking on wood and, of course, the pagan influences on the Christian calendar in the celebration of Christmas and Easter and the Celtic influence we see in Halloween. These are things that are obvious and somewhat trivial examples of the contributions of these Germanic and Celtic people.

In this chapter we're going to look at how these three distinct cultures were blended together in the Middle Ages.

- classical culture
- christian culture
- pagan culture

We're going to illustrate this synthesis of cultures three ways: first, with the figure Charlemagne, the towering historical figure of his age; second, with the dominant style of architecture in the early Middle Ages, the Romanesque; and then finally we'll look at some distinctive art forms of the early Middle Ages to see how this process of synthesis is at work in this period of transition and adjustment.

Charlemagne

Charlemagne (c. 742–812), or "Charles the Great," was the major historical figure of the early Middle Ages. He embodied in his life and career each of these three distinct cultural backgrounds. He was a Germanic chieftain, so when he looked in the mirror, he saw a chieftain such as Beowulf. He happened to rule a much vaster region than Beowulf or any smaller Germanic king would have ruled; but that's what he essentially was—a Germanic chieftain—and these were the core values and beliefs that he carried with him into his reign.

The genius of Charlemagne probably was that he knew exactly who he was and what his background was, and he didn't want to be limited by that. He didn't want to be just another powerful but illiterate and uncultured Germanic chieftain. I would say that a key element of greatness lies in one's ability to identify not one's strength, but one's limitations and weaknesses and then striving to overcome them and compensate for them. And we can certainly see that Charlemagne wanted something more than he was given by birth. He looked beyond the three centuries that had preceded him, all the way back to the greatness and the glory that was once Rome, and he longed for that. He wanted his empire to reflect and rekindle that glory; and thus, even though he was a German and brought that background to his life and his reign, he was also very much in love with classical culture. For example, he studied Latin and Greek and he had the great works of literature read to him. He was also a professing Christian, which at that time basically meant that he had been baptized in the church. Nevertheless, there was still that quality and those values imbued in his character. And so, once again, we see the synthesis of these three sets of values in Charlemagne.

It is important to note that the greatest accomplishment and the greatest legacy that we attribute to Charlemagne is not the territory that he conquered. We don't remember him primarily for the fact that he was a political and military leader. The greatest, most significant legacy that he left behind was the fact that he was like a modern "headhunter." He went out and hired the best talent, put them on the payroll, and brought them to his palace, his court in Aachen, which is in the border region between modern France and Germany. Charlemagne hired the best scholars of Europe in his day. He brought them to his court—and you can imagine what happened. It fostered a revival of learning and the arts and the study of the past, which is why we refer to this as the **Carolingian Renaissance**.

The things that we're now going to be discussing, the architecture, the arts, the copying of manuscripts, and so on, in large measure flowed from the reign of Charlemagne. This is one of his legacies. In the centuries that followed, medieval culture was shaped by that legacy.

Romanesque Architecture

So let's look at our second example, which as I said is one of the outgrowths of the Carolingian Renaissance. I mean the style of architecture that we begin to see in the cathedrals that were built across medieval Europe. The dominant style of architecture in the early Middle Ages is what we call the **Romanesque** style. Let's look at an example (see below). This is the cathedral at Cologne, Germany, which dates from 980. It

dates from at the end of this period, but it's definitely a style of architecture that evokes the synthesis that characterizes this transitional time.

The Romanesque style of architecture displays these three backgrounds. It's not a coincidence that it's called *Romanesque*, because in many ways it's a revival of Roman styles; but it also incorporates Christian values and distinctly Christian elements. It is a church, after all. We're also going to see that it even has Germanic qualities in its design.

In other words, what we're trying to do here is to interpret this building as an expression of the values of this age, much as we interpreted the Pantheon as an expression of Roman culture, the Parthenon as an expression of Greek culture, and the pyramids as an expression of Egyptian culture. We will be looking at these great cathedrals of the Middle Ages to see what is it of this period that we can understand better. The goal will be to penetrate into the mind of the Middle Ages a little deeper.

Note that the style of Romanesque architecture is based on the style of the Roman basilica. You would start with the Roman basilica and then fuse that together with the towers and gates associated with secular fortifications—the kinds of things you'd associate with a castle or with the walls of a fortified city that would have watchtowers and a large, well-defended gateway into the city. These elements are brought together in these Christian buildings in a fusion of styles, a synthesis of different cultures and backgrounds.

Let's look more closely at these towers and gates that we associate with Roman fortifications, even medieval castles. You can see in the cathedral at Cologne that these towers clearly look like watchtowers, and then you see the main entrance into the cathedral looks very much like the gates that you would see in the walled fortifications of cities. What is the meaning of this? In Roman architecture, round, square and octagonal towers were used to reinforce the city walls, and city gates were usually flanked by towers. This is the origin then of these elements. But what about the symbolic meaning of them, the values that are communicated by these? In the Romanesque church, these gateways acquired the symbolic significance of protection and transcendental aspiration. I think we can see the idea of protection pretty clearly. These look, as we said, like watchtowers, which relates to how the church was viewed in the Middle Ages, given that Islam was now emerging on the borderlands of medieval European Christianity and even had a foothold in Spain. It thus makes sense that these watchtowers would symbolize the notion that the church was the bulwark against all of these external threats.

But what about the idea that the gateways also symbolized transcendental aspiration? What does that mean? Simply the hope for something beyond this world, the hope and the promise of something transcendent of the material world that we live in. The idea goes like this: You might be working as a medieval peasant out in the field all week long, but when you pass through this gate,

this central door into that sacred place, the interior of that cathedral, and you make confession to the priest or you receive the bread and the wine from the priest, that's where you enter the spiritual zone. That's where you meet God; that's the place of transcendental aspiration. For the medieval Christian, everything outside the church is material and worldly. It's inside the church where you meet God. Of course, that is a fundamentally unbiblical way of looking at Christianity. Jesus said that wherever two or three gather in his name, he is in the midst of them.

The idea is that we as believers have the presence of God with us, the Holy Spirit dwelling within us, whether you're working out in the field or sitting in the pew of church. You are nowhere nearer to God than you can be right now. And yet, in the Middle Ages, we see this very pervasive error in thinking. We call it dualism, the division between the material realm and the spiritual realm. We see this false idea permeating medieval Christianity and leading to the corruption and the carnality of the church at this time. Once again, the idea is that out there in the world, outside the church, is the material world. It doesn't really have anything to do with God or the church. You can live in any way you like out there as long as you walk through that "gate," confess, and partake of the bread and the wine.

And it's easy for us to look back and condemn the medieval church for that fallacy; but that's the challenge Christians of every age have had to face. How do we recognize that, as Christians, our whole world has to be transformed—not divided into material and spiritual? Paul clearly addresses this in 1 Corinthians 10:31: "Whether therefore you eat or drink or whatever you do, do all to the glory of God." That is, we are to take the most mundane, everyday material thing we can think of—eating and drinking—and it should be an act of worship to God in recognition of his sovereignty and the fact that he provides for everything that we need. That's why we give it back to him in worship.

Medieval Christianity went significantly off track on that point, and the world was divided into the material and into the spiritual realms. The church was where the center of spiritual activity was to be found. Perhaps you have read some of Chaucer's *Canterbury Tales*. You'll recall that there are fun things to read in some of the stories; but you have to recognize how carnal some of those stories are, especially the comic stories that Chaucer wrote; they are basically dirty stories that end with a dirty punch line. You look at that and wonder how it is that in this age in which the church was a dominant institution, literature like this was being produced. Chaucer would have considered himself a good practicing Christian in the Middle Ages. He didn't see any internal contradiction in that. For him, as for most medieval Christians, there was the world and there was spiritual stuff, and never the twain did meet. That's the dualistic fallacy, and you go a long ways toward understanding the corruption of the medieval church when you recognize it. Any time you separate the material from the spiritual you're going to become carnal, and that's a rule that we can see as we look at the church throughout history.

How else did the structure of the Romanesque church function in early medieval Europe? It functioned as a center of **pilgrimage**—a phenomenon we see throughout the Middle Ages. I just mentioned Chaucer, whose stories all revolve around characters on a pilgrimage. What is it that Chaucer's pilgrims hope to see when they get to Canterbury? Or what would it be that pilgrims to the church at Cologne, the church that we've just been looking at, would hope to see? What is it with this medieval tourist industry?

We can only understand this pilgrimage in light of the veneration of saints in the early medieval period. People began to pray to the saints and to ask for their favorite saint to put a good word in for them to God. Think again of how unbiblical this is. We come to the Father through Christ and we have access through him and through his work; but all of these errors are beginning

to creep in through Roman and Germanic pagan influences. The medieval church recognized the lucrative asset that they had in promoting the veneration of saints, and so they exploited it to the fullest potential.

When you arrived at these churches, you expected to see the relics associated with the lives of the apostles, the Virgin Mary, or whatever regional saint was recognized in that local church. What are relics? Any object, any artifact associated with the physical person of a saint. It might be a tooth, St. Thomas's tooth, let's say; it might be the great toe bone of the apostle Peter; it might be a piece of cloth; it might be something as impressive as the Shroud of Turin, which I believe has to be understood as a medieval relic. (I don't believe it's authentic in the sense of going back to the time of Christ. I believe that the Shroud of Turin has to be understood within this context of medieval relics, the veneration of saints, and the production of these kinds of relics during this time.) The relic might be a little bottle, a little vial that contains the "actual tears" that Mary shed at the foot of the cross. That at least is how it would be built up—like a sideshow: pay a quarter and step right up to see this amazing thing. The manufacture of artifacts associated with these venerated figures allowed the church to reap in huge amounts of money.

Incidentally, this is one of the things that worked up the anger of Martin Luther at the end of the medieval period in the fifteenth century. He looked at the state of the Catholic Church—the church which he belonged to before he split with Rome. One of the things that Martin Luther strongly objected to was this profiteering on the part of the church over these fraudulent artifacts. Luther used his common sense and applied simple logic. He argued that if you count up all the great toe bones around Europe that supposedly belong to the apostle Peter, then he would have been one badly deformed apostle. Of course, the point was that these were clearly manufactured artifacts. He rejected this and he said they had no part in the gospel of grace since "the just shall live by faith." This was the great message that Martin Luther preached in the Reformation.

Romanesque Visual Arts

If you put a great value on saints and the relics associated with them, then you've got to have an appropriate way to display these valuable relics; and that's where one of the most distinctive art forms of the early Middle Ages comes in.

A **reliquary** is a little treasure box, the sole purpose of which is to house a tooth, a fragment of a bone, a piece of garment, or some other artifact of the type we've been discussing. Scores of reliquaries survive, and you can see them in most major museums. No two are alike. They are very ornate, sometimes covered with gold, sometimes carved out of ivory, and richly decorated. They are exquisite works of art and are very valuable. If you apply the simple logic that you paint, sculpt and manufacture what you value, it helps to explain what reliquaries are all about. These relics are showcasing something of great value: the idea that the saints give us access to God.

There is another unique contribution in addition to reliquaries that we associate with the early medieval church, and more specifically with the monasteries that began to crop up across Europe in the period after the fall of Rome. I am speaking of the manuscripts that were copied in these monasteries—specifically what we refer to as illuminated manuscripts.

Illuminated manuscript simply means "illustrated manuscript." These manuscripts were copied out by hand on vellum parchment (sheepskin), but they also have beautiful illustrations in them. They are not just functional things like a cheap paperback book. These are works of art in the way they are illustrated and copied and the great care that's lavished upon them.

Of all the negative things we've already said about the medieval church, this is one bright spot associated with the rise of these monasteries. The preservation and transmission of knowledge kept monks, especially the Irish monks, very busy copying out manuscripts. Much of what we know about the ancient world is due to these monks who got up early and would have gone to the chapel at about 4 o'clock in the morning and said their prayers for about an hour. Then there would have been, say, another hour of singing in the chapel, and then off to a silent breakfast and working in the monastic garden for a while. And then finally, as part of their daily routine, ending up in what's known as a **scriptorium**, the room where the manuscripts were copied.

One of the main functions of the monks was to do this, and this is how the manuscripts were copied out. Imagine that we are in a scriptorium right here and I am the head abbott. I've got a manuscript in front of me and you're a monk seated at a desk. You have vellum parchment, a feather quill, and an inkwell in front of you. I read a phrase or sentence in the Latin and you will listen to that, dip your quill in the ink, and then transcribe that phrase. At the end of the copying session, we would have however many manuscripts as monks copying in the room. Obviously, in the age before the printing press was developed, that was the only way to produce manuscripts and to transmit knowledge.

It was of course a method fraught with problems, challenges, and difficulties. If you got up at 4 o'clock in the morning, if you've been working in the garden and have other chores, then by the time you get to the scriptorium you might occasionally nod off while you're copying. What you're going to end up with is a manuscript that maybe doesn't have a sentence or two in it along the way. In fact, we do find this kind of evidence in the manuscript traditions. You might find a manuscript in France which is the same text as a manuscript you find in Germany; scholars will take those two manuscripts and compare them side-by-side and see that this one found in Germany doesn't have a sentence right here. Well, it's an example of human error. Probably a monk nodded off for a minute, shook himself awake, and then picked up where he left off. And so what a scholar does is collect all the manuscript evidence of a given text to weed out the copying errors and to come up with the final text we have. That is the foundation of our translated Bibles; scholars compare the manuscript tradition to get back to the accurate and original form of the text.

This is something I studied in graduate school in my doctoral work at the University of Minnesota. I specialized in the medieval period, and one of the seminars I took was a course in paleography, which is manuscript reading. I had the opportunity as part of my project to work with a thirteenth-century Latin astronomical manuscript in the rare books room of the library. That was a really amazing thing—to hold this 800-year-old manuscript in my hands, to turn the pages and work with this thing that a monk centuries before had written and worked with. It was a fascinating project because I saw how human that manuscript was. It was written by an individual and it was used by individuals who occasionally even doodled in the margins. There were little drawings of dragons and faces peering out from the corners and so on. They would maybe make little marginal notes, and that reminds you of just how human a process the transmission of knowledge over time really is. This knowledge was passed down to us by people who actually lived and breathed and died in a period remote from our own, and it's really important to be reminded of that fact.

I had to figure out where this manuscript came from, because the library didn't have any idea what the history of the manuscript was. They didn't even know what the date of it was. All they knew was that sometime in the years following the Second World War, a GI with a duffle bag in his hand, appeared at the doors of the library and said, "Well, I've got this medieval manuscript here, and I was wondering if you're interested in buying it from me." The librarian didn't ask any questions and offered him a thousand dollars, which was a bargain. It's been part of the University of Minnesota library ever since. And so we don't know the history of it before that point. Obviously the soldier brought it back from his tour in Europe, I would assume; but the specific circumstances of how he acquired it are something of a mystery. I was able to determine some things, however, by close examination of the manuscript, the watermark in the paper, the style of the writing, and the other features of the thing. I was able to date it to the mid-thirteenth century and place it in central Italy. This is how scholars work with the very important textual evidence from the Middle Ages.

Now let's look at a couple of examples here of these illuminated manuscripts. The most famous of these manuscripts is a Celtic manuscript from the British Isles, *The Book of Kells* (see Color Illustration I). I would encourage you to do an online search for the *Book of Kells* and pull up some of the images. You'll see just how beautifully illustrated these manuscripts are. Clearly, these aren't meant to be like cheap paperback books intended just to transmit knowledge. No, they are designed as works of art, and that tells us that these monks placed great value on these artifacts. Again, that's the central idea that we keep coming back to in the study of culture: What is it that a culture places value on? These manuscripts are clearly one of the things that they lavished much care and concern on in the Middle Ages.

Let's look at an example of one of the pages from an illuminated manuscript—the so-called Cross Page from the Lindisfarne Gospels, also from the British Isles. (See above, and Color Illustration J). You can see clearly why it's called the Cross Page. A whole page of very valuable parchment is devoted to this illustration. This page shows us the same kind of cultural synthesis that we saw in the Romanesque style of building. The Christian element is obvious; it's a Cross Page after all. But notice all the swirling elements, the repeated geometric forms. They are highly abstracted, but they are animal body parts that are highly stylized, highly abstracted; these are legs and claws and snouts of dragons and other creatures and snakes, turned into geometric forms. This is the artistic tradition found in the pagan art of both the Celtic and Germanic tribes.

We know about this pagan style of art because we have many surviving examples, such as a wooden prow from a Viking ship, which has the same swirling forms that are abstracted animal shapes (see below). The overall prow is in the form of an animal; but notice again how stylized and abstract it is. This is no particular animal that you could necessarily identify. It's turned into an art form. And so notice what you have: you've got a cross superimposed on the world of these monsters, these pagan ideas, this world of Beowulf. Remember Beowulf's fight? He fights Grendel the monster and then Grendel's mother. And at the end of his life he fights a dragon. This is the world background, and these are the ideas and values, that are being brought into the art of western culture at this time.

Consider what one art historian, A. F. Janson, had to say about this particular work. I like his interpretation a lot. He wrote: "It is as if the world of paganism, embodied in these biting and clawing monsters, had suddenly been subdued by the superior authority of the cross." Notice that concept again. What he's saying here is you've got the pagan world represented by all the geometric forms and shapes. Art historians call this the "interlaced style," which is a weaving metaphor. Then you take the cross and you lay it right down on top of that pagan world, subduing it with "the superior authority of the cross." This is the synthesis of cultures we see in the early Middle Ages—a "weaving together," so to speak, of different cultural elements. These pagan traditions would bring great vitality and dynamism to Christian art in the Middle Ages.

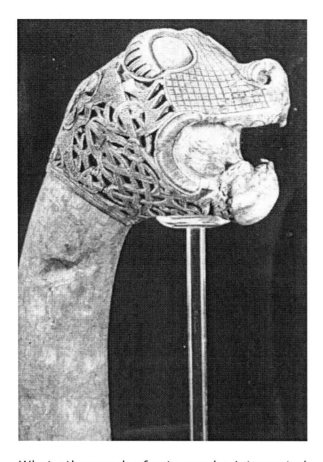

What other work of arts can be interpreted with the same theme of the triumph of Christianity over paganism? Recall the sarcophagus of Junius Bassus in which we see that scene of Christ enthroned, planting his foot on the head of the Roman sky god who is also the god of this world, Satan. The message being conveyed there was that the church had triumphed over Roman paganism. In this manuscript page, we've got the cross triumphant over the paganism of the northern tribes. And again, the synthesis of values is beautifully expressed in these illuminated manuscripts.

We study the names and the dates and the artifacts of the past and it doesn't make much of an impression on us because these are dead cultures that are so far removed from us. But I was reminded of how human these artifacts are when I was able to hold one in my hands and think about the fact that many centuries ago an anonymous monk held this and created it as a work of art. I was reminded of the fact that we have the knowledge of the past because

individual people over time, sometimes at great risk to their own life, preserved that knowledge by copying it—not just the text of the Bible, but also the great classical works of history and philosophy. These things were passed down through their effort and painstaking labor.

I mentioned the marginal notes that we find in these manuscripts. I want to share a few of these that come from Irish manuscripts. These are not the ones that I saw in the manuscript I worked with, but they come from Irish manuscripts, and they clearly show us again that human element that we would do well to remember. These are all translated from the Latin. For example, in the margin of one manuscript, an Irish monk wrote the statement, "Oh my chest, Blessed Virgin." Obviously he was in the damp and dank environment of the monastery and was suffering some respiratory condition such as pneumonia or tuberculosis.

Here is another one, a marginal notation: "Bless the soul of Faergus. Amen. I am very cold." Again, that recognition of the real time and the real life that was lived at that time is what strikes us. You can see that there's kind of a common negative theme that runs throughout a lot of these notations as though they are having second thoughts about their vows of poverty and silence. In fact, a lot of scholars have said that they may have written these marginal notes because the monasteries were pretty silent places, and this is one of the ways they gave expression to their feelings.

Here are three more notations from Irish manuscripts:

Alas, poor hand, how beautifully you have written on this white parchment. It will become famous, but you poor hand will become but small bones on a corpse.

Night is falling, it's supper time.

How sad I am to be myself with no friends but a dog, with no servant but my two hands, and no drinking glass but my shoe.

When we think about the past and study it, looking for clues as to its meaning, we

should always remember that real people—
real flesh-and-blood people—transmitted
this knowledge to us. We owe them a debt
of gratitude, especially these Irish monks
who, under great adversity, and many
times under the threat of Viking raids,
wrote and preserved the great works that
we have, including the Old and the New
Testament and the texts that are the foundation of our translations. Because of them,
we come a little closer to understanding the
past.

THE MEDIEVAL WORLDVIEW

Chapter Objectives

- Contrast the architectural styles of the early and late medieval periods.
- Illustrate how the term hierarchy gives shape to the late medieval worldview.
- Explain how both diversity and conformity were displayed in medieval life.

We've seen that the several hundred years following the collapse of the Roman Empire has been often described as the Dark Ages. There's a little truth in that term, but there's also a lot that's misleading about it. The term "dark ages" is used to denote any period of time when there is a loss in knowledge, a break in cultural. In that sense it's an accurate description of the period immediately following the fall of Rome and of the so-called Great Migrations of the Germanic tribes across Europe. This was very much a period of cultural transition and adjustment.

But the term Dark Ages is also a little misleading because it implies that people back then were in the dark. The term really applies to you and me more than it applies to anybody living 1500 years ago. That is, *we are in the dark* as we look back at that period. Our knowledge is very limited in terms of the historical records from that time. There's much that we don't know. But we do know that it was a formative period, a transitional period. As we have seen, the

term "synthesis" really captures what was happening during the centuries following the chaos brought about by the fall of the Roman Empire. It was a period of the synthesis of different cultures—of Christian culture and the pagan values of Germanic culture, along with whatever remained of classical civilization. We illustrated this principle of synthesis in the life of Charlemagne and in the style of architecture we call Romanesque. We also saw it in the distinctive art forms of the age, such as the reliquaries and, most significantly, the beautiful, illuminated manuscripts.

The period of adjustment and synthesis in the early Middle Ages would lead inevitably to a period of cultural balance. We call this period the High Middle Ages or the late Middle Ages, from about 1000 A.D. to 1400 or 1500 (depending on where you lived in Europe). The closer you were to the Mediterranean, the earlier the Middle Ages came to an end. We see the Renaissance in Italy beginning in the fourteenth and fifteenth centuries; but if you lived in Northern Europe and England, the Middle Ages came to an end a little later. This chapter will be focusing on the culture and worldview of the late Middle Ages.

What is the "balance" that was reached in the late Middle Ages, and what do we mean by that term? A period of balance is achieved when all of the institutions within that culture coalesce around a common worldview held by a majority of the population for a long period of time. This is what gives us the ability to talk about "medieval culture" or "Egyptian culture" or "Greek culture," or any culture at all—namely, that a majority of the population agrees about certain things for a long period of time. So, in this chapter we'll try to put our finger on the worldview that came into focus at the end of the Middle Ages. This worldview will define every aspect and every institution of medieval life, social and political, as well as the things they wrote down, the way they painted and sculpted, and the buildings they built. In other words, *everything* that makes up medieval culture.

Gothic Architecture

Before we label, define, and describe what that worldview was, I want to frame the period of the late Middle Ages around one concrete artifact: the Gothic cathedrals that literally towered over this age. We are going to take the Gothic style of architecture as representative of late medieval culture, and you will see where we are going to go with that in a few moments. But first, let's begin to form an idea of what Gothic architecture is by contrasting the style with the Romanesque. In the illustration below, the cathedral on the right was built in the thirteenth century in Chartres, France, which is during the late medieval period. This cathedral is a classic example of the Gothic style. On the left is the cathedral at Cologne, built around 980, the Romanesque church we looked at in the last chapter. This is just a strategy to simplify things, obviously: take two examples, put them side by side, and see what they can tell us about the periods that produced these two buildings.

If we itemize the different characteristics that directly contrast between these two styles, we can start by making the obvious chronological observation that the Romanesque comes from the early Middle Ages, while the Gothic comes from the late Middle Ages.

What is the most prominent characteristic of the Romanesque style? It's very clearly a plain style, while the Gothic style is ornate. You look at the plain surface of the Romanesque style and compare that to the highly sculpted surface of the Gothic style, where every nook and cranny is sculpted. If you stand right next to a cathedral like this and look up at it there is probably something that's going to be peering down out at you from every angle of that church. It might be an apostle; it might be a saint of the church. It might the Virgin Mary; it might be a gargoyle. But there will be something peering down at you. These are very ornate structures. By contrast, the Romanesque is much plainer, in keeping with the Germanic spirit of the early Middle Ages.

Let's continue to compare the two styles. Which style, Romanesque or Gothic, is going to be darker? The answer "Gothic" tends to come more quickly to us—and that's very revealing. The truth is, however, that the Romanesque is the darker church. We're inclined to say Gothic, however, because of the way we think of the word "Gothic" today, and what it means in contemporary culture. We think of dressing in black, dyeing your hair black, painting your fingernails black, liking vampire movies and so on. This is what Gothic means to many people today. In the Middle Ages, however, it was the Romanesque Church that was dark. Look at the windows and there can be no doubt about it; these are windows that you might see in a fortress—just big enough to fit your bow and arrow through to shoot out at the enemy. But the Gothic cathedrals have more spacious windows, because they wanted to let a lot of light into the church. That's why the Gothic style makes us think of light.

Where did our contemporary idea about Gothic come from? The way people use the word "Gothic" today couldn't be further from the truth of the Gothic style of the late Middle Ages. The answer is a very interesting but convoluted story of the history of an idea. About two hundred years ago in the Romantic period there was a revival of interest in all things medieval, and they fostered a lot of incorrect ideas about the Middle Ages. One of the things that was created at that time was the so-called Gothic novel. These novels are set in dark places—dark abbeys, churches and monasteries. We associate darkness with these spaces, which has created a false understanding of the late medieval style of architecture and the term "Gothic." The truth of the matter is really very different.

What else do we see by comparing these two churches side by side? The towers are very different. In the Romanesque style, they are symmetrical. Look at the towers: they are exact reflections of each other. The Gothic style is asymmetrical. In fact, the towers of the cathedral of Chartres, more accurately referred to as spires, were built in different centuries. This is typical of Gothic cathedrals. They were built over generations and reflect different styles, which is similar to Roman architecture: they loved diversity and they were eclectic.

The Romanesque style of building is considered more massive. I am not saying that the area inside, or the square footage of the building, is greater in the Romanesque; in fact, the Gothic cathedrals are larger in that sense, but the Romanesque buildings give a sense of massiveness. I am referring to the heaviness of construction, the thickness of the walls; the Romanesque is more like a fortress. Another way of expressing this is to say that it has a lower center of gravity. It's a heavier, more massive kind of construction. There is a lighter kind of construction at work in the Gothic cathedral. The walls are thinner. Think of the logic of

that. You have all these windows in the walls. You can't very successfully put in a lot of windows, and bring a lot of light in, when you've got extremely thick walls. You need to narrow the walls down to put these impressive stained-glass windows in.

We are going to see that this leads directly to another problem in the Gothic style. They wanted to build these cathedrals high—the higher the better. They wanted to make the walls thinner to accommodate all that glass. This led to basic support problems. Obviously, you want the building to stand for quite a few years. Some of these cathedrals, however, actually fell down in the thirteenth century, because they hadn't figured out how to accommodate all of those competing interests. We'll talk a little bit more about the style and the techniques that were innovated during this period to accomplish all of these goals later.

For the moment, though, let's look at the history of the Gothic style of architecture. Ultimately we want to see what a Gothic cathedral tells us about the late Middle Ages and its worldview, but we are just trying to work through the more technical and historical aspects of the style right now.

First of all, we are going to look at the history of the style, breaking that down into two periods; and then we're going to specifically define what the main concept at work in the Gothic cathedral is, and how it was achieved through the specific techniques they developed. Finally, we are going to look at the man who is credited with producing the style, Abbot Suger. After this, we'll move on to the question of what it all means and how it provides a window onto the mind of the late Middle Ages.

First of all, let's divide the Gothic style up into two periods, early and late, and identify one key building with each one of these styles. The early Gothic period runs from roughly 1140 to 1200. This is a formative transitional period in developing this new Gothic style as we go from the Romanesque to the Gothic. The most famous example of the early Gothic style is, arguably, the most famous cathedral in the world: Notre-Dame in Paris. Victor Hugo was influential in making it so widely known, and so popularly familiar to us, and it's one of the great landmarks in Paris today. Notre-Dame means "Our Lady," referring to the Virgin Mary. We are going to see that most of these Gothic cathedrals were dedicated to "Notre Dame," that is, Mary. The stained-glass windows in most of these Gothic cathedrals present stories from the life of the Virgin Mary. This was when the cult of the Virgin Mary in the Middle Ages was at its height.

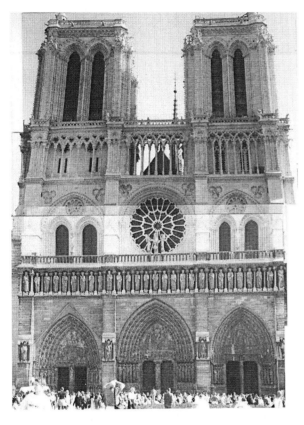

As you look at the illustration of Notre Dame in Paris (above), what about it do you see as Gothic? How do you recognize it as a Gothic cathedral? You see these circular windows that are called rose windows. You see that on either side it's flanked by large stained-glass windows, which would be the case right around the church as well. So that's one of the clearest and most obvious indicators that we are dealing here with the Gothic style—that sense of light, the stained-glass windows. What else do you see? It's very symmetrical. How do you ac-

count for that? This is a Gothic cathedral, but the towers are very symmetrical. How do you explain that? It's a transitional stage. It is *early* Gothic, which means it's still a little bit Romanesque, even while it is becoming fully Gothic. The example I always use is that of a tadpole. If you stare at a tadpole long enough, you are not going to see a point at which it becomes a frog. There is a transition—a period when characteristics are lost and acquired. The styles of art and architecture develop in a similar, organic way. This is partly Romanesque in its symmetry, but we still recognize it as Gothic because it's very ornate and has an abundance of stained-glass windows.

The second period, the High Gothic, runs from 1200 to 1300. This style is best illustrated by the cathedral we've already been looking at—Chartres (see above). This cathedral is again called the Notre Dame of Chartres. We hear the phrase Notre Dame and, unless you are a football fan, you are probably thinking of the cathedral of Paris.

158

But with the term Notre Dame, you really have to say Notre Dame "of Paris," Notre Dame "of Chartres," Notre Dame "of Beauvais," and so on, because this was almost the uniform name for these cathedrals. Chartres is considered the finest expression of the Gothic style, which is why I use it as the example here. Once again look at the highly ornate quality, the use of the stained-glass windows.

During this period these cathedrals were all the rage. Every city in Europe was competing with every other city to see who could build the most spectacular cathedral. The goal was to make it higher, more spectacular, more massive. The little problem, however, was that they hadn't yet mastered the technical aspects of building these structures, even while they were in this mad dash to put all the stone up and to create these impressive structures. Well, the inevitable happened in 1284: the Cathedral at Beauvais collapsed, or at least part of it did. That managed to put the brakes on the building craze while medieval architects and engineers scrambled to figure out how to achieve the different features they were striving after. It was in the solving of these competing problems that we see the ultimate achievement of the Gothic style. So, let's look at exactly what they were trying to accomplish, how they finally mastered it, and what kinds of techniques they came up with to actually integrate all of those qualities into a successful building.

The main concept I would say of a Gothic cathedral, at least in the high Gothic period, can be described as the striving for verticality and elegance. This means that these are like skyscrapers reaching as high as they possibly can. In fact, as you look at the Chartres Cathedral again, these spires were actually called fingers pointing to heaven, pointing to the glory of God. It's a beautiful image of how these buildings were symbolically conceived of as pointing to the majesty of God. They wanted these things to be vertical, but they also wanted them to be elegant, with that kind of ornate, thin quality of construction that allowed for the incorporation of as much glass as possible.

But how do you make it tall? How do you make it thin? And how do you keep it standing?

It was these challenges that led medieval engineers to develop the main techniques that we associate with the Gothic cathedral. We are going to talk about three design elements. The first two are technical support qualities, and the last is just a design feature. The most important technical feature they came up with is called the **flying buttress**. I think this is one of the most curious terms in architectural history, and one that needs to be explained through an illustration.

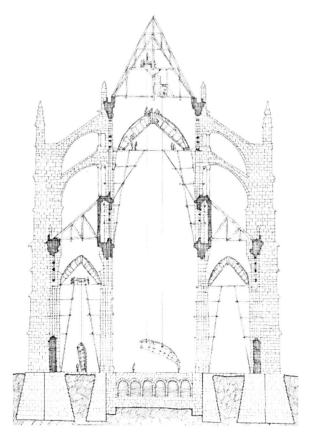

Let's look at a cross section here of a Gothic cathedral. Notice the buttress, as it's called, this massive outer wall. A buttress is a support, and this support is connected by these flying buttresses, flying supports. You can also think of them as braces holding the structure at the point of greatest vulnerability, the back end of the cathedral known as the choir. That region is where most of the glass is found—and, of course, the more glass, the less stable the structure will be.

The second technique that engineers developed is the **pointed arch**. An illustration will be helpful. On the left is a rounded arch, on the right a pointed arch. The simple logic of these labels is easy to see. The rounded arch is what you find in Romanesque cathedrals, the pointed arch is found in Gothic cathedrals.

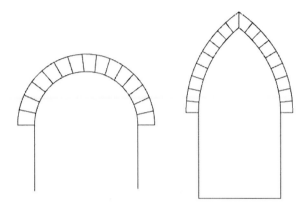

Think for a minute: Why is it that we call it Romanesque? Because it is a revival of Roman architecture. Doesn't it look like the style of arch that we saw in triumphal arches and aqueducts and so on? That's the concept. Notice what you do when you cut that arch and splice it back together and make it pointed: You can increase the height without increasing the footprint of the structure. This is a very simple, elegant solution to the problem of how you can make it more vertical and yet support the structure.

There's one more technical design element that we've already talked about: stained-glass windows. This is a key element that brings light into these Gothic cathedrals. Let's highlight for a moment the man who is credited with developing the Gothic style. His name was Abbot Suger. What was he thinking about, what motivated him to develop the style? In a word, *light*. Abbot Suger redesigned the choir in his church to bring more light into the sanctuary—not because he was having a hard time reading his sermon notes, but because light is a powerful symbol of God. 1 John tells us that

God is light, and in Him is no darkness at all. This profound spiritual truth is given expression by these remarkable stained-glass windows. Like other medieval men and women of his day, Abbott Suger believed that God reveals Himself to us through the intricate details of the natural world; all of God's creation is a grand symbol pointing us to our Creator.

These great cathedrals are impressive structures. I remember when I was studying German in Austria and went to an organ recital in one of these Gothic cathedrals. Think of all that glass and all of that stone—and then add the organ sounds and the organ pipes to that. It's a pretty impressive experience. The interior of a cathedral is an inner sanctum, a little world unto itself. The angle of the light coming through the windows at any point of the day means that the interior never quite looks or feels the same; the infinite play of light through the colored glass reminds us of the infinite nature of God's character. Abbot Suger was very important in developing the Gothic style—a style that eloquently expresses the worldview of the later Middle Ages.

The Symbolism of Medieval Cathedrals

Let's continue looking at the symbolism of church architecture. In the Middle Ages, the entire church building was one big symbol of church teaching and Christian belief. So let's consider five ways in which the medieval church functioned like a symbol.

First, the church is symbolic in that its floor plan is laid out in the form of a cross. This was the pattern from the time of the earliest churches in the post-Constantine age. We call this the **cruciform** pattern, which means "form of a cross." I love the very simple but profound significance of that. Even when that truth of the gospel and the centrality of the cross was lost in medieval Christianity, the irony is that every time a medieval peasant walked into that church, the very floor plan that he was walking on should have reminded him that the cross is at the very heart of what the church is all about. We don't come to God through the church, through the priest, through the sacraments of the church—all those things that the medieval church taught. Rather, we come to God through what Christ did at the cross.

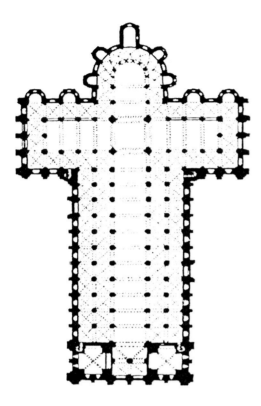

A second way of thinking of the symbolism of the church is that these buildings typically face east. Now this was true of pagan temples as well, but obviously there is a very different meaning in Christian times that points to the resurrection, this orientation towards the rising sun, just as Peter and John ran at break of day to the empty tomb. Just as in the beginning of a new day, we think of new life that we have in Christ through his resurrection. So all of these meanings, once again, very simply but profoundly give expression to Christian faith.

Third, when you enter into this remarkable inner sanctum of stone and glass, it should make you think of the inner life of devotion—the inner life, the religious or spiritual life—just as it did for ancient Romans when they built the Pantheon. In fact, most historians look back at the Roman Pantheon as the beginning of this concept in western architectural history—the idea that when you entered into the Roman Pantheon you're entering into that inner life of devotion, the place of contact with God, with the divine realm. For the medieval Christian, that was the same symbolic meaning that you found within that interior space of the church. Within the church, one received mass and came into direct contact, they believed, with God through this sacrament.

Fourth, as we've noted, the stained-glass windows were symbolic. On the symbolic level, the light represents the nature of God. They also functioned in a practical way as pictorial representations of scripture. What you knew as a medieval peasant, of the Word of God, you knew from what you saw in stained-glass windows or what you saw enacted in a medieval mystery play. You couldn't read, and even if you could read, you couldn't have your own copy of the Bible. And so these were crude ways of communicating church teaching and biblical stories to the peasantry.

Finally, and I would say most significantly, with the Gothic cathedral we see the verticality of these structures, that skyscraper quality, directing our attention clearly to the concept of hierarchy. When you stand before a cathedral, you're meant to think of how big God is, how big the church is, and how small and insignificant you are. Hierarchy is the key concept for understanding late medieval culture. When we reach the later Middle Ages, we come to a period of cultural balance where this hierarchical worldview is expressed in every institution of that culture. I would argue that hierarchy is that key concept.

The Hierarchical Worldview

Now, what is hierarchy? Hierarchy is a top-down ranking of power, a top down ranking of authority. Hierarchies are a reality of life: the executive branch of the federal government is a hierarchy—with the President at the top and the cabinet officials and lower-level officials beneath. A business is another example of a hierarchy. Somebody's got to be in charge, and there are mid-level managers and so on—all the way down to factory workers.

In the Middle Ages, though, this concept of hierarchy became a rigid way of looking at all of reality, the cosmos, truth, everything. They saw the world as a rigidly hierarchical place, extending from God all the way down to the lowest form of life. I want to illustrate how this notion of hierarchy that we see symbolized even in the vertical lines of the cathedral really does reflect the worldview of the late Middle Ages.

First, consider how medieval Catholicism clearly illustrates this idea, since the Catholic Church is a hierarchy. You've got the Pope and the college of cardinals—and all those levels of authority in the Catholic Church, all that hierarchy, really crystallized in the Middle Ages.

Medieval theology, too, presents the cosmos as a rigidly hierarchical place. Dante's *Divine Comedy* gives us the best example of this. The *Divine Comedy*, written in the thirteenth century, is one of the greatest works of literature in the Middle Ages. It's really three books in one. Dante depicts an imaginary journey that he takes, first through hell, the Inferno, in the first book, then through Purgatory in the second book, and finally, through Paradise in the final book.

In Dante's masterpiece, we first journey through the different levels of hell; and

then work our way up through the different levels of purgatory, where Catholics believe that you work off the various sins of your life. Then we continue to journey through the levels of paradise until reaching the presence of God. That is a very structured and hierarchical way of looking at the cosmos within medieval theology. (See illustration below.)

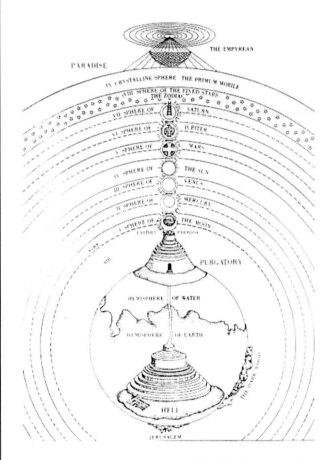

We also see the concept of hierarchy in medieval philosophy. Philosophers spoke of what they called the **Great Chain of Being**, by which they imagine that every living thing in God's creation occupied a distinct place in this chain, all the way from the highest angelic beings down to the lowest flea on the back of the village dog. Everything, including every person, was ranked in this chain of being. This is the really bleak idea here, because you couldn't change your position. In American culture we speak of upward social mobility. Get a good education, work hard, and you can better your position in life and so on; but there was no concept like that in the Middle Ages. In this rigidly hierarchical world, where you were born is where you stayed, where you lived your life. You never had any aspiration that you'd ever be anything else but who you were—a medieval peasant working in a small village in medieval France.

We saw that the medieval Catholic Church as an institution was very hierarchical. We saw that philosophers in the Middle Ages spoke of the great chain of being, by which they meant that you occupy a particular rung on the ladder, a particular link in the chain, all the way from the top created angelic being to the lowest creature. Everything in God's creation, including every one of us, occupies a place in that great chain of being according to medieval philosophers; and the key to keep in mind here, and probably a point that I didn't emphasize enough, is that *you can't move your position*. You can't decide that you're tired of the link in the chain that you occupy, so you're going to migrate to another place in the chain.

All of these notions that we have today that are part of our modern worldview, notions whereby we value equal opportunity, the idea that if you work hard and get a good education and take opportunities and take risks the way an entrepreneur does, then there are rewards for that and you can get ahead within society and change your position in your life. These are basic assumptions that we have as part of our birthright as modern people. In the Middle Ages, peasants living in thirteenth-century France wouldn't have had a clue what we are talking about, because they didn't think of the world that way. It would not have made sense to them, just as it makes no sense to us really when we look back at their lives.

And it's hard for us to wrap our minds around how you could possibly live as a peasant in the thirteenth century, to look around you and not long for something better and not to gripe about the fact that you didn't have access to something better. As far as we can determine, they would never have even considered those thoughts because they understood—at least they believed they understood—the world around them, and it made sense to them; it was highly ordered, highly structured. And I guess you can say that one good thing from that came about from that view—namely, that people didn't struggle with all the anxieties that a lot of people do today. "Who am I?" and "What's my purpose in life?" are common questions today; but people in the Middle Ages just took it for granted that they were who they were born to be. They were born into the peasant class and that's the way they were going to live their life and that's way they were going to die. Furthermore, that's how their children were going to live as well. It kind of took a lot of anxiety out of the picture in one sense. So this is the concept that permeated every aspect of medieval life and thought. We also see it, as we've noted, in their architecture. When you stand in front of a Gothic cathedral, you are meant to feel small before all that that cathedral represents: the majesty of God, but also the power of the church.

The political and social structures of the medieval age were also rigidly hierarchical. It was believed that everybody occupied one of **three estates**, as they were called—one of three positions or statuses in society. Your status was either that you were a member of the kingly class (the nobles), or you were a member of the clergy, or you were a member of the vast unwashed masses, the commoners or peasants. Those were the only three options. These classes were described at the time by their function, as the "those who fight" (noble class), "those who pray" (church class), and "those who work" (peasant class). Unless you joined the church and pursued a career as a cleric, you couldn't simply change your status in life. Everything was rigidly hierarchical.

Medieval Literature

In this chapter we're trying to understand the medieval worldview a little bit better.

Let's look at this from another perspective, however—one that emphasizes the great diversity of life and thought in the Middle Ages. We'll turn to medieval literature for this perspective. I am assuming that you may not have a lot of background in reading medieval literature. You may have read a little Beowulf or a snatch of the Canterbury Tales. But when you start dipping into medieval literature, it dispels a lot of myths that we have with the Middle Ages; and there are number of things that we find that are very surprising in light of our popular assumptions about the Middle Ages.

We think of this period as a time when the church reigned supreme. You might expect that if the church is in control of every aspect of society, then the literature would be kind of clean and sanitized and "churchy." But when you start to read the literature, you find out that's not the case at all. We find some very surprising stuff that paints a very different picture of life as it was really lived in the Middle Ages. Two things in particular surprise us as we start looking at medieval literature. We are going to illustrate both of these as we take this very quick survey of the medieval age.

The first thing that surprises us as I have already suggested is the incredible diversity of medieval literature. It's not all church-related literature, such as sermons and moral fables. It's very diverse, both in style and in content. The other thing is the more puzzling thing that surprises us as we start reading our way through medieval literature—namely, its seeming lack of morality. It is a very carnal literature; it's very worldly, very fleshly in its subject matter. And that again really raises an important question in our mind: How is it that this period of time, the one time in western history when the church pulled all the levers of power and had the best opportunity to impress its values on the world and on western civilization—how is that the art and the literature of the period is so morally corrupt and so worldly in orientation?

The only way we can only explain that is to think back to what we previously saw when we talked about dualism. The great error I would argue of the medieval church was that they fostered this belief that you could divide the world into what is material and what is spiritual, and that those two realms didn't really have any contact. Remember how we looked at that door, that "gate" that leads into the Romanesque church, and we argued that that really symbolizes the fallacy that you leave the world and the flesh behind when you enter into the spiritual realm to partake of mass, confess your sins to the priest, and hear the homily. Inside the church is where you commune with God and receive his favor; and then you go out and you live in the world as though nothing has changed in your life. There was this profound disconnect between the way people lived and what they supposedly believed. I would say that this is the great challenge Christians of every period have had to deal with, namely, to bring the material and the spiritual together the way it is supposed to be. Christ indwelling us should all be about being a new creation, and the way we live should reflect that. We don't see that in the Middle Ages. The church had become a corrupt political and economic institution. It profited from this very fallacy of looking at the world this way, and so you can't really blame the medieval peasant for thinking of the world that way. That's the way the corrupt church hierarchy in a sense taught them and encouraged them to believe. You have got this institution of the church that is so powerful and yet exercised very little influence on the way people really lived their lives. It's really the great tragedy, I would argue, of the church during the medieval period.

Let's look more closely, then, at the diversity of medieval literature. To start with, lyric poems are one category that we have many examples from all of the cultures of medieval Europe. I am going to give you three distinct examples of the short, emotional poems that we call lyrics. In France, we have the tradition of the **troubadours**. Today we still think of a traveling singer-songwriter when we think of a troubadour. You can picture a folk musician of the 1960s. It's kind of what troubadours were eight centuries years ago. They wrote their own songs and traveled around performing them with stringed instruments. This was the popular music of that day. As is the case today, the theme usually revolved around love—and it's not a spiritualized, platonic, idealized kind of love they were singing about. It's pretty carnal stuff, and a lot of these poems are very explicit and detailed in their subject matter. In Germany, there was the tradition of the **Minnesingers** (literally "love singers"). They were writers and singers about love, professional popular poet-musicians. We see a very similar trend in medieval Italy with the rise of the sonnet, the fourteen-line poem which is usually written about love; of course, the sonnet has an important place in English literature as well. Consider the sonnets of Shakespeare. Most of his poems are also about carnal love as it turns out, which is in keeping with the medieval traditions out of which the sonnet developed.

On the other end of the poetic spectrum from the short emotional lyrics, we find epic poems, which are long heroic poems. They are poems that embody the virtues and values of a culture the way Homer's *Iliad* and *Odyssey* and Virgil's *Aeneid* did. We see in the Middle Ages that these various national identities—the English, German, French and so on—are starting to emerge. What will later become the nation states of Europe are taking shape with their distinct national identities and languages; and so logically we see epic poems emerging in response to the question, "Who are we? What do we believe? How are we different from those guys over there?"

In Anglo-Saxon England, we see *Beowulf* as the great epic of early England. In Germany, we see the *Nibelungenlied*, the poem of the Nibelungs. This is the story of Siegfried and so on, and it would become very famous in the nineteenth century as the great composer of operas, Richard Wagner, went back to the story of the Nibelungs for much of his operatic material, the so-called "Ring Cycle." In France, the great medieval epic was the *Song of Roland*. Roland was the fictional hero who served in Charlemagne's

army and fought the infidels along the Spanish border. This is another great epic that relates the values of that culture and that time. Spain, for its part, produced *El Cid* as its national epic.

So again we are starting already to see the diversity, and the secular nature, of a lot of this art and literature. The third type of literature we'll discuss are known as **romances.** Note that we are not talking about romance in the way we use the word today. These are not love stories. Romance means "novel," it means adventure story, and that's what these are. Now sometimes the plot does revolve around a love intrigue; and, as C. S. Lewis, the great Christian apologist, philosopher, and professor of medieval literature, famously noted, these love stories are usually adulterous in nature. He wrote a book in 1936 called *The Allegory of Love*, one of his great scholarly works, in which he deals with the problem of why these medieval love stories always depict an idealized view of love that's adulterous. That's what he tried to understand, especially in the context of the "Age of Faith," as it's sometimes called, the Middle Ages. How would this be tolerated? How would this be looked at favorably? But this is the reality. Consider, for example, the story of King Arthur. Arthurian romances are the most famous type of medieval romance. Recall the story of Arthur and his wife Guinevere and how a knight named Lancelot enters the scene. All of a sudden we have a love triangle. Another example is the famous story of Tristan and Isolt.

So the Arthurian romances are the most famous examples. Most scholars believe that Arthur was a historical figure, but nothing like these stories make him out to have been. He didn't live at Camelot, didn't have a round table and all these other fanciful things. He is believed to have been a fifth-century British chieftain, and there is a lot of controversy about that; but it's fairly well established that there is some kernel of historical truth lying at the base of the memory of King Arthur. That shouldn't surprise us. We found out that this was the case with the Trojan War; and that was the case with Atlantis and King Midas and other stories that we looked at when we discussed ancient civilizations. Usually, there is some small kernel of truth that lies at the heart of a myth.

Probably the most famous adventure stories associated with the court of King Arthur are the quests for the Holy Grail. What is the Holy Grail? Legend has it that Joseph of Arimathea caught the blood of Jesus, flowing from his side on the cross. He caught the blood in the same cup used at the last supper; this cup then embarks on a legendary history. This chalice was believed to have magical properties; in medieval romances, knights went out questing for this, trying to find this artifact because of the great power that was associated with it. Most of us are probably familiar with the Holy Grail from Monty Python or Indiana Jones; the basic story of the Grail was the most popular adventure story of the Middle Ages.

The next category, religious works, is kind of a catch-all category for a lot of different types of religious works that were popular in the Middle Ages. I will give you just one example, **homilies**, which are collections of sermons. We don't normally think of these as our favorite kind of bedtime reading; but in the Middle Ages people loved to read these things and it was a very popular form of literature. This is more in keeping with how we normally think of the Middle Ages.

At the other end of the spectrum we have secular stories. Notice how these things in all of their diversity exist side by side. That's what is so surprising about medieval culture, which takes us back to dualism again. You've got the spiritual and you've got the material, and the two don't really interact. The most famous category of secular stories are what are known as *fabliaux*, which is an old French word. We get our modern English word "fable" from that, but we are not talking about stories about animals like Aesop's Fables here. A **fabliau** is best described as a dirty short story, and that's exactly what they are. The best known examples are those that we see in

Chaucer's *Canterbury Tales*. Chaucer always puts these stories in the mouths of peasants; they are the ones who always tell the dirty stories—the Miller and Reeve and Merchant, and so on. These are the stories that it seems Chaucer had the most fun telling; he expended most of his creative effort on them. So, what we are seeing? We are seeing diversity, we are seeing carnality, and this is why I say this really illustrates the tragic state of affairs of medieval life and the corruption of the medieval church well.

Finally, one last category is medieval drama. There are three types of medieval drama. They all start with "m" so it's an easy outline to commit to memory.

- mystery plays
- miracle plays
- morality plays

All these forms of medieval drama were important in the life of medieval cities, in particular the **mystery plays**. These are plays that were staged annually as part of a pageant, a cycle of plays that every medium to large city in medieval Europe would have. They are called mystery plays because they depict stories from the Old Testament and the New Testament. "Mystery" refers to how the apostle Paul used the word, where he says for example, "Behold, I show you a mystery." And a mystery for the apostle Paul is a great truth that is hidden in the Old Testament but revealed in the New Testament. That's the way he used that word mystery, and so these plays follow that formula. They show you the Old Testament prefiguring of New Testament truth, such as the story of Noah prefiguring the work of Christ as our deliverer. And so that sense of prefigurement and fulfillment defines the mystery cycle of plays that would be staged over a series of days in a medieval city.

Noah is probably the best known example of a mystery play—one that serves to illustrate just how poorly these plays represented scripture. Imagine that you are a medieval peasant. You can't read or write. You certainly don't have a copy of the Bible and you couldn't do anything with it if you had one because you couldn't read. What you know of scripture is very limited. You know what you know by looking at stained glass windows or what the priest tells you in his homily or what you see enacted in these mystery plays. The story of Noah illustrates, however, how distorted that picture of scripture was that these plays presented. In the medieval version of Noah, Noah is not the main character; Noah's wife is the main character. Now, if you remember the account in Genesis, she doesn't play a particularly important or pivotal role and yet she is the central comic figure in the mystery play version of Noah's Flood, which is turned into a comedy. She is depicted as a shrew and a nag. Noah is kind of a henpecked husband and Noah's wife is constantly nagging him. She doesn't want to leave her friends behind; she doesn't want to go on that big boat and he has to drag her, kicking and screaming into the ark; and of course the story has just been turned into a comedy for entertainment. And so what a corrupted view of scripture and biblical truth you get through that medium; but then again that's the tragedy, as I am calling it, of the Middle Ages—corrupting not just the sense of morality, but corrupting even the truth of scripture.

The second type of medieval drama are **miracle plays**. These are reenactments of the lives of saints. Every local region had its favorite local saint and so these were very popular stories and popular plays in the Middle Ages. They are called miracle plays because to become a saint in the Catholic Church, you have to perform miracles. Either you're alive when you do these or your bones do them after your death, and then you can be canonized as a saint. These plays tell the story of these miracles and the lives of these figures that were so revered in the Middle Ages.

Finally, we see the last category, **morality plays**, which are best described as allegories that depict the struggle between the seven vices and the seven virtues in the heart of man. The most famous example of this type of play is the late medieval English morality play *Everyman*. In the heart of Everyman is a struggle between good and evil, between the seven vices and the seven virtues; this again shows us how they understood their faith. They didn't understand the gospel of grace. They understood a religion of works which imposed on you the responsibility of being virtuous and not giving in to the vices. That's what the essence of Christianity was for the average medieval man or woman. It was living a good life as they saw that to be, but they understood nothing of grace. Grace is something that the Reformation would be all about and you can see why the Reformation was long overdue in light of the nature of Christianity in the Middle Ages.

THE END OF THE MIDDLE AGES 16

- Describe how the Crusades affected the development of western culture.
- Explain the conditions under which a worldview collapses.
- Identify some key figures who helped shape the emerging modern worldview.

We've seen how medieval culture reached its high point in the Gothic style of architecture. We've noted how a hierarchical worldview began to define and shape every aspect of medieval culture. We saw as well that the Age of Faith was, paradoxically, an age of great corruption. Medieval literature is an eloquent example of that. Now we're going to turn our attention to how the Middle Ages came to an end. What brought down this system that was several hundred years in the making? How did the church lose its authority? What factors shook the medieval worldview to its foundation?

In this chapter, we're going to consider how western culture transitioned from the medieval to the modern world. We'll do this by looking at two factors—one made-made catastrophe and one natural catastrophe—that contributed to the collapse of the medieval hierarchical system:

- The Crusades
- The Black Death

We'll conclude this chapter by examining how worldviews—or "paradigms," as we'll call them—change within a culture.

The Crusades

The Crusades, which occurred from the eleventh through the thirteenth centuries, had a profound impact on western culture. They were, without a doubt, the greatest blot on medieval Christianity and one of the great blots on the history of the church. You find today that when skeptics and atheists and unbelievers talk with Christians they will say, "Look at how corrupt the church has been over the centuries. Look at the Crusades, what a corrupt thing that was. If that's your faith I don't want to have anything to do with it." And that's one of the great tragedies of that and we as Christians need to know how to respond when somebody wants to take this horrible series of events that we call the Crusades and lay them at the foot of the cross or at that feet of the church and say that Christ or the church is somehow responsible for that.

I think it is an easy argument to reject. I didn't have anything to do with the Crusades. That was the responsibility of so-called Christians who were not really following Christ and it was a product of error and corruption and not the product of truth. But we need to know how to understand this and how to discuss this because this is something that is still referred to today by opponents of Christianity and certainly by Muslims who have a very long list of grievances against the West, which usually go all the way back to what happened in the time of the Crusades.

What were the Crusades? The **Crusades** were a series of military campaigns whereby medieval Christianity attempted to retake the Holy Land from the Muslims. They wanted to take back Jerusalem. They wanted to take back Bethlehem. They wanted to take back the holy sites. The Church of the Holy Sepulchre, the Church of the Nativity—all those things that you see if you go to the Holy Land today—they wanted to take those and bring them back under the control of the church. Well, they failed time and time again in their attempt to do so. We look back at the Crusades and we see them as an unmitigated colossal failure, but it's one of the failures that achieved great consequences nonetheless and we will talk about that as well.

The First Crusade was launched in 1096 when Pope Urban II declared that a campaign should be waged to take back the Holy Land for the Church. There was a lot of excitement; people thought this was doable and they were excited about being a part of it. Armies were raised and knights led their troops and they headed to the Middle East, to the Holy Land, and they were successful in the short run. The First Crusade was the only one of the crusades that achieved any measure of success at all. Jerusalem was captured, and it and much of the Holy Land was held by European Christian forces for at least a generation, and then eventually the Muslims defeated them once again and that obviously made necessary the following series of Crusades.

The first Crusade though, really set the tenor and the tone for all the Crusades that would follow. It was a bloodbath. When Jerusalem was captured, the Muslim and the Jewish populations were slaughtered. It was a horrible massacre and a dark stain on medieval Christianity. It should be noted that in the Middle East in Arab cities at this time Jews were not generally persecuted,

nor were Christians. Arabic cultures in the Middle Ages were reasonably tolerant and Christians and Jews lived side by side with Muslims; of course, this is something that tragically, unfortunately, has changed over the centuries in ways that affect us deeply to this day.

The second, third and fourth Crusades were then were launched in subsequent generations to try to do what the first Crusade could not manage to succeed at. There were other minor crusades. There was even a Children's Crusade, and it absolutely defies explanation. This occurred when a couple of young boys began traveling around and preaching that they had received a vision from God to raise an army, and a little ragtag band of children and teenagers started following them. We don't know how many there actually were but they marched their way to the Mediterranean and they believed in their delusion that the Mediterranean would part like the Red Sea had for Moses when they got there. They were expecting to just march right across to the Holy Land and be able to accomplish what the best knights in Europe weren't able to do. What happened was that they were given passage on ships and probably sold in the slavery when they sailed into the Mediterranean. Many died at sea; it was a horrible event. But, again, how do you explain this? What kind of mass hysteria had taken over the mind of medieval Europe to engage in these foolhardy adventures, even to the point where children's crusades would be launched with no hope of success? That tells us something about the mind of the Middle Ages, the corruption of this age and the willingness to believe a lie. That's what we see about the blindness. It's going to characterize the end times as well that people will believe a lie and you certainly see that in the Middle Ages.

The crusades did not accomplish their goal, not by a long shot, but they accomplished a lot of other things. I would say that the crusades are one of the best examples in history of what is sometimes called the law of unintended consequences. The law of unintended consequences refers to a situation in which you set out to do one thing and you don't accomplish the one thing you set out to do—but along the way a lot of other things happen that you never intended, for good or for bad. History is like that. For example, Alexander set out to conquer the world and did it, though he didn't hold it for very long; but in the process he spread Greek culture throughout the world. Of course, that was something Alexander was clearly trying to do—but not maybe in the same way that he ultimately accomplished.

The Crusades were like that, setting out to impose the authority of medieval Christianity on the Holy Land and not succeeding; but some very important things were done nonetheless, unintentionally. These are things that on the one hand would help to bring down the medieval worldview and on the other hand lay the foundation for the emergence of the modern world in the centuries to follow. We are going to look very quickly at four unintended consequences of the Crusades.

There was first of all a *political impact*. Who issues the call for the Crusades? The Pope, but the Pope doesn't command any armies. Where is the army going to come from? It is going to come from the kings and the knights of Europe, the secular political powers. What happens generation after generation when you're sending troops off to the Middle East and nothing good is coming out of it and you don't see any benefits coming from this policy? It's costing you a lot of money and a lot of men. Are you going to start being skeptical when the Pope issues yet another call for a Holy Crusade for which you have to pony up the troops and the money? Yes, you are, and that's what we see.

We see a political impact in the increasing conflict between church and state, between Pope and king. It increases the tension between religious and secular power. Why is that significant? Because, if we are going to make it from the Middle Ages to the modern period, the power of the church is going to have to be brought down a few notches.

The connection between church and state is going to have to be severed. We live in a modern world where we assume a disconnect between church and state. For that to come about, you have got to have this kind of tension, this political impact that the Crusades helped to foster at the end of the medieval period.

Secondly, we see a profound *intellectual impact*. These Christian knights came into contact with all kinds of things, physical things, but also abstract ideas, bodies of knowledge, that were preserved in the Middle East, that had been lost to western Europe for centuries; and those things were rediscovered when they came into contact with Middle Eastern Islamic, Arabic culture. I am referring specifically to the rediscovery of Greek learning. What happened after the fall of the Roman Empire to these ancient books and all this knowledge? Did all this stuff get burnt and lost forever to history? No, it was preserved in the East and ultimately preserved. The irony of this is that it was preserved by Arabic Muslim scholars who translated the works of Greek antiquity, works of science and astronomy and philosophy and so on, into Arabic.

And so these Christian knights come and they find all this stuff and slowly it begins to make its way back into medieval Europe. Why is that important? Because the period that we know as the Renaissance is a rebirth of knowledge of the classical world, and for that rebirth to happen, these books had to be discovered and make their way back into Europe. The Crusades were one of the factors that led to that knowledge making its way back into western culture. So, it is ultimately thanks to Arabic scholarship that this knowledge was rediscovered in the West, which then laid the foundation for the Renaissance and with that the rise of the modern world.

There was also a very important *economic impact*—unintended, but very real nonetheless. I said that these knights came into contact with a lot of things they weren't familiar with in the Holy Land when they met up with Arabic culture. One of the things they no doubt noted was that the food tasted very different and very flavorful, because of the spices that they didn't have back in Europe—the kinds of spices that, if you open your kitchen cabinet at home, you'll see that we cook with today. Where did these spices come from that fill our pantry? They entered into European cuisine at the end of the Middle Ages and this led to new trade routes for things like spices, new textiles, new dyes—things that you can buy and sell.

These commodities entered into Europe from the south, the ports of Italy for example. If you take a culinary trip through Europe, starting in the south from the Mediterranean regions and migrate towards the north, you're going to find that the food gets blander the farther north you go. Down in the south where all these spices first made their entry into the ports in Italy, Greece, and Spain, the foods are pretty flavorful, pretty spicy and so on. European cuisine kind of reflects the old trade patterns that go all the way back to the Middle Ages. The way the spices transformed the national cuisines of these cultures at this time is still apparent today.

What happens when you have a lot of trade? It's kind of a truism that free trade and a lot of trade activity is good because it creates wealth, and this is what we see in the Middle Ages as well. If all of this buying and selling is occurring, then somebody has got to be doing the buying and the selling. What is going to happen as a result of this?

This will lead to a fourth profound *social impact*, namely, a new class of people is going to emerge in late medieval society: the merchant class, the people who do the buying and the selling. We know them as the middle class. Most of us here ourselves are products of the middle class. In fact, American culture is a very much a middle class culture and we can trace our values as a people several hundred years back to this very important transformation in Western culture when the middle class emerges.

I would argue that the emergence of the middle class is the single most important development in understanding the rise of the modern world. It's a debatable point, but I really want to stress the importance of it. The middle class begins small as a merchant class and it grows in power over the centuries. By the time you reach the eighteenth century, the middle class will have become the most important and most powerful class within Western European societies. When you've got economic power, what's the next thing you're going to ask for and demand? The answer is political power. What do you see at the end of the eighteenth century? You see two middle class revolutions. One is the American Revolution, over the issue of no taxation without representation. Having attained economic power they now wanted to be able to determine their destiny themselves; and in France you see another middle class revolution, the French revolution of 1789. We understand the ground work of these revolutions and the causes of these revolutions as lying all the way back hundreds of years before in the great transformation that we are looking at—the end of the Middle Ages.

How about that for complexity in history? When you start looking at historical events, you realize how highly leveraged everything really is—how completely interconnected it all is, and how you have to take the long view and be very patient when you look at history.

The Fourteenth Century

As we've already noted, great cultural change grows out of periods of chaos—and we have that in spades in the fourteenth century. We are going to see how this period of time, the fourteenth century, followed by the great changes of the fifteenth and sixteenth centuries, brought about a transition to the modern world. As we go through this I will be introducing or defining some more conceptual terms that are not terribly complex or difficult in and of themselves, but which are abstract. So we will be defining those. So stay focused on the big picture as we go through this material. I am going to try to use some concrete examples as well to break through the abstraction of it a little bit along the way.

If you could travel back in time, you would want to make sure that your time machine was fixed in such a way that it could not possibly take you back to the fourteenth century. You wouldn't want to be dropped off in that century for anything. It was a really truly horrible time to live in the western world for a lot of reasons, which we are going to look at in due course.

People who lived through it could have sworn they saw the four horsemen of the apocalypse on the horizon. That's how bad things were. If you think of wars and pestilence and famine and all those, they had it. They also had a major population adjustment in the fourteenth century. In fact, this is one of the most interesting facts that introduces us to just how bad things were in the fourteenth century. At the beginning of the fourteenth century, the population of Europe was as great as it would be for several hundred years. The population rose to the highest point it had ever been at the beginning of the fourteenth century and then it significantly drops off. So much so that it would take several hundred years for it to rise to that level again. Well, you are clearly going to have to have some pretty catastrophic events for that to occur. There was really overpopulation in Europe in the late Middle Ages, and that led to a problem of how to feed all these people, similar to what happened in the late Roman Empire. History is not very imaginative; it keeps bringing out the same set of problems over and over again. And then at the beginning of the fourteenth century you have a few bad years of drought, which brings about a famine that kills we believe about ten percent of the population of Europe.

Well, that's a pretty bad beginning, but things just go from bad to worse. In the 1340s, something very terrifying appeared in the ports of southern Italy, those great trade ports where all the trade was flowing in. Along with all the goodies that they were bringing—spices and textiles and all the other things that they were trading and im-

porting into Europe at that time—along with this came something else that would shake European civilization to its foundation.

What am I talking about? The Black Death, bubonic plague as it's normally believed to have been. But we usually refer to the medieval experience of this plague as "the Black Death," and that pretty much tells you everything. It's as though death is not bad enough, so you call it the Black Death. That was a reference to the physiology of what happened with that disease and how the skin would blacken. It was a horrifying disease and a terrifying way to die, a very painful way to die, and a very quick way to die too. Medieval men and women didn't have a clue what caused it, why it was striking them, or how it spread. We're going to see that this experience contributed greatly to the breakdown of the medieval worldview. In a three-year period, this disease had entered from the fleas on the rats that came into the port cities of Italy primarily. The Black Death spread within three years across Europe to kill one third of the population. That's the best estimate. It's a little hard to arrive at precise figures, but that's the closest estimate that we have.

It's hard to wrap our minds around that, isn't it? But let's translate it in terms that you and I can understand. I mean, after 9/11 there has been a lot of talk about bio-terrorism. What would happen if there was a coordinated release in major metropolitan cities of the smallpox virus? Well, nobody is vaccinated against smallpox anymore. It's an extraordinarily contagious and virulent disease, with a very high mortality rate. But what would happen is that, depending on how quickly it was detected and people were quarantined, it's conceivable that a third of the American population could die in such a pandemic, such an outbreak. That would be about 100 million Americans dying in a two- or three-year period. Do you think that would have a profound impact upon American society? Do you think that would shake everything that we are to the foundation, our political institutions, our social or economic institutions, religious institutions? It would turn everything upside down. We cannot even imagine what our country or the world would look like in the aftermath of something like that. Not to mention a terrorist attack with nuclear weapons. What would that do? It's not enough to say it would have a major impact. It would be transformative in a way that we can't even conceive.

And this is the kind of scale we're talking about. This outbreak wasn't a terrorist thing at all; it wasn't man-made or man driven. It occurred as diseases do. But the impact of it was very similar. It shook to the foundation the certainty that medieval men and women had that they understood the world. It turned their world upside down. They thought they understood the world, this hierarchical world where everything was in its place—this great chain of being that they understood where everything was ranked according to power and authority, where God rewarded those who were good, the favored ones who occupied certain positions in life and so on.

And then comes the Black Death and it completely blows away all those expectations of what the world is like. How does it do that? This plague, like every plague, doesn't spread rationally; it spreads in ways that really defy explanation. And the Black Death spread in such a way that on one side of the street in a village everybody might die and on the other side of the street everybody might live; or everybody in one house might have been affected and everybody in the house right next to it was spared. Or in one valley one village was wiped out and the next village was left untouched. It made no sense, in other words. It didn't fit the way in which they understood the world through their worldview.

And when you encounter something that you can't explain in your worldview it turns everything upside down. I've mentioned C. S. Lewis in another context, but he's a good example of this. He was a great Christian apologist, one who wrote defenses of the faith that are still read and remain powerful today. But when his wife died of cancer, it shook his worldview to the foundation, and he didn't understand why God would bring this woman into his life only to take her away in a very short period of time. He went through a period of great doubt in searching and wondering about God and about the world, and he wrote some really beautiful and searching books in the aftermath of that experience. This is a good example on the small scale of what happens to one person when disaster strikes; But we're talking about a much bigger scale with the Black Death—an entire culture suddenly being faced with a massive challenge to its worldview. This is a picture I am trying to paint of this world in crisis in the late Middle Ages in the fourteenth century. Chaos has the ability to bring about this kind of radical systemic change in every aspect of society. Let's talk a little bit more about worldviews.

Paradigms and Paradigm Shifts

I'm going to introduce another term, which is probably not going to be a new term, but which we'll be using in a very particular way. The term I want to work with is **paradigm**, because when I am talking about worldviews, I will really be referring to "paradigms of reality." So, let's define paradigms in three ways.

First, consider the narrow, technical meaning of the word. Paradigms are grammatical sets you learn when you study a foreign language. When you study Spanish or French or Latin, you study paradigms of how to conjugate a verb. The first person singular, second person singular, third person singular, etc. That's a conjugation, a paradigm. It tells you what the proper form of the verb is for the context in which you are using it. So the first way that you can define a paradigm is to think of a grammatical model. In English the conjugation of a verb is pretty simple in the present tense. But here's the paradigm, nonetheless.

	Singular	Plural
1st	I sing	we sing
2nd	you sing	you sing
3rd	he, she, it sings	they sing

It's a simple paradigm; but note what the paradigm tells you. In the third person singular, it tells you to do something to the verb. It tells you to add an ending to it, to add an -s to the verb: he/she/ it sings. We sing, you sing, they sing. That's a paradigm in its most basic sense. It's a model that you plug information into in order to get an answer back from. So you have this model here which tells you how to conjugate a verb. You plug a question in—"How do you conjugate the verb *to sing* in the third-person singular"—and the paradigm gives you the answer. You put an -s on the end: he/she/it sings. This point is essential to how we are going to be defining a paradigm as an explanatory model into which you plug information or questions and out of which you're expecting to get answers. So, this leads logically to the second extended meaning that was mentioned a minute ago.

We also use the word *paradigm* to mean worldview—a set of assumptions, concepts, values, and practices that constitutes a way of viewing reality for the community that shares them. Well, that's just another definition of a worldview. But now think of a how a worldview is like that grammatical paradigm. Think of it as an explanatory model into which you plug a question or a problem and out of which you expect to get an answer.

Let's say that I, as a Christian, face some challenge in my life. Maybe I face some tragic events in my life. That's a challenge, that's the question that I have. What do I do? I take that, I plug it into the paradigm—my Christian faith, my biblical worldview—and out of that I get an answer to that situation. That answer will probably be something like, "God is Sovereign," "God is good," "There's sin in the world." Those things that the Bible affirms that are part of my worldview as a believer are the answers that I get as I plug my experiences, my questions, my challenges, into that Christian worldview. You can see why we can't live without worldviews. They're the structure that helps us to understand ourselves, our experience, the world around us, and even history.

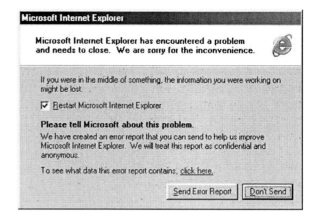

Related to this is a third definition, which is kind of putting a little twist on it and using an example or a metaphor here. We can think of a paradigm or a worldview as an intellectual computer—if not the hardware then at least the software that runs that computer. How do you use a computer? You sit down and you type data into a computer. Why? Typically, you want to process that information. You want to get something out of that. You might be plugging figures in. Those figures are processed and you get some kind of answer out of it.

You can see where I am going with this and how it's going to relate back to the fourteenth century. What happens when you plug data into your computer that the software program can't handle? We have all experienced this. We wanted to throw our computer out the window and then when we get rational about it we realize that we probably just have to upgrade our software. If it's not powerful enough to handle the things we are plugging into it, then it freezes up, it locks up, and you get one of those error messages that we dread.

Then you've got to reboot your computer. If that happens often enough, you're going to just give up on that system and you're going to get a more powerful computer or a better software package. That's why this metaphor of an intellectual computer makes a lot of sense, because at the end of the Middle Ages, their computer locked up. They were faced with things like the Black Death that they couldn't explain and the medieval system locked up.

Now why couldn't they explain what was happening? The Black Death, as I said, seemed completely random. They couldn't figure it out. Some tried to figure out the theology behind it, or the significance behind it, by saying that maybe God was judging them, that it was some kind of divine judgment; but even that didn't seem to make sense, because why is the village drunk who hangs out in the tavern all the time doing perfectly okay while the parish priest is dying of the Black Death? People high up in the church hierarchy were dying and lowlifes in the tavern were getting along just fine. Everything was upside down; it didn't make sense to them. The hierarchical model didn't explain it. So the computer froze up, locked up, and crashed. That's the picture I am trying to paint here. It's just a very simple way drawn from our own everyday experience of working with computers, but it helps us to understand the nature of what's happening here, the kind of change that's occurring at the end of the medieval period and the beginning of the modern. So what I want us to do now, having crashed the computer in the fourteenth century, is to look at how western culture began to reprogram its software in the fifteenth and sixteenth centuries.

What we are going to see now are what are call **paradigm shifts**, shifts in worldview, shifts in knowledge, shifts in ways of looking at the world. It's kind of a buzz term that's used in scholarship and has been through the last generation. But that's all that a paradigm shift means—a radical turning around and shifting in your way of looking at the world or your way of looking at a particular problem. I want to focus on four specific paradigm shifts and see how each one of these contributed to the re-making of the western world as we transition from the medieval hierarchical model to a new modern model of understanding reality. We'll associate four names with the paradigm shifts we examine. Most of these names will be familiar to you:

- Copernicus
- Columbus
- Gutenberg
- Luther

The most important thing that we are going to be doing is to look at these four figures and look at four paradigm shifts that followed on the heels of the chaos of the fourteenth century. The main thing to take from this is what each one of these men contributed to the making of the modern worldview.

The first figure is probably known to most of you: *Copernicus*. What field are we talking about? Astronomy. What was the view that was held in the ancient World and the medieval world about the structure of the cosmos in a physical sense? It's known as the **geocentric** or Ptolemaic view, in which the earth is at the center of everything and the planets and the sun are revolving around the earth. The stars were seen as fixed points rotating around the earth. They pictured them like little pinholes of light in a black curtain. This is the conception that they had in the ancient and the medieval world. Copernicus comes along and he observes and he calculates and he observes again. He says: "We've got it all wrong; we have had it wrong for hundreds of years. Actually, the geocentric view," he says, "is flat out wrong. The earth is not at the center. Rather, in our solar system at least, the sun is at the center and the earth is going around the sun and all the other planets are as well." This is a radical change in thinking and it's called the **Copernican Revolution**, which tells you that scholars and historians measure this as a highly significant moment in the history of western thought.

It was like an intellectual earthquake in its significance, in the way it rattled people's view of the world. It took a few hundred years for it to settle into people's consciousness. Galileo later picked up the Copernican idea and developed it more and had to battle with the authority of the Catholic Church on this point. But really, what Copernicus is saying and going from the geocentric to the **heliocentric** view of astronomy is that the old books of astronomy are wrong. The old authorities are wrong. We have to throw those old books out. I mean he didn't literally say that, but this is the implication of it. We've got to get rid of the old books; we've got to rewrite them. We've got to observe, we've got to calculate, we've got to figure out what the truth is, and we can't just believe something to be true because somebody authoritative high up the hierarchies told us it's true.

You can see how this is starting to chip away at the old hierarchical medieval worldview. Before, you just received what's true passed down to you through the chain of command. Copernicus and all those who followed in his wake say, "Now, we've got to figure what's true out for ourselves." This is one of the watchwords of the modern world, that we come to truth individually. We come to it through our own experience, we come to it through the scientific method, and we see this as a powerful implication of the Copernican Revolution.

Let me give one more implication as well, one more consequence of the Copernican Revolution. This is the one that's taken a few hundred years to really settle into the consciousness of the Western mind. If you live in the Middle Ages and you believe the Earth is the center of everything, then that's a pretty important and privileged place to be, right in the middle of God's creation. You can't get any more important than that, everything revolves around you.

Copernicus and all of those who followed him are basically challenging that view and saying, "Well, how significant is man? How significant is man really?" Now, with the

scientific materialist worldview today, it's not uncommon to hear scientists, astronomers, and so on, describing man as just a rather insignificant byproduct of random natural forces crawling on this little rock known as Earth. In others words, there is nothing special about us. That's the view that has settled into the western mind after five hundred or six hundred years of thinking about Copernicus. And that's again part of the modern worldview. Obviously the Middle Ages had it wrong about the geocentric view, but they had it right about the idea that man is the crowning achievement of God's creation made in the image of God. The problem is that this theology got thrown out too.

Let's move onto the next name on the list, and a name that we all recognize: *Columbus*. We're using him as a representative of all the other discoverers as well in that period that's known as the Age of Discovery, the discovery of the New World. Just as men were looking at the stars and the planets and trying to figure out the universe, so also they're looking at their own world and trying to understand it better and not just taking what some old books says about it. The goal is to see and understand the world for themselves; and so they head out in ships to do this.

And what do you know; they run into continents that nobody knew existed. And they

177

find people living on those continents that nobody have ever heard of. That would be profoundly disorienting. You think you are finding a passage to India, and you run smack into this major continent, and you go look at your old maps and you look at your geography books, and you try to figure out what this land mass is—but it's not there. Complete continents are found: North America, South America, and then, in the eighteenth century when Australia was discovered, at least by western Europeans. What are these places and who are these people? Are they the lost tribes of Israel? I mean all these kinds of crazy ideas emerge trying to figure these things out. And there were plants and animals in these places that you don't recognize, so you go to the books of botany and zoology and you can't find what these animals and these plants are. So what do you do? Just as Copernicus did: if your astronomy books are wrong, then throw them out and rewrite them. Now you've got to rewrite your maps, too; and you've got to rewrite your histories. You've got to rewrite all of this stuff and go back to the drawing board.

In other words, authority is being challenged in many different ways. In the Middle Ages, how do you know something is true? If you are a medieval peasant how do you know what do you take for granted about the world? Whatever you were told, what somebody higher up the chain of command tells you. The earth is the center of the universe and Europe is the center of the globe; this is what is told about the world and people believe that. It's what's passed down in the old books. But we don't accept authority like this anymore, and so these paradigm shifts help us to understand where we're at right now in the western world. You and I are expected to find things out for ourselves. You don't accept something to be true because somebody has told you, but rather because you figured it out for yourself. That's what the scientific method is all about. You test it, you experience it, you put it to the test in a laboratory, and you see if it's true. You don't just accept it as true because somebody said so.

So look at what we've done: we've thrown out the old astronomy books, we've thrown out the old maps, the old geography books, the old history books, the old zoology books, the old botany books. What is the ultimate old book that's going to get thrown out in the modern period while we're throwing everything else out? The Bible is the oldest and the most authoritative of these books that's going to get thrown out in the modern age. Do you see how that's part of a pattern? And so modern secular people don't accept the authority of an old book any longer just because somebody says so; from their perspective, it's just another old book and it doesn't have any claim over our modern lives. This is a trend of modern thinking and you can see how it's all part of this process of these paradigm shifts, different ways of looking at the world around us, different ways of understanding what is true about the world.

The next figure on our list is a little bit different in terms of his contribution, but we'll see how this connects up as well. *Gutenberg* is credited with the development of movable type, or printing. Well, let me ask you another leading question. In the Middle Ages who had books? The clergy had books, monks had books, priests had ac-

178

cess to books. You and I in the Middle Ages would not have had access to books. You couldn't just go to a public library; they didn't have public libraries back then. People didn't know how to read and write. There wasn't widespread literacy in the medieval world, and so what happens with Gutenberg is that suddenly books can be mass-produced. What is that going to do? It's going to take books out of the hands of the church. It's going to take books out of the hierarchy, right? Because now you don't have to have a roomful of monks who are copying manuscripts in a very costly process; now you can mass produce. The price is going to go down and access will go up.

We see a rise of literacy, and now people will have access to books starting in the late Middle Ages and the early modern period. It's an amazing thing. We go from this vertical model of the hierarchy where only people in the hierarchy had access to knowledge and held it pretty close to their chest. Here in the modern age we expect to have equal access to knowledge and literacy, public education and public libraries, newspapers and all the various forms of media. Now in our lifetime the rise of the Internet is keeping in line with this trend. It's just another extension of what Gutenberg was trying to do six hundred years ago: bringing knowledge to everybody, making it more democratic, making it more horizontal, breaking the stranglehold on knowledge held by the hierarchy.

So with each one of these paradigm shifts we're going from this top-down vertical model to a horizontal one. Although the horizontal model may be a better way of learning, isn't the vertical hierarchy needed in society? Absolutely, and this is where I think the Christian has a lot to say to society today as we look at this, because radical individualism ultimately leads to anarchy. If everybody is searching for his own truth for himself, isn't that kind of the world we live in? People increasingly define truth around themselves: "That might be true for you," people will say, "but it's not true for me." It's one of the classic clichés of postmodernism. But what on earth does that

mean? I mean it obviously shows a very limited knowledge of what truth is if truth can be so easily altered from one person to the next. What the Christian affirms is that there is something that is hierarchically known and it's divine revelation, passed down from God to man.

But, let's look at the last figure on our list, *Luther*, and see if we can balance this out a little bit. As necessary as hierarchies still are for us today, we clearly don't accept all these other hierarchical notions of the Middle Ages such as the oppressive and repressive notions of medieval Catholicism. I think we would, as modern Christians, want to reject the worst aspects of hierarchical thinking, even while we affirm the fact that God has revealed Himself to us divinely. Well, let's look at the fourth figure on our list. I think it can help us see our way to the resolution of this dilemma—this tension between vertical and horizontal approaches to truth. Martin Luther is one of the great figures of the Reformation. Notice how Martin Luther, like all these other figures, is challenging the medieval hierarchy. Let me ask you one more leading question. If you're a medieval Catholic, how do you think you come to God? What is the basis of your relationship with God? Through the priest, through the church, through the hierarchy; that's how you're supposed to come to God. Martin Luther says that is absolutely wrong; he goes back to scripture and challenges that. He says, "Forget that hierarchical stuff. We come to God as individuals." You've heard the expression, "The ground is level at the foot of the cross." What Martin Luther is saying, what the Reformation is all about, is that we don't come to God through some hierarchy; we come to God as individuals by faith, through the grace that we see in the work of Christ on the cross. We come to God through Christ as individuals. Notice how the Reformation can even be seen as part of this larger process of shifting from this medieval hierarchical view to a horizontal modern view of looking at the world. And that's the great shift—from vertical to horizontal—that defines the transition from the medieval to the modern world.

PORTAL TO THE MODERN AGE
17

Chapter Objectives

- Give a concise explanation for how the Renaissance initiated the modern age.
- Describe how Leonardo da Vinci illustrates key ideas of the Renaissance.
- Define and illustrate the central value of Renaissance thought--humanism.

As we saw in the last chapter, the Middle Ages came to a rather bleak end. Within the medieval hierarchical system, people couldn't make sense of what was happening to them. A different worldview—the modern worldview—is going to emerge from all this chaos; and although there will be much "truth" in the new way of looking at the world in terms of the scientific advances and so on, there is going to be much error that we are going to want to see as well, primarily as we see the rise of humanism in modern culture.

Once again, we are at a period of change, a period of transition as we're leaving the Middle Ages and entering the modern world. So all those old questions of how a culture changes come right at us again, and we don't have simple answers to any of those questions. We are going to try to define some things, we are going to label some things, and we are going to mark off historical periods and talk about them as if we know what we are talking about. But really, the emperor has no clothes as we

study the past and the reality is we don't have much of a clue about how and why things change the way they do. Our attitude when we look at a historical phenomenon this complex should be one of humility as we approach it from a scholarly point of view. We should recognize how little we really know in the face of the sovereignty of God over history.

Historians grapple with complex problems like this and they give it their best shot; but we always fall short of a complete answer. The Renaissance is like that. Literally, a period of cultural "rebirth," the **Renaissance** is the portal into the modern age. We leave the Middle Ages and the rubble of the hierarchical worldview behind and we see in the Renaissance that men are struggling to create a new world. That's why we will be referring to the Renaissance as the portal, or gateway into the modern age. The humanists we'll be studying—artists and intellectuals of the fifteenth and sixteenth centuries—saw themselves as "modern" men. That was their word; they coined it to describe the time they lived in. They knew they were leaving the Middle Ages behind and they were struggling to figure out what are going to be the values now of this new world they were helping to create. We want to look at where they got inspiration from and what motivated them. What were the values that resonated with them as they looked at the past? These are the questions we'll be exploring in this chapter.

Background to the Renaissance

But as we enter into this portal, I want to emphasize once again that the Renaissance, like the fall of Rome, is a great historical problem. That's a description I don't use lightly or casually. It means something very specific. We defined it once before but let's define it again in this context so that we can be reminded of the difficulty of what we are doing when we try to make sense of a period like this. *A historical problem is a set of circumstances so complex that it defies easy explanation*. And having said that, I always quickly add that an easy explanation is exactly what you and I, as human beings, want. We simplify, we generalize; sometimes we oversimplify and overgeneralize in our attempt to understand and make sense of things. But we want the easy answer—and history doesn't give easy answers up very easily. Certainly, not as you look at the fall of Rome; what caused it? We don't have a clue.

What caused the Renaissance? We don't know. We have ideas, of course, but we can't explain all the complexity of what was going on in western culture that led to a "rebirth." We don't necessarily have explanations; but we have interpretations and theories, and that's what I'll be giving you as we go through this. Obviously, we know there was something that happened that was transforming in Europe in the fourteenth, fifteenth and sixteenth centuries. We know it because we see the change in culture, we see the change in art, we see the change in all the institutions of western culture. We labeled it the Renaissance and we are going to be trying our best to make sense of that. Let me start with the definition. We will just go with a textbook definition of the Renaissance. We will go through this carefully and draw out the meaning of the different phrases and terms that we are going to use.

The Renaissance was a great cultural movement that brought about a period of scientific revolution and artistic transformation at the dawn of modern European history.

Now, you and I think that we live in the modern world. We think the modern world is synonymous with our generation. It's kind of a way in which people have always thought about these things; but history teaches us to take a very long view. The modern age is actually several hundred years in the making. Historians usually date is as five or six hundred years. We are probably at the tail end of the modern age; actually, we are entering into something different as we analyze the historical trends that we see. The Renaissance as I said is the portal that gets us into the modern age. If we are going to understand the values of this world we live in right now, then we will have to come to terms with how these humanistic thinkers at the dawn of the modern age were looking at the world and looking at the past.

Let's isolate two aspects of the Renaissance from this definition. First, note the phrase "scientific revolution." Science really does define much of the modern age. We look at the world right now on the breathtaking pace of technological advance. We look at the phenomenal scientific accomplishments of the twentieth century, and science is very much a reality of the last half a millennium. We see that coming to fruition in the period of the Renaissance. The scientific revolution of the seventeenth century is something we'll examine more fully in a few chapters.

The second thing to note is the phrase, "artistic transformation." Clearly, the art of the Renaissance is going to undergo a major facelift, and it's going to be defined by new styles and new ways of looking at the world. This is the age of Michelangelo, of Leonardo da Vinci. Other great artists of this period that we're going to be looking at are Raphael and Botticelli. This is one of the high points in all of Western cultural history. So clearly, we think of these two things as direct outgrowths and consequences of whatever this phenomenon is that we're calling the "Renaissance."

Scientific revolution points us to the notion of rationalism, the faculty of human reasoning. This is the belief that the human mind, reason, the critical faculty can comprehend the world, can figure out the mysteries of the universe. We found that the Greeks believed that their rational minds could do that. Rationalism was one of those keywords that we used to understand Greek culture, their philosophy, the way they produced their art and their architecture as an expression of human reason. And we're going to see that in the modern age, rationalism is clearly a philosophy of our time as well. You look around at modern scientific thinking and in our own time, and there is this extraordinary pride, this hubris about what man can do and what man can figure out, the notion that science will unlock and unravel the great mysteries of human life and the origins of the cosmos. And that rationalism, so typical of the ancient Greeks, is reborn in the modern age in this period that we call the Renaissance.

There's another word that should come to mind; and that is "humanism." We can relate this concept to the phrase "artistic transformation" in our definition. We're going to see in the art of the Renaissance, in the art of Michelangelo, da Vinci, and so on, that humanism is the hallmark. It's the philosophy that motivates them in all they do. They believe deeply in the dignity and worth of human beings and human existence, and they are setting that up as the standard for all that they do in culture— in the way they paint, in the way they sculpt, in the way they philosophize about the world. This is true of the Renaissance and it was also true of the ancient Greeks. The ancient Greeks were humanists, just as the ancient Greeks were rationalists. What is this pointing us to? The Renaissance is the rebirth of classical values and classical ideas having to do with ancient Greek and Roman culture.

Well, what about the Middle Ages? Didn't these artists and intellectuals, standing at the dawn of the modern age, draw inspiration from the Middle Ages as well? No. The Renaissance humanists looked back at the period that immediately preceded them with contempt. The last thing they wanted to be was *medieval*. That old hierarchical

way of looking at the world was something they were rejecting. People like Michelangelo and da Vinci saw themselves as Christians, but they didn't want to be like medieval Christians. They wanted to be more like the ancient Greeks—rationalists and humanists. We're going to see them trying to do that, to be Christians on the one hand as well as being classical humanists on the other. Good luck trying to mix truth and error, but that's what they're trying to do. It will be a fool's errand to try to be a "Christian humanist." But we're going to see that a whole lot of really good art will be produced in pursuit of that unattainable goal.

Ultimately, that project will fail, as Michelangelo, late in his life, would acknowledge. He looked back at the works that he created, so full of humanistic ideas and philosophy, and he looked back at that with regret and realized that it was a failure. He would in a sense repent of those motives. We are going to be able to look back and see what they were trying to do as they tried to synthesize these two values that just don't go together at all—Christianity and pagan classical humanism. They had contempt for the Middle Ages, and by the way, with that in mind, let me just say a couple of things about the terminology that we are using here.

These men that I am referring to, these Renaissance humanists of the fifteenth century, they pretty much came up with the terms that we are using. They invented the word "modern," as we've seen. They also came up with the terms "Middle Ages" and "medieval." As they looked at this period that they had contempt for and wanted to get away from, they called it the Middle Ages. They viewed it as the unfortunate period of time between the classical age of the Greeks and Romans and their own age, the modern age. The Middle Ages—that was just the forgettable stuff in between, in the middle of two glorious periods.

These Renaissance humanists also gave us the word "classical." They looked back at the Greeks and the Romans and they said, "Those guys were the classics. That was the

Classic Age. We want to be like them." Finally, they also gave us the word "Gothic," as in Gothic architecture. Remember those great cathedrals, those masterpieces of stone and glass? These Renaissances humanists of the fifteenth century weren't terribly impressed by those at all. They looked at them as decadent, as everything that classical architecture was not. They judged Gothic architecture by the standards of Greek architecture, which is a foolish thing to do. Gothic churches weren't trying to be Greek temples; and yet they looked at it that way and they demeaned and downgraded the style as *Gothic*—that is, the style (as they wrongly believed it to be) of the Gothic tribes that destroyed Rome. They wanted to revive Greek and Roman styles of architecture in opposition to the medieval styles in building cathedrals.

So they are looking at the Middle Ages contemptuously, and they are looking at the classical world with reverence and trying to draw their inspiration from those values. That's why they are rationalists. That's why they are humanists as the Greeks were.

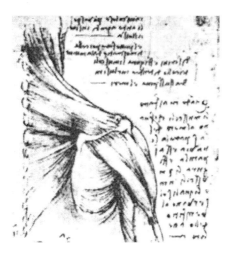

Can you think of a Renaissance figure right off the top of your head who would best illustrate both of these qualities of rationalism and humanism of scientific revolution and artistic transformation, these two aspects of the renaissance? Leonardo da Vinci is called a Renaissance man. What we mean by that is somebody who is deeply curious about the world and all aspects of knowledge, art and science alike—and da

Vinci really illustrates that. This deep curiosity about the world is reflected in his notebooks. These are drawings from the notebooks of Leonardo da Vinci, our classic Renaissance man, who illustrates the new science and new art. Look at what he is drawing and thinking about. He is sketching out the human body and the muscle structure, for example. (See above.) He knew what the muscle structure was like because he would actually dissect cadavers so that he could get a better understanding of the underlying muscular and skeletal structure of the human body. He didn't have some macabre interest in that. That's not what motivated him. It was a scientific curiosity to understand the human body as a scientific phenomenon, but he was also thinking as an artist, not just as a scientist. He figured that if he could see the skeletal structure and the muscular structure of the body, he would able to draw and paint the body more realistically as an artist.

So you see both of these qualities at work, science and art. He is trying to figure out how we can harness the laws of nature, and scientific knowledge and principles of mathematics, to create helicopters, to create parachutes. (See above.) He is studying and measuring the structure of trees and plants. The mind of science, the mind of art, bringing these things together, blending them together, trying to understand the world, not just receiving the knowledge that's passed down through the old medieval hierarchy, but rather as a modern man trying to figure it out for himself, scientifically, putting it to the test, calculating, checking in out for himself. We see that new spirit of modern thinking very clearly illustrated in da Vinci. There's much more to da Vinci than the "Mona Lisa." Behind that famous painting lies a boundless curiosity about the world.

The Renaissance is divided into three periods: early, middle, and late. The early Renaissance period is usually dated from 1400 to 1475. The most important form of art that's driving the Renaissance at this point is architecture. Artists are rediscovering the architectural forms of the ancient world, and as they do that, they make certain discoveries about perspective and then they bring that into art and it transforms the way they paint, the way they sculpt. But architecture is really the leading edge of what's going on in the early Renaissance.

The High Renaissance period is a 50-year period from 1475 to 1525. This is the period of greatest achievement in the Renaissance, the period of Michelangelo, of Leonardo da Vinci, of Raphael, the greatest masters of the Renaissance. This is the period of the greatest works of the Renaissance. If you think of da Vinci's paintings, the "Mona Lisa" is unquestionably one of the two or three most famous paintings in the world: it has a whole life of its own, and legends abound about this work, and all kinds of myths associated with it. Without a doubt the greatest work of the High Renaissance is by Michelangelo, and it's really a series of works. It's the great paintings of the Sistine Chapel in the Vatican. These are the great paintings that he did on the walls and on the ceilings of that chapel in the Vatican, where he recounts the whole story from creation to last judgment that we see in scripture. Arguably, this is the single greatest work of art in the entire history of the West, and it's associated with this period of the High Renaissance.

Finally, the Late Renaissance runs from roughly 1525 to 1600. It's another period of change, obviously. We see the Renaissance style becoming exaggerated as it changes into later forms. We are not going to say a whole lot about this period, certainly not at this point. Rather, our focus is going to be on the High Renaissance. Most of the works of art that we are going to analyze come from that period, from 1475 to 1525.

Humanism and the Renaissance

Let's come back to the question of what motivated these humanists at the dawn of the modern age. What did they see as they looked past the Middle Ages, leap-frogging that age all the way back to the classical world? What did they see in the Greeks and the Romans that inspired them so much? I want to focus here on Renaissance humanism, because I think this is an important key to understanding this age, its art, all of the things that they produced, their philosophy, and so on. To do this, let's go back and see what they saw when they looked at the Greeks. What kind of humanism was modeled for them in ancient culture? What is the formula, as I would put it, of humanism, and how do we see that in Greek and then in Renaissance life? Again, this is a key to the Renaissance. That's why I am focusing on this philosophy. I would argue that humanism has two aspects to it. It starts with something and it ends with something, and again, the Greeks are our guide here.

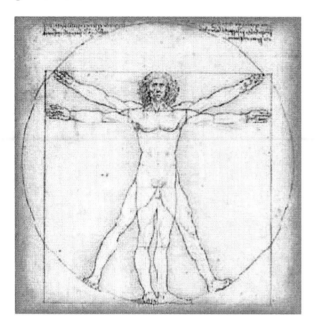

First, we see that humanism begins with what I would call introspection. You look inward: self-examination, self-knowledge, self-discovery, or a less flattering way to call it would be navel-gazing, but looking at yourself, fixated on yourself, looking inward, obsessed with who you are, taking yourself as the point of departure. Does that sound like the ancient Greeks? Yes, that was what they thought was the beginning of wisdom. That's why Socrates said, "Know thyself." You look inward, and you believe that the philosophical life is the life of self-knowledge and self-discovery. You can see how that's going to breed a philosophy of humanism, but you don't stop there. You begin with that, looking inward, and then you take what you find inside and you project it on the world.

Second, we see that humanism ends with projection. It begins with introspection and it ends with the projection outward of what you find inside. Protagoras said, "Man is the measure of all things." Man is the measuring stick, the standard by which all things are gauged. You figure out who you are, you figure out what man is, and then you measure the world by that. You project that out on the world. That sounds like the Greeks, it sounds like the Renaissance, and it sounds like modern humanism too. So this is the formula of what humanism is. This is what motivated these Renaissance humanists, as we are going to see.

Well, let's look at that humanism as they defined it, and as the Renaissance gave expression to that. What I want to do is, first, to look at a literary expression of that humanism in the Renaissance and, second, to look at a visual example of that humanism. We've defined what humanism is, and we see that the Renaissance is taking its cues from the Greeks. Now let's see how they gave expression to that—first in literature and secondly in their art.

The literary example that I want to give comes from a humanist writer named Pico della Mirandola. In 1486 he wrote an essay called *"Oration on the Dignity of Man."* This falls right in the period of the High Renaissance, the greatest period of achievement. This is when Mirandola is making this famous statement of Renaissance humanism. Mirandola is imagining God speaking to His creation, Adam. Mirandola is going to put a lot of words in the mouth of God that don't belong there. He is offering a kind of humanistic commentary on the opening chapters of Genesis, and it's very revealing to see how he interprets the story of the creation of man. Here's what Mirandola's God says to Adam:

"The nature of all other beings is limited and constrained within the bounds of laws prescribed by Us. Thou, constrained by no limits, in accordance with thine own free will, in whose hands We have placed thee, shalt ordain for thyself the limits of thy nature. We have made thee neither of heaven nor of earth, neither mortal nor immortal, so that with freedom of choice and with honor, as though the maker and molder of thyself, thou mayest fashion thyself in whatever shape thou shalt prefer. Thou shalt have the power to degenerate into the lower forms of life, which are brutish. Thou shalt have the power, out of thy soul's judgment, to be reborn into the higher forms, which are divine."

God is saying to Adam: "Look around you, look at the animals. Every other creature that I've made is bound by laws that are written into those creatures." We call those laws instinct; they live according to instinct, and they live by impulse. God is saying to Adam, "You're different from that. You are not determined by your nature, not determined by your instincts, you are indeterminate." God is saying: "Adam, you can pretty much define what you want to be. The sky is the limit. I have created you; I have given you free will. I've given you the opportunity to take that and run with it." It's like the old army ads that used to be on TV said, "Be all that you can be." That's what God is saying to Adam. Take this free will and see how far you can run with it.

Well, I have got a lot of problems with that way of interpreting what God is saying to Adam but it gets worse as we move along. You know, if we just stop here, I mean it's like God is telling to Adam, "The reason why I created you is just to see what you can make of yourself, to see how far you could pull yourself up by your own bootstraps, to see how glorious a creature you could make of yourself." What a profane thing to put in the mouth of God. Scripture clearly teaches that man is made for the glory not of himself but of God, that we are to be vassals reflecting God's glory. It's not about you and me and how much we can make of our lives, and look at what we made of our lives. It's all about what God can make of us.

And certainly, as we look at the work of Christ, it's what Christ can make of us as he indwells us. You can see where this is just going wrong from the get-go here as an interpretation of Genesis. It gets worse. God tells Adam that he is the "maker and molder" of himself. It's as though God wants to see Adam turn himself into a work of art by his own effort. God gives the raw material, and we do the rest. This was a very key idea in the Renaissance. People like da Vinci and Mirandola and Michelangelo saw their lives as works of art. They saw themselves as making and molding themselves as a Renaissance man. That's what

da Vinci was doing. That's why he pursued knowledge and science; he was trying to make of his life a work of art, to be a self-made man, to give expression to what Mirandola is putting in the mouth of God here.

God finally says to Adam, "Thou shalt have the power to degenerate into the lower forms of life which are brutish. Thou shalt have the power out of thy soul's judgment"—notice this—"to be reborn into the higher forms which are divine." It is amazing to think that Mirandola would have considered himself a good Christian. He doesn't see himself as some heretic, or someone who is way off the path of truth, and yet, this is how he is interpreting what God says to Adam, "You will be reborn into the higher forms which are divine." What is so incredible about that? It's because somebody in Genesis does say that very thing to Adam, and he is not God. Who says that to Adam? The serpent does. These are the words of Satan. "Here, disregard what God said, take this fruit because God's withholding this good thing from you, take this fruit and you will be like God," the Serpent says to Adam and Eve.

And here we have got Mirandola: Does he not know what he is saying? He puts these words in the mouth of God. It's so profane, it's so blasphemous when you think of it, and this is a good introduction to the arrogance and the humanism of the Renaissance. This is how they thought. This is how they evaluated themselves. This is what they thought they could do with their lives. No thanks to God, they are going to do it on their own effort. Kind of sounds like the ancient Greeks again. You can certainly see where they are taking their cues from.

Well, we've seen a literary example of this humanism, this emphasis on man is the standard and the measuring stick of reality and all things. Let's look finally now at a visual example of this same concept, the same humanism, the very famous illustration of Michelangelo's Creation of Adam. It's the same story that Mirandola was telling us about. I am sure you recognize this very famous painting. Here, Michelangelo depicts

Adam in that split second before he becomes a living soul, and notice how he's leaning forward. There's a languid, sluggish look to him. He leans forward, he is looking towards God. God floats in on His bank of clouds, very much looking like this old man in the sky with this beard and everything—all these stereotypical ways of depicting God. He is floating in on this cloud, He is reaching out towards Adam and Adam is reaching out towards God, and as you can see, the fingers have not yet touched. It's that split second before life has breathed into him and he becomes a living soul.

But what's amazing about this beautiful artistic rendering of this, is that it's absolutely wrong on one level, the same way that Mirandola's interpretation is absolutely wrong. We see Michelangelo giving expression to this same idea of man as a self-creating being, one who participates in his own creation. Look at Adam again. He is in a sense leaning out to meet God halfway. You might say that God's drawing him, maybe you could argue that. I think that in the context of what Mirandola said, however, you have to see Adam participating in his own creation, and this is how they really saw man in the world, as the highest of God's creation. That's true, that much is biblical; but somewhere along the way they lose the sense of the fact that man is created out of clay. We are created out of dust, and we are nothing apart from God.

We are to be vessels that reflect the glory of God. We are not the subject of creation. Humanism says that. Humanism says it's all about us. The Bible says it's all about God. So you see Michelangelo giving this man-centered take on creation the same way that Mirandola did. And we see, illustrated beautifully in the heart of Catholicism, right in the heart of the Vatican, this tribute to pagan humanism. A lot of irony right there, and we see it expressed as well in the oration of Mirandola.

Now as we pick up on this theme in the next chapter, we're going to see that the art that they created was a glorious art, like no art of any other period in all of western history, motivated by these values that are so off-base theologically. But we'll see that it's a brilliant art nonetheless.

ART AND HUMANISM

Chapter Objectives

- Define the art of the Renaissance by listing four key characteristics.
- Demonstrate how we see the modern age emerging in the art of this period.
- Show how Renaissance artists were reviving classical ideas in their art.

Among the few things we can say with any certainty about the Renaissance is that it is a revival of interest in the ancient world and a revival of the values of ancient Greece and Rome. Foremost among those are the values of rationalism and humanism. Humanism always begins with the self looking inward; and then what you do with that is you take it and project it out on the world as a kind of measuring stick and your understanding of the world is based on your understanding of yourself. That really is the core idea of what humanist philosophy is all about.

Certainly that's the case with the Renaissance and we are going to see this illustrated in the works of art that we'll be exploring in this chapter. We saw that "The Oration on Human Dignity" by Mirandola challenged us to think about humanism with its bold declaration that man is the "maker and molder of himself." That phrase that we highlighted is a key that really unlocks so much of Renaissance philosophy, art and culture. What we see in a figure like Leo-

nardo da Vinci is nothing less than a Renaissance humanist who is trying to be the maker and the molder of himself. What we see in the case of Michelangelo is a life dedicated to arts and beauty, a life dedicated to the humanistic pursuits of self-knowledge. What we see here is nothing less than man attempting to be the maker and the molder of himself. But these are really values that are foundational to the modern world. This notion of being a self-made man, of taking the resources of human thought, ingenuity and rationalism and building a life on that, and building a culture and a society on that, and these are the things that we see today just as surely as we see those same humanistic values in the Renaissance and beyond that among the ancient Greeks.

We're going to be looking now in greater detail at the Renaissance achievement, and we'll see once again these values of rationalism and humanism everywhere we look as we work through the art of the Renaissance. We are going to isolate four qualities, four aspects that make up the Renaissance achievement. What should emerge from this very brief overview of Renaissance art—too brief an overview for so vast a subject—is a clear picture of how these men like Mirandola and Michelangelo and da Vinci looked at the world around them and themselves. How they asked the big questions about the nature of reality and how they sought for answers to those questions and then how they expressed that in the beautiful art that they produced.

A Revival of Interest in Classical Subjects

The first quality that we see in Renaissance art is the logical beginning point for everything that follows, and really builds on the things that we said up until this point. This is the revival of interest in classical themes and subjects. If you were an artist in the Middle Ages, what would be the subjects that you would spend your time painting or sculpting? Biblical themes, church subjects. You could paint the Virgin Mary and then you could paint the Virgin Mary and then you could paint maybe a saint and then you could paint the Virgin Mary and so on. It's very repetitive, the list of subjects that you can paint or sculpt as a medieval artist.

It would be absolutely inconceivable for you as a young medieval artist, just starting out as an apprentice in a studio to walk in there on your first day and say, "You know what, I've got some new ideas about art. I think we've really done the Virgin Mary theme to death and I've got this idea, maybe we should start painting some new themes, maybe some pagan classical goddesses would be a good theme for us to explore and paint." You could never consider that option as a medieval painter, it couldn't even occur to you in that hierarchical worldview that we talked about, because what the church sanctioned is what you thought and what you did, and you would not even have conceived of the possibility of painting anything else. So the kinds of things we're looking at here are truly radical and truly revolutionary, in the sense that they break out of the mold of medieval subject matter, medieval values, and medieval ideas that were sanctioned within the hierarchy of the church of the Middle Ages. A late medieval masterpiece, "Madonna and Child Enthroned" by the Italian master Cimabue (c. 1280) illustrates well the art of the late Middle Ages.

We are going to look at two examples of these radical new subjects in Renaissance painting. The first of these, and it's the best example to start with really and it's one that you will find in any textbook on the Renaissance, is a painting by Sandro Botticelli that he did in 1482 known as "The Birth of Venus." (See Color Illustration K.) The title alone tells you that this is something completely new. It's not the Virgin Mary, it's not this saint or that saint, it is Venus, classical pagan fertility goddess. Now to you and me that just looks like an old painting by an old master. It doesn't knock us back on our feet as we look at it, or take our breath away without radical and revolutionary laws, but in the fifteenth century this was something entirely new.

It is a pretty marked departure from the norm, and this is the point I am emphasizing here: there is a revival of interest in classical themes. Venus is a classical goddess. Now, you can imagine how exciting that would be for an artist. You can now explore all kinds of themes that have been painted for hundreds of years and you can develop your craft and your skill in depicting the human form in the way the wind that blows through Venus' hair and so on, is the nymphs, the gods of the air and so on, and the wind pushing her forward. This is a depiction of a mythological birth, and here she emerges from the ocean riding onto land on an open clamshell.

That's a ridiculous story, just on the face of it, as far as subject matter goes. But the point is that it's something new and it allows the artist to explore the human form, the human figure, new styles and subject matter, and to do so with a completely new set of ideas and values. But the amazing thing is that as fresh and new and revolutionary as this work of art is, it's also old.

There is something of the old in this very new painting. The more you look at Venus, in the center of the canvas, the more she starts to look familiar to you, that is, if you are looking at it from the vantage point of medieval art. Look at Cimabue and Botticelli side by side, and you realize what Botticelli has done. Here we've got the Virgin Mary, here we have got Venus, and suddenly we realize what's going on here, Botticelli is creating something that is revolutionary, that is new, but it's based on the traditions of the past. Where did he learn to paint this kind of archetypal female form? He learned it from the medieval style that he inherits. It's the style Renaissance painters learned and studied in the studios and are now moving beyond. Let's isolate the features of this that are similar as we compare Venus

and the Virgin Mary side by side.

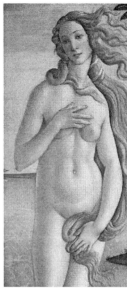

Let me give you three shared characteristics that we could isolate here. Let's start with the most basic thing we can see. First of all notice the oval shape to the head, very characteristic of the Virgin Mary, and you can see that here in this medieval painting, you can see that in the Venus painting right here.

Second, notice the slight tilting of the head. This is very characteristic of the iconic portrayals of the Virgin Mary. The head is slightly at an angle, and this softens her image a little; it brings a maternal quality to her form. She is usually holding the Christ Child and her head is slightly at an angle as she looks down at Him. But we see that the head of Venus is slightly tilted as well in that same style of the traditional medieval depictions of the Virgin Mary.

Third, and this is the one that really interests me—notice the position of the arms and the hands, which is like the very traditional way of the medieval painting of the Virgin Mary. Now there is a very practical reason for this in the medieval portraits. She is cradling the Christ Child with the lower arm and with the upper arm she is pointing to Him. But we come now to the Renaissance depiction of Venus and we see that her arms and her hands are positioned very similarly. There is another very practical reason for that; she is covering herself

191

up. But beyond that we see that Botticelli has taken this traditional form and he is adapting it. Remember, this is the quality of genius that we identified in Myron's "Discus Thrower," that great fifth century Greek work of the athlete hurling the discus. As revolutionary as that was, it was also very traditional in that you could see the old form of the Egyptian style kouros of frontality in that style of art. We are looking at something very similar. We are looking at a work that's a transitional work from an older form to a newer form, and it still exhibits many of the stylistic features of the old form.

Now, let's take that and turn it into a symbol of the Renaissance. What is it that these humanists in the Renaissance are trying to do? What is it that Mirandola was trying to do? Mirandola would have considered himself a good Christian and yet, as we see in his interpretation of the Genesis account of the creation of man, gives us a very humanistic account of that story. What are all of these Renaissance figures trying to do? They are trying to bring their Christianity and their classical pagan humanism over here and bring the two of them together. That's something that they're not going to be successful at doing. We saw that Mirandola wasn't too successful and we're seeing that it's not a very successful thing even in a work of art like this. It creates a beautiful work of art, but, there are a lot of internal contradictions here. Again, turning it into a symbol, this figure of Venus is both a pagan classical goddess, but she is also the Virgin Mary. Another way of putting that is that these humanists are trying to put a Christian head on a pagan goddess. They are trying to bring Christianity and paganism together. It's not going to work. A lot of great art is produced in the process, but it is bound to fail. It is bound to fail because the biblical message is all about the glory of God. Humanism is all about the glory of man, and you can't mix the glory of God and the glory of man. It's going to compromise the truth and so we are going to see that.

Let's look at a second example of this Re-

naissance obsession with classical culture, Raphael's "The School of Athens." (See below, and Color Illustration L.) This is a great work of art painted around 1510.

What Raphael is trying to do here is pay tribute to the classical world. Let's look in greater detail at some of the figures that are in this painting just to get a sense of what Raphael is trying to do. He is basically saying, "This is where we're drawing our inspiration from, the world of the Greeks, the classical world."

We are going to see some interesting things as we go through this. The figures in the painting are poets and playwrights and philosophers and mathematicians and politicians and so on, from the ancient world—with Plato and Aristotle right in the middle. We are going to just take a very quick overview of this incredible cast of characters.

Let's first focus on the left side of the painting and as we hone in on it a little bit more, notice this grouping of figures (see above). Let's take a closer look at that, and this is what we see. This is Socrates; he is obviously the best known figure in this grouping, but he is depicted pretty much as we would imagine him, in the marketplace debating philosophy with whoever was willing to take him on. But there are other figures, less well known to most of us, but well known in the classical world. If you look down on the right side you'll see a couple of figures stooping down towards the floor. This is a depiction of Euclid, the great ancient mathematician, and here he is with a compass working out some geometric formulas on a piece of slate. And so we have a whole range of figures, not just poets and philosophers, but scientists and mathematicians depicted in this school of Athens as well.

Let's look at another grouping, also on the right side (see below). On the extreme right side we see Zoroaster and Ptolemy, but the most interesting figure probably is this young man who is looking out of the painting at you and me. This is a self-portrait of Raphael. He has painted himself into this painting, which is a pretty bold thing to do if you think about that: to put yourself in the company of Socrates and Plato and Aristotle and Euclid and so on. But this is how the Renaissance humanists thought. They saw themselves as modern men, but modern men who were re-creating the values of the ancient world. They saw themselves as belonging in this company, and Raphael is putting himself with great pride, certainly, but also a real sense of self-confidence in this group. The larger message that he's communicating by this is: "I'm drawing my inspiration from them and I rightly belong in this company, is really."

Let me point out a couple of more figures to look for in this great painting. The figure sprawled out on the steps is the philosopher Diogenes, the man who told Alexander the Great to get out of the light and stop blocking the sun. Also in the foreground, on Plato's side, is Raphael's portrait of Michelangelo. So he doesn't just paint himself into this painting, but also his friends, his competitor, and it's a great tribute to him to put him in the same company and say Michelangelo belongs with the great figures of the ancient world. These men that we are going to be looking at, these artists like Raphael and Botticelli and Michelangelo, lived at the same time. Most of them lived in Florence or in Rome. They knew each other, they were not so much friends as they were competitors, vying for the same lucrative commissions from families like the Medici or from the Pope himself, and so it's quite a tribute for Raphael to put his competitor Michelangelo in this scene. Here he is very reflective. It's quite an accurate depiction of what we know of Michelangelo. It's a brooding, melancholy, reflective man and it's as though he is reflecting on what he is going to turn that slab of marble into, what his next work of art is going to be. So *The*

School of Athens is really best described as a tribute to the ancient world, an expression of the veneration that these humanist artists of the Renaissance had for the classical world. As I said, that's the logical starting point as we try to understand the nature of Renaissance art.

The Emergence of the Individual

Let's move onto the second quality. In addition to the revival of the interest in the classical world, a second quality that we identify in Renaissance art and culture, and a very important one, is the emergence of the individual in Renaissance art. We are going to look at three quick examples of this phenomenon that should give a better sense of what we are talking about here. In the Middle Ages, people didn't see themselves as individuals, they saw themselves as occupying a place in the great Chain of Being. They are part of this big, vast hierarchical structure. They didn't see themselves as a unique personality with a unique creative genius and something to contribute to the world. This is very different from what Michelangelo, da Vinci and the other humanists saw themselves as being.

Our first example is another painting by Botticelli. This time it is not a classical painting like "The Birth of Venus," but a traditional theme that you could see in medieval art and you could still see in Renaissance art, a biblical theme, "The Adoration of the Magi," painted around 1475 by Sandro Botticelli. (See Color Illustration M.) As we go through this, we are going to see that it's a very complex painting. It's in a sense no less revolutionary than "The Birth of Venus" in the way Botticelli handles this traditional subject. We'll analyze the painting very briefly and then what should come into focus is that element of individuality that is so characteristic of Renaissance culture. The adoration of the Magi refers to the wise men presenting their gifts at the birth of Christ. We see the Holy Family in the upper central portion of the painting. Notice the traditional depictions of the Virgin Mary, her face, the slight tilt to her head, all those things that we identified a moment ago.

You see the Christ Child looking very much like a little adult, which is how they depicted him both in medieval and Renaissance art. You see a disinterested, sleepy looking Joseph resting his head in his hand and his palm and looking down on the scene. He is one of the interesting figures to look at in these Holy Family portraits. Nobody really knows what to do with Joseph. He is part of the scene, he is connected to it and he is not connected to it; he is on the margins. And here he is looking with a fatherly gaze down on the scene. In the lower central portion of the painting you see one old wise man kneeling before Christ in the immediate center with and impressive red cloak, and you see a younger wise man and you see a third one dressed in white right of center.

These were the three wise men, but interestingly we know who these wise men are or rather who they were. These are contemporary figures in Florence, Italy, at the time that Botticelli was painting this in 1475. These are members of the Medici family. The Medici family was the powerful, wealthy ruling family of Late Medieval and Early Modern Florence, Italy. The elderly man, the one closest to Baby Jesus, is the "godfather" of the Medici family. I use that term because that's a very accurate way to refer to them, almost like a kind of a mob family. They had their hands on pretty much every aspect of civic, political and economic life and they were patrons of the arts. So if you are telling the story of the Renaissance in Italy, you inevitably have to tell the story of the Medici family, because they funded many of the great art projects. The ones that weren't funded by the church were funded by the Medici, and the Medici. Cosimo, the one kneeling before Christ, is the one that signed Botticelli's paychecks. So it's not surprising, given that he is the one commissioning this work of art, that Botticelli paint them as individuals into his painting. You start to see this element of Renaissance individuality and humanism coming out of this painting.

The fact that these Medici family members are depicted as wise men really raises the question as to what the painting is about. On the surface the adoration of a Magi on the surface means worship. But if you start looking at it a little bit more, that title becomes significantly ambiguous. Is it the adoration of the Magi of the Christ Child or are we adoring the Magi? Is it the adoration of the Medici family? And that's really what's going on here. The focus should be on Christ, the "Word made flesh." This is the most amazing moment in history, where God became man, and everybody seems to have other things that are capturing their interest and attention.

This becomes a painting about Renaissance life, power and culture, and the last thing it's a painting about is Christ, the Incarnation. Well, let's explore this a little bit further. Look at this group of Renaissance courtiers and figures over here and noblemen dressed up in their finery and so on. The man on the extreme left, preening himself and puffing his chest out, seems completely unimpressed by the fact that the "Word is made flesh and dwells among us." People are carrying on conversations and so on, they are talking about all kinds of things, probably that have nothing to do with this remarkable miracle that's in their midst. In other words, look at how all of these vain humanistic qualities of the Renaissance are becoming the subject matter in the foreground of this painting.

Then, to top it all off, on the extreme right hand side, we see this figure in a brown cloak, and he's looking at you and me. This is Botticelli painting himself, as Raphael had done, into his own painting. And so for hundreds of years these people have looked at this painting, Botticelli is looking back out to see what our reaction to his masterpiece is. He is laying claim to it, saying, "This is my work, this is my vision. This is an expression of my individual created genius." This is the quality of individuality that this points us to. But notice here again how in this traditional Christian theme, where the focus should be on Christ, the painting is compromised by all of these individual and humanistic values: the power of the Cosimo Medici clan, the values of Renaissance culture, the values of individual humanism that we see in the artist himself. This is happening because the Renaissance humanists are trying to take their Christian faith and their Classical Humanism and bring the two together, and this is what you get. You get a compromised faith.

Let's look at a second example of the emergence of the individual in Renaissance art. Here we are going to leave Italy and go to the northern countries. We are going to go to the Low Countries, Flanders, and look at a painting by a Flemish master named Jan Van Eyck that we usually just call, "The Arnolfini Wedding Portrait," painted in 1434. (See above, and Color Illustration N.) It's an early Renaissance painting, fully a generation before Botticelli is painting his masterpieces, and it reminds us that the Renaissance is not just an Italian phenomenon, but it's actually occurring in other places in Europe as well.

This is unquestionably one of the most famous paintings in all of Western art, and you can see this in the National Gallery of Art in London. Your first reaction on looking at it might be to wonder why this is the case. But there are good reasons for it and as we examine this you are going to see that this is a masterful as well as a revolutionary painting in a lot of ways.

This is Mr. and Mrs. Arnolfini on their wedding day and Jan Van Eyck is painting this wedding portrait to commemorate that happy occasion. Mr. and Mrs. Arnolfini are in their home and we start seeing some of the signs of middle-class affluence. The rise of a middle-class in the late Middle Ages was so important to the making of the modern world. We see the sense of wealth in the things that are in their home. Even a little thing like the oranges on a windowsill speak of affluence by way of the fact that they have enough money to buy oranges. There are little domestic touches, such as the slippers in the foreground, and the little dog in the immediate foreground is a traditional symbol of fidelity, and thus an appropriate symbol commemorating this marriage. Mrs. Arnolfini looks like she is about four months along, but that is the traditional way in this period of depicting female beauty, not that she's pregnant, but that she certainly has the potential to become pregnant. She is fertile. In fact, women would artificially pad themselves in their lower abdomen to create that kind of effect, and to you and me that seems very strange, but I can guarantee you that if Jan Van Eyck were to get in a time machine and

come forward five or six hundred years to our time he would look at our standards of female beauty and he'd think they are equally bizarre. So these notions are very much culturally dictated, the way we look at beauty, and especially female beauty is something very subject to cultural change throughout human history.

Let's see if we can find a few more interesting things that point us towards this theme of individuality. This is a detail you see on the wall, and before we look at the mirror, look at the chandelier. One of the reasons this is such a famous painting is the extraordinary detail and the shading that you see in that chandelier painted with oil. This is one of the first paintings to use oil, and with oil you could create that extraordinary detail. Then you see the mirror and as you might expect Mr. and Mrs. Arnolfini reflected in the mirror from behind, but in between them you see a couple of figures. These are Jan Van Eyck, the painter, and next to him a young man who is probably his apprentice.

So Jan Van Eyck is doing the same thing Raphael and Botticelli did in painting themselves into their painting. There is that sense of the artist as an individual. But he doesn't want us to lose the message here, so across the wall he writes, "Johannes de Eyck fuit hic 1434", *Jan Van Eyck was here*, and he dates it. It's not like a little piece of graffiti that he is writing on the wall, like some kind of "Kilroy was here" message. Scholars believe that in a sense it's like signing your name as a witness to a marriage certificate and that this painting really commemorates, witnesses, and authenticates that marriage.

As we've seen, the Renaissance was a much broader cultural phenomenon than what just occurred in Italy, but we are kind of focusing on what's happening in Italy, in Florence, in Rome, in the circles that Michelangelo and da Vinci were in, in that period of time in the late 15th and early 16th century. As we look at the art, our point is not just to become lovers of great art and to become able to appreciate it as we talk through the galleries of a museum. As good as that might be, I would say that has really limited usefulness to you and me. It's much more important to be able to understand a work of art, a work of literature, a work of music than it is to appreciate it. What we are trying to do is to take it apart to see how it is a reflection of the values of the age that produced it. We've talked about how the Renaissance was inspired by the classical world, how they looked back at the Greeks and the Romans and they sought to imitate them, and we are going to continue with that theme today as we see how their art was in fact humanistic and rationalistic.

As we have pointed out, another characteristic that emerges in the art of this period is the representation of individuality. Let's look at the third example of this quality of individuality. In addition to Botticelli's "Adoration of the Magi" and Jan Van Eyck's "Arnolfini Wedding Portrait," let's stay in the northern countries and look at a painting by Albrecht Dürer, who was a great German painter contemporary with Michelangelo. He traveled from Germany to Italy where he no doubt saw many of the great works of Renaissance art that were being produced at that time, around the year 1500. He is a worthy contemporary of Michelangelo, and a great artist. He is by no means a second tier artist after the Italian artist. He is one of the greats of the Renaissance, and this is his "Self-Portrait at Twenty-Eight," which he painted around the year 1500. (See Color Illustration O.)

Once again, we are illustrating the quality of individuality. The obvious thing to note here is that this is a self-portrait. It's pretty bold to take yourself as a subject. Again, we don't have any medieval self-portraits; it's incomprehensible within the medieval world view, where any given individual was seen as an inconsequential and insignificant player in the great cosmic hierarchy of things. Thus something very radical has clearly changed as we go from medieval to modern, and that's the thing to keep our eye on.

Then we look at various other little indicators. The fact is, as I mentioned a minute ago, that artists are signing their names to their works of art. Here you see it right up here, signing his name in the Latin form, and then interestingly Albrecht Dürer, who was a great wood-cut artist as well as a great painter, he developed his own little personal logo such that if he had this practice back then he certainly would have trade-marked his logo. Here it is, a big capital A with a little D tucked underneath it and then he puts the date across the top. It's just as good as a little C with a circle around it, always copyrighting that circle, trade-marking this and imprinting that with his own individual sense of ownership.

Now as we look at this painting of himself, the self-portrait at twenty-eight, what is it about this image that you find most surprising when you look at it? It's so life-like, and again he is painting in oil, this new technique. Look at the hand in the foreground. Self-portraits by artists are very interesting to look at because they are always trying to showcase their talent, and the hand is important because you see this in Rembrandt self-portraits. The hand is very prominently displayed, because it is after all the hand that picks up the brush; it's the hand that executes the work of art, the hand that is—symbolically at least—the repository of creative artistic genius. And so the hand is important. Note the hand, he is drawing our attention to something, he is holding or pointing to the fur collar. He is drawing attention to that fancy coat and in particular the fur because this is the most difficult part of the painting to do. Every little strand of that fur is executed precisely with oil, and he wants you to see the skill of the artist in that.

Who does it look like that you are looking at when you look at Albrecht Dürer? I think we all intuitively feel that this looks like a traditional Christian depiction of Christ, that there is that image that it's not a historical or a biblical image, but in the history of Christian art this is very much what we see in the picture of Albrecht Dürer. That's a little disturbing when you recognize that. Is he suffering from some kind of messianic complex here? I mean, is it not bold enough to paint yourself as a subject, but you are going to paint yourself and make yourself look like Christ? What's going on with that? I think that we can come up with a couple of answers. One is that this just takes this sense of Renaissance hubris to a new level. That could be one possibility, but I am not comfortable with that interpretation.

The other interpretation would be to recognize what we know about Albrecht Dürer: he was a very devout Christian. And we have to interpret his painting in light of this. When you look at Albrecht Dürer, who do you see? You see Christ. Now think about the implications of that, think of what Albrecht Dürer might be communicating by that. Possibly what he is communicating is what the Apostle Paul communicates in Galatians when he speaks about how he is dead to himself, right, but he is alive and Christ is the one who is living within him, that Christ life indwelling us such that when you look at the Christian you were to see Christ. And so when we look at Albrecht Dürer we see Christ. It becomes rather a beautiful expression of what the essence of our faith is all about, and I think that's an accurate way to understand what Dürer is saying here, such that this is not some kind of vain Renaissance boast necessarily about his artistic gift and talent, but rather maybe he is saying, "Look at the skill here, my inspiration comes from Christ, my talent comes from Christ." And this painting then can be understood as an active worship being given back to God.

Capturing a Dramatic Moment

Let's move on from this second point to look at the third quality that we see. Renaissance artists tried to capture a dramatic moment in what they painted and sculpted. And again we are going to use a couple of examples to illustrate what we are talking about.

They were very interested that their art capture the reality of life, the vitality of life, the energy of human existence and experience. The medieval painting by Cimabue is a good example of what these Renaissance artists were reacting against, these medieval types of depictions which are the antithesis of life-likeness and dynamic human experience. In Cimabue's painting of the Virgin Mary there is nothing dramatic happening. She looks like a mannequin propped up in a store window and nothing dramatic has happened to her for hundreds of years and nothing dramatic is going to happen for another hundred years in this particular painting. It is a fixed, static, unchanging artistic tradition. It's dead and lifeless, and Renaissance painters didn't want to paint that way. They saw themselves as active people and players within the world, much as the ancient Greeks did.

We'll discuss three examples of this. The first is the painting that we've already looked at, the very famous painting by Michelangelo from the Sistine Chapel. This of course is the creation of Adam. This qualifies as a pretty dramatic moment. That split second before Adam became a living soul. I sometimes call this a Kodak moment. We have to snap the picture in just the right moment, when something very dramatic has just happened or is just about to happen, and that's what they are trying to freeze-frame in their art in the Renaissance and capture that intensity of experience and drama.

Let's look at another example, also from Michelangelo. This one is a work of sculpture. We think of Michelangelo for his great paintings but he would have described himself first and foremost as a sculptor, and Michelangelo's "Moses" (c. 1515) is a good

example of this quality. This is a massive marble statue that he produced for the crypt of one of the popes that commissioned this particular work of art. This is in the Vatican in Rome and is part of a much larger sculptural project.

It's a very impressive statue. I want to start from the top and work our way down and see what we can find about this that will point us to this dramatic quality Renaissance artists such as Michelangelo are building into their work. As we go through this, I want you to try to figure out what moment in the life of Moses Michelangelo is depicting. And if we can identify that, then we will put our finger on the dramatic moment that he is trying to capture. Let's start at the top.

The face of Moses presents a pretty stern aspect. I think we've even described it as an angry look on his face as he is looking off to the side. If it looks like he has horns on this head, that's because he does have horns on his head, which certainly adds to the fierceness of his demeanor. What is the reason for that? It's a very long story in the history of art that lies behind that traditional way in which Moses is depicted, and it has to do with a mistranslation in the Vulgate. Going back to the Septuagint, the passage that describes how, when Moses came down from Mount Sinai, he was radiating the glory of God in his countenance ended up getting garbled to read he had horns on his head. This thus became the iconic way to depict Moses within the tradition of Christian art.

It certainly adds to the effect here. Now, let's look at his body. Look at the size of his arms. This is one muscular figure. And in fact this is how Michelangelo sculpted and painted everything that he did. He himself was a very large man, and so he painted and sculpted everyone that he painted this way. His women are big massive amazons and certainly here Moses is very strong. It's always been noticed that his female charac-

ters are very muscular, very masculine, and as great an artist as he was that was the one area that he had a difficulty: bringing that sense of realism to the female form. But here it really serves him well to bring this muscularity into the form of Moses. What is tucked under his right arm? Well, he's got the tablets of stone, so let's start to put the picture together. He is looking off in the distance, he is seated, he has the tablets of stone under his arm. Now look at his legs and his feet. The right foot is firmly planted. The left foot however as you can see is beginning to press down for leverage and pressing himself up. He is in the process of getting ready to stand. So he is looking at something, he is angry, he has got the tablets of stone, he is getting ready to stand and he is about to do something very dramatic. What does he see in a distance?

He sees the Children of Israel dancing around the golden calf that they made. They have fallen into idolatry while he was on Mount Sinai. The anger is welling up inside him. All of that drama comes into play as you reconstruct where this falls in the story of Moses. And all that drama, all that energy, life and vitality, is chiseled into the form, which is very different from that kind of static, dead, mannequin quality that we saw in medieval art. This is what motivates them, this is what they are inspired by. Where do they get this inspiration from? From the ancient Greeks. Think of those statues of athletes that we looked at. Think of the discus-thrower, who is also about to do something very dramatic: hurl that discus. Here Moses is ready to hurl these tablets. They are very similar kinds of depiction.

One more thing to notice is which foot is moving. It's the left foot. Remember what we said about that. You go all the way back five thousand years, and in Egyptian art it's always the left foot that moves. You see that in the Egyptian forms, you see that in the Greek forms they copied from the Egyptians: the left foot is always the one that slightly advances. Here Michelangelo is copying that classical tradition by putting the movement in the left foot. It's never been satisfactorily explained why it's the left foot that's moving, especially given the bias in favor of right-handedness that we see in culture.

Let me give you one final example here before we move on, the very, very famous painting by Leonardo da Vinci: "The Last Supper" (1498). (See Color Illustration P.) Look at the illustration here of *The Last Supper*. Christ in the center, with six disciples on the left and six disciples on the right. It looks like a very tranquil and static scene to you and me, but as you begin to look at the disciples you realize there is a lot of activity going on.

They are looking at one another, they are questioning, they're talking, they are gesturing. Da Vinci went back to the gospel narrative to reinterpret this scene that has been painted traditionally for hundreds of years in a very static way. He wanted to do something new with the story. He went back to the gospel narrative and what caught his eye was the moment when Jesus said to His disciples in the upper room, "One of you will betray Me." That's the dramatic moment that he is trying to capture, and the disciples are turning to one another and saying, "Is it I Lord?" and they are questioning one another. And so the room is filled with that kind of drama and characteristically that's what da Vinci is interested in trying to portray.

Notice how for each one of these points we've seen that the Renaissance painters are getting their inspiration from the ancient Greeks, the classical tradition. They start getting the themes and subject matter

and the values from the classical times as we noted. The high value they placed on the individual is something that they also see in the Greco-Roman period, as is this sense of drama and intensity in art.

The Development of Perspective

The fourth point is the most technical. We see the development of realistic perspective in Renaissance art. That quality of realism that you and I take for granted when we look at a painting is something that artists in the fifteenth century figured out on the basis of mathematical principles and so on as they scientifically tried to understand the way in which we optically comprehend the world and then to translate that into visual form. They came up with certain principles of perspective that defined Renaissance art.

We are going to identify two types of perspective and both of these are going to be illustrated by this very important early Renaissance work, "The Tribute Money" by Masaccio, dated around 1425. (See Color Illustration D.) It's a painting that we have looked at once before when we talked about Roman art and the style of continuous narrative. We are now going to use this to illustrate something entirely different. We are going to look at the principle of perspective as it's emerging in early Renaissance art. To recall the subject matter, Jesus is here confronted in the center by the scribes and Pharisees and the question is asked whether it is lawful to pay tribute to Caesar? On the left side of the painting we see Peter getting a coin from the fish's mouth and then delivering that on the right side of the painting to the tax collector. That's that Roman principle of continuous narrative. You've got three separate scenes layered in one particular painting and if you don't realize that it becomes a very confusing painting to try to figure out. It's almost like three separate frames in a comic strip.

Let's focus on the element of perspective. You could divide this painting right in half and illustrate the two types of perspective, one on the left hand and one on the right hand. It's almost like Masaccio was deliberately painting this to showcase these new principles of perspective. Let's define what they are. On the left side of the painting we see first of all the principle of atmospheric perspective. The principle of **atmospheric perspective** is a known optical phenomenon. We experience it every single day. Atmospheric perspective relates to the fact that distant objects appear smaller and less clear than objects that are close. You go out at night, you look up at the sky, you see the moon and you can take your hand and you can cover up the moon. Now we know that our hand is not bigger than the moon, we know that it's the great distance that makes it appear small. And similarly you look at the mountains and they are scaled in keeping with a distance and so it's an optical phenomenon of how we view the world.

On the left side of the painting we see atmospheric perspective in the distant mountains. They are scaled according to size and they're less distinct and less clear. Now let's briefly mention how different perspective is in medieval art. Look again at the Virgin Mary. She is not several times bigger than anyone else in this painting because she's close and everyone else is far away, as the scientific optical approach would give us. Rather, she is bigger because she is more important. So it's a completely different basis on which medieval art is functioning. It is not a scientific basis, but with the rise of scientific thinking and out of the Renaissance they are starting to look at the world with these optical principles in mind, and da Vinci is a good example. He is a scientist as well as an artist. He is trying to understand through art the way the world actually is and the way we understand art and then trying to represent that accurately and scientifically in the painting. So that's why we

see in Masaccio's painting the world realistically represented with these principles.

Now the second type of perspective is seen on the right side of the painting, and this is what we call linear perspective. Again, it's a known optical phenomenon; it's based on mathematical formulas that were discovered in the fifteenth century, so it has a basis in scientific discovery. **Linear perspective** is the use of straight lines to create the illusion of three-dimensionality. Notice what you have on the right side of the painting. You have a building. Now if you go back to the gospel account of this story, you are not going to find that the building factors into the story. There is no reason for a building to be in this painting except that it gives the straight lines that Masaccio needs to showcase this new technique of linear perspective. You've got the straight lines up here in the top of the building. The straight lines in the steps down here, notice how these are all at a diagonal and they're all emerging at the head of Christ. There is a tunneling effect that gives you that illusion, just as when you stand in a long hallway. The straight lines in the floor where the wall and the floor meet, and the straight lines where the ceiling when the wall meet, tunnel inward. That's the illusion that creates that sense of distance and depth. It's almost like you could walk into that scene, like you could walk down that hall. That's what Renaissance artists are trying to create here. And so as you look at Renaissance paintings note that they always put buildings in their paintings whether they belong or not because again they give you the convenience of a lot of straight lines, which will give you that feeling of three dimensionality.

Let's look at Leonardo da Vinci's *Last Supper* once again with that in mind. Notice how in the ceiling you have all of these straight lines, and if you take a ruler and follow them they emerge at the head of Christ.

So it's highly significant: da Vinci is saying that at this moment in time, in this moment in history, all the lines of history in a sense are converging at that place where the crown of thorns is going to be placed, just as the lines of this room emerge at that vanishing point. So it becomes a very profound kind of theological statement that da Vinci is making as he uses this new technique of linear perspective to support and convey the doctrinal message that he wants to communicate with this painting.

Finally, we'll consider an early da Vinci painting that does something very similar. This is a da Vinci painting on a very traditional theme done early in his career, when he is a young man of probably about twenty years old, in 1472, and it's called "The Annunciation." (See Color Illustration Q.) The angel Gabriel is announcing to Mary that she is with child. So it looks like a very traditional painting until you realize that it's also using this new technique of linear perspective.

Let's isolate this and see what's going on. There are three terms I want to very quickly introduce to you by way of using this painting. Da Vinci is showcasing all these techniques by superimposing these lines. We can see what those techniques are. The first point that's very important in perspective as Renaissance masters employed is the **horizon line**. As we walk around the world we're not aware of this, but the horizon is how we orient ourselves. The horizon line is very important to orient where you're at. We just do this naturally and intuitively, but Renaissance artists turned that into a methodology and the horizon line is very, very significant. And so, as you look off into the distance, this line that runs right through here is the first principle of construction that we see. Interestingly, note where that horizon line runs. All of these

things are very deliberate, very significant. It runs through the head of the angel Gabriel and through the heart of the Virgin Mary. It's like this message that's been given to her comes from the mind of God into the heart of Mary. And again, da Vinci knows exactly what he is doing. The second set of lines that's important are the diagonal lines known as **orthogonal lines**, and these are the straight lines that the building gives you. If you follow those out you notice they meet in a distance at the **vanishing point**, which is the third point. When you find the vanishing point, you've found the heart of the Renaissance painting.

Well, where is that vanishing point in this painting? Again, da Vinci knows what he is doing. We see a mountain in the distance right here. The straight lines are emerging at that mountain. What is that mountain? Scholars believe what he is depicting there is Calvary. And so suddenly again the theology comes richly into focus here because even though da Vinci is portraying the Annunciation, he is already looking ahead to why Christ is coming to earth. The whole purpose is so that in the future, in the distance, all of those lines will merge at Calvary.

So as you begin to take these paintings apart and look at them and analyze them, this is how we interpret them; but in order to do that well, we've got to understand what the Renaissance painters are striving after, what they're trying to accomplish, what the values that are motivating them. As we do this, we realize that these are the values that have shaped the modern age—and this is why we can describe the Renaissance as the "portal" to our own time.

THE NORTHERN RENAISSANCE

Chapter Objectives

- Compare and contrast the Renaissance in the South and the North.
- Identify the key ideas and figures in the Protestant Reformation.
- Demonstrate how the Reformation shaped modern western values.

Up to this point, almost everything we've said about the Renaissance has been focused on the Southern or the Italian Renaissance. I now want to focus our attention on the North. As we look at what's happening in Germany, England, and Holland, we see that there is a reawakening, a revival in arts and culture that we describe with the same word, *Renaissance*. We are going to see that in some ways, this is similar to what was happening in Italy in the fifteenth and early sixteenth centuries; but in some important ways it's very different as well.

The first things to consider are how the Southern and the Northern Renaissance are different, and then secondly, we will go on very logically to ask how they are similar. What binds them together? What justifies our speaking of both of them with a single word, Renaissance? We are going to find that one of the ways in which the Renaissance in the North is different from the Renaissance in the South was the particularly religious nature of the arts and the culture in the North. There is a much more of a religious flavor to the Northern Renaissance than in Italy. In Italy it's much more secular, much more pagan and classical in theme and subject matter. Understanding the religious nature of the Renaissance in the North is also helpful for understanding the Reformation, which is focused on what happens in Germany, England and to some lesser extent, the countries of the North.

We will next turn to the subject of the Reformation and analyze it as natural outgrowth of the Renaissance. We should not think about the Reformation as an event that only has significance if you are studying church history. Rather it has cultural significance and it can be understood as an outgrowth or an expression of the same values that can also be identified as Renaissance values. Finally, we are going to ask the question, Why does all this matter? Why does it matter that we know what was happening during the Reformation and the Northern Renaissance 400 years ago?

We are going to see that it profoundly affects our understanding of how our own culture is today. What do we mean when we describe someone as having a good work ethic? Where do those ideas come from? What about the notions that we take for granted as qualities and values of middle class America? We are going to see, again, that it is in this period, in the culture and the values of the Northern Renaissance and the Reformation, where we can isolate and identify the values that were so important in shaping our own country and our own time. And so, yes, it does matter.

Once again, the same theme that we have been exploring from the very beginning is once again on display. That the more closely we look at the past, the more clearly we see the present. The past does matter, and it does help us. It gives us the tools and the resources, in some cases simply the vocabulary to talk about our own times, our own values, our own conflicts and challenges with greater clarity and with a greater understanding.

The North and South: A Contrast

First of all, what is the Northern Renaissance? How is it different from, how is it similar to, what was happening in Italy? The first thing that we should note is that, when we talk about the Northern Renaissance, we are thinking of a slightly later period. Remember those years for the Renaissance; they were pretty expansive, 1400-1600, roughly 200 years. That timeframe is very misleading, because it really depends on what part of Europe you are talking about. The Renaissance was best understood as a kind of wave that swept from South to North over these 200 years. It's occurring first in the South, in Italy. 1400 is not early enough for Italy, already in the 1300s in Italy we are seeing things that we look back and say, this is a shift in thinking. This is kind of Renaissance. We just conveniently put the date 1400 to it. As you head north to England, 200 years later, at the end of this period, around the year 1600, this is when Shakespeare was writing his plays. There is much that's renaissance about Shakespeare, but there's also a lot that's still very medieval about Shakespeare and still very medieval about the Elizabethan world in the England of his day and age. Renaissance is a very elastic term. As we head to the North, the Renaissance is a much later phenomenon;

it occurs at the tail end of this period that we designated the Renaissance.

Let's focus now more specifically on what is different from and what is similar between these two Renaissances, North and South. What can we say? First of all, the Italian Renaissance (as a generalization) is more secular in tone and nature. It is more obviously humanistic. The subject matter was more deeply classical, even pagan and classical in its themes. Botticelli's "Birth of Venus" sums up these values, these classical humanistic pagan values that are so typical of the Italian Renaissance painting. Scholars have often noticed that there is much more of a religious quality and tone to the Northern Renaissance. The art is more devotional, more obviously religious in feeling. They weren't just painting religious themes; they were painting them with more emotion, with more feeling. In the South they were into drama: Michelangelo's "Moses," Leonardo da Vinci's "Last Supper," capture that sense of a dramatic moment. In the Northern Renaissance we see a more internalized sense of emotion that is a religious experience and an expression of faith. This forms an obvious connection to the Reformation in the North.

In the Italian South, they were just falling in love with classical humanism. And so the ground was more fertile really for the Reformation in the North because of this tradition, this more deeply rooted tradition of emotional and religious art. This is clearly on display in one of the masterpieces of the Northern Renaissance, a painting by the German, Matthias Grünewald—not a name that is widely known. In fact, Grünewald was not well known until the twentieth century. He was really, through art scholarship and the work of historians, rescued from relative anonymity. There are only thirteen or fourteen of his paintings that have survived, and he was largely unknown until just a hundred years ago. The famous "Crucifixion of Christ" from the "Isenheim Altarpiece," painted in 1510-1515, wasn't even attributed to Grünewald until the twentieth century; it was believed to be a work by Albrecht Dürer. (See Color Illustration R.)

Matthias Grünewald's central panel in the "Isenheim Altarpiece" is the "Crucifixion of Christ." What's interesting is not just that it's a religious theme, since Botticelli painted religious things too; "The Adoration of the Magi" is a biblical account that he is painting, but Botticelli painted it in a very secular manner and its very focused on Renaissance humanistic values. In Grünewald's painting there are no Renaissance humanistic values. What's on display are Gothic medieval devotional values. It's a more medieval painting than a Renaissance one, and yet it's painted in the early sixteenth century. Look at the depiction of Christ: the body of Christ is deeply wounded. You see the blood, you see the wounds, and you see the stripes—very uncharacteristic for what you see in other traditions in Christian art. It's certainly not something widely depicted in Italian Renaissance art, to see the body of Christ so violently and brutally and realistically portrayed. In this deeply devotional and highly emotional style of religious art of the Northern Renaissance, Christ was depicted as the "Man of Sorrows" prophesied in Isaiah 53. This is what Grünewald wants to give us. This is very characteristic of the Northern Renaissance, and we are going to see the spirit of this even in the Reformation. Notice the figures to the left who are also deeply emo-

tional, grieving the death of Christ. And on the right you see John the Baptist portrayed, holding a book in his hands, the Old Testament prophecies. He is pointing to Christ as the last of the prophets, the forerunner to Christ. The symbolism is very medieval; but the spirit and the feeling of it is in keeping with the devotional nature of the Northern Renaissance and the spirit even of the Reformation.

If that's one of the primary ways in which we see the difference between the Northern and the Southern Renaissance, does that mean that all of the arts in the North were all about deeply emotional religious scenes like this? Well, the answer is no. I want to caution us against overgeneralizing here. There is a very famous Northern Renaissance painting that has nothing to do with these religious themes: "Hunters in the Snow," painted in 1565 by Pieter Brueghel. (See Color Illustration S.) It is simply a painting of a village scene in winter. It's a beautiful painting in its evocative nature, the way it calls forth the quiet, everyday routines of life in a village. The hunters are coming back, apparently, unsuccessfully from the hunt; the fires are burning and the meal is being prepared. Everything expresses the sense of the warmth of human society and the contrast of that warmth with the cold of winter. It's a very rich painting in many ways.

Look at the direction the hunters and the dogs are going as they enter stage left as it were, and they are moving along the base of these trees in a diagonal direction. It's a very subtle, very beautiful use of that line of composition to give you that sense of movement across the canvas. And in that sense then you contrast and compare the foreground with the extreme background of the painting. It's a painting of an everyday scene. We wouldn't look at this and say, "Well, this is obviously a Northern Renaissance religious painting." No, not at all. But it points us to the fact that there's a lot more going on in the Renaissance of the north besides just this religious quality of the Reformation. There is also the rise of a whole class of people, the middle classes, who were becoming increasingly affluent. The merchant class is now commissioning works of art. It's not just the church that's paying artists to produce works like Grünewald's Altarpiece. It's now individuals who are saying, "I want you to paint a beautiful winter scene." "I want you to paint this portrait." That's also occurring as part of the Northern Renaissance. The merchant class will reach its height in the seventeenth century in Holland, where we begin to see the great paintings of Rembrandt, for example, all commissioned by individuals.

The North and South: A Comparison

Let's turn from the differences between the Italian and the Northern Renaissance to the similarities. What binds them together? What justifies our saying these are both expressions of this movement that we call the Renaissance? There are two things I want to identify here, by way of noting how they were similar. We know, for example, that in both the north and the south there was a profound emphasis upon individuality. We recognize that we have clearly shifted from the medieval to the modern when we identify this quality. We see this in the way that Botticelli and Raphael are bringing themselves into their paintings, the way in which individuals now are objects to be painted. The individual is now something you can focus on as a subject, because the individual is seen as having worth and dignity, apart from any kind of hierarchical system with which that individual might be associated. This is something we see in the North as well. Once again, I would argue that this is one of the most important concepts that helps us to understand the modern age. We cannot account for the rise of social institutions like the middle class; we cannot account for the rise of political institutions, democratic institutions, economic institutions, and capitalism, apart from this shift towards the emphasis on the individual that we see in the Renaissance, in the early modern age.

We see the concept of individualism documented in the art of the North, just as surely as it's documented in the art of the South. Recall the great self-portrait of Albrecht Dürer, which, among other things, bears witness to this new perspective of individuality. But note the twist here. Being a Northern Renaissance painter, being a devout Christian, we see that even Dürer takes this humanistic theme and value of individuality and gives it a devotional interpretation. He depicts himself as Christ, and this becomes an act of worship, and that's so typical of the religious tenor and quality of the Renaissance in the North. Recall, as well, Jan van Eyck's Arnolfini wedding portrait. This is a Northern painting, and it shows that these qualities of individuality and humanism are clearly percolating in the culture of the North and being given expression in the arts of this period.

Let's look at a third example, not an example from painting or sculpture here, but the works of Shakespeare, who was arguably, the greatest figure in all of the arts of the Northern Renaissance. If you think of his great plays, if you think of his poetry, this Renaissance value of individuality is on display everywhere in Shakespeare's great body of work. His tragedies are explorations of individual personalities. Consider the psychology of Macbeth or Hamlet, King Lear or Othello when you read or watch those plays. Shakespeare's drama very much displays this preoccupation of seeing one as an individual with a unique perspective on the world, not just as part of a system, but as an individual.

Mr. WILLIAM
SHAKESPEARES
COMEDIES,
HISTORIES, &
TRAGEDIES.

Published according to the True Originall Copies.

LONDON
Printed by Isaac Iaggard, and Ed. Blount. 1623.

Secondly, in addition to the rise of this individual value, we see that both the Northern and the Southern Renaissance were steeped in classical learning. This revival of classical knowledge defines the North as well as the South. We see scholars going back to the old texts, going back to the old histories, back to the old languages, Greek and Latin. They are studying and learning those and reviving the scholarship of those things. What you and I normally think of as modern scholarship—going to the library and doing research by going back to the original sources—all of these scholarly practices developed in this period through the classical scholarship of the Renaissance. It's one of the legacies that we can trace back to this time. Biblical scholarship was anchored in this period as well—that practice of going back to the manuscripts and comparing them in the original languages.

Let me just give you a few names that we associate with a Northern classical revival of knowledge and learning. Erasmus—he's best known for his book in "Praise of Folly," which is a satiric book that he wrote about Renaissance values. He was a great humanist scholar in the classical tradition. In England, Sir Thomas More, also a great classical scholar, was the author of *Utopia*, another Renaissance satire. More coined the word "utopia," which means, "no place." More was making the point that this perfect society, one made perfect by man's reason, is really "no place."

In addition to Erasmus and Sir Thomas More, we can cite the great reformers. Martin Luther and John Calvin were also humanists and classical scholars; they went back not only to the original languages, but also to the original manuscripts. Finally, once again, we must mention Shakespeare. He is kind of a universal man of this age and is typical of the Northern Renaissance in so many ways. We see in his plays this revival of classical themes and subjects. Some of his plays are on classical subjects, such as "Julius Caesar" and "Titus Andronicus." We also see in Shakespeare an awareness and knowledge of classical sources that he drew upon when writing his plays and his poetry.

What do we conclude then, by comparing the Northern and the Southern Renaissance? We can conclude that the Renaissance was a broad cultural development. It was not just an isolated occurrence in Italy or in Florence. Florence, in particular, and Italy in general may have been the epicenter of the Renaissance, out of which this movement radiated to the rest of Europe. But it's not to be understood as a purely Southern or Italian event. The Renaissance affected all of Europe and all of Western civilization.

The Reformation

As we look at the North, we now turn to one of the ways in which the Reformation developed out of the Renaissance. We have already noted the uniquely religious nature of the Renaissance in the North. This gives us an opportunity to explore that in greater detail, by looking at the Reformation. First, I'll define it, before looking at a couple of the key figures of the Reformation. And then I'll finally ask the question: How has the Reformation affected and shaped the values of Western culture and Western civilization?

The perspective that I am bringing to this is that the story of the Northern Renaissance cannot be separated from the story of the Reformation. But what was the Reformation? Look at the word itself. It has to do with reforming. The **Reformation** was the attempt to reform the Catholic Church. Note that it's an attempt to reform the Church from the inside. Martin Luther wasn't throwing stones at the Church from the outside. He was operating initially within the Catholic Church. Martin Luther was a priest in the Church. So we are going to have to ask the question, Why did Church need to be reformed? What the reformers were trying to do was to bring the Church back to the Bible, back to the foundation and the authority of scripture. Why did this have to be done? Why was it in need of Reformation? There were many ways in which the medieval Church had veered seriously off course over the centuries with the practices, teachings, and doctrines that had emerged during the Middle Ages. We can identify four main ways that the medieval Catholic Church had become corrupt and was in need of the kind of reform that Martin Luther and John Calvin were preaching from their pulpits.

- Political corruption
- Financial corruption
- Moral corruption
- Theological corruption

The Church had become a corrupt political institution. You know that something is wrong when the Church becomes a political player. Christ did not commission his disciples in Acts 1:8 to go out and be politicians in the world, but to be witnesses of his resurrection and proclaimers of the Gospel.

This is not to say that Christians do not have a role in the political sphere; it's not to say the Christians cannot be involved in political activity. The Church, however, is not a political institution. Its primary function is not political, and cannot correctly and biblically be seen in that light. Yet it became a political power based institution in the Middle Ages.

It was also the biggest bank in the Middle Ages. It had become financially corrupt. It had become all about money and wealth, and they raked in the wealth during the Middle Ages. This was one of the things that most outraged a young Martin Luther, as he looked at the abuses of the late medieval Catholic Church.

If you are politically corrupt and financially corrupt, then you are going to be morally corrupt as well. We see that outrageous careers of many of the late medieval and early modern popes. They wheeled and dealed and bought and sold offices. Some popes who had mistresses and fathered illegitimate children, whom they then tried to put on the career path towards the papacy themselves. The really horrible thing was that the Church had no moral authority, because it had become a corrupt institution. Finally, the church was theologically corrupt. Many false teachings had entered the church through the Middle Ages—the veneration of saints, the cult of the Virgin Mary, the doctrine of purgatory, and many more. These doctrines had corrupted the message of grace and faith. So the church was in desperate need of reformation. That's when Martin Luther steps onto the stage.

Martin Luther lived from 1483-1546 and was a priest and monk in the Catholic Church. As an infant he had been baptized in the Catholic Church and raised in its teachings. I emphasize this because to me that's the most remarkable thing about this whole story of the Reformation. How could somebody like Martin Luther see through all that blindness to the truth? Do not just look at Luther as a historical figure and the Reformation as a historical period. You should see the hand of God in history, as we look at the Reformation and see the work of the Holy Spirit doing what Christ promised the Holy Spirit would do: lead us into truth. I don't know how else you can account for how Martin Luther arrived at the truth and that understanding and then had the boldness to challenge the Pope and the authority of the Catholic Church. He was not the first reformer, and he would not be the last reformer. There are others who went before—men like Wycliffe, men who in many cases died a martyr's death as they sought to reform the teachings and practices of the Church.

But Martin Luther certainly towers over the history of the Reformation as the single greatest figure. The singular event that really was the watershed of the Reformation occurred in 1517 when Martin Luther nailed what are known as the 95 Theses to the church door at Wittenberg. These 95 statements addressed one of the practices of the church that Luther found most repugnant—the buying and the selling of indulgences. In a very methodical way, Luther argued through 95 statements and refuted the church's teaching and practice on this point.

Indulgences are pardons doled out by the Church for a fee. You could pay for so many years off your stay in purgatory. You can see how conveniently the Church had a monopoly in this. It's not like you could go to the discount indulgence store to buy lower priced indulgences to get ten years off. To translate this into modern terms, it would be like purchasing a little credit card which you could swipe at the door of purgatory to get, say, ten years off your stay in purgatory. That's how it was in the Middle Ages, as these indulgences were sold by the church and sanctioned by papal edict. The church profited and gained enormously and became, as I said, the biggest banking system in medieval Europe. Martin Luther found this repugnant and he railed against this and preached against it. He also published his objections, using the new technology that Gutenberg had invented—the printing press.

As we look at his teachings more specifically, we're going to see what the nature of the Reformation was all about. Let's look at Martin Luther's own conversion, the transformation in his understanding of his faith before we look at the heart of the teaching itself. He was a priest and a scholar. He was also a Professor of Theology; and as he was teaching through the book of Romans, he experienced a great life-changing event. Romans is a great doctrinal book—all about the work of salvation, the law and grace. Luther could not shake loose from a statement he found in scripture: "The just shall live by faith." He could not understand that verse in light of Church's teachings. It seemed obvious to him, as he reflected, that the Church had gone way off track in its understanding. He wanted to bring the Church back to Ephesians 2:8-9 and Titus 3:5: "Not by works of righteousness which we have done, but according to his mercy he saved us." The work of justification in our lives is the work of God's grace, not the product of our work.

Luther's teaching and the heart of the Reformation are really summed up in two Latin phrases. The first phrase is **sola scriptura**, which means "only scripture," or "by scripture alone." The idea here is that only scripture is authoritative for life and practice, for faith and doctrine. Not the teachings of the Church, not the edicts of the pope, but only scripture. If you can't justify it from scripture, then what business do you have teaching it as the doctrine of the Church? The other Latin phrase, so important to understanding the teaching of the Reformation, is **sola fide**, which means "by faith alone." This means that we come to salvation only through faith in Christ—not through our works, not through the Church's mediation, but only through faith. How did he arrive at that, while blinded within the teachings of the church? Again, we have to see in this the work of the Holy Spirit.

There were other reformers as well. There was the great Frenchman John Calvin, who preached in Geneva, Switzerland. We remember him as a great theologian, more than probably any of the other reformers. In a popular sense, when we think of Calvin and Calvinistic teaching we think of the doctrine of election; but that's just part of the vast tradition of the reformed theology we associate with his life and teaching.

In England the Reformation was very real as well, but for different reasons. The English Church broke with the Church of Rome, not over some high theological dispute over justification. Rather, the Church of England broke with Rome because King Henry VIII couldn't get the pope to sanction his divorce. Henry was having a hard time producing a male heir, and so he decided, since the Pope wouldn't authorize it, he would separate the Church of England from the Church of Rome. What began in that very petty personal political context, we have to see as part of the larger Reformation in England. The great legacy and tradition of the English Reformation, certainly, is the magisterial translation of the Bible, the King James Version of 1611.

Max Weber's Theory

The question remains, *Why does the Reformation matter?* How has the Refor-

mation influenced the direction of Western culture? That's why we go back to the past. That's why we study something that occurred 500 years ago, as the Reformation did, not just because we are interested in knowing the details of a long past historical event. What would be the value of that if it doesn't have any application to our lives today? So the question for us is: How does it impact our culture? What has been the lasting legacy of something like the Reformation on the direction of Western culture?

Let's start with a simple observation. As one travels across Europe, one can see profound differences between the culture of northern Europe and the culture of southern Europe. As you move towards the Mediterranean, time seems to slow down, people take a little bit longer lunch breaks. The trains and the buses don't run maybe as much on time as they do in Germany and in Scandinavia. All kinds of little cultural things are noticeable as you move from North to South. What accounts for these kinds of differences? A hundred years ago, Max Weber, a German historian and sociologist, formulated a thesis to try and account for these great cultural differences between North and South. We are going to see how they help us to understand the unique nature of American culture as well.

The gist of his argument was contained in the title of his book, published in 1905. The title gives the whole thesis away, *The Protestant Ethic and the Spirit of Capitalism*. We still refer to the Protestant work ethic today. We recognize what we mean by that, the sense of thriftiness and working hard and putting in an honest day's work, of getting ahead through hard work and individual effort and so on. All of these things are so essential to the capitalistic system of economics that emerged in the early modern period in the West. Max Weber associates these qualities with the Reformation.

His argument went something like this. The doctrinal teaching of the Reformation emphasized that one is not saved through works; one is not saved through the church—by being baptized in the church and taking communion in the church. Those are the things that medieval Christians in the Catholic system believed saved them. Instead, Luther and Calvin taught that one is saved through the work of God in your life; it's a work of grace. One is saved if one is part of the elect—if one is elected to salvation. But how do you know you are one of the elect? That's the question that drives Max Weber's understanding of the Protestant ethic. Hard work, the acquisition and growth of capital, were seen as signs of God's blessings on His elect. They "confirmed" what the church could never confirm—that you were, indeed, elected by God to salvation.

Weber contended that the theology of the Reformation conditioned people to seek the blessing of God in their life through hard work, labor, discipline, and thriftiness. These are the qualities that make up what Weber called the Protestant Ethic. Thereby, through the acquisition of wealth, and all the capitalistic virtues that go with that, one could demonstrate that there was the blessing of God in your life. Then you must be one of the elect if that is the case. That's his main argument. He is trying to connect the rise of capitalistic systems in the North, the rise of these ethical principles, with reformed doctrine and reformed theology.

Weber was claiming that the North is different from the South because the North is Protestant and the South is Catholic. All these German merchants and workers in the little German cities are working hard and being very thrifty and saving, because they see themselves as part of the elect; their values were influenced and shaped by this powerful doctrinal idea of the Reformation. This is the central argument, the thesis that Max Weber set forth. It has been a very controversial thesis. It has weathered well over the century since he first put it forth, and I think it's a very powerful interpretation.

Let's now think ahead to the application of this thesis to our own American culture.

Who is it that settled North America? We think back to the pilgrims and the Protestant work ethic they brought with them from Northern Europe. It is these values of hard work, frugality, and thriftiness that we associate with that culture. These qualities that we are calling the Protestant ethic have probably never been better expressed as they were by Benjamin Franklin.

The emphasis in these familiar, pithy statements is on hard work, saving money, and keeping your hands busy doing worthwhile things so that God will bless you.

- Idleness is the devil's workshop.
- Cleanliness is next to Godliness.
- A penny saved is a penny earned.
- Haste makes waste.
- The early bird catches the worm.
- A stitch in time saves nine.

Whether you accept Weber's theory of not, and it has been very controversial, it's nonetheless a very clever way, I think, to account for the profound cultural differences between northern and southern Europe, and ultimately as we look at American culture as well. So does the Reformation matter? It does matter—in ways that continue to shape western culture today.

A CENTURY OF GENIUS

Chapter Objectives

- Define the Scientific Revolution as a shift in worldview.
- Identify some of the key thinkers in the "century of genius."
- Demonstrate how Bacon's "Idols" express the spirit of modern science.

In the last chapter we noted that the Reformation has exercised a lasting impact on western culture—one that is still felt today. That's the perspective we need to bring to our study of the past. We should be asking, "Why does it matter? How does it help us to understand the way people live and think and behave in the world right now? What have we inherited from these earlier cultures?" Remember how we did asked those questions of the Greeks and the Romans. We did as well when we surveyed the Middle Ages, the Renaissance, and the Reformation. Now, we'll continue to do that as we carry on the story of the emergence of the modern age. Once again, we are going to ask the question, "Why do the developments in these remote centuries matter to us today?"

We'll be moving in the seventeenth century in this chapter. The seventeenth century is sometimes called "a century of genius." This was the century of Milton and Galileo, Cervantes and Descartes. In this chapter, however, we're going to focus on one aspect of that genius—the Scientific Revolu-

tion which, in many ways, came to a head during this century. As we go through this, we are going to be looking back at the roots of modern science, as well as looking ahead to our own time to see what the implications are for how people look at the world today. The Scientific Revolution was a natural outgrowth of the Renaissance. Leonardo da Vinci, for example, as a typical Renaissance man, was deeply curious about the world around him. So it shouldn't surprise us that this focus on materialism should give rise to the Scientific Revolution.

The Scientific Revolution: Overview

What are the dates that we associate with the Scientific Revolution? Roughly, the period is from 1550-1700. What is the significance of those dates? 1550 is right around the time when Copernicus, the great Polish astronomer, published his great book, which challenged the longstanding view of astronomy—the old notion that the earth was the center of the universe. Copernicus said, "No, we're just a planet going around the sun." So, we swapped out the geocentric view for the heliocentric view. That's the significance of the date 1550. The "New Science," as it's sometimes called, had begun.

What about on the other end of the period, the date 1700? That's associated with the life of Isaac Newton, who, until Einstein, was arguably the greatest scientist in the Western tradition. With Newton, we have the emergence of the whole mechanical model of the universe and its physical laws.

Why did the Scientific Revolution occur? What caused this great shift in thinking about the natural world and the physical world to come about? It happened as a natural byproduct of the shift from the medieval to the modern world view, from that vertical hierarchical model in the middle ages to the modern world view. This brought about a new emphasis on scientific knowledge and scientific investigation. This shift was vividly demonstrated when Galileo (1564-1642) championed the views of Copernicus, and ran afoul of the authority of the church.

So that's just a quick overview: the time period, the causes behind the Scientific Revolution, and some of the great figures associated with this shift and knowledge about the physical world.

But what, more specifically, is the Scientific Revolution and how does it break from the ancient and medieval practice of science? First of all, the question that we need to consider is, "How is ancient science different from modern science?" Let's consider this question based upon what we said about the Middle Ages. Consider that you're a medieval man or woman. On what basis would you "know" something to be true

about the world around you? Quite simply this: *Someone tells you that it's true.* Somebody higher up the chain of command than you tells you. That somebody might be the church, it might be an old authoritative book that you look to, but that's how you know. At least you think you know. That's how you would know, for example, that the earth is the center of the universe, because you go to an old book on astronomy written by Ptolemy 1,500 years earlier. Some ancient authority tells you, or the authority of the church tells you that something is true. It's very important to understand that way of thinking. We can't make sense of the modern way of looking at these things unless we have that contrast in mind.

What about modern science? What is its basis for truth? Observation and experimentation. You figure it out for yourself. You investigate it for yourself. Something is true not because somebody tells you, but because you can go into a laboratory, you can test it, and you can experiment. You can repeat that experiment, and you can say that, "Yes, this is true; I can see it with my own eyes that it's true." That's the profound difference in thinking between ancient and medieval science and the modern scientific method. This shift in thinking toward experience and observation is captured in Rembrandt's famous "The Anatomy Lesson of Dr. Tulp" (1632).

The Scientific Method

Let's hone in on the **scientific method** then. The scientific method is based upon

216

what we call inductive reasoning. What is inductive reasoning? Well, let's illustrate it.

First of all, inductive reasoning is usually contrasted with another kind of reasoning known as deductive reasoning. Let's use an example to try to illustrate what both of these modes of reasoning are and then apply it to modern scientific thinking. You go to a grocery store and you buy a bag of oranges, ten oranges in the bag, and you take those oranges home. Of course, you bought the bag because you are hoping for really good, sweet tasting oranges. So you open the bag up, you peel the first orange, and you eat it. It's pulpy, it's sour, it's not worth eating, and you throw it away. You try a second orange. It's the same thing; it's not worth eating and you throw it away, too. You try a third orange, but have the same problem. What might you conclude after trying the first three oranges in that ten-orange bag? That's how they all are. They are all not worth eating. They are all pulpy and sour and so on. You have just reasoned inductively. When you reason inductively, you reason from specific pieces of evidence to general conclusions. In a sense, you have performed a basic kind of scientific experiment. Is this bag of oranges worth eating? You put it to the test? How do you arrive at the truth? By testing it for yourself. You try the oranges, and after three sour oranges, you reason inductively, from these specific pieces of evidence, that the rest of the bag is also sour.

Now let's say you go to the grocery store and you want to buy a bag of oranges and you are debating whether or not to spend money on a bag of oranges. Obviously, you want to make sure that they are worth eating if you are going to spend a lot of money on them. You ask the guy who is putting the oranges out there, and based upon his authority he says, "Yeah, these are worth eating." Now, in this case you would be taking it on authority, wouldn't you? That's a good way to illustrate that difference between medieval and modern scientific approaches. Somebody in authority tells you, as opposed to putting it to the test through your own observation and experimentation.

Let's more specifically illustrate deductive reasoning. Let's say some authority is not around for you to ask. How might you arrive at an answer deductively? You might stop and reason as you stand there in front of this bag of oranges. You might say, "Well, let's see, this time of year usually bags of oranges are sweet. Usually bags of oranges that come from Florida, in particular, are sweet. Considering the kind of weather they have had down there over the last few months, which is very favorable to sweet oranges, I would deduce that this bag of oranges is going to be sweet." So you buy it on that basis; whether it is or not is an entirely different matter. But what you have done is reasoned deductively. Where inductive reasoning is going from specific pieces of evidence to general conclusions, reasoning deductively is reasoning from general statements to specific conclusions—in this case, general statements about the time of year, the place that these oranges are coming from, the weather conditions, and so on. Those are general foundational statements from which you deduct a specific conclusion; hence, deductive reasoning.

Again, think of a scientist, going into the classroom, putting something to the test. Then, based upon those specific pieces of data he or she arrives at a general conclusion—the hypothesis that's testable or a scientific law that is demonstrable and provable in some way. So that is really the foundation of the scientific method, this inductive approach to truth. Notice how it takes knowledge out of the realm of authority and brings it down to the level of you and me. What we observe, what we reason, what we test, what we see with our own eyes, what we can handle with our own hands—all of these things make up modern the approach to scientific investigation and also make up, in large part, the modern materialistic world view.

Look at the big picture. Why is it that the modern scientific materialistic worldview is so hostile to the supernatural, to faith, to religion? We start to see why as we look at the nature of this thought process. Modern science believes what it can handle. It believes what can be testable. It believes what can be studied in the laboratory, what can be arrived at through inductive reasoning.

This scientific method is sometimes called the empirical method; **empiricism** refers to how we arrive at knowledge through experience. The experience of what we see, of what we can touch, of what we know about the world. An English philosopher, named Francis Bacon, gave us a great formulation of this method about four hundred years ago. Let's turn to what Francis Bacon had to say about empiricism. He presented the classic statement about the scientific method in the early modern period. Bacon's critique and analysis of the new science gives us a blueprint, really, to understanding how the modern mind thinks about the world.

For us as Christians in the modern world, it's very important for us to understand how, when you are talking with somebody who is not a believer and who just believes in science, how that person thinks about the world. What, for that individual is the basis of truth? That's really what we are trying to understand.

Bacon's Idols of the Mind

Francis Bacon (1561-1626), whose dates correspond almost exactly to William Shakespeare's, laid out the issue four centuries ago when he talked about how we arrive at true statements about the world through the scientific method. One of things he emphasized was how hard it is to do that. He spoke of this as a process of coming to knowledge about the world, where we have to really knock down a bunch of false ideas. You start by having to smash these false gods, false ideas in our minds. Bacon used this concrete metaphor to help us understand what's at stake.

Bacon identified four false ideas, four false ways of thinking, that modern science has to smash and get rid of before we can arrive at true statements about the world. The first of these is the **Idol of the Tribe**. Bacon is speaking about false beliefs that are common to all men; that is to the tribe.

In other words, false ways of looking at the world, which come about just because this is how we look at the world through our eyes, and how we are limited by our senses. We are limited by our faculties of reason, and so we see the world through own natural, physical limitations.

Let me give you one very quick simple example. We talk about the sun rising. The sun doesn't rise and yet, even today knowing that the sun doesn't rise, and yet we use that expression. Why do we say that? Why do we speak that way? Why in ancient times was there the belief that the sun rose and why do we still speak of it in those terms? Because that's how it looks like to us. You look at the eastern horizon and it looks like the sun is rising. We are limited by what we see. We are limited by just how we look at the world and those natural limitations are built into our senses, built into our framework. This is what Bacon is talking about when he speaks of the Idols of the Tribe. The scientist has to set those aside and say, "I know that what I am seeing looks like the sun is rising, but I have got to test it, I have got to calculate, I have got to observe. I can't just rely upon what my eyes are telling me here, because that's an idol of the tribe. That's a natural limitation of who I am in the world."

Second, Francis Bacon identified another kind of problem that the scientific method

218

has to deal with and he called these the **Idols of the Cave**. He spoke of these as false beliefs, shaped by personal experience, in the mind of the individual. These are idols that are unique to me as an individual—false beliefs that may arise out of the way I was raised or what my personal experience with the world has been. I can't carry into the laboratory my personal biases. I have to set my own personal biases aside. The way I was raised has shaped my way of looking at things; and the scientific method tries to set those aside.

The third idol that Bacon speaks of, the **Idols of the Marketplace**, are false beliefs that arise from language. He uses the word marketplace, because language is kind of like a marketplace of ideas. We exchange words like we exchange goods. What Bacon is saying is that language is imprecise. We know the world imperfectly through language. Language doesn't give us an accurate description of the world. We know that to be true. We argue over words all the time, and we are arguing over the imprecision of words. How do scientists try to deal with that when they speak of scientific laws? They try to reduce scientific laws not to words, but to mathematics. To formulas, to equations, to mathematical statements—using math as a kind of pure language that's not subject to ambiguity and misunderstanding. Scientists like to reduce things to something you can write on a chalkboard—an equation like e=mc2, that's not bound by language and misunderstanding. That's really what we see Bacon talking about, that we have got to work beyond those, false beliefs and imperfections. The scientific method tries to take us to that point, so we can understand and then describe the world as it actually is.

Finally, Francis Bacon speaks of what he calls **Idols of the Theatre**. These are systems of belief. They might be theological systems, they might be philosophical systems, they might be political systems, like Marxism, let's say, or an ideological system like feminism. They might be a religious system like Christianity. Bacon would see all these as the same kind of a thing, *systems of belief*. The idea is this: When you

go into the laboratory, you are supposed to take your system of belief and check it at the door and go in and practice the supposedly neutral and objective scientific method in the pursuit of truth.

We are justified in asking, however, whether it's ever possible to actually do this. Now, Science, with a capital S, and the scientific method, has itself become a kind of Idol of the Theatre. It has become a system of belief, with its materialistic assumptions about the world. It is almost a kind of religious system in our own day. And that's the irony; that's something that Francis Bacon didn't foresee happening.

Well, let's talk about that a little bit more and ask, "What are some of the basic ways in which this revolution in scientific knowledge has shaped our culture?"

First of all, we see the elevation of science as the measure of truth. People appeal to science now as the final statement and the final word as to whether or not something is true. This leads us to the next two points. Second, we see skepticism of authority, which is one of the significant things to note in the transition from medieval to modern. If science is now the basis of truth, the measure of truth, then everything, including authority, has got to be judged by science. But who will question the authority of science?

Finally, we see skepticism of the supernatural. Think about it. If science is the ultimate measure of truth, then only things that can be tested, only things that are subject to scientific inquiry, are real and are true. By definition then, there is no such thing as the miraculous. What then happens to miracles? What happens to personal conversion? We can't test these things in the laboratory? The reality of one's own personal salvation in Christ can't be tested in the laboratory. So somebody who is steeped in scientific thinking would discount that as not real or as not true, not subject to scientific analysis.

What we have been tracing here in this great development of seventeenth-century thought, the Scientific Revolution, is really the foundation for so much of the conflict that we see today between Science with a capital S and Faith with a capital F. You really can't account for the modern age without talking about this profound intellectual shift. It's the foundation for the direction of the last few centuries. We need to understand that scientific thinking about the world has become, in many ways, the dominant filter through which modern man sees reality and formulates his understanding of truth in the world.

THE SECULAR TURN

Chapter Objectives

- Describe the connection between the Enlightenment and the new science.
- List three terms that describe different aspects of 18th-century culture.
- Analyze three key Enlightenment ideas and their impact on western culture.

On the heels of the Scientific Revolution, the western world took a decidedly secular turn as the eighteenth century approached. Once again, our focus in this chapter will be on how the intellectual and cultural developments in this century still matter to us today. Why, after all, should we care what the philosophers in the eighteenth century believed about things? These dead philosophers like Voltaire and Rousseau that we're going to be talking about: Why should we bother with what they thought? We're going to see that they cast a pretty long shadow over the world we live in today. It does matter what they thought and that's what we need to consider in greater detail.

Defining the Eighteenth Century

I want to first of all cover a few introductory things about this century. We'll start by listing the different terms and labels that we use to describe the eighteenth century. Then we are going to focus more specifically on two or three key doctrines or beliefs of the philosophers of the Enlightenment. Finally, we are going to look at Voltaire and

Rousseau as two eminent examples of eighteenth-century philosophers. They believed some very influential things that have shaped much of the direction of modern thought, down to our own present day. There are several different labels that we use for the eighteenth century. I want to briefly discuss each one of these. One term that we use to describe this century is the Age of Reason. Right there that kind of clues us in to this important theme, this important idea that we've been tracking since the Renaissance. The revival of rationalism is a way of looking at the world—the belief in human reason, which is so much a part of what Mirandola says and what Michelangelo and Da Vinci illustrate in their art. This belief in the rational faculty goes back ultimately to the ancient Greeks. We are going to see that this just carries right on through the scientific revolution right into the Age of Reason. Rationalism is going to become the dominant value, the dominant idea that man puts great stock in, in the eighteenth century. Taking their cues from science is what they are going to be doing—looking at the great achievements of the figure like Newton and then on that basis believing that the human mind, the faculty of reason, is capable of understanding all things.

The second term that we use for this age is neoclassicism or the Neoclassical Age. When we use the phrase Age of Reason, we are specifically referring to the philosophical values of the eighteenth century. When we use the term the Neoclassical Age, we are emphasizing something different in eighteenth-century culture; we're emphasizing the arts, music, painting, literature, and architecture. We use the term neoclassical because we see a revival of classical art, of classical forms. The emphasis in classical art is on balance and harmony, things that are reasonable and rational. The neoclassical age sees those qualities as *classical* values that are grounded in reason.

Consider a few examples of neoclassical art in the eighteenth century. This is the age of Mozart and what we normally refer to as classical music. Mozart's symphonies are structured around complex principles of order and balance, again reflecting those classical values. We see this in the painting, in the sculpture, of the age as well. We see it in the architecture of the period. Thomas Jefferson was a neoclassical architect, going back to the balanced and orderly rational forms of Greco-Roman architecture. When we use the term neoclassicism, that's what we are referring to. We are looking at those sorts of rational qualities in the arts as we have illustrated.

Finally, the third term is the most general term and it's the one that's usually used as a kind of catchall term for eighteenth-century culture: the **Enlightenment**. Where does that term come from? Well the metaphor kind of gives it away in a sense, the idea of opening your eyes to the light and coming out of darkness into the light. That's how in the eighteenth-century, these very optimistic philosophers saw the condition of man at that time. Leaving the superstition, the darkness, as they saw it, of medieval religion behind and moving into the full light of reason. That's where the light

comes from as they believed you leave the darkness of religion behind and you walk into the light of reason.

The imagery is so powerful there when you put it in contrast with what Scripture says about the light and the darkness. Men love darkness, the Bible says, because their deeds are evil; and Christ is the light, the light of the world. All of that imagery is just something that you have to keep in mind as you think of this age of Enlightenment. These rationalists, who were steeped in human reason, believed that reason provided the light for mankind. But they were really just stumbling headlong in to the darkness and had no idea of the irony of that. Tragically they dragged all of western culture with them for the last couple of hundred years, as we are going to see momentarily.

Key Ideas of the Enlightenment

Let's look at the key ideas of the enlightenment. The eighteenth century, for the philosophers, was the crowning capstone of all of the achievements of science in the previous century. These eighteenth-century Enlightenment philosophers believed that reason and science were the foundation of truth for modern man; tradition and faith were increasingly being rejected as superstition.

Note clearly what's being said here. It's not being implied that if you are going to be a Christian in the twenty-first century that you are going to reject science. No, the idea here is not that science is something that the Christian rejects, but rather the notion that science and reason are the foundations of truth is the idea being rejected. The notion that they are the foundation of what we ultimately know to be true about the world. The biblical belief is that Christ is the foundation, the way, the truth, and the life. What we ultimately know about truth is what God has chosen to reveal to us in creation through the Word of God and through His son Jesus Christ. That's really what's at stake, the foundation of truth. In the eighteenth century, reason and science became sort of the bottom plank on which everything else that man believes is true was going to be built on. When you use that phrase "something is true," in the modern world, what is usually meant is that it can be verified by scientific methodology. This concept of truth became well established in the eighteenth century.

Also during the eighteenth century, philosophers began to teach the idea that man is born good, that he comes into the world good and that man—through his good instincts, his good nature, and his rational faculty—can make a better perfect world approaching social perfection. Man's nature is now deemed to be essentially good by the eighteenth-century philosophers; they believed that man is basically good and capable of social perfection. Well, you know that we've come a long way, far away from the truth of Scripture, when we start putting forth that idea.

The third doctrine that we are going to isolate here is that the goal of Enlightenment philosophy was to unify all knowledge under the all-seeing eye of reason. Look at the illustration taken from the back of the dollar bill. You see the eye of reason at the top of that pyramid; look at the light radiating out from that eye. That's what the human mind, with the rational faculty, can understand—the world of knowledge, organized within the human mind. This was the belief of Enlightenment philosophy. In the mid-eighteenth century, a group of French enlightenment philosophers decided that they were going to write a big encyclopedia, which we refer to by the French term, **encyclopédie**.

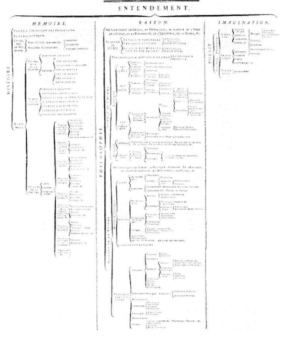

The French encyclopedia in the mid-eighteenth century was meant to be a compendium of all human knowledge. You can't do that now obviously, and you couldn't even do it then—and there was a lot less scientific knowledge then. It would be fair to say we don't have the storage capability, even with the growth of computer technology and the way the computers can process data in just milliseconds. We still don't have the capacity to store all knowledge. How could you possibly write an encyclopedia of, say, twelve volumes or so, and claim that this is all knowledge unified by the mind of reason? But that's exactly what they tried to do. We can look back smugly at the degree of arrogance that this displays, and yet the modern materialist also believes in the unifying power of human reason.

These two illustrations side-by-side really document the arrogance of what these men were trying to accomplish in the eighteenth century, and how much they thought the human mind is capable of. On the left, you see a painting of early seventeenth century by Peter Paul Rubens, with a traditional religious theme. You have the Virgin Mary and child and throne with Saints. It's very much a celestial painting of the glory of the Virgin Mary and so on. It's very much a Catholic painting in that sense, but very religious in orientation, and traditional in its theme. Would you say that the illustration right next to that looks similar to that in form and style and structure? It does look very similar to it in a lot of ways. But instead of the Virgin Mary being in the upper center of this illustration, which is the frontispiece to the encyclopedia, up in the upper center of the painting with light radiating out from its figure is a personification of reason, reason turned into a god.

They swapped out a religious icon for a new God—the God of Reason. And that tells the story of the modern age, of how religion was swapped out for another set of religious beliefs, another set of values. Revelation was swapped out for reason.

Voltaire and Rousseau

Let's start looking at the two towering figures of the eighteenth-century Enlightenment: Voltaire and Rousseau. Both of these men were very influential, but in the different ways. Voltaire was a kind of happy-go-lucky atheist. He was an atheist in an age where it was still a pretty uncommon thing

to be. There were not a lot of atheists in the eighteenth century, but it's not so uncommon today. One of the things that's really amazing is that you can see how much has changed in Western culture by Voltaire's time; he wasn't burned at the stake for some of the things he said. Clearly the world had changed a lot, including the role and the status of the Church within Western culture.

Voltaire, lived from 1694 to 1778, was a very brilliant man, a very witty man, and a great writer. He is known for his great literary style, and is also known as a philosopher of sorts. One of his very familiar statements is that "If God did not exist, it would be necessary to invent Him." That expresses a lot of what Voltaire believed—that God was a construct of the human imagination made because we need a moral standard in society. If we didn't have that, we would all tear each other apart; so we invented God. He was a very outspoken man in his beliefs and a brilliant man, but a man who was also a blasphemer. I think it's important to put what he said in context. My approach to him is always from a Christian perspective, so to look at him from another perspective, pick up humanities text written from a secular point of view. It's not going to describe him as a blasphemer. It's going to fall down in front of him and worship the memory of Voltaire. He is considered one of the great secular figures of the modern age. He is looked to and idolized by the secular modern world, because he was so hostile to faith. He was so hostile to the Church, what he described as called the tyranny of the Church. He was a "free thinker" in that sense, and so he's a hero to that secular mindset. But I see him as a blasphemer.

I want to give you a phrase that will make it much clearer. It's a statement of his, that's very hard for me even to state, because it is so blasphemous, but I want you to know who Voltaire is. If you run into him in other readings along the way, especially readings that celebrate this great and wonderful figure of Voltaire, I want you to think about this man who said "The blood of Christ, the blood of pigs, it makes no difference." That's a pretty remarkable statement. That's an incredibly blasphemous statement to make and this is the man, this is the atheist Voltaire. He said those things, because he was challenging in most radical way he possibly could, the authority of the Church. You can see why secular humanists and so on look to a figure like Voltaire with such approval. You can see how he inspired them, because the very same kinds of hostility that Voltaire expressed, which was uncommon in the eighteenth century, is now common today.

Look at how you can't call it "Christmas" in a public place anymore. It's just a secularized holiday. Christmas trees aren't Christmas trees anymore. They are holiday trees— whatever that is. In public schools, you can't sing Christmas carols that are of a religious nature. We are seeing the emasculation of the Christian heritage and the culture that lies behind it. This is Voltaire's legacy in many ways—not that he created all of that, but rather that he is indicative of that trend. You can see in him on the leading edge of Western culture. You can see that though his hostility to Christian faith was uncommon two hundred years ago, it is quite familiar to us now.
That's why it's important to talk about Voltaire and Rousseau. That's why it's important to see Voltaire for what he was, and to recognize that while he looks like a witty, genial, and brilliant figure—and certainly the history books make him out to be this wonderful figure—there is a darker reality

behind the façade. I don't for minute deny that he was a brilliant writer and intellect. But as a Christian, I also see him as a man who said terrible and destructive things about faith. Let's turn now to the equally important legacy of Rousseau who lived from 1712 to 1778.

In many ways, Rousseau was even more influential than Voltaire. He was not as brilliant a thinker, a man slightly demented in a number of ways. He was a very troubled man. That's pretty sad when somebody has been so influential and yet lived some a troubled life. You think about men like Freud and so on in the twentieth century who similarly have exerted tremendous impact on Western society. We don't take our clues from the right people, do we? Roussea said that "Man is born free, and everywhere he is in chains." Rousseau more than anyone believed that man is born good and man is born free. Those notions of goodness and freedom are really, for him, interchangeable. When we come into this world you are good; your nature is good, or at least it's not bad. If you believe that, look around you for a moment. You have a problem, don't you? You have a big problem in accounting for the nature of the world around you. If man comes into this world good, why is everything is so messed up wherever we look? How do you account for not just individual acts of wrong, but how do you account for the big historic acts of evil in the twentieth century? How do you account for that? I believe that Rousseau has been proven wrong by both theology and by history. You can't look back at the last couple of hundred years and conclude otherwise. Nonetheless, even though the twentieth century seems to have completely disproven him, you can stop and ask people on the street and find that people still believe that man is basically good.

It's a widespread belief—and so, again, you can see how far we have come from what scripture teaches. Scripture doesn't teach that man is basically good, and not even that that man is basically bad; scripture teaches that man is entirely depraved. How did Rousseau account for the sorry state of the world if he believed that man is good? He believed that it's society's fault. Man is good, but institutions are bad. So you come into this world good and you find yourself in a rotten family that ruins you. Then you go to school and you have rotten teachers, who turn you into a rotten and cruel person. Then you go into the world, into society, into a political and economic system that's unjust. No wonder people steal and kill and so on, according to Rousseau, because they've been made that way by society. Bad families and bad schools and bad social and political institutions have made them that way. Thus, man is born free but he gets enslaved. Think of how that contrasts with Scripture. Man is not born free; man is born in bondage to sin. You can see again just how clearly these philosophers are rejecting Scripture and the concept of personal, individual responsibility. Institutions, not individuals, are to blame.

This is important to note, as we look at Rousseau and the powerful legacy of his thinking. This way of thinking is still out there. It's how people think. Today, we call it social and political liberalism. Just think of the kind of the political debates in our own country that track along the spectrum from liberal to conservative philosophy. What is that the liberals believe about social problems? Liberals generally believe that bad institutions cause social problems. Bad things don't happen in society because people are bad, but because they've been conditioned that way by bad schools and bad neighborhoods. They've been conditioned that way by not having access to good jobs and good health care. And if you

think that way, it's very logical within its own system of assumptions. Liberals believe that man is basically good and institutions are bad; therefore, you become a creature of government. You think government is the institution that is going to tinker with these bad institutions and things better. So you try to legislate change; you try to make better people through better schools and better social benefits. If people have better homes and neighborhoods to live in, better access to healthcare, and so on, then they will be better people. We can trace that line of thinking back to Rousseau. He's the godfather of modern social liberalism. Liberalism is based fundamentally on a false view of human nature and that's the biggest split between conservatives and liberals. The conservative tradition has always been to view human nature as something that has to be restrained because man is not naturally good; whereas liberalism believes in the basic goodness of men.

So what are the consequences of this? Well, Rousseau had a profound impact on American education and the way we teach our kids. We don't want to screw them up with facts and so on; we just want them to bloom and blossom into the good little creatures they were meant to be. We want them to be individuals and so we don't want them to teach them facts; we want them just to develop. This is a very much an American theory of education that's had horrible consequences on American education—and these were Rousseau's ideas about education. Think as well of the consequences in the legal system. Somebody is brought into court, charged with murder. He stands before the judge and says, "It's not my fault. My parents messed me up." The jury agrees with that, and so he is acquitted of the crime. This is Rousseau's philosophy and its devastating legacy for us today—not just in education, but in the legal system and the political arena as well.

These are some of the profound impacts of the Enlightenment right down to today. Just as we found with the Scientific Revolution, the influence continues on. And so that's why we study it; that's why we go to the past to try to figure out the present world.

226

ROMANTICISM AND REVOLUTION

Chapter Objectives

- List and describe four ways that the late 18th-century was "revolutionary."
- Define and illustrate the concept of a "romantic hero."
- Demonstrate how the values of romanticism still shape the modern world.

In this chapter we're going to examine the Romantic period, which is one of the most important modern movements in western cultural history. In many ways romanticism is just as important as the Enlightenment or even the Renaissance. As we've looked at each one of these periods, we've seen that they cast a very long shadow over our culture. The philosophical presuppositions of the Scientific Revolution are with us today. The values and beliefs of the Enlightenment, the Age of Reason, are with us today. The humanism of the Renaissance is with us today. And this is how we're going to look at romanticism. We want to figure out what the movement was all about, but how it affects us in the world we're living in right now.

The period that we'll be looking at in this chapter is roughly between 1775 and 1825. Let me give you two quick points for how we're going to proceed. First of all, we'll define romanticism in light of what comes before it. We can't just take these fifty years, put it in a box, label it romanticism, and understand it by itself. We've got to see how this cultural movement is connected to everything that came before it. Secondly, we're going to then define romanticism in light of everything that came after it. We'll consider what the implications are for you and me today, how we still think like romantics today, and how we view the role of art and nature today. We are going to see many ways in which we've inherited romantic beliefs and values.

Understanding Romanticism

First, let's place romanticism in its historical setting. How would we define this period from 1775-1825 in light of what comes before it? Let's use the method of comparison and contrast to get at some answers to this question. When you compare you focus on similarities. When you contrast, you focus on differences. It's a very logical kind of way for us to proceed.

Let's start then with the comparison. How does romanticism reflect the values of the periods that came before? How does it reflect the values of the modern age that we have been talking about ever since the Renaissance, the seventeenth century and the eighteenth century? Two key values come to mind: individualism and nature. The first one is the most important, that's the familiar theme of individualism or the old theme of individuality. Individualism is a constant theme throughout western culture. Certainly we made much of it when we examined the ancient Greeks. We looked at it in the Renaissance, and we find it here again in Romanticism. Individualism is a very important theme in the romantic period and in romantic art. It is a natural outgrowth of the modern emphasis on individualism.

The second value is the theme of nature and the natural world. How does this also follow from what we said about the modern world so far? In the Renaissance we found that men like Da Vinci were opening their eyes to the natural world around them. If you doubt that, just look at Da Vinci's sketchbooks. What is he sketching? He is sketching the human body. He is sketching nature. He is sketching trees and flowers and trying to understand their intricate forms. People are looking at nature as something important. Consider, took how the Scientific Revolution refocuses attention on the natural world. Modern science is all about trying to understand nature, trying to focus on the world around you. So it shouldn't be real surprising then, that we see nature as an important theme as we move into the period of romanticism.

What do we see when we contrast romanticism with what came before? The difference really lies in the extremity. The Romantics took these ideas to the extreme. Yes, we'll see the familiar idea of individualism once again, but it will be an individualism like none we've seen before. It will be individualism taken to the nth degree. It's going to be a radical kind of individualism—an assertion of one's own identity even in the face of God. We're going to see that Romantic artists really do that and they believe that reality is reducible to who I am living right now in this moment. That's a pretty radical kind of individualism, and that's what we'll be seeing in this period. It may be an old theme, but it's given a significant facelift in the romantic period. It's a much more extreme version of that kind of individualism.

Similarly with nature, the Romantics didn't view nature anywhere near the way Da Vinci did or Copernicus and the great scientists of that age who were studying the material world. The Romantics viewed nature as a goddess to be worshipped and to draw in-

spiration from. Again, this is a very extreme way of looking at nature, equally as extreme as the way they viewed individualism. The point I am stressing here is, these are old themes; we've seen them percolating up in western culture. But these are themes that the Romantics took to an extreme end point.

There is another way in which romanticism differed from what came immediately before it—the Enlightenment and its central belief in human reason. Reason is all about order and structure and the kinds of things that science can investigate and study. The culture of the eighteenth century, the period of the Enlightenment, was steeped in rationalism. Human reason, it was believed, would guide man toward progress. We'll see that the Romantics moved in the other direction. They would react vehemently against the rationalism of the eighteenth century. Instead of saying that the "head" and rationalism are the primary things, they would emphasize the "heart." I am simplifying here, but it's a useful simplification nonetheless. This helps us to see the nature of this profound difference between the romantics and the rationalists of the eighteenth century. Where the Enlightenment philosophers were all about the power of human reason, the romantic artists will focus on the power of the human heart. This emphasis will be expressed in political revolutions like the American and French Revolution. We'll see the power of the individual will celebrated within human society and expressed most clearly in the art, music, and literature of this period. For the Romantics, the passions of the heart, the will of the individual, will reign supreme. The Romantics were not even striving for balance—that value that was so important to the ancient Greeks. Remember how the Greeks were trying to find that balance between the head and heart, between the moment and the eternal. The Romantics didn't strive for that kind of balance; for them, it's all about the heart. They wanted to define the world they lived in according to the passions, dictates, and the will of the individual human heart. That is a pretty radical departure within western culture, and we can see that contrast in the dissimilarity between romanticism and the rationalism of the Enlightenment. In many ways romanticism did grow naturally out of Enlightenment culture; but the contrast is nonetheless very striking and reactionary.

Our second goal will be to see how romanticism connects with our world today. Why does it matter to us what the Romantics thought two hundred years ago? Ultimately, it wouldn't be worth studying if it didn't speak to us today, right? It would just be facts for a game of trivia, if it didn't have some impact and some relevance to understanding our lives. We're going to see, for example, that you can't really understand how artists are today, how they view themselves, how they seem to be so out of sync with the rest of society (and we'll use the culture of Hollywood as an example of that)—you can't really understand modern artists without referring back to the Romantics. We are going to see that that's one of the shadows that romanticism has cast over our world. We are going to see that this radical notion of individualism is something that we've inherited, I think, to our detriment. I don't think we are the better for it at all; and the notion that everybody is just out there marching to his own drum and creating his own truth and so on is a very radical postmodern notion. These ideas make up a significant part of the legacy of the Romantic movement.

As you can see I'm not a Romantic. It should be obvious by now from everything we've said in the way that we talked about the Greeks and the classical legacy. I very much admire what the Greeks were striving to do, to find that balance between head and heart, between reason and passion, and that was the genius of Greek culture. The Romantics really are playing with fire, literally. I've deliberately chosen that metaphor, because one of the great romantic myths is that of Prometheus. The English romantic poet Shelley talks about Prometheus, who stole fire from the gods—and this is what the Romantics are really trying to do. Romanticism, as I am going to present it, is a kind of false religion that worships the individual and nature. These are the two themes that we're going to emphasize as we examine the Romantics.

Let's look now at the historical context of Romanticism, the period from 1775-1825. This period in which Romanticism emerged is a period of revolution, and that's really the theme that we're going to explore here. We are going to focus on the arts obviously, and the culture and the philosophical beliefs of Romanticism; but to get at that, we've got to talk about the historical context as well. Let's talk about several of the ways in which the period of Romanticism was a revolutionary period. It was revolutionary in the political sense, in an economic and a social sense. Finally, we're going to focus on how it was a revolutionary period, culturally and artistically.

The Revolutionary Spirit

The dates speak for themselves: This was a period of political revolution. It was a period in which we see the assertion of individual rights. The American Revolution of 1776 and the French Revolution of 1789 make this clear. These are the most significant examples of political revolution in this period; but there was a widespread spirit of revolution that extended beyond the borders of France. One of the great paintings of this era, Francisco Goya's "Third of May 1808" captures this reality. (See Color Illustration T.)

The genius of the American constitutional system is that it struck a balance and that's really the important contrast to note, as we think of this period of political revolution. Something has to control those passions, or society would be a pretty scary place to live. As you look at the American system, the constitutional system of checks and balances and so on, we see how it enshrines the needs for individual freedom and individual rights, but balances them against the necessary structure and order of society. That's the genius there. And so we can see these themes of individualism playing out against the political landscape, and we can contrast the American and the French Revolutions as a way of seeing how these themes of individualism matter in the world of experience.

This was also a period of profound economic revolution, the time of the industrial revolution. I again mention Alvin Toffler and his book *The Third Wave* (1980). Alvin Toffler is a futurist, and he tries to understand the direction of future history by looking at the trends of the past. He argued that you could look at all of human civilization as having developed under one of three economic waves that have swept over civilization and have controlled every aspect of human life. The first wave was the longest, The Agricultural Revolution. Most of human history has occurred under that "wave," as Toffler calls it, up until the late eighteenth century, when people began leaving the rural countryside with its farms and migrated to the cities where factories were being built. Every aspect of society would be transformed; it would be like a wave flowing over human culture. The way people live, the way they relate to one another, the way they understand the world—everything would change. And that's the point Toffler was making. We see in this period of great economic revolution the ongoing process of urbanization. People were leaving the country, moving to the cities, working long hours in factories, and it would have a tremendous political and social impact upon society.

Art and literature gave expression to the upheaval. Poets and painters documented that and reflect the great revolutions and upheavals that were occurring in the western world at this time. This is very much a period of upheaval; people were being dislocated as they move to the cities for work. All sorts of social problems emerge from that disruption of the social fabric. People are working long hours in factories—dangerous factories, polluted factories—not having the normal protection of the law that is now built into our system. We see activist social movements beginning to emerge out of all this chaos in an attempt to address these issues.

First of all, we see the workers' rights movement emerging in this period of time. People were working twelve, fourteen, even sixteen hours in dark, polluted factories around dangerous machines. There wasn't any government oversight—not OSHA (the Occupational Safety and Health Administration) protecting people's rights in the workplace then. Workers basically had no rights. We take many things for granted today that had their origin in this period of change, such as the idea that workers, too, are individuals who have rights.

In addition to the workers' rights movement, we see the emergence of the feminist movement in this period. We are used to thinking of feminism as a very recent phenomenon. We think of it within the current American political landscape, and associate it with the 1960s and 1970s, when the American feminist movement as we know it came into being. But feminism as a modern movement goes back two hundred years to a woman named Mary Wollstonecraft. She is usually cited as the first feminist. In 1792, she wrote a book called *A Vindication of the Rights of Woman* in which she argued that women need to be treated with equal respect as men. It doesn't sound too radical to you or me today, but that notion that was pretty revolutionary back then—that women should be treated on equal terms and not treated as second class citizens. As a side note, Mary Wollstonecraft was the mother of Mary Shelley, the author of *Frankenstein*.

Third, in addition to the rise of the workers' rights movement and the feminist movement, we see another response to the social upheaval of this period—the enactment of child labor laws. Children as young as nine or ten years old were working twelve hours a day in factories when they should have been in schools. The desire to protect these children grew out of the belief that they, too, were individuals whose rights needed to be protected. This is the core belief—individualism—lying at the heart of this revolutionary period in western culture.

We see this in the poetry of William Blake, an English romantic poet at the end of the 18th and early 19th century. One of the things that appalled him was the tragedy of child labor. If you take a British literature class, you will read the famous poems of William Blake that he wrote about chimney sweeps. These orphaned children, all boys, only eight or nine years old, were employed as chimney sweepers. They were small enough to climb down into the chimneys and do the dirty work. The lived just horrible lives; they were not only robbed of their childhood, they were dying in childhood of the various conditions and diseases and health conditions that they acquired as a result of their work. Blake was appalled by that, and so he wrote these poems which passionately spoke to those problems and asserted their rights to be treated as children in the right way. So, whether we are talking about the economic, social, or political upheavals of this period, we're seeing that people are thinking about the new role of individuals within society.

Perhaps the most significant of all of these social movements is the rise of abolitionism, the anti-slavery movement which arose first in Great Britain and then finally in North America. It's a natural and logical extension of your philosophy of individualism to extend rights to those who are not free. Rights are being gradually extended to every other disadvantaged and vulnerable group: factory workers, women, and children. No other group was more deprived of their dignity and worth as individuals than those who were bought and sold as property. These social movements, then, represent one of the best legacies of this sea change of thinking associated with the romantic period. We need to keep this balance in our thinking. There is a positive quality in focusing on the individual and good things can come from that—such as the "revolutionary" idea that one individual doesn't have the right to abuse another individual and deprive him of his rights.

The Romantic Hero

Now let's look at the negative side of all this emphasis on the individual. We'll turn to another revolutionary aspect of the romantic period—its artistic and cultural legacy. I'm not going to be claiming that romantic art is morally "bad," but I will be arguing that it is deeply humanistic in its philosophy. Consider the great romantic poets like William Wordsworth, Keats and Shelley. Or think of the great romantic painters or the great romantic composers like Beethoven. I am definitely not saying that the romantic movement and its art are bad; what I am talking about is the philosophy of romanticism. That's where we are going to be shining the spotlight. The philosophy, the values that give expression to the art itself, is clearly what I want us to not lose sight of. As we do this, we're going to focus once again on individualism and on nature. These will become false gods for the romantic artists. The modern western world has inherited this false religion as one of the legacies of romanticism. So, in addition to this being a period of political, economic and social revolution, romanticism is a period of cultural and artistic revolution. To get at that, we are going to have to look at the values, the belief system of the romantic artists, the poets, the painters, the musicians. What did they think? What did they believe?

The unique twist that the romantics gave the theme of individualism is that they took it to the extreme—to the nth degree. Individualism, for them, became a way of life; it was their philosophy, even their religion to the point where you can see romantic artists, in a sense, worshipping the individual and the idea of the individual. For them, the ultimate expression of human experience was to live your life as you see it—not as society tells you, not as some old book of religion tells you, but as you see fit. That's going to be the new religion of individualism, which we can trace back to the romantic period.

Let's look at the labels developed in this period to describe this radical type of individualism. The term **romantic hero** was developed to give expression to what they meant when they talked about individualism. Using the word "hero" pretty much suggests that you are elevating something to an ideal—a high standard that you look up to. The romantic hero then was the ideal of what their notion of individualism was. Our first example we'll cite was not a poet, musician, or an artist; he is none other than Napoleon. In many ways, Napoleon is the prototypical romantic hero, a man of this age. We look back at him as a man who, in his life, is giving expression to the radical individualist values that we associate with romanticism.

Let's identify the three qualities in Napoleon's career that we can see as qualities of the romantic hero. Napoleon was definitely a well-defined individual, and we can see him as the first romantic hero in the following three ways. First, in his sweeping ambition, which is a pretty fair characterization of somebody who sets out to conquer the world. Second, we see a powerful individualism in Napoleon—the sense of being a unique identity. That's how the romantic artists saw themselves and their ideal of living life as an individual. It was to be different, totally unique and to give expression to that individualism within society.

One of the ways you gave expression to your own unique identity in the world was to make sure you were not like anybody else. That's why we see a third element in Napoleon as well: an arrogant disdain for all that is ordinary. Just think about that for a minute. If you're a practicing artist in America today, the last thing that you want to have said about you in a review—whether you're an actor, a painter, or a musician—is that your performance is ordinary, typical, routine, or conventional. The romantic wants his art to be defined by his individualism. Notice the extreme to which that idea has been taken in our day. Art has become a kind of a caricature today, because artists strive for this individuality so much. They want to make sure that they're not routine and ordinary, as they see in the rest of society to be; and so they set out to actually offend through their art. This is why there is so much controversy about contemporary avant-garde art that offends social values and moral beliefs. It's also why actors in Hollywood espouse the views that they do and live their lives the way they do, which is so much out of step with the rest of society. We can trace these ideas back to this radical individualistic notion of the romantic hero. Though not an artist, Napoleon is a remarkable prototype of this radical individualism; he's not your ordinary individual, but he transcends (and transgresses) the ordinariness of social conventions.

Let's look at another historical figure in the world of literature. We've looked at a political figure, but let's look at another man of this age, Lord Byron. He was one of the great English romantic poets, and again, he was a man with a sweeping ambition and a powerful sense of individual identity. Most importantly, he was very disdainful of the social and moral standards of his day. He rejected them and lived his life by his own moral values. He lived in accordance with what he chose to call "moral," and not what society or what religion defined as moral. We would call him a libertine, a man who lived his life for sensuality and pleasure. We call this kind of person a "Byronic hero," somebody who abandons traditional and conventional notions of social behavior and moral behavior. Again, this is an example of individualism taken to the extreme.

Let's look at a fictional example. I mentioned Mary Shelly and her great novel *Frankenstein*. So, let's now consider the central protagonist, Dr Frankenstein, the mad scientist who creates the monster. It's a little jarring to think that Dr. Frankenstein could be considered a romantic hero. But think of his "sweeping ambition." I would say that anybody who goes into the laboratory with the goal of creating life has a pretty sweeping ambition. It is not your ordinary pursuit in life. There is nothing conventional or routine about that at all. When you apply each one of these Napoleonic qualities, you see that Dr. Frankenstein is very much a romantic hero. Mary Shelley was married to Percy Bysshe Shelley, one of the leading English romantic poets of this period. One of Shelley's great poems is "Prometheus Unbound," which is a retelling of an ancient myth. Prometheus is so sweeping in his ambition, so powerfully individualistic in his life, so, discontented with the ordinary, that he dares to steal fire from the gods. The story of Prometheus is adopted as a romantic myth about what man in his individualism tries to achieve through his own genius and ambition.

In addition to Dr. Frankenstein and Prometheus, we can cite another fictional example of the romantic hero—Dr. Faust, the man who sold his soul to the devil so that he can experience the full range of human experience. Again, that sounds like a typical romantic quest; once again, we see the sweeping ambition, a disdain for all that is ordinary, and the desire to define life and morality for oneself.

In addition to the term "romantic hero," we often encounter the phrase "romantic genius" as a description of how the creative intellectuals of his period saw themselves. They believed that art was an expression of the individual's unique life, and that art, therefore, was an expression of individual genius. This quality of genius is what sets the artist apart from the ordinariness of society, which is why the romantic genius is usually depicted as a loner, cut off from society. He is like the starving artist who is pursuing, in a lonely way in some garret somewhere, his own vision of reality. This is a romantic stereotype that we've inherited—the poet, for example, who has to give expression to his heart and lives to do that, regardless of what an unaccepting and unforgiving society might think.

As we look back at this period, we can identify one of the greatest composers of this or any period as a kind of a prototypical romantic genius. Beethoven is a remarkably interesting figure, because if you look at his early compositions, his symphonies, they are much more classical, much more similar to the style we associate with Mozart. Then you hit that famous fifth symphony, and we begin to see Beethoven the romantic emerging in his later compositions.

Let's put our finger on these qualities of the solitary artist struggling to express a sweeping ambition. The romantic genius is conceived of as a solitary isolated figure, struggling for creative autonomy against the interference of outside bodies. Those outside bodies might be the norms of society and the values of conventional morality. The artist wants only to be bound by the dictates of his own heart—that's the notion I am stressing here. That's the idea of the romantic hero, the romantic genius in art. Here's where we see a direct application to our own culture today. You really can't understand the offensiveness of so much of contemporary art, unless you understand this idea of turning art in a religion of individualism. It's as though the purpose of contemporary art is to assault the values of ordinary people. Artists see themselves as playing the role of consciously being out of step with the rest of the society. The notion of the romantic hero, or romantic genius, persists in popular culture most clearly with the cult of celebrities—especially pop musicians and Hollywood actors. Once again, we see the long shadow that has been cast by the romantic period. We're seeing that you really can't understand much of our own world without understanding that it came from this period of time.

The Power of Nature

Without a doubt, individualism is one of the most important values of romanticism. But let's consider one more, and that's the value of nature. Nature was a source of inspiration for them; it was the source of all that was pure and original. The purity of nature reminded the romantics of their lost innocence, their alienation from the natural world. They looked to nature for the inspiration of their art. We see this in a painting by Caspar David Friedrich, a German Romantic painter. Take a look at his painting "Wanderer above a Sea of Fog" (1818). Here you've got a man, whom we can describe as a typical romantic figure of that age, looking out into the awesomeness of nature and taking it all in. The point is to see the power of nature as a source of inspiration. We see this quality in the English romantic poets like William Wordsworth who wrote about nature; Wordsworth's great sonnet, "The World Is Too Much With Us" is one of the most profound expressions of the romantic rejection of the "modern" world and embrace of the "natural" world. We see this quality, too, in romantic painters such as Friedrich, and even in romantic composers who drew much inspiration from the natural world. Nature is one of the dominant themes of romanticism.

What shadow has this love affair with nature cast upon the modern world? What are some of the modern movements that have grown naturally out of this celebration of nature, even this idealization of nature? I would say that the environmental movement is perhaps the best example of this. We talk about radical environmentalists as "tree huggers," suggesting that they love nature and they love it in the sense of worshiping it. Modern environmentalism has turned nature into a goddess to be worshipped. We can trace this back to this romantic love of nature as a source of inspiration. If you think about it in the modern world, if you've turned your back on God, then what are you going to replace Him with? When we talked about that in the aftermath of the Scientific Revolution, we saw that science for some people became a God. During the Enlightenment, Reason became a God. And we're seeing that Nature, for the romantics, has become a goddess—and this idolatry has persisted down into the modern world.

THE TRIUMPH AND MATERIALISM

Chapter Objectives

- Understand how realism was a reaction to the excesses of romanticism.
- Analyze how Darwin and Marx both expressed a materialistic philosophy.
- Describe and critique the optimism that was typical of the late 19th century.

In the last few chapters we've been tracing the progress of some of the key values that emerged during and after the Renaissance. We've seen that each period, each century of the modern age found new ways to express the humanistic and rationalistic impulses that define the modern secular world. Following the Renaissance, we have the rationalism of the Scientific Revolution and the belief that the scientific method can unlock the nature of reality. We see reason coming into focus again in the Age of Enlightenment, the Age of Reason of the eighteenth century. We looked at romanticism and saw the humanistic values of individualism on display. The romantics took individualism to an extreme; they celebrated the notion of the "romantic hero," and they believed that all reality was to be understood through one's own experience of living. Figures like Napoleon really illustrate the radical individualism of the romantic era; but we also saw this quality clearly in the poets and artists of that age as well.

As we move to the middle of the nineteenth century, we're going to see that the arts

and philosophy of the era will be reacting strongly to romanticism. That's the approach I want you to have as we look at the period of the mid-nineteenth century. We'll be looking at the philosophies and the arts of that age. I want us to start by considering how the culture of this period can be seen as a reaction to the excesses, if you will, of romanticism.

The excesses of romanticism with its radical emphasis upon the individual, led artists in the mid-nineteenth century to see the romantics as people who were narcissistic—people who were living for themselves and for their own subjective visions of reality. We're going to see that the artists and the philosophers of the mid-nineteenth century rejected that. Instead, they believed that you can't just be focused exclusively on yourself as the romantics were. This reaction will define the period in the arts that we call "realism." We'll be examining this movement from various points of view in this chapter.

Reaction to Romanticism

As we've seen, the romantic poets and artists created art that was really all about themselves; their art was an expression of their own individual visions of reality taken to the extreme. One of the most curious sources of inspiration for them were the opium dens of London, where they smoked and then wrote poetry based on their hallucinations. Where do you think that the musicians and poets and artists of the 1960s got their inspiration? I mean it's nothing new; they looked back 150 years to the romantic poets for their drug-induced inspiration. When I describe these romantic poets as living in their own world and then writing about their own visions, I mean this in a very literal sense. They were obsessed with themselves and their own notions of reality with very little regard to the world outside. As we move into the mid-nineteenth century, the realist reaction to romanticism was to say, "Enough of that. Let's look out at the world. Let's look at society and let's look at the world that's filled with people other than yourself."

This is the reaction that we see. The fanciful and exotic world of the romantic poets is contrasted with an emphasis upon *what is real*. Of course, this is why we call the movement "realism." This new generation of artists and writers were reacting to that obsession with the self and one's own view of reality that was so much a part of the romantic age. As we look at this period, we are going to see the contrast between a subjective focus on reality and objective focus, or "looking outward at the world" as I put it, and trying to understand the world as it really is. We are going to see that this is the case in the literature of this period. It's also what we see in the visual arts of the mid-nineteenth century.

In literature, this is the period of Charles Dickens. Writing in the mid-nineteenth century, Dickens wasn't writing like a romantic; he wasn't focused entirely upon himself, hanging out in opium dens and concocting stories based upon whatever hallucination he had. People like Dickens were reacting against that, and saying, "No, we have to look around us. We have to look at society. We have to look at the state of the world as it is." Consider the novels of Charles Dickens. He was describing life in London in the mid-nineteenth century, the way it was really lived on the streets. One of the things you would see when opening your eyes to the world around you in the mid-nineteenth century was just how bad things were. You would see all the negative consequences of the Industrial Revolution—

and these are the kinds of things that Charles Dickens was documenting. But it's not enough just to look at the world and see how it is. The realists also wanted to change the world.

A social agenda lies behind the writings of Charles Dickens. His novel *Oliver Twist*, for example, portrays what it was like to be an orphan on the streets of a modern city. But the larger idea behind this was to conclude that this is not right—that this should not be the case and we should do something about it. Laws should be passed in order to change these horrible conditions. A very real social conscience lies behind this movement in literature and art. Note the contrast again between romanticism and realism. Artists, in particular, are moving outside themselves, outside that subjective world of romantic art and experience. They are looking at the world as it really is and then wanting to change that world. We also see in France, the great novelist, Gustave Flaubert, as another realist writer. He is considered one to be one of the greatest of all of the modern novelists. His novel, *Madame Bovary*, is considered by many to be the greatest modern novel. Like Dickens, he was trying to depict what life was really like. But instead of depicting it as Dickens did—life in a big city in London—Flaubert has given us insight into what life was like in the small towns and villages of France.

I have mentioned a social consciousness, of looking at the world around you objectively and seeing the conditions of the industrial age. This will lead naturally to the rise of modern journalism during this time. It is really no surprise, if you think about what journalism is supposed to be; journalists are supposed to look at the world and report what they actually see. They are supposed to relate and report objectively the situation that's out there in the world.

There is even this strain of journalism that we call investigative journalism, like the show "60 Minutes," for example, or other similar types of shows on television where the whole point is to investigate in an almost adversarial way the nature of a problem or a social issue. Many journalists consider it their job to determine what the problems in the real world are and how can they be addressed. You can see how that mentality grows naturally out of this mid-nineteenth century realism.

We should also note that this is the age when photography emerges as a technology, and this too is in keeping with the spirit of realism. If your goal is to see the world as it actually is, then this new technology allows you to take a picture of the world as it actually is and relate it more accurately than any painter could ever achieve. Thus, photography as a medium becomes very important in the mid-nineteenth century as a means of documenting the world and we see it. Photographic journalism in the nineteenth century began documenting the reality of life on the streets of London and New York. Towards the end of the nineteenth century, some of the great photojournalists documented their life in New York. Their extraordinary black-and-white photographs are very moving records of what it was like to be an orphan on the streets of New York. These are very graphic photographs of the poverty and the squalor of life in the industrialized city; the children living on the streets and sleeping on the grills where the steam comes up and gives them some warmth. You can see the social consciousness again behind all of this. The idea is not just to see how the world is, but what can we do to change it and make it better. Lurking behind the realistic impulse is the notion of progress, the belief that man is going to make a better modern world through science and technology, guided by human reason. The idea of progress will be one of the dominant themes that we'll be exploring from this point on.

The Crystal Palace

In addition to this new spirit of realism in the literature of the age and the emergence of modern journalism, what do we see in the arts of the nineteenth century that reflects this new emphasis upon the world as it actually is?

We're going to look at architecture briefly, and one of the most famous buildings I would say of the entire nineteenth century—the Crystal Palace. We're going to see what this structure tells us about this new spirit. How does the Crystal Palace fit into this movement that we're calling realism? First, a little bit of background. The Crystal Palace was built in London in 1851. It was an enormous structure. The Crystal Palace was built in London, early in the reign of Queen Victoria. Its purpose was to house what was known as the Great Exhibition. The Great Exhibition is usually described as the First World Fair; different countries sent exhibits, showcasing the leading technology and commercial products of the day.

In 1851, hundreds of different countries were represented, including the United States. The various countries exhibited the material products of their factories. Remember that one of the great revolutions we talked about earlier was the Industrial Revolution. Factories were now being built all over the western world and were churning out products—all of which were now proudly on display in the Crystal Palace in 1851. This is really in a sense a celebration of the achievements of man and this notion of progress. The sense of—"Look at what we're producing, look at where we're going, look at what the modern age is becoming." That's really what the Crystal Palace with the Great Exhibition was all about.

The entire structure was made out of a steel superstructure with glass panels—a very modern mode of construction. You think of a skyscraper today and all of the glass and steel. This is really what was meant to be conveyed—the spirit of progress in the modern age. Let's consider the scale of the building. It's an enormous structure and the interior housed all of the exhibits. You couldn't cover it in a day obviously, if you're going there to look at all the exhibits from all the different countries. The European nations formed the leading edge of the Industrial Revolution, so they had the most impressive displays of machines and steam engines and other kinds of technology. The exhibit from North America was pretty modest. It wasn't terribly impressive in light of the machines that were being produced by European factories at that time. As you look at the nineteenth century, there is very much a lagging quality to American culture. It's a good generation or so behind what's going on in Great Britain. Romanticism hit America later, in mid-nineteenth century. People like Thoreau and Emerson in the middle part of the century were really romantics, and then the Realist Movement takes root in America towards the end of the 20th century. The same is true for the industrialization of America—so there wasn't much to display that could impress the sophisticated, progressive Europeans. The Crystal Palace celebrated the products of the factories of the western world, and it expressed the spirit of progress that is so much a part of the nineteenth-century. The world seemed to be becoming better and better; optimism was widespread throughout mid-nineteenth and late- nineteenth century western culture.

We've described what the Crystal Palace was—but what does it mean? How do we understand it is an expression of culture? As we've already seen, buildings are not haphazardly produced; they are meaningful structures. They give expression to the values of their age. Pyramids give expression to an Ancient Egyptian values; Greek temples give expression to the Greek way of looking at the world. And similarly Roman buildings express the imperialism and practicality of the Romans. Medieval cathedrals express notions of hierarchy. This is true of every period. So, what is it that this incredible structure, the Crystal Palace, was expressing? The meaning starts to come into focus when we compare it to Gothic cathedrals built in Europe some six centuries before. Glass was very important to the design and the symbolism of Gothic cathedrals; glass is also pretty important to the Crystal Palace. With all that glass and all that steel, it's as though they were expressing the confidence of the modern age in strength of scientific progress. The steel structure can be thought of as symbolizing the framework that science provides to the modern secular mind. You've also got the glass, the clear glass that you can look right through—the idea being that with reason, you're looking right through to the truth of things and seeing the world as it actually is. It's a very different symbolic meaning than we see in Gothic cathedrals, where the glass symbolizes God and the glory of His nature. Now glass has been turned into a secular symbol reflecting the rational faculty of man—that is, the ability to see the world through the clear glass of science. We see the same values of the modern age reflected in the skyscrapers of our own age; these, too, express great confidence in man's ability to understand the world and to harness the powers of science.

Realism in Painting

Let's turn from architecture to painting and see what we can see of this movement documented in the paintings of this age. We're going to look at two paintings. The first is Gustave Courbet's "A Burial at Ornans." Courbet is capturing a typical scene of village life, a funeral in a village. But he's expressing more than this; there's a subtle social critique that lies behind the image.

Courbet is showing that when it comes to death, everybody is equal—the priest, the merchants, the peasants, the village dog. Death takes everybody equally; there is no respect to your persons. That's also very much part of the spirit of realism—that is, looking at things objectively, neutrally, not trying to alter things in the light of some belief, but showing exactly how the world is. This painting was commissioned around the time of the Crystal Palace, the same time that Charles Dickens was writing his novels. This is very much the spirit of the age in the mid-nineteenth century.

Let's look at the second example of a realist painting: French painter, Jean-Francois Millet's "Gleaners," painted in 1857. This painting was produced within a decade of the very things we've been describing. Millet is painting an ordinary country scene here of workers in the field, gleaning and harvesting. Notice that the emphasis is not upon them as individuals; we don't see their faces, and their identities are hidden from us. The idea is just to document life as it is actually lived by real people; but beyond that, Millet wants to portray these field workers having value in themselves.

Intellectual Developments

Let's turn to what is going on in other areas and branches of knowledge in the mid-nineteenth century? How is this emphasis upon the natural world, the emphasis on the realities of society and the world around us, being expressed in other areas of intellectual development? Well, consider the names we'll be looking at: Marx and Darwin. It's interesting and insightful to link these two names in the same breath, as we are going to be doing. These were very much men of their age—men who were trying to look at the world as it actually was, not as the romantics had done. This is certainly the case with Karl Marx and the very influential book that he wrote in wrote in 1848, *Communist Manifesto*.

Again, look at the date, 1848—the very middle of the century. In three years, the Crystal Palace is going to be built. Courbet is painting his realist landscapes, and Dickens is writing his novels at this time. We need to keep all this in mind, as these values run across all of the arts and even into the sciences. People are looking at the world this way; they're looking at it "realistically," as it were. Karl Marx, in writing the *Communist Manifesto*, was focusing on the problems within society and prescribing changes that he thought had to be made. Karl Marx wrote as a materialist, and so we'll need to define that term in order to understand him. As we do, you'll see why materialism became such a defining part of the philosophy of the nineteenth century.

239

What is the definition of materialism as it relates to Karl Marx? **Materialism** is the belief that man is the product of the material world, of material things. In a sense, it's a belief that man's nature can only be understood by reference to things that are material. Who is man? What is man? Man is the product of the material environment around him. Karl Marx very much believed that who you are in society is a function of what you have in a material sense. You are made by your material environment. We talk today about the haves and the have not's. That's what Karl Marx was also talking about. What a man is can be reduced to what he has and doesn't have. As Marx looked around at mid-nineteenth century Europe, he saw the flourishing factories of the industrial age; he saw that some people were factory owners and had a lot of money. He also saw the people who worked in the factories didn't have much at all. As he looked at society, he saw all the social problems. Karl Marx would look at problems like crime and he would ask, "Why is there crime in society?" A typical Marxist reply to that is: "Well, there's crime because some people don't have things and other people do." In other words, people turn out to be thieves and steal because of the structural inequalities that exist within society, the inequalities between what some people have and other people don't have.

Marx approached society as a materialist, believing that our very nature is material, that we're not in fact spiritual beings at all. Marx believed that religion (as we can see in a famous quote from the *Communist Manifesto*) is "the opiate of the masses"— that is, religion is something that drugs people so they can't see clearly the nature of the world around them and the nature of society. This is the logical thing for the materialist, like Marx, to conclude; that is, it's the natural end point of their reasoning. If the world is only material, then what you should do is make sure that all things are equal in society. If crime and other social problems are produced by inequalities within society, then how do you address these social ills? Make things equal. Make things "common," which is of course the essence of what communism espouses as a philosophy. In that sense, we can see that communism and Marxism are absolutely logical systems of belief. They're false—but they're logical. They're logical because they are internally consistent; Marxism flows naturally from its foundational assumptions about man. If you accept that man is nothing but a material being, then all the problems in society must have purely material causes and they can be addressed through purely material means. Of course, the belief system is false, because man is not just a material being. Man is a spiritual being as well as a material being. That's the one central thing that Marxism denied. Communist ideology also declared that all of human history could be understood as the struggle of man, this material being, towards a "workers' paradise." Obviously, the twentieth century has disproved Marx and disproved the theories and the philosophies that he espoused.

Let's turn to another great thinker of the mid-nineteenth century, Charles Darwin. Notice I use the word "great." When I use this word, I am not expressing approval, but rather acknowledging the profound influence of these men and the long shadows they have cast. Charles Darwin certainly fits the definition of a great, influential thinker of this period who is expressive of his age. Consider his monumental achievement, *Origin of Species*, which was published in 1859. Note how this work is from the same mid-century period that we've been focusing on—the period that produced Dickens and Courbet and the Crystal Palace.

What do Darwin and Marx have in common? One was looking at the world of society, politics, and economics; the other was looking at the world of science and nature. Both men, however, fundamentally shared the same materialistic view of human nature. Karl Marx believed that we're nothing but material stuff; and Charles Darwin certainly viewed man as a material being. Another way to put it is that both Marx and Darwin believed that the material environment shapes man. Now, think about that: *Man is shaped by his material environment.* Earlier we noted how Marx believed that you'll be defined by whether you have and don't have material things. Note how this is a pretty good description of natural selection—the belief that man is shaped by interacting with his material environment. At the heart of evolutionary theory, then, is a materialistic view of man's nature.

The Humanistic Response

You can see that Darwin and Marx are really giving expressions of the same idea that man is not a spiritual being, but that man is a material being, the idea that man has to be understood as an economic and political being, as Marx put it. He is to be understood as a biological organism as Darwin argued—nothing but a bundle of biology and chemistry. What we are seeing, then, is that the whole spiritual dimension of who man is has been taken out of the equation; and this will lead to what I'm calling "the humanistic critique" in the latter part of the nineteenth century. This will be the reaction of those who question where this negation of the human soul will ultimately lead us. So, what is it that poets and novelists of that age had to say about all of this?

We'll look briefly at two examples, two ways of critiquing this materialistic optimism that Marxist philosophy expressed. Darwin, too, in his own way offered an optimistic appraisal of man's progress in his view that man and society are evolving. Progress was the watchword of the nineteenth century. Of course, not everybody was caught up in the hoopla and the hype about man's inevitable progress. There was one figure in particular, Matthew Arnold, the British poet, who had some negative and cautionary things to say as he looked out at the landscape of the nineteenth century. He wasn't persuaded that man was progressing; he wasn't persuaded that the society was getting better. He wasn't persuaded that man was on some ever-inclining evolutionary spiral toward perfection. Like a prophet, he was looking at his own age and critiquing its values; but he was also looking ahead and anticipating what is going to come. Arnold's most famous poem, "Dover Beach" (1867) expressed his views most clearly.

"Dover Beach" is considered by many to be the first truly modern poem. If you look at any standard anthology of English literature, you are going to find this poem positioned at the beginning of the modern era as a kind of a harbinger of things to come. Let's read the poem and see how Arnold goes about critiquing this optimism, this sense of progress that was so pervasive in the second half of the nineteenth century. The setting here is that Arnold is looking out across the sea. He is looking out where the cliffs meet the beach, looking out over the channel at night, and seeing the moon reflected on the waves as they come in. That image causes him to reflect back on history and he is going to go all the way back to ancient Greece, thinking about the waves in the Aegean Sea. Then he is going to think symbolically about what he calls the Sea of Faith. Then he is going to ask, "What have we lost?" What have we as modern people who believe in progress and materialism—what have lost in the bargain? That's really what he is going to be asking.

The sea is calm to-night.
The tide is full, the moon lies fair
Upon the straits; on the French coast the light
Gleams and is gone; the cliffs of England stand;
Glimmering and vast, out in the tranquil bay.
Come to the window, sweet is the night-air!
Only, from the long line of spray
Where the sea meets the moon-blanched land,
Listen! you hear the grating roar
Of pebbles which the waves draw back, and fling,
At their return, up the high strand,
Begin, and cease, and then again begin,
With tremulous cadence slow, and bring
The eternal note of sadness in.

As he looks at the scene, he sees the moon on the English Channel and the ebb and the flow of the waves on the coast. He reflects on this, and a kind of melancholy begins to set in as he reflects on the condition of man in the modern age. That's really where he is going to go with this. These thoughts take him back to ancient Greece.

Sophocles long ago
Heard it on the Aegean, and it brought
Into his mind the turbid ebb and flow
Of human misery; we
Find also in the sound a thought,
Hearing it by this distant northern sea.

He is really beginning to ask the question, what has changed? Nothing has changed.

Human nature is the same now as it was then. We might build spectacular things like the Crystal Palace, and we can witness all of the great advances of modern science; but how much is man really advancing? That's the question that Arnold is asking. "What have we lost with all this progress?" He thinks back to how faith has been lost in the modern western world. That's one of the really unfortunate developments of the modern age—that man has moved away from his belief in God.

The Sea of Faith
Was once, too, at the full, and round earth's shore
Lay like the folds of a bright girdle furled.
But now I only hear
Its melancholy, long, withdrawing roar,
Retreating, to the breath
Of the night-wind, down the vast edges drear
And naked shingles of the world.

The Sea of Faith, now just a remote memory, doesn't exist anymore. You can't sail on that sea any more. So what can we do? How can the modern man live his life? That's really where Arnold ends the poem. He tries to find some way that we can live in a world that has stolen our souls away.

Ah, love, let us be true
To one another!
for the world, which seems
To lie before us like a land of dreams,
So various, so beautiful, so new,
Hath really neither joy, nor love, nor light,
Nor certitude, nor peace, nor help for pain
And we are here as on a darkling plain
Swept with confused alarms of struggle and flight,
Where ignorant armies clash by night.

That's a pretty bleak critique of the modern age. In the midst of all of this optimism about the world, this is what Arnold is concluding. That's why you can look at this poem and see that Arnold is speaking with an almost prophetic voice as he critiques his own age. But he is also anticipating what's going to happen in the twentieth century. These are the beliefs; this is the way the world is viewed. The world is a place where nothing is certain any longer.

And so the point here is that though the nineteenth century was an age of great optimism, there were some dissenting voices. People like Marx and Darwin in their own respective fields had charted this new view of man as a creature of progress, a material being who is going to be defined by ever-increasing material prosperity. The most optimistically minded believed that we were on track towards a better world, towards what would come to be called in the twentieth century "a brave new world." But clearly, as Arnold demonstrates, there were those who fundamentally questioned this.

Matthew Arnold was one of those skeptics. Dostoyevsky, the great Russian author, was another. He traveled to England in 1862, saw the Crystal Palace, and was depressed by all it represented. Contrary to those who viewed this architectural wonder as a great testimony to man's achievement and progress, Dostoyevsky believed that man had given up his soul. That's what he saw: not what man had gained, but what he had lost. He concluded that man had become soulless—defining himself by reason, defining himself by material prosperity, and no longer defining himself as a spiritual being. That's the great theme of Dostoevsky's novels, *Crime and Punishment* and *The Brothers Karamazov*, as he examined the heart of man, and, like a prophet, questioned this false idea of the nineteenth century. Of course, as we trace these themes into the twentieth century, we're going to see some interesting things.

At the beginning of the twentieth century this notion of progress is going to be pervasive—the idea that man is on a track towards a better society. The most respected intellectuals in Europe and America believed that the twentieth century was going to be the dawning of a utopian age and wars would cease to exist in the twentieth century; man was just going to evolve beyond the primitive barbarism of his past. Of course that idealism and optimism, that notion of progress which is so characteristic of the nineteenth century, would run into a brick wall in the early twentieth century— World War I, the Great War. This war had a devastating impact in shaking people back to the realization that we are not really progressing, and that human nature is not evolving towards perfection.

MODERNISM AND POSTMODERNISM

Chapter Objectives

- Describe how the Great War shattered the optimistic claims of progress.
- Illustrate how fragmentation became the norm within modern art.
- Explain how the modern western world is trying to find a new direction.

In our final chapter we'll be turning our attention to the period of Modernism—the movement in western culture at the beginning of the twentieth century. As we've gone through western culture—and especially the modern era—we have to conclude that each one of these periods requires much more time to develop than we've been able to devote. We've just been dipping into these centuries and pulling out a theme or two as a way of trying to understand more fully the progression of western culture since the Middle Ages.

Consider the main themes again that we've been following: rationalism, humanism, and materialism. We've seen how these themes have defined the modern secular age. We've seen how in the centuries following the Renaissance, each of these themes is developed and taken in different directions. For example, in the seventeenth century, we traced the rise of scientific thinking and the scientific method, which really gave flesh and blood to the rationalism of the modern age. As we moved into the eighteenth century, reason became enshrined as the standard of truth for the modern age. In the period of romanticism, in the late eighteenth and early nineteenth century, we saw that the humanistic belief in individualism was expressed in the notions of the romantic hero. Then as we moved further into the nineteenth century, we saw that materialism, the belief that "man is nothing but matter," began to take center stage in western secular thought. By the end of the nineteenth century, thoughtful men and women started to question whether western culture was on the right track or not. Were we heading for a brave new world? Or had we lost our soul along the way? This is the cultural and intellectual backdrop as a new century—the twentieth—began to dawn in the western world.

The Legacy of Materialism

The dominant spirit in the late nineteenth century, on the heels of all of this material progress and new scientific theories, was one of great optimism about what the future held. I really want to stress this point, because it's critical to understanding the direction that western culture will go as we enter the early twentieth century. The cultural movement we call Modernism, will be a reaction, in part, to this unbridled and unfounded optimism.

If we don't understand just how optimistic people were—that is, the intellectuals in Europe and America at the dawning of the twentieth century—then nothing that follows will really make a lot of sense. Among the leading intellectuals and artists, there was a very widespread belief that we were going to enter a new age, a utopia of sorts, as the twentieth century dawned. You see this feeling in the world fairs and exhibits that were held at this time in places like Chicago. Once again, the cutting edge of technology was on display—evidence that man would bring this about through his own reason and effort. People believed that society would get better, that the human condition would improve, that man would even become in a sense more moral. It was widely believed even that war would cease to exist, since it's the most "unreasonable" thing that a rational, modern human being could possibly do. After all, who would want to destroy all this progress? Modern society was governed by the dictates of reason, and war was viewed as fundamentally irrational. It's hard for us today to see how people could have believed this. But look at it from their point of view. As they looked around the world of progress, they saw what reason had accomplished, what science had produced—and it was pretty spectacular. In one sense, they were emboldened to think that reason would take us to the next obvious level, whereby it would improve our interactions with one another. It's not just that we can make better machines and better products, but also that we will become better people.

Having expended so much effort to create this modern world, people believed that we would not possibly stoop to war, because war is so destructive. After all, war would destroy factories and cities. It would destroy all of the things that we have created through our rationality. Therefore, they concluded, it's not reasonable to go to war. Man would just agree to stop fighting. But we should emphasize right now how this naïve hope was premised upon a false view of man's nature.

What was this false premise? It was the view of human nature first advanced by those eighteenth-century philosophers, Voltaire and Rousseau—the notion that man is basically good. Man was viewed as a creature of nature, but also creature of reason;

man was believed to be capable of social perfection. If you accept that as your premise, then the idea of moral progress does indeed make sense. Of course, we have the advantage today of knowing the history of the twentieth century. That leads us to wonder how intelligent men could have been so naïve. Yet there are still people today who harbor those same fantasies about man being on some inevitable career track towards perfection. Many secularists believe that man is capable not just of bettering his lot in life, but also his moral condition. You would think that the twentieth century would have pretty much disproved that idea and convinced us that that is not the case. But this continues to be a very seductive idea today. We see all around us the tangible benefits of technology in the twentieth century which go way beyond what anyone in the nineteenth century could possibly dream about. We see how life has gotten much easier in a material sense. Life is more comfortable and the human condition has materially improved; there is no question about that. But we are absolutely wrong to make the next leap, as they did a hundred years ago and some people still do today, to think that just bettering our material condition will translate into bettering our moral condition. But that was the dominant view at the turn of the twentieth century.

All of that optimism, however, slammed right into a brick wall in the early twentieth century. That brick wall was the Great War, which we now call World War I. We're going to see that this world war was so devastating in its consequences that it pretty much shook that optimism to the foundation. It radically and drastically affected the direction of western culture—its art, philosophy, and politics—in the modern age in the twentieth century.

The Impact of the Great War

The Great War was utterly devastating. It was more devastating, really, than World War II—not in loss of life but on the cultural psyche of the western world. It had a more profound impact. The devastation and irrationality of World War I was so unexpected.

If you're just sort of whistling along, as people were in the early twentieth century, thinking the world is getting better and better, that war is going to cease to exist, and then along comes the most devastating war ever, then you can see what the impact of that is going to be. It had a profound impact for a lot of reasons—among which is how it showcased the worst aspects of nationalism.

Nationalism was what people were fighting over; people on opposite sides of the trenches were fighting just because of the nation that they belonged to. This is one of the great causes of disillusionment that came out of this war; ordinary Frenchmen were fighting ordinary Germans, and they suddenly realized, "I don't have anything against you, so why am I killing you?" And the only answer was: "I am killing you because my nation is at war with your nation." This ugly side of nationalism is one of the main reasons why Europe has been striving for the last few decades to unify itself through a common market and common currency. Europeans look back at the twentieth century and they see the devastating legacy of nationalistic wars. One of the driving rationales behind the European Union is that they've experienced the alternative, and they don't like what it led to. So now they're trying something different.

I should emphasize that along with the worst aspects of nationalism, we also see the worst aspects of materialism. For the fifty years or so leading up to the Great War, everybody was singing the praises of the great factories that were producing better machines and better products. Suddenly factories are producing not just things that make life better, but machines that kill people more efficiently and effectively. Just when material prosperity was looking like the answer to a better life, it enables the production of killing machines the likes of which the world had never seen. That devastation would cross the military lines and directly impact civilian populations through new technologies like airplanes. In most of human history, wars have been fought on the front lines. Wars were fought by one army arraying itself against another army.

As devastating as that war might be, it affected the soldiers on the frontlines most directly. We know, of course, that civilian populations suffered as well throughout the centuries of human warfare as cities were captured and burned. But World War I affected civilians in a new and terrifying way. New kinds of weapons enabled enemy combatants to fly over the front lines and take the battle directly to the civilian populations. Of course, this will become much more significant in World War II, but we see the beginnings of this in World War I. With such profound effects upon the civilian population, all of this is going to lead to an incredible amount of intellectual disillusionment. The optimistic worldview—the belief that saw reason, science and material prosperity would make the world better—began to fall apart in the brutal reality of the World War I.

As we said, factories were not just making better products that make life better for everybody; they're also making more efficient killing machines that are food in the hands of armies. And this led to a profound intellectual disillusionment. This disillusionment can be seen as naturally evolving out of two premises. First of all, the God of the Bible had been rejected systematically over the previous centuries. Voltaire in the eighteenth century had audaciously declared that if God did not exist, then we'd have to invent Him. Then we go on to see secular man inventing his own God in the nineteenth century. Marx was certainly inventing his own God—the State. Darwin was inventing his own God—the blind forces of nature. And so the God of the Bible was rejected. And if you reject God, if you reject the Creator, then you've got to put some false god up in His place.

That's one of the clearest things you can see in the Old Testament, that when you turn from the true God, then you start worshiping some false god. And that's true in the modern age as well. The kicker here is that when man puts that false god—Science—up on his pedestal, then this new god shows himself to have a pretty savage and brutal face. We've seen how science, factories, technology, and material prosperity were put to a very cruel and immoral end—the efficient killing of large numbers of people in warfare. So what does that lead you think of your new god? Do you just run back to the God that you've abandoned in the centuries before? You think you might do that; but in the modern age that's not what happened. Western society didn't wake up and realize the folly of the path that they were pursuing and say, "We've got to go back to recognizing our Creator and our dependence on Him for all we are." No, man just continued in his rationalism and humanism and went searching for new gods in the twentieth century.

This is where we're at in the early twentieth century. One God is rejected and another god proves to not be quite as nice as everybody thought he was. Let's illustrate this with a couple of very quick examples. We are going to look first at a somewhat unexpected illustration—an illustration by Norman Rockwell. He was a great illustrator for many years for the *Saturday Evening Post*; his illustrations captured the sentiment and spirit of life in America in the middle of the twentieth century. One of his illustrations, in particular, gives us a wonderful metaphor of disillusionment. It's called "Bottom Drawer." Of course, Rockwell is not literally depicting in this illustration the subjects we're talking about; but I am going to use it as a metaphor for the experience of disillusionment. Rockwell painted "Bottom Door" for the cover of the *Saturday Evening Post* in 1956. It depicts what a little boy finds when he is snooping around in his father's dresser and opens the bottom drawer. You can see the red cap with white fur and the red outfit; what he's found, of course, is a Santa Claus outfit in the bottom drawer of his father's room. The expression on the little boy's face says it all. I'd argue that this is the expression of western man in the early twentieth century. This is the expression of profound disillusionment when you suddenly realize who Santa Claus is—or when you suddenly realize who the god of science really turns out to be in the hands of cruel and violent men.

The Great War imposed this moment of great disillusionment on western society,

much as opening that bottom drawer and seeing the truth did for that little boy in Norman Rockwell's painting. It's a beautiful illustration that we can use to visualize what we are talking about.

Let's look at a second example, one drawn from the literature of the early twentieth century. I'm referring to one of the most famous war poems in the English language, "Dulce et Decorum Est," by Wilfred Owen. Owen was a soldier in the British army—so he knew what he was talking about.

The title is a Latin phrase taken from a Latin poem by Horace, a great Roman poet. "Dulce et decorum est" means, "It is sweet and fitting." The rest of the phrase is "pro patria mori." The whole Latin phrase, then, means, "It is sweet and fitting to die for one's country." This complete phrase is found in the last line of Owen's poem. It's a statement of nationalism—a statement of patriotism. Consider how the Romans viewed warfare and honor and what they thought about their own imperial destiny. Horace is giving expression to that Roman sentiment. The idea that the highest thing for a man is to die for one's country was typical of the nationalism that led to the Great War. Nations sent their young men off to die in the horrible trenches of World War I where they would face gas warfare— one of the most wicked innovations of World War I—and the "sweetness" of this honor would be severely tested.

Owen lived between 1893 and 1918. He not only fought in World War I, but he died in battle—just days before the armistice was signed. But during his time in the trenches, Owen documented the disillusionment of what it was like to fight in the front lines, the terrifying nature of warfare in World War I, and how it was capable of imposing this kind of radical shift of thinking on the whole of western culture. What Wilfred Owen experienced as an individual was really the experience of an entire generation. What he is depicting here is what he witnessed himself. He's depicting in this poem the effects of a gas attack. It's a pretty horrifying depiction that he gives.

Bent double, like old beggars under sacks,
Knock-kneed, coughing like hags, we cursed through sludge,
Till on the haunting flares we turned our backs
And towards our distant rest began to trudge.

Owens is depicting the incredible fatigue of hours, even days, of fighting on the front lines. You think of the Battle of Verdun, for example, which is one of the most extraordinarily devastating battles ever fought in any war of any time of any century. It's not the one he's describing here, but it very much goes to the heart of the things he's talking about. The Battle of Verdun was fought in northern France, where a million men fought for a year and only advanced maybe one hundred yards in either direction. The earth was chewed up to a depth of about twenty feet or so over the course of the year as the two armies went back and forth, back and forth. It's recognized as maybe one of the most devastating single battles of any war ever fought. Keep that in mind as we are looking at what Owen is talking about: battles that raged for days and weeks and months without end, with no sense of progress in sight and nothing really being accomplished.

Men marched asleep. Many had lost their boots
But limped on, blood-shod. All went lame; all blind;
Drunk with fatigue; deaf even to the hoots
Of tired, outstripped Five-Nines that dropped behind.
Gas! Gas! Quick, boys-An ecstasy of fumbling,
Fitting the clumsy helmets just in time;
But someone still was yelling out and stumbling
And flound'ring like a man in fire or lime...
Dim, through the mist panes and thick green light,
As under a green sea, I saw him drowning.

This is beautiful, lyrical poetry. The poem is one of the most widely anthologized of all early twentieth-century poems for a couple of reasons—the greatness of the lyricism certainly, but also the depth of what it expresses. Also, look at the music of those last two lines, specifically the repetition of the M sound. The irony of this is that although it is very beautiful, very musical, what Owen is describing is the most horrifying nightmare that you could depict. A man is drowning in a gas attack as his lungs are being eaten up and he can't breathe.

Dim, through the misty panes and thick green light,
As under a green sea, I saw him drowning.
In all my dreams, before my helpless sight,
He plunges at me, guttering, choking, drowning.

Then he goes on to the whole point of the poem now, the disillusionment that this experience is leading him, Wilfred Owen, and his whole generation to conclude:

If in some smothering dreams, you too could pace
Behind the wagon that we flung him in,
And watch the white eyes writhing in his face,
His hanging face, like a devil's sick of sin,
If you could hear, at every jolt, the blood
Come gargling from the froth-corrupted lungs
Obscene as cancer, bitter as the cud
Of vile, incurable sores on innocent tongues,--
My friend, you would not tell with such high zest
To children ardent for some desperate glory,
The old Lie: Dulce et decorum est
Pro patria mori.

In these lines, he is turns and addressing from the frontlines his friends back in England—schoolteachers sending school children off to die, teaching them their Latin lessons, teaching them Horace, and teaching them this phrase. Teaching them that "it is sweet and fitting to die for the Father-land." Owen is saying that they wouldn't teach their students this belief, if they were haunted by the nightmares of this man who died, this man who is unable to breathe as his lungs were destroyed in a mustard gas attack. It's a powerful poem, a powerful indictment and an expression of the depth of the disillusionment that was felt in the early twentieth century.

Fragmentation in Modern Art

We started by looking at the optimism at the turn-of-the-century followed by the devastating impact of the Great War. In the generation after the World War I, we see the profound impact that this war had on western culture. We see this impact specifically in the emergence of modern art. We see it as well in literature, the so-called "lost generation" of American writers who gave expression to the question, "Where do we go now and what does the future hold for us?" We think of writers like Ernest Hemingway who expressed that bleak outlook in the heroes he depicted in his novels—solitary men who were adrift on the landscape of the western world. Hemingway's heroes have no sense of direction, and this really captures that sense of where western culture found itself in the aftermath of the Great War.

Modernism, I am arguing, is a movement in art, literature, and music, that grows directly out of this experience of disillusionment. The world was no longer viewed as a unified rational place that mankind was conquering through his own energy and his own goodness. The world has suddenly become radically fragmented. Fragmentation, I would argue is the most important concept that we can see in the art, literature, music, and philosophy of the early twentieth century. You can't find a better quote that gives a more eloquent expression to this than a very famous line from a poem by W. B. Yeats, the great Irish poet. This line stands as an expression of modern man in the twentieth century: "Things fall apart, the center cannot hold." Yeats goes on to say, "Mere anarchy is loosed upon the world." In its most extreme form, this view

of fragmentation—and the notion that the world was simply falling apart—led to a curious movement in art, which we call Dada-ism or Dada Art. It's essentially nonsense art, randomly produced, and it can be seen as a reaction to a world that no longer seems to make sense. And so, the fragmented and random productions of art tried to give concrete expression to this.

Let's quickly look at some well-known and pivotal works of modern art and literature that expressed this theme of a fragmented world. First, we see this theme in T. S. Eliot, the great Anglo-American poet, who was one of the greatest of all the early twentieth-century modern poets. He was a man who longed for order and lamented how the western world was falling apart at the seams. In his groundbreaking poem, "The Waste Land," written in 1922, Eliot describes the intellectual and cultural landscape of the post-World War I world. Eliot pieces his poem together from the fragments of the literary classics of the past, pasting them together as a collage. The style, then, really reflects the theme of fragmentation that he is conveying. In the same year, James Joyce wrote his influential novel *Ulysses*, which is also a work of fragmentation. It is probably the most difficult novel written to read, because it's so much a patchwork of ideas and fragmented pieces of other works. You enter the stream of consciousness of the central character, and it's a world that lacks cohesiveness and order. Again, the style of Joyce's writing gives expression to this theme of modernism, where things are falling apart.

We see this theme in art as well as in literature. The movement in painting known as of Cubism, which we associate with Pablo Picasso, is a style of fragmentation. One of Picasso's greatest early works, from 1907, is "Les Demoiselles d'Avignon." This painting, of course, was produced before World War I, so it's already anticipating this theme that would become so important after the war. Modern art was already trending towards fragmentation before the Great War. This famous painting, an example of the Cubist style, depicts prostitutes on the street. But notice how fragmented the human form is becoming as Picasso paints the human body. He is taking objects apart, taking the human form apart, piece-by-piece, fragment-by-fragment, and then re-assembling them.

Where did Picasso get the inspiration for doing this? Look at this figure on the left, the face looking in one direction. But notice the eye and the side of the head. Picasso is trying to reinvent modern art, and where did he go for inspiration? He doesn't go back to Leonardo da Vinci and Michelangelo. He doesn't go back to Myron and the other Greek sculptors and painters. He goes all the way back before western art, to the ancient Egyptians. And this shows just how revolutionary this movement of modernism really was. Picasso was trying to reinvent art by looking for inspiration from before western art even began. The world was fragmenting—we see this in the art, the way the forms are coming apart. Just as in Egyptian art, the bodies are fragmented according to characteristic elements.

We also see this fragmentation in the music of the early twentieth century. One of the most important early twentieth-century musicians is Stravinsky. Schoenberg is another who really illustrates this notion of fragmentation in his principle of atonality. By completely moving away from the traditional harmonic patterns that had developed in the classical music of the previous centuries, atonality was really a reinvention of the entire harmonic basis for modern music. This is why the classical music of this period strikes us as so jarring and so dissident, because it's exploring and trying to invent a completely new harmonic sys-tem. These composers were fragmenting the harmonies of the past, much as Picasso was fragmenting the artistic tradition and Eliot and Joyce were fragmenting the literary tradition. All of this is an expression of an early modern post-World War I world, in which things seem to have fallen apart.

What happens to the soul of man, the spiritual aspect of who we are? We talked about how that seemed to have been lost in the headlong rush of the nineteenth century towards materialism. We saw the basis for that in the philosophy of Marx and the theories of Darwin. Man had become a purely material creature who was no longer viewed as a spiritual being. Throughout the twentieth century, western culture would explore new directions, new patterns, and (in a sense) new gods that he could worship. After the Second World War, for example, the philosophical movement known as existentialism defined much of the cultural output of the western world in the middle of the twentieth century; existentialism was the ultimate "end point" of the rejection of God—the view that life is essentially meaningless apart from what we ourselves make of it. More recently, the movement known as postmodernism has rejected the idea that there is any such thing as absolute truth. And this is the tragic dead-end position where the western world finds itself at the outset of the new millennium.

Color Illustration A (above). "Painting of a Pond" (Egyptian, c. 1400 B.C.). British Museum.
Color Illustration B (below). "The Death of Socrates" by Jacques-Louis David (1787).
The Metropolitan Museum of Art (New York).

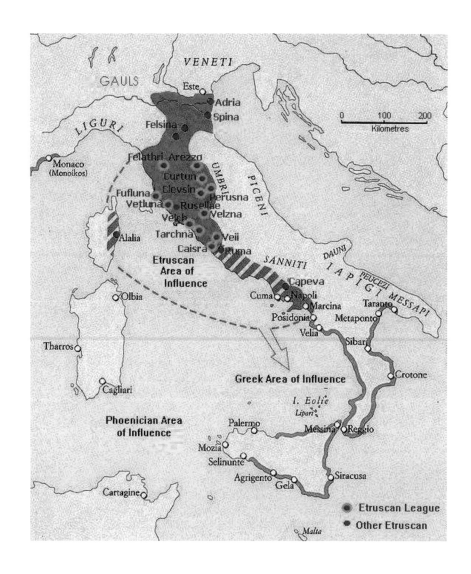

Color Illustration C (above). Map showing the political divisions on the Italian Peninsula in the 6th century B.C.
Color Illustration D (below). Masaccio, "The Tribute Money" (c. 1425). Fresco: Florence, Italy.

Color Illustration E (above). The Three Hebrews in the Fiery Furnace.
Color Illustration F (below). Moses Parting the Red Sea.
Catacomb of St. Priscilla, Rome, Italy (late 3rd, early 4th century).

Color Illustration E . The Story of Jonah (with the Good Shepherd in the center).
Catacomb of St. Peter and St. Marcellinus (early 4th century).
Below (below): Detail of Jonah being cash into the sea to be swallowed by a sea creature.

Color Illustration H . The Sarcophagus of Junius Bassus (c. 359 A.D.).
Vatican, Rome.

Color Illustration I. Page from the Book of Kells (Irish, c. 800 A.D.).

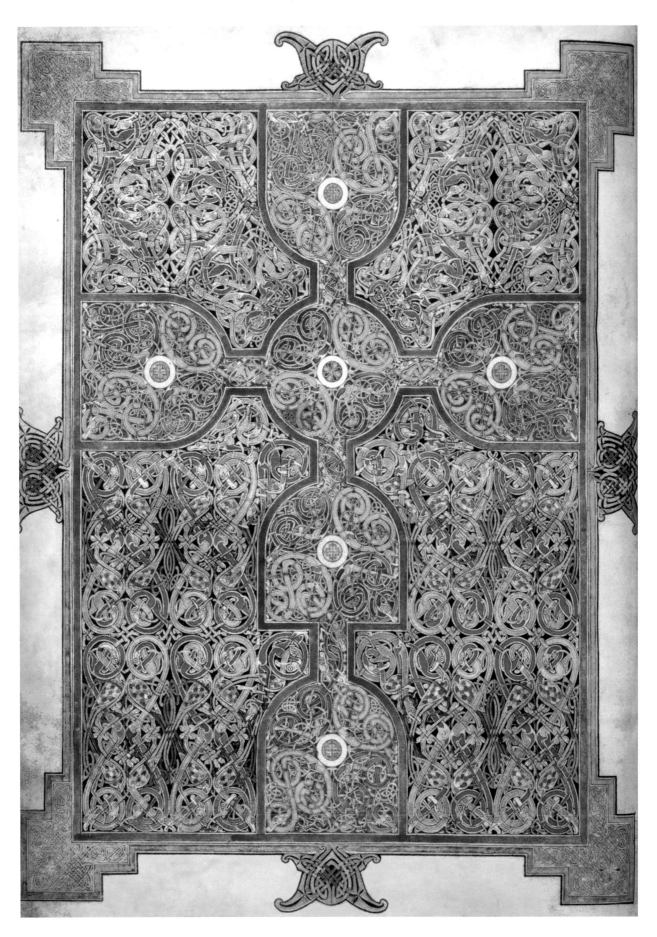

Color Illustration J. The "Cross Page" from the Lindisfarne Gospels (British, c. 800 A.D.).

Color Illustration K (top). Sandro Botticelli, "The Birth of Venus" (c. 1485).
Color Illustration L (bottom). Raphael, "The School of Athens" (c. 1510).

Color Illustration M (top). Sandro Botticelli, "The Adoration of the Magi" (c. 1475). Detail (bottom) of the artist, Botticelli.

Color Illustration N. Jan van Eyck, "The Arnolfini Wedding Portrait" (1434).

Color Illustration O. Albrecht Durer, "Self-Portrait at 28" (1500).

Color Illustration P (top). Leonardo da Vinci, "The Last Supper" (c. 1498).
Color Illustration Q (bottom). Leonardo da Vinci, "The Annunciation" (c. 1475). With details.

Color Illustration R (top). Matthias Gruenewald, "The Crucifixion," Isenheim Altarpiece (1515).
Color Illustration S (bottom). Pieter Brueghel, "Hunters in the Snow" (c. 1525).

Appendix

Great Books in the Western Tradition

AENEID (ca. 19 B.C.), by Virgil (Publius Virgilius Maro). Virgil's epic of the beginnings of the Roman state is the most celebrated work in Latin literature. Its materials are drawn from the Trojan legend and earlier Roman poets and its form from Homer, but the *Aeneid* reflects the more deliberative and personal spirit of the literature of the sophisticated Augustan age. It retells the story of Aeneas' flight from fallen Troy and his final settlement in Latium. There are twelve books, the first six modeled on the *Odyssey* and the last on the *Iliad.* Book I tells how Aeneas and his followers were driven ashore at Carthage and there hospitably received by Queen Dido. In Book II Aeneas relates to Dido how Troy was captured by the ruse of the wooden horse; how he himself escaped from the burning city bearing his aged father, Anchises, on his back and leading his little son, Ascanius, by the hand; and how he lost his wife on the way and finally reached the slopes of Mt. Ida, where he joined other refugees. In Book III he continues with the narrative of his voyage and many adventures as leader of the Trojan exiles, and how he lost his father and finally reached Carthage. In Book IV Dido has fallen desperately in love with Aeneas, but the restless hero feels himself led by the will of the gods to pursue his quest for the fated goal of his travels. He sails away from Carthage, and the heart-broken Dido immolates herself upon a pyre. Book V tells of his arrival at Sicily, where funeral games are celebrated in honor of Anchises, and how he sailed on and reached Cumae in Italy. Book VI is an account of his descent to the infernal regions under the guidance of the Cumaean Sibyl. There the shade of Anchises foretells the future of his line and the destined greatness of Rome. In Book VII Aeneas reaches Latium at the mouth of the Tiber and is welcomed by Latinus, who offers him the hand of his daughter Lavinia. This princess had already been betrothed to Turnus, king of the Rutulians, who now raises an army of allies against Latinus and Aeneas. Book VIII tells how Aeneas visited the neighboring king Evander and enlisted his aid and that of the Etruscans. Books IX-XI describe the war with the forces of Turnus, and XII, the single combat between Aeneas and Turnus, resulting in the death of Turnus and the victory of Aeneas. The purpose of the poem is to celebrate the high destiny of the Roman state in general, and in particular of the reign of Augustus, for whom descent is claimed through Aeneas from the Trojans on one side and on the other the gods.

BEOWULF (ca. 700). This is the oldest epic poem in any modern European language, and the "beginning" of English literature. Of unknown authorship, most of the material was circulated orally, then written down by two unidentified tenth-century scribes. That the Beowulf epic may have been a development of older sagas is apparent in its Scandinavian background and structural form. Hrothgar, King of the Danes, builds a palace, Heorot, which is visited nightly by the monster, Grendel, who devours Hrothgar's thanes and haunts the palace for twelve years. Beowulf, nephew of Higelac, King of the Geats (a tribe in southern Sweden), arrives with fourteen companions to get rid of Grendel. As they are sleeping in the hall of Heorot, Grendel breaks in and devours Hondscio, one of Beowulf's men. Beowulf struggles with the monster, who loses an arm and flees to his cavern beneath a lake, to die. As Hrothgar and his men celebrate, Grendel's mother enters the hall to avenge her son's death. She carries off Aeschere, one of Hrothgar's followers, and Beowulf pursues her to her lair. Using an enchanted sword, Beowulf cuts off the witch's head and also Grendel's, and returns to Hrothgar with his prizes. After the deaths of Hrothgar and his son, Heardred, Beowulf succeeds to the throne and reigns for fifty peaceful years. Then a dragon devastates the kingdom, and Beowulf, with eleven companions, searches for him. Deserted by all his men except Wiglaf, Beowulf kills the dragon but is mortally wounded in the struggle. His body is burned on a funeral pyre with his armor and the dragon's treasure. Many details of Germanic court life are included in the saga. Christian spirit pervades the work; yet the background material is derived from ancient pagan legends.

BLEAK HOUSE (1853), by Charles Dickens. The novel contains sharp criticism of the courts of chancery through its story of the involved case of Jarndyce vs. Jarndyce. As in similar cases, the litigants spend years trying to conclude the proceedings, during which time the estate is consumed by court costs. The two suitors in Jarndyce vs. Jarndyce are Richard Carstone and his pretty cousin, Ada Clare. The two young people are kindly treated by John Jarndyce, an older relative. He takes them to his home, Bleak House, to live. Richard and Ada secretly marry, and Richard slowly allows nervous anxiety and deferred hope over the expected fortune, still "in chancery," to ruin his health. Continually excited about his prospects, he is unable to settle down to any serious work. Finally, sunk in misery, he dies. Shortly thereafter, news is received that the case is finished, but that the money has been dissipated! With Ada at Bleak House is Esther

Summerson, one of the narrators of the story. Esther believes herself to be an orphan; she is a person of great common sense, sweetness, and generosity. Lady Dedlock, adored wife of Sir Leicester Dedlock, appears to be a bored and indifferent member of society. However, she has a guilty past which she is anxious to conceal. In her youth she had been engaged to a Captain Rawdon. As a result of their affair, a daughter was born to her shortly after Rawdon's reported death at sea. She believes her child is dead, too. Rawdon, in fact, 'is not dead but has returned, a poverty-stricken scrivener. In the presence of her crafty and malicious lawyer, Mr. Tulkinghorn, Lady Dedlock glimpses Rawdon's handwriting on a legal paper and starts violently. Tulkinghorn takes note of her reaction and is determined to find the cause. Lady Dedlock tries to find Rawdon, and finally, with the help of Jo, a pathetic little street-sweeper, she locates his newly-covered grave in a pauper's field. From Jo's unwitting information, Tulkinghorn immediately proceeds to unravel all the facts about Lady Dedlock. He threatens to expose her to her husband, but is murdered by a former maidservant of Lady Dedlock's before he can do so. Bucket, a policeman, then tells Sir Leicester the truth about his wife. Lady Dedlock, discovering that her husband knows her secret after all, escapes from the house. Her husband and Esther, who now knows that Lady Dedlock is her mother, search for her, but are too late to save her. She is found dead near Rawdon's grave. Esther, while living at Bleak House, has succumbed to smallpox and is afraid her good looks have vanished. She and her physician, young Dr. Woodcourt, have fallen in love. Mr. Jarndyce also loves her and asks her to marry him, and she, grateful for his unfailing kindness and trust, feels she must accept. But when Mr. Jarndyce learns that she really loves the young doctor, he withdraws his suit. Dickens' gallery of characters includes Mrs. Jellyby, whose family suffers from neglect because of her foolish philanthropic activities; Miss Flite, the pathetic and crazed little woman who was driven out of her mind by a chancery case; Krook, the dealer in rags who dies spectacularly and horribly of "spontaneous combustion"; Jo, the slum-child, one of Dickens' most pitiful and heart-rending characters; and Mr. Chadband, the pious hypocrite.

BOOK OF THE DEAD, THE (2500 B.C.). The Book of the Dead contains ancient prayers and hymns which had been learned by heart and recited from memory long before the emergence of historical writing in Egypt. They prove conclusively that not only the worship of Isis and Osiris, but all of the mythological philosophy connected with it,

were accepted more than five thousand years ago. They form one of the oldest and most complete documents of primitive belief concerning man's hopes and fears of the world beyond the grave. The work is essentially mythological, and assumes the reader's thorough knowledge of the myths and legends of ancient Egypt. It was considered by Egyptians to be an inspired work. It is the god Thoth himself who speaks, revealing to man the will of the gods and the mysterious nature of divine things. Portions of the book are expressly stated to have been written by the very finger of Thoth himself. The Book of the Dead has neither beginning nor end; the chapters were thrown together without method, and the parts have no organic connection. It includes a description of the judgment and a list of the sins of which the deceased must be able to declare himself innocent, as well as prayers and incantations. Texts from it were written upon coffins and inscribed upon the walls of tombs or laid, in papyrus form, in the grave for the departed to carry with him as a passport and an aid to slipping memory. For it was believed necessary to sing hymns of praise in the other world as well as in this one. The right word could ward off demons and hostile beasts, open gates, procure food and drink, justify a man's life before the dread god Osiris and the forty-two judges, and secure for him the status and privileges of a god. As with all other scriptural writings handed down from father to son, in the course of time exegetical commentaries were required to clarify, reconcile and explain away inconsistencies. It was not given final form as an authoritative canon until about the seventh century B.C. The English translation was done by E. A. Wallis Budge.

BRAVE NEW WORLD (1932), by Aldous Huxley. In the "brave new world," reproduction is a standard laboratory matter, turning out people systematically conditioned for the several strata of life. Sex and all other sensory matters are exploited contentment media. Production and consumption are the purposes of life; the commonplace is apotheosized. Literature, art, philosophy are suppressed; and a variety of pacifying sensory gratifications, all standardized, are substituted. Ford (sometimes called Freud), legendary father of standardization, has been deified. Workers are content because they are so conditioned, possessing no aspiration beyond the sops of drugs. Near this environment is reared a "savage," on an Indian reservation kept as a scientific museum. Meanwhile, even in Utopia, there is some dissatisfaction. In the Psychological Bureau, Bernard Marx feels socially isolated because of slight physical deficiencies, and the resultant insecurity makes him cynical. His Alpha Plus friend, Helmholtz Watson, feels a vague creative restlessness and isolation caused by his very superiority. With Lenina Crowne (who is proud that men think her "pneumatic") Bernard is disgusted, and Helmholtz bored. When Bernard brings John, the savage, into the new world, there are immediate repercussions. Helmholtz, hearing the youth recite Shakespeare, first questions his own long-conditioned set of artificial values. He and Bernard join John in an abortive demonstration against the use of "soma," the universal drug; the three are summoned before Mustapha Mond, the Resident World Con troller for Western Europe. The Controller is an understanding man. A radical in his youth, he had accepted a governmental position and "conventionality" rather than exile, that he might further his dearest interest, pure science. Bernard and Helmholtz, however, now choose differently. The latter welcomes exile, the stimulation of physical hardship and mental freedom; the cowardly Bernard must be drugged and dragged away. John is maddened by the soulless horror of the new world. Retained as the subject of scientific experimentation, and trapped by the ambivalence of a physical attraction to and mental repulsion from Lenina, he commits suicide. The harshly ironic fantasy of. Brave New World has gained in impact with the years rather than diminished.

BROTHERS KARAMAZOV, THE (188()), by Feodor Dostoevsky. Regarded as his outstanding work, this psychological novel is Dostoevsky's final judgment on modern times, on a humanity succumbing to what he calls "socialist materialism," on individuals abandoning true Christianity. A deeply religious work, obsessed with man's search for faith, it is also a sordid story of crime, and an account of the struggle within the soul of man for truth and virtue. The tragedy is dominated by the patriarchal Father Zossima, who has achieved holiness by renouncing his reason and will. The elder Karamazov is a roue and sot who has sunk into a swamp of corruption and has dragged his young mistress, Grushenka, with him. A cunning old reprobate, he is intelligent enough to understand the deeper motives of his behavior, and suffers maudlin pangs of conscience. The struggle between him and his eldest son, Dmitri, for the carnal love of Grushenka, is the pivotal motive for the crime that ensues. Under the sly promptings of another son, Ivan, the old man's epileptic, illegitimate son, Smerdyakov, murders his father. Dmitri is suspected, and is sentenced to die for the crime on the grounds of circumstantial evidence. All three legitimate sons of Karamazov,

Dmitri, Ivan and Alyosha, are tainted in varying degrees with the Karamazov hereditary weakness of character. It is most pronounced in Dmitri. He is a fine, simple soul, tormented by inner conflicts, and in his quest for ideal values, treads the sorrowful way of the blundering heart. At his trial, overwhelmed by the spectacle of crime and spiritual confusion, he at last finds God and inner peace. He publicly flays his soul for its shortcomings. He admits with gratitude that in order to see the light, it is first necessary to undergo purgation by tragedy: "I accept the torture of accusation, and my public shame. I want to suffer, and by suffering I shall purify myself. But listen, for the last time, I am not guilty of my father's blood." Dostoevsky argues that it was really Ivan who was the murderer of his father, rather than the weak minded Smerdyakov who actually committed the crime, or the brooding Dmitri who vicariously suffered for it. It was Ivan who planted the seed of evil in Smerdyakov's mind. Everyone shared in the crime, for the whole world must be held responsible for all the evil that passes under the sun. In the questioning, doubting Ivan, Dostoevsky wished to castigate the rationalism of his time, which he saw as bereft of feeling and faith, and which would turn into a demoniacal force if let loose. Ivan, too, had the Karamazov taint in him, but it was intellectual rather than sensual. The youngest Karamazov, Alyosha, as a novice in a monastery, seeks spiritual

rapture, guided by Father Zossima. He too bears the Karamazov rot in his otherwise pure young soul. He, like his brothers, wrestles with the Evil One, but emerges triumphant: "He longed to forgive everyone and for everything, and to beg forgiveness. Oh, not for himself, but for all men, for all and for everything." It is this novel that contains the famous story of "The Grand Inquisitor," so much anthologized, and it is in the equally famous chapter preceding this-"Ivan Karamazov's Confession of Faith"-that Ivan utters the celebrated and oft-quoted phrase: "It is not God that I don't accept, Alyosha, only I most respectfully return Him the ticket."

CANDIDE (1758), by Voltaire. In Westphalia, where the story starts, the preternaturally earnest and simple Candide is very happy. He has just learned the joys of love from Cunegunde, daughter of the Baron of Thunderten-Tronckh, and the Leibnitzian doctrine that "all is for the best in this best of possible worlds" from the philosopher Pangloss. But the Baron kicks Candide off his estate, and when war breaks out, Candide is pressed into the army. Cunegunde becomes booty of war. Misfortune follows all three characters in their attempts to find each other. Pangloss survives illness, shipwreck, earthquake and the torture of the Inquisition; Cunegunde is raped by soldiers, made the mistress of an Inquisitor, mutilated by pirates. In the best of possible worlds they see an auto-da-fe, the Lisbon disaster, the shooting of Admiral Byng for losing a battle, Huguenots sent to the galleys, missionaries exploiting the natives in South America-in fact, every kind of intolerance and injustice. The one happy land they find is El Dorado, which of course does not exist. Old and worn, Candide and Cunegunde end in Constantinople, where they settle down to "cultivate their garden." Voltaire gave this tale the subtitle "-or Optimism." Others of his philosophical tales are *ZadiB* (1747), a series of episodes in which a wise man of Bagdad learns that Providence, if it exists, is entirely inscrutable; *Micromeoas* (1752 or earlier), a Swiftian story of a visit to the Earth by giants from other planets who find humans and their concerns to be of microscopic importance; and *The Huron* (1767), the story of a simple Indian who visits Europe and finds its alleged civilization frequently offensive to common sense.

CITY OF GOD, THE (426), by St. Augustine (Aurelius Augustinus). Not until the appearance of the Summa Theologica of Thomas Aquinas in the thirteenth century was St. Augustine's City of God rivaled in the universal esteem of Christendom. For one thousand years it reigned as the most influential apologia for Christianity. Augustine was one of the most cultured and profound of the church fathers, and one of the most genuinely pious. A teacher of rhetoric and a man of broad learning, he brought eloquence and loftiness to Patristic writings. The City of God was evoked by the chaos of the times in which Augustine lived. The sack of Rome by the Goths under Alaric in 410 stirred the imagination of all thinking men as a sign of the disintegration of the Roman Empire. Defeatism poisoned the atmosphere. Men's hearts, wrote Augustine, were "failing them for fear and for looking after those things that were coming on the earth." Moral and intellectual confusion accompanied the imperial downfall of the "Eternal City." Augustine at last saw his opportunity to win over, by marshaling historical proof and eloquence, the multitudes of cultivated pagans who could no longer find comfort and assurance in the pagan pantheon. Augustine divided his work into twenty-two books. Books 1-V present a refutation of the belief of the pagan masses that polytheism was necessary to mortal happiness. Books VI-X meet the assertion of the philosophers that the worship of the gods was advantageous in

view of the prospect of life after death. The latter part of the work concerns itself with the presentation- of a constructive philosophy of life to take the place of pagan worship. Books XI-XIV contain "the origin of the two cities, the City of God and the city of the world." Books XV to XVIII contain "their process or progress." Books XIX-XXII reveal their "appointed ends." Augustine finds much wretchedness in the city of the world in contrast to the splendor of the City of God. He finds there is one commonwealth for all Christian men: "That heavenly city which has Truth for its King, Love for its Law, and Eternity for its Measure...."

CODE OF HAMMURABI (ca. 2067 B.C.) by Hammurabi. In all Oriental research no event can compare in importance with the chance discovery of the Code of Hammurabi in 1902, on the site of the Acropolis of Susa which was the capital of ancient Elam in Persia. The zenith of Babylonian civilization was reached during the time of Hammurabi, who reigned supreme for 43 years (2067-2025 B.C.) over a united and highly centralized Babylonian Empire. He was a model Oriental despot with strongly benevolent inclinations toward his subjects, as can be seen in his Code which consists of 282 paragraphs, preceded by a Prologue and concluded by an Epilogue. His object in promulgating the Code, he tells us, is to insure "that the strong oppress not the weak, that the orphan and widow be protected." The outstanding merit of the Code as an historical document is that it affords a contemporary insight into the cultural and social life of Babylonians some 4,000 years ago. The laws do not resolve themselves into general principles of jurisprudence; they have practical application to human conduct, social and economic relations. They deal with witchcraft, legal evidence, duties and privileges of royal servants, tenure, rents and cultivated lands, trade and commerce, deposit and prosecution for debt, family law, marriage settlements, divorce, inheritance, adoption, criminal law, slavery, care of canals and wages of architects, surgeons and boat men. It is to be assumed that Hammurabi did not start with a clean legal slate. He grafted his new concepts on the old, deriving from the civic institutions that had hitherto shaped people's lives. His Code was an adaptation, as well as the amalgam, of several systems of ancient ethics.

COMMUNIST MANIFESTO, THE (1848), by Karl Marx and Friedrich Engels. As a document the Manifesto is the most concise and influential statement of Marxism. It is written with epigrammatic force and literary skill. Published on the eve of the epidemic of social revolutions in Europe in 1848, it was designed as a program for the Communist League, a workers' organization, which, although German at first, soon achieved international scope. The Manifesto embodied the materialistic conception of history evolved by its authors. It states its thesis with the directness of a challenge: "The history of all hitherto existing societies is the history of class struggles." It then attempts to array all historical proof for such a theory, finally bringing it down to nineteenth-century capitalistic Europe, arguing that even as the bourgeois revolution destroyed feudalism, so in its turn capitalism would be displaced by a workers' society. This, the authors stated, was an historical inevitability: "The proletarian movement is the self-conscious, independent movement of the immense majority, in the interest of the immense majority." According to the Manifesto, the Communists were the most advanced and determined section of all working class parties, "that section which pushes forward all others." Their aim was the "abolition of private property." Just as the first step of the bourgeois revolution was the overthrow of the feudal power, so the later proletarian revolution would strive "to raise the proletariat to the position of ruling class, to win the battle of democracy." Most dramatic is the Manifesto's introductory sentence: "A spectre is haunting Europe," and equally apocalyptic are its concluding words: "The workers have nothing to lose but their chains; they have a whole world to gain. Workers of all countries, unite." The Communist Manifesto has gone through countless editions, and has been translated into almost all languages.

CONFESSIONS (ca. 400), by St. Augustine (Aurelius Augustinus). "Confession of sin all know," declared St. Augustine, "but confession of praise few attend to....The former but showeth the wound to the physician, the latter giveth thanks for health." This, in brief, expresses the aim of Augustine in writing his *Confessions*. It treats of his deep religious experiences against a background of personal unhappiness and moral conflict. The work created a new literary genre: the confessional autobiography. Its main object, however, was a defense of the Latin Church against the heretical sects of his day. The author had in mind the Roman intellectuals whom he was eager to win over from paganism. He also wished that his book might serve as a

source of spiritual edification to his brethren in their evangelical labors. He commented ruefully upon the one-sidedness and aridity of contemporary intellectualism: "Men desire to learn the rules of learning, but neglect the eternal rules of everlasting salvation." The early chapters of the *Confessions* are extraordinarily moving. Augustine was a great man who could expose his weaknesses and errors without attempting to justify them. He had a sensitive, probing mind, a philosophical passion for objective truth. His work breathes a devotional and penitential mood. In his early years he had fallen into licentious habits. Although he had an avid desire for learning, and even wrote Latin treatises on the arts and on the *Catenaries* of Aristotle in his twenties, he had lacked a unifying world view. His love of pleasure, which had manifested itself since his boyhood, was constantly opposed to his guilty conscience, which craved a spiritual reality. After stubbornly resisting the preaching of St. Ambrose, Augustine finally accepted Christian baptism at his hands in his thirty-second year. The rest of the *Confessions* (Books X-XIII) is an apologia for the Roman Church. He examines and illuminates the Scriptural texts with the dialectical skill and learning he had formerly lavished on his Aristotelian commentaries. He attempts to expose the contradictions and untenable doctrines of the Christian sects regarded by the Latin Church as heretical. The *Confessions* is one of the foundation stones of Catholicism.

CONFESSIONS (1781-1788), by Jean Jacques Rousseau. Rousseau's *Confessions* inaugurated a new school of autobiographic literature based on an attempt at scrupulously honest self-analysis. Whether he succeeded in being candid in this work is open to question. Sometimes he is over-facile in justifying his "misdeeds." The very fact that he, Rousseau, a great and wise man, should fearlessly lay his soul bare regardless of the consequences, fills him with childish pride: "I undertake an unexampled enterprise, the execution of which can never be imitated." Regardless of the motive, Rousseau's *Confessions* is an extraordinary portrait of a genius who was not a fraction as lovable or as noble as he fondly thought he was, but a vain, jealous, calculating individual. To his credit it must be remembered that this is only one aspect of his baffling, contradictory character-that he also struggled for a free world, championed intellectual freedom and social responsibility and justice. The *Confessions* was written when Rousseau was already middle-aged, some parts going back to his childhood forty years before, and his memory was not trustworthy. He was sick, and possibly a little insane. His *Confessions* frequently document his philosophical works, furnish a fascinating view of people he loved or hated Hume, Voltaire, Diderot, Grimm, Mme. d'Houditot, etc. and contain passages of great lyric beauty; they are more readable than many novels.

CONSOLATIONS OF PHILOSOPHY, THE (ca.523), by Amicius Manlius Severinus Boethius. Boethius lived at a transitional point between two historical epochs-the ancient and the medieval. He was a great scholar, and a reverent student of Greek philosophy. He is best remembered for his Consolations, which he wrote in the prison at Pavia while awaiting his execution at the hands of Theodoric. Its five books have been characterized as "the last work of Roman literature." Book I tells of a vision the philosopher had. A woman appeared before him, holding a book in one hand and a scepter in the other. She offers him the promise of solace. He recognizes her; she is his lifelong companion, Philosophy. He pours out to her his tale of woe, and she listens with sympathy. In Book II Philosophy upbraids Boethius for his foolish ambition to achieve eminence as a statesman and philosopher, showing that greatness has no enduring value. In Book III there is a discussion of the Supreme Good. The conclusion is that it does not consist of riches, power or pleasure, but that it resides in God. In Book IV the problems of evil and the freedom of the will come under scrutiny. The subject of the freedom of the will is further pursued in the fifth and final book, and is reconciled with predestination. In the ninth century Alfred the Great translated the book into Anglo-Saxon. Chaucer made an English translation which was published by Caxton in 1480.

COURTIER, THE (1518), by Baldassare Castiglione. Castiglione, one of the most accomplished courtiers and diplomats of his time (Emperor Charles the Fifth called him "one of the best knights in the world"), served the Duke of Urbina, and typified Italian refinement at the English court, where he was sent to receive the Garter for his sovereign. When he wrote *The Courtier,* Castiglione was the Duke's ambassador to the splendid court of Pope Leo X and an intimate friend of the most cultured men and women of his age. The book is a report of dialogues presumably held at the court of Urbino among the distinguished guests who visited the Duke on various occasions and spent short or long periods of time in his magnificent palace. Through the dialogues, the author conveys the idea of what a perfect courtier, a very accomplished and refined gentleman, must be; what habits he has to follow, and how he has to profess courtesy and civility. But, although this is the main theme of the book, often the conversation deals with important social and political problems of the time, such as the best form of government, the condition of women, etc. The dialogues are also interspersed with pleasant stories which give a fascinating picture of Italian court life.

CRIME AND PUNISHMENT (1866), by Feodor Dostoevsky. One of the great psychological crime novels, this book has probably never been surpassed in its field. Raskolnikov, a student, is suffering severely from poverty and ill-health. His life seems thwarted and crushed. As a last straw comes word that his sister is contemplating an obviously distasteful marriage in the hope of bringing some financial benefit to her mother and brother. In a morbid state approaching delirium, he plans the murder of a repellent, aged woman pawnbroker who preys, harpy-like, upon such poor students as he. He rationalizes himself into believing that it is his right to kill the old woman on the ground that she is a parasite, in fact a positive evil in society, and that she hoards means which could be used to further his own progress in some constructive career. After elaborate preparations he commits the crime. Utter panic overwhelms him, and the neat structure of his plan crumbles. The pawnbroker's sister returns unexpectedly and he kills her as well. He fails to find the money chest and at last flees with merely a purse and a handful of trinkets, almost being detected in his escape. He hides his trifling haul under a stone and never touches it again. The book follows the course of his slow breakdown under the pressure of remorse. He begins to indulge in cryptic, suspicion-arousing eccentricities. In the course of time he enters into a prolonged intellectual game of cat-and-mouse with Inspector Porfiry Petrovitch, with whom he is first thrown into contact socially. No account can do credit to the suspense and terror of this subtle conflict, known only to the two men involved. Inevitably Raskolnikov is tracked down. He confesses to Sonya, an unfortunate girl whose family he has aided. She urges him to give himself up. At last Porfiry extracts a tacit acknowledgment from him, but withholds arrest, advising voluntary surrender. Raskolnikov accepts this course and purges his soul. He is sentenced to eight years in Siberia where, with Sonya's love and loyalty, he struggles to remake himself spiritually.

CRITIQUE OF PURE REASON (1781), by Immanuel Kant. The title itself suggests Kant's objective, i.e., to discover the scope as well as the limitations of the rational power. He concluded from his investigation that reason had transcended its own sphere and was the source of speculative error and mental confusion. The *Critique* was written to remedy this Condition. The philosopher's motive may be said to have been ethical in the beginning. He was perturbed by contemporary philosophical skepticism which corroded belief in God, in immortality and in freedom. This he regarded as speculative chaos and falsehood. He finally concluded that reason is only a limited faculty and that it cannot serve as a means by which we may demonstrate those ideas upon which life is based. If critically used, however, it can be an effective instrument. The outcome of this critical inquiry, says Kant, is to destroy knowledge and substitute be lief for it. Reflection by itself cannot produce conviction. By dogmatic objections the religious faith of people is destroyed. By disproving these objections people will be able to follow their higher spiritual instincts, and to believe in the practical implications of life without any need of philosophical demonstration. Kant described his philosophy as critical philosophy, distinct from the philosophy that preceded his, which he called empirical as well as dogmatic. The empiricism of Locke had reached a nihilistic development with David Hume. Locke based his philosophy on experience; Hume demonstrated that when the mind remains passive, experience itself is only a disappearing phantasm which makes all knowledge impossible. Kant said that Hume aroused him out of his dogmatism. He found a new instrument of inquiry: the critical mind. He attempted to show that all scientific knowledge is of phenomena and that this knowledge is a product of sense perception (its material) and thought (its order and system). The nature of the world independent of mind can never be discovered by science.

DE MOTU CORDIS ET SANGUINIS (published 1628), by William Harvey. This work is one of the greatest and most famous contributions to physiology, for it introduced into biology the doctrine of the complete circulation of the blood. Partial anticipations of Harvey's great discovery go back to the thirteenth century, when the pulmonary or lesser circulation was proposed by lbn-an-Nafis. In 1553, Servetus said that blood flows from the heart to the lungs, and that here it mixes with air to form the arterial blood which flows back to the heart. Between 1570 and 1590, Cesalpino suggested, in controversy with Galenists, that the movement of the blood was more like a circulation than an oscillation; but his views lack clarity. In 1603, Fabricius of Acquapendente published a work clearly describing the valves in the veins and showing that they hinder the flow of blood away from the heart. From 1597 to 1602, Harvey had studied at Padua, and he made a careful study of the heart and the movement of the blood. By 1616, he was presenting in lectures his case for the circulation of the blood, but it was not until 1628 that he published it in his classical work, *De Motu Cordis et Sanguinis.* This book is important both for the discovery of the complete circulation and for the experimental, quantitative and mechanistic methodology which Harvey introduced. He looked upon the heart, not as a mystical seat of the spirit and faculties, but as a pump analyzable along mechanical lines; and he measured the amount of blood which it sent out to the body. He observed that with each beat two ounces of blood leave the heart; so that with 72 heart-beats per minute, the heart throws into the system 540 pounds of blood every hour! Where could all this blood come from? The answer seems to be that it is the same blood that is always returning. Moreover, the one-way valves in the heart, like those in the veins, indicate that, following the pulmonary circulation, the blood goes out to all parts of the body through the arteries and returns by way of the veins. The blood thus makes a complete closed circuit. As Harvey expressed it, "There must be a motion, as it were, in a circle." There was, however, one stage in the circulation which Harvey was not able to see-that in which the veins and arteries lose themselves by sub division into the tiny capillary vessels. It was in 1660, three years after Harvey's death, that Malpighi saw the blood moving in the capillary vessels of the frog's lung, and thus supplied the missing link in Harvey's proof of the circulation of the blood.

DE REVOLUTIONIBUS ORBIUM COELESTIUM (1543), by Nicolaus Copernicus. Copernicus was born in 1473 at Thorn, on the Vistula, and after attending schools there and at Cracow, he studied at universities in Italy. At Bologna he was in close touch with Domenico di Novara, a professor of astronomy who was strongly neo-Pythagorean in viewpoint. With him Copernicus discussed the errors in Ptolemy's *Almagest* (q.v.) and the possibility of improving upon the Ptolemaic system. He became familiar with various ancient astronomical schemes including the heliocentric system of Aristarchus. He also studied law, and after his return to Poland he became canon of the cathedral at Frauenberg. Here he spent the last thirty years of his life, much of his time devoted to administrative affairs. But it was in this period that Copernicus worked out the details of his astronomical scheme which was to be decisive in showing that the earth moved about the sun. About 1529 he circulated among his friends a manuscript, entitled *Commentariolus,* in which he presented his system with the calculations omitted. About ten years later a young astronomer named Rheticus visited Copernicus and published an account of the system in a book entitled *Narratio Prima* (1540). To Rheticus the old and ailing Copernicus committed for publication the manuscript of his great work, the *De Revolutionibus*. The printed book appeared in 1543, and the story goes that the first copy was placed in the hands of Copernicus a few hours before he died. In the dedicatory apologia, addressed to Pope Paul III, Copernicus states: "I too began to reflect on the earth's capacity for motion. And though the idea appeared absurd, yet I knew that others before me had been allowed freedom to imagine what circles they pleased in order to represent the phenomena of the heavenly bodies. I therefore deemed that it would readily be granted to me also to try whether, by assuming the earth to have a certain motion, representations more valid than those of others could be found for the revolution of the heavenly spheres." The body of this work falls into six books. In Book I Copernicus sets forth his general arguments for believing in the mobility of the earth, and for substituting the heliocentric for the geocentric point of view. He sketches the heliocentric arrangement of the solar system in broad out line and gives the modern explanation of the seasons. Book II deals with spherical astronomy and treats of the problems connected with the rising and setting of the sun. In Book III Copernicus treats of the earth's several motions and the elements of its orbit. Book IV deals with the theory of the moon's motions and the determination of the distances of the sun and moon. Books V and VI, in which Copernicus investigates the motions of the five planets and the sizes of their orbits in relation to that of the earth, are the most significant part of the work. Rheticus, to whom Copernicus entrusted the printing of his book, was unable to see the whole work through the press, and he left the supervision to Osiander, a Lutheran clergyman. Osiander, afraid that the Copernican doctrine would offend philosophers and churchmen, undertook to insert in the preface a statement that the whole work was to be regarded as a device of computation rather than as a statement of physical truth. Not until long afterward was it discovered that this interpolation had been made against the expressed wishes of Copernicus. This disarming passage probably accounts for the fact that the book was not immediately banned. The Catholic Church, for example, tolerated Copernican astronomy until the days of Galileo. The new astronomy spread slowly at first, for the evidence at hand made a decision between this and Ptolemaic astronomy difficult. The chief advantage of the Copernican scheme was, at that time, a greater degree of mathematical harmony and simplicity. Only when the calculations of Kepler and the telescopic

observations of Galileo came to its support did the preponderance of evidence very clearly favor the heliocentric system. By that time, moreover, the elaborate scheme of circles which Copernicus proposed was giving way to the far simpler Keplerian system of ellipses. Nevertheless, with the possible exception of Ptolemy's *Almagest* (q.v.) and Newton's *Principia* (q.v.) the *De Revolutionibus* represents the most important single treatise in the history of astronomy.

DEATH OF A SALESMAN (1949), by Arthur Miller. Willy Loman is a salesman whose escapist tendencies have blinded him to his real mediocrity. At sixty-three, the company which has employed him for thirty-four years takes him off salary; and on commission only, the financial distress of the family, which has always purchased on the installment plan, be comes even more acute. His son Happy is a moderate business success, but lonely Biff, whom Willy has educated to consider the world a jungle, has tried many jobs, but at thirty-four is antagonistic toward Willy, who by his belief that success and happiness depend on deceit and ruthlessness, has warped the lives of his wife Linda and the two boys. Final attempts are futile, as Willy is fired and Biff cannot get a good job. Biff believes himself a failure, but finally tells Willy that he is to blame also. Willy, whose mind is failing, commits suicide to give the family insurance money. He leaves Linda, who has just made the last payment on the house after twenty-five years, confused and lonely, and Happy infected with the fatal success compulsion.

DECAMERON, THE (ca. 1350), by Giovanni Boccaccio. Boccaccio's epoch-making *Decameron* is composed of a hundred stories told by seven young women and three young men in ten successive days. They all gather in the country outside the city of Florence, to escape the Great Plague. Boccaccio takes the originals of his stories from traditional folklore, or French fabliaux, or Oriental tales. The ten stories of the first day are freely chosen by the party; those of the second day tell of adversities finally overcome, with a happy ending for each story. On the third day, the reader encounters people realizing their dreams through their ingenuity; on the fourth, unhappy lovers; on the fifth, lovers able to achieve their desires. The sixth day describes dangerous events cunningly avoided with the help of brilliant ideas and solutions; on the seventh day, unfaithful wives are portrayed; on the eighth, unfaithful husbands. The ninth day is again left free to the narrator's will, and the tenth recounts liberal deeds of illustrious knights and liberal-minded men. Boccaccio's greatness as a master of narrative has made his *Decameron* one of the most popular books of all times, and for many centuries the supreme model for many storytellers.

DECLINE AND FALL OF THE ROMAN EMPIRE, THE HISTORY OF THE (1776-1788), by Edward Gibbon. Gibbon's History, although it was written over two hundred years ago, in many ways remains today an unequaled historical study of ancient Roman society. Gibbon epitomizes his subject with the tart bold epigram: "I have described the triumph of barbarism and religion." He held that human progress entered into its decline with the advent of Christianity, which he treats (notably in Chapter XV) with a stately irony that has been repeatedly resented by believing Christians as slanderous and "wicked," and, conversely, has been defended with an equal amount of warmth by the nonreligious. Gibbon's views of society and the universe were shaped by the liberal French thought of the day, which was anticlerical, antifeudal and democratic. In the outmoded tradition of eighteenth century historical writing, Gibbon's fine historical balance was frequently tipped by his didactic air, his satirical analyses and his soliloquies. He was very erudite, and his work is still regarded as substantially accurate. His historical method was quite novel to England, whatever the influence on him of such French writers as Voltaire and Montesquieu. *The Decline and Fall* is in seven volumes, and it runs in continuous unity from the time of the Antonines (180) to the fall of Constantinople in 1453. Gibbon was an enthusiast for Roman civilization at its best: "In the second century of the Christian era, the empire of Rome comprehended the fairest part of the earth, and the most civilized portion of mankind. The frontiers of that extensive monarchy were guarded by ancient renown and disciplined valour. The gentle but powerful influence of laws and manners had gradually cemented the union of the provinces. Their peaceful inhabitants enjoyed and abused the advantages of wealth and luxury. The image of a free constitution was preserved with decent reverence." Gibbon saw the forces of disintegration as setting in upon the death of Marcus Aurelius. However, he was not a particularly profound student of Roman life. He had an unfortunate tendency to romanticize the Roman rulers and their administrators as starkly good or bad, without giving enough emphasis to the social decay around them. But his work is an unrivaled monument in the grand style; it stands in the forefront of both history and literature.

DECLINE OF THE WEST, THE (1918), by Oswald Spengler. Spengler attempted to combine information from many fields (mathematics, natural sciences, the arts, history) into a systematic philosophy of history. In his conception, cultures are similar to living things that are born, grow to maturity, decline, and die. He studied a variety of cultures, tried to plot their life courses, and found many interesting parallels from one to an other. As the title of his book indicates, he believed that western civilization was in the declining phase of its life-cycle, and was to be replaced by a new and more vigorous culture.

DEMOCRACY IN AMERICA (1835-1840), by Alexis de Tocqueville. Tocqueville, a young French aristocrat, and his friend Beaumont came to the United States in the 1830's with a commission from their government to study the prison systems of this country. While traveling here, Tocqueville made extensive observations of all phases of American life economic, political, social, religious and intellectual. *Democracy in America* is his report to the French on how democracy was faring on the other side of the Atlantic. He was neither a violent critic nor a rabid supporter of the American way of life. His standards of evaluation· enabled him to see virtues and defects, and to present a balanced estimate. In the course of his analysis of American institutions, Tocqueville indicated the outlines of his general philosophy of history. He felt that Western society showed a providential trend toward democracy, which for him meant equalitarian ism. In itself, this was neither good nor evil. If the tendency of democracy to create a tyranny of the majority was not curbed, the consequences would be disastrous for society. If this tendency was curbed, and Tocqueville felt that this was possible, then the future of democracy was indeed bright. This sociological and historical study, perhaps the best ever written on this country, was ignored for many years after its appearance, but it was revived in the last century and has been studied by social scientists with renewed interest. This is partly explained by the accuracy of many of Tocqueville's predictions.

DIALOGUES (399-347 B.C.), by Plato. There are extant today forty one dialogues ascribed to Plato (ca. 428-347), but fourteen of them are certainly forgeries or imitations and the authenticity of three others is doubtful. Of all the dialogues deemed genuine, it is not possible to affix a definite date of composition for a single one; consequently, only a few can be read in any time-sequence. The dialogues represent no rigid philosophic system, being rather an effort at the apprehension of wisdom, virtue, truth and beauty. In a large measure they are not original, as Plato himself testified in his Seventh Epistle: "The opinions called by the name of Plato are those of Socrates in his days of youthful vigor and glory." The profound spell the oral teachings of Socrates cast on Plato during his youthful years endured throughout his life and is fully revealed in the dialogues. Socrates not only appears as the protagonist in many of them but the Socratic outlook on life, the Socratic moral and intellectual aims, are stamped on all of them. Furthermore, the famed Socratic dialectical method is uniformly used by Plato. Although Plato was deeply disheartened by the execution of his master and took little active part in public life because of it, the precepts and example of Socrates inspired his life and philosophy. It is, however, possible to observe a progression toward a higher degree of dogmatism evidenced and accompanied by a diminished importance of Socrates' role in the dialogues and his final disappearance, as in the *Laws*. The dialogue as a vehicle for the expression of philosophic ideas was not Plato's invention. He probably selected it because it was so well adapted to Socrates' customary manner of discussion. His artistic mastery of the form is unsurpassed. He chooses the most homely and unpretentious incidents or remarks upon which to build his speculations on the nature of wisdom, virtue and knowledge. Many of the characters that people his dialogues are his friends, relatives, pupils, and fellow philosophers. Plato was an earnest searcher after the eternal truths. Like Socrates he believed virtue is synonymous with knowledge. Constantly he dwells upon man's capacity for good derived from his ability to discriminate and reason. The following are the dialogues of Plato about whose authenticity there is no doubt: *Euthyphro, ApoloBJ, Crito, Phaedo, Crao/lus, Theaetetus, Sophist, Statesman, Parmenides. Philebus, Symposium, Phaedrus, Charmides, Laches, Lysis, Euthydemus, Protagoras, Gorgias, Meno, Jon, Republic, Timaeus, Critias, Laws.*

DISCOURSE ON METHOD (1637), by Rene Descartes. The *Discourse* is divided into six parts and touches upon various matters concerning the sciences: the principal rules of Descartes' method, the rules of morality deduced from this method, proof of the existence of God and the soul, investigations in the field of physics, conclusions concerning the motion of the heart and other anatomical problems, and finally, a program for the further investigation of nature. Descartes stresses constantly the fundamental importance of method: "For to be possessed of a vigorous mind is not enough; the prime requisite is rightly to apply it." As a mathematician, Descartes was concerned to discover the method which enabled him to make his discoveries. He proceeded as follows: he started by attempting to doubt everything, and finds grounds for doubting the evidence of the senses, nature in general, and even mathematics. What he cannot doubt, in the very process of his doubting, is the fact that he is thinking. From this he derives his basic philosophical principle, "I think, therefore I am." Upon this basis, using a rigorous mathematical method, Descartes builds his philosophy. This philosophy is dualistic in character; mind and body are conceived of as distinct. The movement of bodies is mechanical and can be described by mathematical laws. Mind is independent of this mechanical system, but through reason can grasp its structure. The problem of the relation of mind to matter was Descartes' legacy to modern philosophers. When he comes to summarize his method, Descartes lists four principles: 1) accept only that which is clear and distinct as true; 2) divide each difficulty into as many parts as possible; 3) start with the simplest elements and move by an orderly procedure to the more complex; and 4) make complete enumerations and reviews to make certain that nothing was omitted. The philosophical implications of these principles were further elaborated by Descartes in his *Meditations* (1642).

DIVINE COMEDY, THE (1314-1321), by Dante Alighieri. *The Divine Comedy* is a grandiose monument of the Middle Ages, symbolizing the allegory of the human soul which from error and ignorance can reach the highest degree of perfection-contemplation of God. The *Comedy* is divided into three Canticas: *Hell, Purgatory* and *Paradise.* Each Cantica consists of thirty-three Cantos. Another Canto, preceding the whole poem as an introduction, makes a total of a hundred, a number which for Dante is symbolic of true perfection. In the introduction Dante explains that he finds himself in a dark, tangled forest (symbolizing error). At its edge there is an illuminated hill, but a leopard, a lion and a wolf oppose the poet's ascent. Virgil, the great Roman poet, for whom Dante had the deepest admiration, and whom he selects as his guide through the voyage in Hell, appears. He guides Dante to the entrance of the Inferno, which is the figure of a gigantic inverted cone having its top at the center of the earth. Inferno: In the outer court of Hell, Dante sees countless legions of spirits bitten by wasps until their blood mingles with their tears. They are the cowards and the undecided. In the First Circle are the virtuous who died un-baptized, and good heathens, such as Homer, Horace, Ovid and Lucan. Hell actually begins in the Second Circle of the descending cone, where a whirlwind blows the spirits of those who sinned with carnal lust, among whom Dante finds the unhappy lovers Paolo and Francesca da Rimini. In the Third Circle Dante encounters the gourmands who lie in the mud watched by the fierce Cerberus; in the Fourth, misers and spend-thrifts collide, as they push huge rocks forward. Virgil then leads Dante into the swamp of Styx which constitutes the Fifth Circle. Here the ill tempered dwell in mud and filth. The Sixth Circle is a strange city, the City of Dis. Thousands of devils prevent the two poets from entering until an angel sent by God breaks their resistance. As they proceed, Dante and Virgil see a vast graveyard in which heretics and teachers of errors, with their disciples, lie in red-hot tombs. Dante recognizes Farinatadegli Uberti, a great Florentine patriot, and Cavalcante Cavalcanti, the father of his intimate friend and fellow-poet Guido Cavalcanti. In the Seventh Circle tyrants and murderers are doused in a stream of boiling blood. The Eighth is inhabited by deceivers, a category comprising seducers, flatterers, simoniacs, soothsayers, barrators, hypocrites, thieves, evil counselors, schismatics and falsifiers. In the Ninth Circle the most grievous of all crimes, treachery, is expiated. There are traitors to their kindred, traitors to their country, traitors to their friends and traitors to their lords and bene factors. Especially impressive for its poetical beauty, among the encounters of Dante with traitors, is the episode of Count Ugolino, who died of starvation with his children in the tower of Pisa. Now, in the Inferno, he rabidly devours the head of his fatal enemy, Archbishop Ruggero. At the very end of Inferno--the top of the inverted cone-is the giant Lucifer who champs with his teeth Brutus, Cassius and Judas Iscariot, the three arch-sinners. Purgatory: Purgatory has the shape of a mountain divided into seven terraces. At the peak is the divine forest of earthly Paradise. Outside the gate of Purgatory Dante finds four classes of negligents waiting to be admitted into the place of penance and purification. On the seven terraces are punished the Deadly Sins: Pride, Envy, Anger, Sloth, Avarice and Prodigality, Gluttony, Lust. On the stairs leading to the gate of Purgatory stands an angel who, with the point of his sword, traces on Dante's forehead seven p's-the initial of the Latin word *peccata,* sins. Dante is bidden to wash the seven letters off, one by one, in the seven circles of Purgatory. During the ascent, as Dante wanders from one circle to another, an angelic choir sings the Beatitudes in contrast to the Seven Deadly Sins. When Dante reaches the Seventh Circle, where the sins of carnal lust are cleansed, he is moved by the sight of penitents moving in flame and singing the hymn of divine clemency. On the other side of the flame stands the angel of chastity who, with the cry "Blessed are the pure in heart" bids the poet to go through the fire. He is now purged of all sins and the last P has been erased from his brow. Dante and Virgil have now reached the mountain summit and they enter the forest of earthly Paradise. Beatrice, the woman whom Dante most loved in his life and who represents in his eyes the embodiment of human perfection, appears adorned with heavenly beauty. He then is immersed in the waters of Lethe and thus purified is ready for his flight to Paradise. Beatrice now replaces Virgil as Dante's guide. Paradise: Dante's Paradise consists of nine Heavens all surrounded by the Empyrean Sphere where dwells the Divine Presence. The earth, with its Inferno and Purgatory, is the center around which they revolve. Led now by the spirit of Beatrice, Dante is flooded by an ocean of light. His inner hearing is opened to receive the celestial harmonies of the Spheres. Beatrice informs him that now he is in Heaven, borne there by the longing of his purified soul for the presence of God. As they journey from Sphere to Sphere, Beatrice's beauty grows ever more radiant. In the First Sphere, that of the Moon, Beatrice dis courses learnedly on the mystic powers of the moon and the stars. The first of the blessed souls appears. In the Second Sphere, the Sphere of Mercury, Dante is joyfully surrounded by the blessed spirits who, seeing that he is blessed by God, wish to increase their love through him. As they soar to the Third Sphere, Beatrice imparts to him all the secrets of the Redemption, which are hidden from all except those who have been purified by the flames of love. In the Fourth Sphere, that of the Sun, reside the great teachers of the Church: Albertus Magnus, Thomas Aquinas, Peter Lombard, King Solomon, Boethius, Isidore of Seville and the Venerable Bede. St. Thomas then proceeds to instruct the poet in the manner of the risen body of saints. In the Sphere of Mars, the Fifth Heaven, and surrounding the Cross, appear the spirits of those who have borne arms in the service of the Lord. Dante meets Joshua, Judas Maccabeus, Charlemagne and Roland. In the Sixth Heaven, of Jupiter, appear the blessed spirits of upright monarchs. In the next, the Sphere of Saturn, appear the saints of the contemplative life. In the Eighth Heaven, that of the fixed stars, Dante beholds in awe the splendor of Christ, surrounded by the Virgin Mother and the Apostles. When he finally rises to the Ninthor crystalline Heaven, Dante can behold its glories only through the pure eyes of Beatrice. He sees the nine choirs of angels moving in concentric circles around the throne of God. He receives instructions on the various hierarchies of angels and on their creation and fall. Then Beatrice leads him to the Empyrean where he gazes on the seat of God and the blessed who surround him. In the heavenly zone Beatrice bids him farewell and takes her place among the blessed. St. Bernard de Clairvaux assumes the role of guide and reveals to Dante the final aim of man. St. Bernard utters a prayer of intercession to the Virgin for him. Dante then obtains, in an outburst of ecstasy, the grace to plunge himself into the contemplation of God, the highest, the supreme goal of man. The poet ends on a lofty note: "But now my desire and my will were revolved, like a wheel which is moved evenly, by the Love which moves the sun and the other stars." Dante's immortal poem reveals, in their highest form and essence, the religion, philosophy and morality of the Middle Ages. It is like a gigantic cathedral, built on the spacious road of human history, to indicate that a whole epoch is finished and another begins. But it is not to these qualities, no matter how important, that *The Divine Comedy* owes its immortal fame. Dante the philosopher, Dante the theologian, and Dante the political theorist are all surpassed by an even greater Dante the poet. Throughout the marvelous voyage, in its dramatic encounters with the damned, the spirits in penance or the blessed, Dante gives vent to his individual passions and feelings, revealing a vehemence hardly equaled, never surpassed, both in hatred and love. His artistic capacity to translate this passionate feeling into beauty makes of Dante one of the outstanding poets of all time.

DOLL'S HOUSE, A (1879), by Henrik Ibsen. One of the best known of Ibsen's plays and one of the most widely discussed, it raised a furor at the time it was first produced, as it dealt with the question of woman's social position and was far in advance of its day. An almost perfect example of a realistic three-act drama, the action takes place at Christmastide in Christiania in the space of three days. Torvald Helmer, a vain but conscientious lawyer, has just received a promotion at the bank, and his wife, Nora, pretty, lighthearted and seemingly frivolous, feels that they can squander a little money on Christmas festivities. Helmer, who treats her like a child and calls her his "little lark," warns her that she must be more careful, as money always slips through her fingers, and she is continually asking him for more. Mrs. Linden, an old widowed friend of Nora's, calls and admits that she had heard of Helmer's improved position and had hoped that maybe Nora could find her a place in her husband's bank. Nora proudly tells her friend that she has been earning money too. Helmer was very ill the first year of their marriage and to save his life it was necessary to take him to

Italy. Nora borrowed the necessary money, but told Helmer that she had received a small legacy from her father. She has managed to pay the interest out of her clothes allowance, and sometimes found work unknown to her husband. But now the debt is almost paid off. Helmer agrees to employ Mrs. Linden and gives her the position in the bank held by Nils Krogstad, a lawyer of shady character who had been convicted of forgery. Krogstad is the man from whom Nora had borrowed the money and he threatens to reveal the loan to her husband if he loses his job. He points out that her father, who was supposed to have signed the paper for the loan, was dead at the time. Nora finally admits that she forged her father's signature. She tries to coax her husband to keep Krogstad, who is trying to regain his position in society, but Helmer says the former was a forger and insists on replacing him. Mrs. Linden, an old friend of Krogstad's, promises to appeal to him in Nora's behalf, but discovers that he has gone out of town. In the meantime Krogstad has written Helmer a letter telling him the story, and Nora is desperate. She sees the letter in the letter-box, but cannot remove it as her husband has the key. She does everything to prevent his reading it. They go to a fancy dress party in the apartment above with a friend, Dr. Rank, who knows he is dying, and is hopelessly in love with Nora. She wears an Italian costume and dances the tarantella, trying to keep her husband diverted by her feverish gaiety. In a despairing mood she plans to slip out and commit suicide at the moment Helmer discovers the letter. When he reads it he accuses her of having committed a serious crime which will ruin him, and tells her she is not fit to associate with their children. His self-righteousness exceeds even her anticipation. Krogstad sends back the promissory note, and Helmer cries that he is saved. But Nora has been too deeply shocked to return to her husband, and in a dramatic scene leaves him to support herself, and learn to do her own thinking. She gives him a ray of hope that if a miracle should occur perhaps they can be reunited.

DON QUIXOTE OF LA MANCHA (1605, 1615), by Miguel de Cervantes. An elderly country gentleman of La Mancha becomes so utterly mad reading romances of chivalry that he finally believes them to be true and, considering himself a knight-errant, goes forth into the world to defend the oppressed and to undo wrongs. Since knights-errant cannot exist without lady-loves, he chooses as the lady of his thoughts a peasant girl he had known in former years and gives her the name of Dulcinea. After his first sortie, in which he is knighted, he urges an ignorant and credulous but good-natured middle-aged peasant of his village, by name Sancho Panza, to follow him as esquire. Knight and esquire sally forth in search of adventures and there is no dearth of them, thanks to the imagination of the Don, who forever transforms the common into the extraordinary: windmills become giants; inns, castles; galley-slaves, oppressed gentlemen. The esquire's more pedestrian perception of the truth forms a contrast to the illusions of his masters, but both suffer the most excruciating discomfitures and are brought home somewhat crushed in body and spirit. Ten years later, spurred by the appearance of a spurious Don Quixote, Cer-vantes published the second part of his novel. This is perhaps superior to Part I, showing more invention, vigor and richer material: Don Quixote's dream in the cave of Montesinos, the puppet show of Maese Pedro, the adventures at the castle of the Duke, Sancho as governor of his island, the scenes with the Robin Hood Roque Gulllart, and the final de feat of Don Quixote. By the time of the death of the Knight, Sancho Panza has become an altogether lovable, quixotic character, so that the reader parts from them and their exciting world of marvels with deeply felt regret. The novel which obviously had for its genesis the satire of romances of chivalry, gradually grew into a vast panorama of Spanish life and into a most entertaining work of fiction, the first modern novel, read and admired to this day as one of the world's great literary achievements.

ECCLESIASTICAL HISTORY OF THE ENGLISH NATION, THE (731), by Bede. Precious both as history and as literature, this work was written in Latin at the monastery of]arrow, and its author is often referred to as the Venerable Bede. Divided into five books, it begins, after a dedication, with a physical description of Britain, mentions briefly the early Roman conquerors and persecutors, becomes detailed with the be ginning of the fourth century, and proceeds very closely from the year 596 when Pope Gregory the Great sent Augustine to King Ethelbert's court to introduce Christianity. The story of the gradual conversion of the English is continued until within four years of Bede's death. It is in many ways a pagan story of violence and invasion, of relapses into idolatry, of abject superstition. But the faith gradually spreads, aided, apparently, by many visions and miracles, such as the wonders wrought before and after death by St. Cuthbert. One of King Edwin's counselors, when Paulinus comes before them, compares the life of man "to the swift flight of a sparrow through the room wherein you sit at supper in winter," while the hearth is burning and outside there is a storm. Also memorable is the anecdote about the sudden power of song

given the ignorant herdsman Caedmon, the first poet in English literature whose name we know.

ELEMENTS OF GEOMETRY (3rd c.), by Euclid. The author of these thirteen books taught and founded a school at Alexandria, where his fame as a geometer drew many students from all parts of the Hellenic world. The famous mathematician De Morgan wrote in 1848: "There never has been, and till we see it we never shall believe that there can be, a system of geometry worthy of the name, which has any material departures from the plan laid down by Euclid." Geometry did not originate wholly with Euclid but reached its highest development in his mathematical genius. His early Greek editor Proclus states that Euclid "put together the *Elements,* collecting many of Eudoxus' theorems, perfecting many of Theaetetus; and also bringing to irrefragable demonstration the things which were only somewhat loosely proved by his predecessors." When King Ptolemy of Alexandria asked Euclid if there was in geometry any shorter cut than that of his *Elements,* the mathematician replied, "There is no royal road to geometry." The first six books of the *Elements* were long used as a modern introductory text to geometry and in England it was customary to speak of studying Euclid, rather than geometry. The first two books of the *Elements* are on the geometry of the straight line, much of the material probably being derived from the Pythagoreans. · Books three and four, on the circle, may have been due largely to Hippocrates of Chios; and books five and six, on the theory of proportion, probably were based on the methods of Eudoxus. One thinks of the *Elements* as exclusively devoted to geometry, but books seven to nine summarize the knowledge in Euclid's day on the theory of numbers, including the well-known "Euclidean algorithm" and a proof that the number of primes is infinite. Book ten, on incommensurable magnitudes, is one of the most finished and remarkable of the thirteen. The last three books are devoted to solid geometry, and the Elements closes with the proof that there are five, and only five, regular solids. Some editions of the *Elements* include two further books-a fourteenth and fifteenth-but these are later interpolations. Euclid, the "Elementator," was the author of a number of other mathematical works, including one on the conic sections and another on optics; but most of these have been lost. The *Elements* of Euclid is without any doubt the best-known mathematical work. It is the oldest of the ancient Greek treatises on mathematics which have survived; and it was widely used by the Arabs and by medieval Latin scholars. It was one of the earliest books on mathematics to be printed, appearing in an edition of 1482. Since then it has been published in over a thousand editions-more, probably, than can be boasted by any book with the exception of the Bible.

EMILE (1762), by Jean Jacques Rousseau. This description of the education of Emile and Sophie presents Rousseau's views on the fundamental principles of education so necessary for producing the morally noble individuals required by a free society. In general Rousseau's views on this subject would today be called "progressive." He is against discipline, formal training, and restriction in general. Since the child is born morally good, our aim should be to prevent civilization from corrupting him. His only discipline should be natural punishment. His natural tendencies should be allowed free development. This book was influential on later philosophers of education Pestalozzi, Proebel, and others.

ESSAY CONCERNING HUMAN UNDERSTANDING (1690), by John Locke. The purpose of this essay was "to inquire into the origin, certainty, and extent of human knowledge, together with the grounds and degrees of belief, opinion, and assent." Locke argues against the doctrine of innate ideas, that is, knowledge preceding experience. He starts by assuming that at birth the mind is blank, like a sheet of white paper, and attempts to show how all our knowledge is engraved upon it by experience. In working out this empiricist theory, Locke develops a dualistic metaphysics. He conceives of the universe as made up of particles of matter in motion. There are certain qualities which these bodies possess in themselves the primary qualities: solidity, extension, figure, motion or rest, and number. When we perceive the world, these qualities are imprinted on the mind together with other qualities which exist for the perceiver only and do not reside in the bodies. These latter are the secondary qualities: color, sound, size, etc., which exist only where there is a proper organ to perceive them. This distinction between primary and secondary qualities, which proved to be unsatisfactory to later philosophers, served as the philosophic foundation for the Newtonian world view, and rationalized the investigations of physical scientists. Locke never did make clear his view as to the exact nature of knowledge. Sometimes he held that it consisted in the agreement of ideas with one another. At other times he seemed to believe that it consisted in the agreement between ideas and things. This latter view is difficult to understand, since, according to Locke, all we can ever know is the ideas in our own minds. This ambiguity gave rise to two subsequent traditions in philosophy. The French followers of Locke, em

phasizing the primary qualities, developed in the direction of mechanical materialism. His English followers, accepting his view that ideas exist only in the mind, rejected the distinction between primary and secondary qualities, and turned toward subjective idealism (Berkeley) and phenomenalism (Hume). Locke may be said to be a philosopher of common sense; many of his postulates and principles are credible, but their philosophic implications lead to perplexing difficulties.

EVERYMAN (15th c.), Anonymous. At the opening of this morality play, God, discouraged by Mankind's neglect of spiritual matters, determines to demand a reckoning of Everyman. He sends Death forth with a summons. Everyman is taken by surprise. He is dismayed when Death identifies himself and orders him to prepare for the long journey. He pleads for more time, which Death refuses him. When Death will give him no stay, Everyman next asks for the right to ask his friends to accompany him. This request Death grants, saying that he may have the companionship of anyone who will venture forth with him. Everyman approaches Good Fellowship, who, seeing him cast down, offers to do him any service even to laying down his life. But when Everyman explains the nature of his journey and begs his company, Good Fellowship flatly refuses. Everyman then has the same experience with Kindred and Goods, who abandon him. In despair Everyman looks for Good Deeds, but Good Deeds cannot rise from the ground; he is weak, weighted down helplessly by Everyman's sins. Good Deeds would go with him but cannot. Knowledge enters, bringing Confession. By their advice, through penance, Good Deeds is allowed to rise to accompany Everyman. They are joined by Strength, Discretion and Five Wits; after Everyman has gone to a priest for the last rites, they set out upon the journey. When they come in sight of the grave, Strength, Discretion and Five Wits desert. Knowledge says that he can go no farther than the grave's edge, although he has no fear. Only Good Deeds can go the whole way. Thus Everyman, realizing how misguided he has been in not loving Good Deeds most through all his life, enters the grave with this true companion, with his book of reckoning in order, certain of being saved. *Everyman* is the work of an unknown author, in all probability a priest. It antedates the reign of Henry VIII. It is the perfect type of the morality play, the most famous of its kind. It is still alive in the theatre and has had a number of modern American productions. For all its archaic phrasing and moralistic content, *Everyman* is astonishingly moving and human. This is because it is rooted in one of the profound and basic experiences common to all men, or to "every man": the final reckoning with Death and the mystery of the hereafter.

FAREWELL TO ARMS, A (1929), by Ernest Hemingway. Frederic Henry is a lieutenant in the Ambulance Corps of the Italian Army during World War I. He meets Catherine Barkley, an English nurse, with whom he contemplates a casual affair. Henry sustains a severe wound. Nursed in the hospital by Catherine, he perceives a new meaning to their relationship: they find themselves very much in love. By the time he returns to active service, she is pregnant. The Italian Army disintegrates in the course of a retreat from Caporetto. Soured by the war, like his depressed Italian friend Rinaldi, and seeing no point to remaining with the shattered and impotent army, Henry deserts and escapes to Switzerland with Catherine. They live an idyllic life for a few months until their child is due. Both Catherine and the child die in childbirth. Henry is left stunned by the completeness of the disaster.

FAUST (Part I, 1808; Part II, 1831), by Johann Wolfgang von Goethe. This epic drama is truly the lifework of the versatile poet, dramatist, novelist, philosopher, statesman, scientist, art critic and theater manager Goethe. Not-withstanding the preoccupations of so diversified a career, the writing of *Faust* was begun in his youth and the finishing touches were put to the second part just before his death in 1832 at the age of 82. Part I begins like a mystery play with the celebrated prologue in Heaven, essentially a paraphrase of the first part of the Book of Job. The same bar gain is struck, in both cases. The Lord, at Satan's challenge, gives him permission to make a test of the integrity of God's servant, Faust. Mephistopheles makes a bargain with the aged Faust. If Faust is granted one moment of complete contentment, he loses his soul. Faust regains his youth, and with Mephistopheles he travels about enjoying every form of earthly pleasure. He has a love affair with a simple girl, Margaret, whom he betrays and for whose downfall and death he is responsible. Mephistopheles thinks he will capture the soul of Margaret, but the purity of her betrayed love for Faust and her refusal to be rescued from death by Mephistopheles cause her to be saved. As the first part of the play ends, Faust has not yet found, in the world of desire and passion, that wonderful moment of existence to which he could really wish to cling. The second part of Faust, that of the world of public life and aesthetic beauty, is a profound philosophical poem, less of a familiar drama than the first. In it Faust tastes every form of intellectual and worldly power, but still fails to find the moment for which he so eagerly seeks, even in the love of Helen of Troy. Mephistopheles has almost despaired of his bargain. At last, once again an old man, the weary, sated Faust takes an interest in a project to reclaim land from the sea, a project which will mean little to him person ally, but which will bring untold good to countless numbers of people. Here to his astonishment, in this disinterested and socially constructive occupation, Faust finds truly profound happiness. So noble is this impulse that Mephistopheles at the end is deprived of the soul of Faust, who, like the unfortunate Margaret of the first part, is redeemed. Faust is a monument that will stand as long as literature endures. It is not of great importance on the actual stage, for its difficulties of production are enormous. Primarily it is a literary-poetic work. However, on rare occasions, both parts have been performed in careful adaptations. The first part, by itself, has received fairly frequent performances, and is the basis of Gounod's popular opera *Faust,* also of the opera *Mifist Jele* by Boito, and the *Damnation of Faust* by Berlioz. The semi-legendary figure of the magician and charlatan Faustus has not only attracted many poets (Marlowe, Lessing), but the adjective "Faustian" has become synonymous (since Oswald Spengler's use of it) for the striving quality of modern Western civilization. The latest prose variation of the theme is Thomas Mann's novel Doctor Faustus.

FRANKENSTEIN, OR THE MODERN PROMETHEUS (1818), by Mary Wollstonecraft Shelley. This is one of the world's favorite terror stories, yet its stature is greater than such a classification implies. It is a highly imaginative, poetic novel. In the summer of 1816, the Shelleys and Byron were in Switzerland. For want of something more diverting to do they entered into a friendly ghost-story competition. Mary claimed that she had dreamed her story of Frankenstein. The plot is developed in the course of a series of letters from the Arctic by Robert Walton to his sister, Margaret. Upon coming into his inheritance, Walton goes off to the North Pole on an expedition of exploration. One night he encounters a remarkably big man on a dogsled. The latter comes on board Walton's ship, on being told that the expedition is Pole-bound. This stranger is Frankenstein, a Swiss. Frankenstein tells Walton that he is the son of a nobleman and has dabbled in the mystic sciences of the medieval Paracelsus, Cornelius Agrippa and Albertus Magnus. His principal obsession was to discover the elixir of life. By means of his knowledge of the esoteric, he has actually created a living man. Horrified by the sight of this huge and revolting creature, Frankenstein flees from it. Later he receives word from his father that his little brother, William, has been found murdered. Hurrying home, he catches his monster lurking in the woods. Frankenstein realizes in a flash that his creature was the murderer, not the accused maidservant, Justine. But, as he is certain that no one will believe him, he does nothing about it. At Chamonix Frankenstein comes face to face with the monster. He wants to kill him, but the creature restrains him with the words: "All men hate the wretched." As his creator, argues the monster, Frankenstein has a responsibility which he cannot evade. He promises to leave him in peace provided he creates for him a wife, for he wishes to be like other men. He feels frustrated and rejected, which is the cause of his bestiality. Frankenstein accordingly sets about making a wife, for he is moved by the story of the monster. But, at the very moment of breathing life into her, he recoils from the thought that he is creating the possibility of a race of monsters which might yet destroy mankind. In revenge, the monster kills Frankenstein's best friend and his bride. Horrified and maddened with hatred, Frankenstein seeks him in the frozen North. But in the end Walton finds the monster standing grief stricken over Frankenstein, whom he has murdered.

FREUD, SIGMUND (1856-1939). Freud was the founder of that school of psychiatry known as psychoanalysis. Led to his investigations through observations on the use of hypnosis in the cure of hysteria, Freud eventually abandoned hypnosis as a method and replaced it with "free association." In this method, a patient suffering from a nervous disorder thinks aloud before a trained analyst, who attempts to discover the pattern of his thought. If the analyst is successful in tracing the present disorder back to the original situation (usually in childhood) which gave rise to it, he can then, according to this theory, explain the matter to the patient, who will be relieved of his burden and cured. In developing this approach, Freud formulated a theory of the mind which had several distinctive features. He postulated the existence of an unconscious level in the mind which influenced conscious thought and behavior. The view that the sexual instinct is the basic one in the human personality led Freud to discover and describe the presence of sexual behavior even in infants. He developed the theory that there are various forces in the personality, "ego," "id," "super-ego," and that mental disorders come about through conflicts that arise among these forces, or through the repression of one by another. Freud had great influence on medicine, psychology, philosophy, social thought, and especially on literature. The

most easily accessible of his books for the general public is *Psychopathology of Everyday Life* (1904; Eng. tr. 1914). A large school of analysts grew up around him, including Adler, Jung, Jones and others, most of whom differed from the master in more or less important respects.

GOLDEN BOUGH, THE (1890; 1907-1915), by James G. Frazer. In many respects this is a unique work in the field of anthropology. The author's purpose is to give an extended description and explanation of magic, religion, cults and folklore. An indefatigable collector of information on ancient and "primitive" beliefs, practices and social institutions, Frazer attempted to weave this data into a series of integrated pictures of various cultures. His sympathetic approach and his talented pen made the book a work of art as much as a treatise in anthropology. Prefatory to and lying behind all of Frazer's accounts is a conceptual framework that has not stood up under the critical scrutiny of later and more analytic anthropologists. Thus Frazer is valued most today for his uncanny insight and imaginative re-creation of other cultures, rather than for any theoretical contributions he may have made. His book is still used as a source book by other students, and has been used by specialists outside his own field. Freud went to it for data to support his psychological theories, though Frazer rejected psychoanalysis. Originally a two-volume work, *The Golden Bough* was gradually expanded to twelve volumes. In 1922 a one-volume abridgment which has proved to be very popular appeared under the same title .

HAMLET (1603), by William Shakespeare. Hamlet was published in 1603 in quarto and again in 1604, but had been acted before these dates. The story was known to Elizabethans through Francois de Belleforest's *Histoires Tragiques* and Saxo Grammaticus. An earlier, now lost, play about Hamlet had been written by 1589, possibly by Thomas Kyd. Shakespeare's *Hamlet* is the most famous play of the modern world. The story is laid in Denmark. Hamlet, the royal Prince, is mourning the death of his father, and the hasty marriage of his mother, Gertrude, to Claudius; her husband's brother, now king. The former king's ghost has appeared to sentinels on the battlements of the castle at Elsinore. They report this to Hamlet, who waits to verify their statements. He meets the ghost and learns that his suspicions about his uncle's bad character are true: Claudius had killed his brother while he was sleeping in an orchard so that he could marry the queen and seize the kingdom. Hamlet makes his friend, Horatio, and the officer, Marcellus, swear to secrecy regarding the appearance of the ghost. The ghost demands revenge and Hamlet swears he will execute it. How ever, his brooding and his melancholy, together with his soul searching, and his stated fear that the ghost may be a devil, prevent him from immediate action. Hamlet feigns madness. The court takes this to be caused by his love for Ophelia, daughter of the chancellor, Polonius. Hamlet hears that players have come to the castle, and asks them to give a drama, reenacting the murder of his father, before the king and queen. Claudius, as he watches the play unfold, is tormented by his conscience. Hamlet, observing him closely, is now sure he is guilty. The king leaves the play hastily and is followed by the queen, who asks for an interview with her son. The king, now angry and suspicious, arranges for Hamlet to be sent to En gland. He plans to have him executed there. When Hamlet visits the queen, she begins the interview by upbraiding him. He turns on her and accuses her of falsity to the memory of her dead husband. Polonius, always meddlesome, is hiding behind the arras in the queen's chamber. Hamlet, detecting his presence and mistaking him for Claudius, stabs him to death. He departs for England with two courtiers, Rosencrantz and Guildenstern. Ophelia, in the meantime, goes mad, overwhelmed by the death of her father, Hamlet's strange actions toward her, and her brother's long continued absence in France. Her brother, Laertes, returns, incensed over the murder of his father and vowing revenge. Claudius puts the blame on Hamlet. To her brother's grief, Ophelia drowns herself. Hamlet's ship, in the meantime, is attacked by pirates, who send him back to Denmark. When he arrives he witnesses Ophelia's funeral procession. He and Laertes, both frantic with sorrow, leap into her grave and fight over which shall be chief mourner. Claudius, knowing Laertes' desire for revenge, suggests that he challenge Hamlet to a fencing match. Not suspecting that the king has had Laertes' sword tip poisoned, Hamlet accepts. In the match, the queen, to do her son honor, drinks to him from a poisoned cup the king had prepared for Ham let. Laertes wounds Hamlet, and in the scuffle they exchange swords and Hamlet wounds Laertes. The queen dies; Laertes falls, and, dying, confesses Claudius is to blame and asks Hamlet's forgiveness. Hamlet stabs the king and bids Horatio tell Fortinbras, Prince of Norway, whose martial music is heard in the distance, that he has his dying voice for his election as next king. Fortinbras arrives after the death of the young prince and promises to give him a soldier's funeral. Sir Laurence Olivier's film version of Hamlet is one of the most masterful dramatizations of this tragedy.

HISTORY OF THE PELOPONNESIAN WAR, by Thucydides (ca. 455-399 B.C.). Thucydides was the first truly critical historian with an ad equate conception of historical causation. His famous narrative analyzes with surgical incisiveness the long and bloody struggle between the Athenians and the Peloponnesians to the year 411 B.C. When the war first broke out, Thucydides, grasping its great historical importance, began to take notes of all events with singular objectivity. "I have described nothing," he wrote, "but what I either saw myself or learned from others of whom I made the most careful and particular inquiry." The history is largely a study of the downfall of the imperialistic Athenian state, which, by its arrogance and tyranny, brought upon itself the bitter opposition of the conservative Spartans fighting to assert their hegemony among the Greeks. As Thucydides puts it, "The real, though unavowed cause, I believe to have been the growth of the Athenian power, which termed the Lacedaemonians [Spartans] and forced them into war." Although Thucydides' aim was to record the events of the war from its beginning in 431 B.C. to the fall of Athens in 404 B.C., his narrative breaks off abruptly without explanation at the end of the twenty-first year of hostilities. The whole work is arranged in eight books. Books 1-4 and part of 5 bring the chronicle down to the Peace of Nicias in 421 B.C. The rest of Books 5, 6 and 7 cover the six years of the truce, which actually was no truce at all, since it was devoted to diplomatic maneuvers on both sides, the Athenians encouraging Argos to attack Sparta in order further to weaken her. Book 8 opens on the third phase of the war, when, the truce being terminated, the two enemies were again at each other's throats. An interesting feature of the history is the introduction of speeches attributed to the various actors in this real tragedy. Thucydides writes: "As to the speeches which were made either before or during the war, it was hard for me, and for others who reported them to me, to recollect the exact words. I have therefore put into the mouth of each speaker the sentiments proper to the occasion, expressed as I thought he would be likely to express them." Thus these speeches serve as Thucydides' interpretation of the motive forces at work behind events. Probably the most famous of all these speeches is the funeral oration (Book 1) of Pericles over the Athenians who died in the first campaign. Proud of Athens' greatness and scorning the enemy, he said: "For we have compelled every land and every sea to open a path for our valor, and have everywhere planted eternal memorials of our friend ship and our enmity." Powerful scenes are drawn everywhere, particularly in Book 2, which carries a description of the plague that struck Athens; in Book 5, which details the alleged treachery of Alcibiades; and in Book 7, which gives a breathless account of the naval engagement be tween the Athenian and Syracusan fleets with both contending armies watching anxiously from opposite shores.

HISTORY OF THE PERSIAN WARS, by Herodotus (ca. 490-425 B.C.). Herodotus well deserves his title, the "Father of History." His nine books are the earliest extant Greek prose, and in them he lifts himself from the level of his predecessors, who were still retailing myth for history, to the eminence of that title. The work that we have is his history of the conflict between the Persians and Greeks culminating in the great battles of Thermopylae and Salamis. To make this conflict understandable he goes back to the beginnings of oriental aggression and traces the growth of the Persian empire. The first six books are devoted to this background, while the last three narrate the actual expedition and invasion of Greece under Xerxes. Herodotus was the first man anywhere to write history in our sense of the word, sifting reports, searching for the truth and thereby exalting man's intelligence. Perhaps his greatest accomplishment lies in the very conception of the events he narrates as a historic unit. But Herodotus is much more than a historian, or rather his history is much more than an arid chronicle of events; he is an enthusiastic and fascinating storyteller. The customs and traditions of strange and distant peoples such as the Egyptians and Scythians, some of which he knew from his own extensive travels, always intrigued him. Thus he gives us such stories as that of Rhampsinitus in Book II, a story to match anything from the *Arabian Niohts,* but remarks with a saving grace, "It is my business to tell what was told me, but not necessarily to believe it." The familiar motto of the Post Office Department, "Not snow, nor rain, nor heat, nor gloom of night stays these couriers from the swift completion of their appointed rounds" is taken from Herodotus' description of the courier system of the Persian king Darius.

ILIAD (9th c. B.C.?), by Homer. This magnificent Greek epic is one of the unquestionably great poems of all time, ranking in literary importance and influence with the Bible and Shakespeare. Its origin remains obscure despite the devoted efforts of generations of scholars. It is the earliest extant literature, and in fact the first written record of Western civilization. From its very perfection it must have had a long tradition of predecessors, and was almost certainly preserved by oral tradition before it was ever reduced to writing. Herodotus believed that Homer lived about 850 B.C., and that

may not be far from the actual date of the poem. The incidents, however, of the Trojan war which it describes, and which have been made to seem far more substantial and real by archaeological discoveries of the nineteenth century both at Troy and in Greece, belong apparently to the twelfth century B.C. The materials for the epic were drawn from the Trojan legend which told how the barbarian city of Troy, or Ilium, was besieged for ten years by an army of Greeks and finally captured and sacked to regain Helen and avenge her abduction from King Menelaus by the Trojan prince, Paris. The story unfolded by the *Iliad* is but an incident, lasting some seven weeks, in the tenth year of the war. The unifying theme is the wrath of the Greek hero, Achilles, and throughout the twenty-four books of the poem we see its cause and effects. Agamemnon, the commander of the Greek force, injures the sensitive pride of Achilles by demanding from him a captive handmaiden, his share of the spoils of war. Achilles is forced by the gods to comply, but in his heroic wrath he swears to withdraw himself and his Myrmidons from further combat until Agamemnon sorely feels the need of him. Through the interference of the gods the Greek army is brought to dire extremities by the Trojans under the leadership of Hector. Agamemnon humbles himself so far as to send an embassy imploring Achilles to return to the battle but cannot bend his will. Achilles does consent reluctantly to the importunate pleas of his bosom companion, Patroclus, and permits him to join the conflict. Heedless of warnings Patroclus involves himself in conflict with Hector and is slain. As the Greeks are now truly humbled, Achilles rejoins the fray, defeats and kills Hector. The spirit of Patroclus is appeased by an elaborate burial; and the epic ends on a chivalrous note of reconciliation with the ransoming of the corpse of Hector to Priam, his aged father. The pace of the poem is stately and majestic. The heroes are made to speak dramatically for themselves and the poet never obtrudes himself upon one's consciousness. He presents the Trojans with as great if not greater sympathy than he does the Greeks. Hector becomes at times, indeed, as in the famous scene of his parting from his wife and infant son, the most humanly moving character in the epic. The lasting popularity of the *Iliad* is evidenced by the frequency with which it has been translated. Chapman's translation, which inspired Keats' sonnet, is hardly read today. Among the poetic versions may be mentioned those of Alexander Pope and William Cullen Bryant.

INSTITUTES OF THE CHRISTIAN RELIGION, THE (1536), by John Calvin. In the realm of Protestant doctrinal literature the *Institutes* of Calvin occupy a position similar to that of the *Summa Theolooiae* of Aquinas in Catholic dogma. It is authoritarian, systematic and comprehensive. First published in 1536, when Calvin was only 26, as merely a sketch of the enlarged form of later years, it has gone through innumerable editions in all countries of the world. The emphasis in the *Institutes* is on God's will, His holiness, and His majesty, unrelieved by the traditional conception of Christian love or mercy. Man's function in life is to serve his God in the manner prescribed by the Bible, eschew pleasure and happiness, and fulfill faithfully and unquestioningly the role "divine providence" assigns to him. The central doctrine enunciated in the *Institutes* is that of absolute predestination, which is the foundation stone of Calvinism. Anticipating criticism from theologians, Calvin denies that his doctrine of predestination makes God the author of sin, since He leaves mankind helpless without free will: "Their [sinners'] perdition depends on the divine predestination in such a manner that the cause and matter of it are found in themselves. For the first man fell because the Lord had determined it should so happen." The *Institutes* is written with elegant simplicity and its meanings are very lucid. Calvin's literary, philosophical and legal training were of a very high order and endowed all his writings with a clarity and readability unexcelled in his day. The work is a distinguished one purely on literary grounds. Undoubtedly he was one of the great molding forces of modern times. He was to Western Europe what Luther was to Germany. His influence on American civilization and religious life was effected through the New England Puritans and the Scotch Presbyterians, who interpreted his doctrine of obedience to God's will as a justification for resistance to earthly tyrants.

JEWISH WAR, THE (ca. 79), by Flavius Josephus. This history gives our most complete and detailed account of the war in which the Jews were defeated and subjected to the rule of the Roman Empire; it is written by a Jew, a Pharisee of a priestly family, who had commanded against the Romans. The first two books review the history of the Jews from the capture of Jerusalem by Antiochus Epiphanes to the beginning of the war with Rome in 67. Much space is devoted to the dynastic squabbles in which the Romans from the time of Pompey were invited to intercede until Judea was finally constituted as a Roman imperial province under Augustus. The remaining five books describe the war as prosecuted by the Emperors Vespasian and Titus from 67 to 73 and as witnessed and participated in by Josephus himself. He was captured at the siege of Jotapata in the first year of the war, succeeded in ingratiating himself with Vespasian, and after Vespasian became emperor remained with Titus and served as an intermediary with the Jews. After the war he lived as a pensioner of Rome, where he did much of his writing. He has been quite justifiably regarded by the Jews as a renegade. *The Jewish War* was written first in Aramaic and then translated into the Greek form in which we have it. His express purpose in writing was to arouse the interest of the Graeco-Roman world in the history and character of his despised people.

KING LEAR (ca. 1605), by William Shakespeare. In many ways the most powerful of Shakespeare's tragedies, *Kina Lear* has been criticized for being obscure of plot and arbitrary in motivation, and Charles Lamb thought it burst the bounds of the theater. Yet it is without question one of the greatest plays. The story of Lear and his daughters is found in Geoffrey of Monmouth's *History,* in Holinshed, and in an older play. King Lear determines to give over to his daughters and their husbands all the wealth and powers of his rank, retaining only his title. He proposes to retire and live with his various daughters in rotation. As a guide to division of his kingdom he demands an expression of their love. Regan and Goneril hypocritically protest great love and are richly rewarded. Honest Cordelia, apple of his eye, says plainly that she loves him "according to my bond; no more nor less." Infuriated, Lear disinherits her and bestows her dower on the other two. Cordelia is wedded, powerless, by the King of France, who perceives her fine qualities. The rest of the play traces Lear's swift mental deterioration as he is betrayed and cast out by first one and then the other of his unnatural daughters. He goes mad while shelterless in a storm. In a parallel subplot the Earl of Gloucester, almost the only still faithful follower the old king has, has done injustice to his true son Edgar in favor of his villainous bastard son Edmund. All these unfortunates, Lear, Gloucester, whose eyes have been put out, the disinherited Edgar pretending to be mad, and Lear's fool form a pathetic party whose wrongs are righted too late. At last the King of France, together with a handful of Lear's loyal adherents, crushes the forces of villainy. Regan, Goneril, and Edmund are justly dead. Cordelia has been slain. Lear, utterly demented, dies of grief.

KORAN (ca. 660), by Mohammed. The Koran, meaning "that which is recited," is the production of Mohammed as set down by his scribes, among them the devoted Abu Bakr, who collected "from palm-leaves; skins, blade bones" fragments which various hearers had copied. The Koran is the sacred book of Islam, believed to be the word of God, dictated to Mohammed by Gabriel, the Angel of Revelation in both Persian and later Jewish and Christian thought. Mohammed was afflicted with epilepsy, which was regarded until modern times as supernatural evidence' of sanctity or demon possession. Written in the purest Arabic, the Koran consists of 114 suras, varying in length from 4 to 285 verses, and abounding in repetitions of ideas, personal experiences, dire warnings by Mohammed to his enemies, and exhortations to his followers. To the believer, the Koran is a miraculous work containing the utterances of God. The orthodox think that it should never be translated into another language. One may not touch the Koran without previous bodily purification; it is forbidden to hold it below the waist. Many buildings and decorative objects are blazoned with quotations from the suras. Two dominant ideas stand out in the Koran: the certainty of a Day of Judgment, when good and bad will be separated; and the unity and majesty of one God. The Koran prescribes the forms of prayer, five times a day; the month of fasting; the pilgrimage to Mecca; and almsgiving; all of which have given the Moslems, wide spread as they are throughout the world, a sense of community and a civil and moral code permeating their entire society. Disjointed, crude as the Koran may sound to the modern ear, it is nonetheless the only one of the great religious scriptures to be the creation of one man, given to his followers within the brief period of twenty years. It is the source of truth and wisdom for a billion people.

LEVIATHAN (1651), by Thomas Hobbes. Subtitled *The Matter, Forme, and Power if a Commonwealth, Ecclesiasticall and Civill,* this book, divided into four parts, treats respectively: Of Man, Of Commonwealth, Of a Christian Commonwealth, and of the Kingdom of Darkness. In the first part Hobbes presents a mechanistic theory of human nature and describes man's natural state as one in which all men strive to acquire as much as they can with no government to keep them at peace. This is the war of all against all. Through man's power of reason he learns that the first law of nature is to seek peace and follow it; and from this emerges the second law, that, for the sake of peace, a man should be willing to lay down his right to all things when other men are also willing to do so. In the second part, Hobbes discusses the ways in which commonwealths are instituted. Central is the doctrine of the social contract in accordance with which men confer all their power and strength on one man or one assembly (the Sovereign) so that with absolute power that Sovereign may preserve order among men. There is no peace among men unless there is a supreme power to keep them all in awe. In the third and fourth parts of the *Leviathan,* Hobbes outlines the principles which should govern the relation be tween the state and church, and attacks the universal claims of the Roman Catholic Church. Hobbes' writings on political theory were extremely influential and served as the basis for modern realistic political theory and political science.

MACBETH (1606? Folio, 1623), by William Shakespeare. Shakespeare drew his material from Holinshed's *Chronicles.* The play was written in honor of James I. It is one of the most popular and powerful of Shakespeare's tragedies, closely knit in structure, direct and concentrated in impact. Macbeth, victorious Scottish warrior and Thane of Glamis, is confronted on a heath by three witches. They prophesy that he will be come Thane of Cawdor, then King of Scotland. It is also said that the sons of his friend, Banquo, shall enjoy the subsequent succession to the throne. Immediately thereafter Macbeth does acquire the title, Thane of Cawdor. He becomes obsessed with fulfilling the prophecy that he will be King. Lady Macbeth becomes inflamed with the same lust for power. When Macbeth's spirit quails before the consequences of his ambition, she fiercely impels him onward. Together they murder King Duncan as he sleeps, a guest in their own castle. Macbeth is now launched upon a bloody course. His fears and suspicions drive him to a series of murders. Banquo is slain in an attempt by Macbeth to frustrate the witches' prophecy that his own line shall not inherit the throne, but Banquo's son Fleance escapes. Macbeth cruelly slays the wife and son of Macduff, one of his mortal foes. He takes comfort in the assurance of the witches that he will not be overthrown "till Birnam wood do come to Dunsinane," and that he cannot be slain by man born of woman. But catastrophe follows. Lady Macbeth, tortured by guilt, slays herself. His enemies advance upon Dunsinane under the camouflage of boughs torn from Birnam wood. Finally he is slain in combat by Macduff, who "was from his mother's womb untimely ripp'd." The philosophical content of the play is of great interest. Both Macbeth and Lady Macbeth, contrary to their superficial ruthlessness, are complex studies of disintegration of the will under the pressure of remorse. Lady Macbeth's famous sleepwalking scene, and the growing realization of Macbeth that the game has not been worth the candle, testify to this. Shakespeare further presents a fascinating pattern in the symbolic figures of the witches, who betray men to folly by cryptic half-truths, treacherous to him who counts upon them. Of great significance is the subtle snare into which Macbeth falls by gambling on presumptive fate and seeking foolishly to avert part of the same prophecy, that Banquo's sons shall be the kingly line. On these counts the play is susceptible to varied and stimulating interpretations. But so universal are its motivations, and so vividly alive in all eras are the phenomena of the ruthless will to power, that the vigor of the play remains unabated.

MADAME BOVARY (1865), by Gustave Haubert. Emma Rouault, the convent-bred daughter of a Norman farmer, marries a dull and uninteresting young doctor, Charles Bovary. Naturally the marriage fails to give Emma the exalted happiness which she has read and dreamed about. Discontented with her small-town surroundings and tedious family life, she rushes from one folly to another, dallying first with a timid law clerk named Leon, then embarking on a genuine affair with the cynical, wealthy Rodolphe. Jilted by Rodolphe, she again turns to Leon, but the latter, after the first thrill of their liaison, becomes frightened of Emma's desperate enthusiasm. Morally bankrupt and hopelessly involved in debt, blackmailed by the cunning merchant L'Heureux, who has encouraged her extravagant gifts to her lovers, Emma takes arsenic. Charles, never truly knowing what it is all about, dies shortly thereafter, leaving their hapless child adrift on the same ocean of bourgeois mediocrity which has swallowed up her parents. The book's power comes from Haubert's masterly, savage picture of the mediocrity of his time-of which Emma is at once an example and a victim. The one character who emerges from the story successful and honored, the pharmacist Homais, is the most bombastically mediocre of all. Haubert was obsessed by style, and *Madame Bovary,* which took him more than five years to write, is called his artistic triumph. Many prefer it to his other works: *Salammbo, The Temptation of Saint-Anthony, The Sentimental Education, Three Tales* and *Bouvard and Pecuchet.*

MEDITATIONS (ca. 170-180), by Marcus Aurelius Antoninus. This is a rare work of its kind, a book of philosophical meditations written in Greek by a Roman Emperor while commanding his legions on the distant and barbaric borders of his empire. Marcus Aurelius was thoroughly steeped in later Stoic moral philosophy as represented by Epictetus, and his *Meditations* are, as the name suggests, his reflections along Stoic lines on ethical problems. Typical both of the personal tone and of the benevolent character of the work is one of his thoughts on the brotherhood of man: "My nature is rational and social, and my city and my country, so far as I am Antoninus, is Rome; but so far as I am a man, it is the world." Neither Marcus Aurelius nor the world was ready for the practical application of what has always remained an ideal, and he cannot justly be censured for his persecution of the Christians, which fell within his duty as head of the Roman state.

ODYSSEY, THE (9th c. B.C.), by Homer. The *Odyssey* is a companion piece to the *Iliad.* Its poetic style is the same but its interests are far different. The *Iliad* is truly heroic in its devotion to martial incident, whereas the *Odyssey* shows a more romantic interest in adventure. The story covers the ten years of Odysseus' return to Ithaca after the capture of Troy. At the opening a council of the gods determines to restore Odysseus to his home despite Poseidon, who has delayed him. In Ithaca Penelope, his faithful wife, is plagued by a host of overbearing suitors who hope that Odysseus is dead. Books I-IV tell of the quest of the faithful Telemachus for his father. Books V-VIII recount how Odysseus was released from the island of the beauteous Calypso at the command of the gods and was shipwrecked on the island of the Phaeacians, where he is warmly received. In Books IX-XII Odysseus relates to his Phaeacian hosts all the adventures that befell him after his departure from Troy until he reached their shore. Books XIII-XVI describe how he was miraculously returned to Ithaca by the Phaeacians, and his welcome in the hut of the swineherd Eumaeus, where Telemachus meets and recognizes him. In Books XVII-XX Odysseus returns to his own house in the disguise of a beggar, and endures for a time the insolence of the suitors. The last four books tell of his vengeance in slaying the suitors and his reestablishment in his realm with Penelope. Odysseus is always presented as the man of many wiles and ever-ready cunning under the sternest buffetings of misfortune. Always fascinating are the tall tales of his adventures in strange and distant lands amid fanciful men and monsters, which served for the model of Virgil's account of the wanderings of Aeneas. This central point of interest is reserved for the midpoint of the poem by use of the device of the narrative flashback. Among the famous English translations may be mentioned those of Pope and William Cullen Bryant.

OEDIPUS THE KING (ca. 430 B.C.?), by Sophocles. *Oedipus the Kina,* or *Oedipus Rex,* is Sophocles' masterpiece. Structurally the play is unrivaled in dramatic literature. The characters are drawn with humanity and warmth. Creon is a manly character, though in *Antiaone* and *Oedipus at Colonus* Sophocles represents him as mean, treacherous, and a braggart. Jocasta, Oedipus' Queen, the widow of the former King, Laius, is portrayed as a dutiful wife, with a slightly maternal attitude toward her younger husband. She tries vainly to comfort him and to convince him that the gods govern wisely. Oedipus dominates the play. In the beginning he is rash, proud, and obstinate and, as the drama mounts in horror, is overcome by the awfulness of his fate. The play opens in Thebes before the royal palace where Oedipus rules, having won the throne and the hand of the widowed Jocasta years before by ridding the city of the Sphinx. In front of the central doors is an altar, and seated on the steps are men and youths dressed as suppliants. The elderly priest of Zeus stands facing the palace. Oedipus comes forth and asks the priest why the suppliants are there. The priest replies that the city is suffering from a plague and they have appealed to their gods. Oedipus has sent his brother-in-law, Creon, to the shrine of Apollo; Creon now returns with word that the murderer of Laius, the former king of Thebes, is in their midst and must be driven forth from the city before the plague will pass. The King has also sent for the blind old seer, Teiresias, who tells Oedipus that he is the slayer of Laius, the man whom they seek. He also tells Oedipus that he is the unwitting slayer of his father, who was Laius, and that he is the incestuous husband of his own mother. The very suddenness of the revelation makes it incredible to all. Oedipus thinks Creon is in league with the seer, and unjustly accuses him of wishing to seize the kingdom. Creon answers with restraint and dignity, but Oedipus' unrestrained rage brings them close to blows until Jocasta comes out from the palace and stops the quarrel between the two men. Now the story sweeps forward with rapidly accelerating dramatic pace. The very things Jocasta tells Oedipus to reassure him that Teiresias' charge cannot be true arouse Oedipus to apprehension. He had been reared as the son of Polybus, King of Corinth, but the oracle of Delphi had warned him he would kill his father and wed his mother. To avoid such a hideous fate, he refused to return to Corinth. As he departed from Delphi, however, he had encountered an unknown man and killed him and his retinue in a quarrel on the road, allowing only one survivor to escape. The circumstances of the killing seem to correspond with those of the death of Laius. A messenger now arrives with word of the death of Polybus, at which Oedipus rejoices, since he thinks he cannot now kill his father. To still his fear that he may yet wed his mother, the messenger reveals that Oedipus is not the true son of these parents. Under questioning he tells how he had found Oedipus as an abandoned child and taken him to Corinth and Polybus. Jocasta now perceives the full truth that Oedipus is indeed her son, for Laius had abandoned their child in fear of a prophecy that he would die at the child's hand. She rushes into the palace and leaves Oedipus to piece together the rest of his story. The missing link is provided by the survivor of Laius' murder, who proves to be the same servant who had exposed the child Oedipus to die. At this discovery of the complete fulfillment of the dreaded oracle Oedipus rushes into the palace after Jocasta. A servant soon reports that Jocasta has hanged herself and Oedipus has struck out his own eyes so as to look no longer upon the scene of his abomination. Oedipus himself soon reappears with blood-stained cheeks, cursing his fate and calling upon Creon to send him into the exile he had himself decreed for the murderer of Laius.

ON THE NATURE OF THINGS (ca. 54 B.C.), by Lucretius (Titus Lucretius Carus). Lucretius' didactic poem is an exposition of the philosophy of Epicurus. The poetic treatment of such subject matter was no novelty, for verse had been a common vehicle for the thought of the pre Socratics, and Lucretius took Empedocles as one of his models. He surpassed by far, however, the poetic genius of his predecessors, was the idol of Virgil, and even elicited praise from Cicero, who despised Epicurean ism. The invocation to Venus which opens the first book is a passage of unrivaled beauty, and there are many other fine passages throughout the book. The exposition of a close-knit philosophical system in verse makes tremendous demands on the art of any poet and sheer poetry must often yield to these demands, but nowhere does Lucretius become completely pedestrian; his varied rhythms and vivid imagery always sustain the burden of his serious task. He speaks always in terms of divine awe and reverence of the master whose system had fired his imagination. His purpose in writing the poem was to show the unhappy Roman of the generation of the Civil War the senseless folly of his ways, and reclaim him for the untroubled and philosophic calm of Epicurus' rational hedonism. To do this he must clear the ground of all manner of degrading fears and superstitions. The ethical precepts of Epicurus rested squarely upon his natural philosophy, which was a startling if oversimplified anticipation of modern atomic theory. The first book treats of the fundamental characteristics of matter and void in the universe. The second book explains the nature and properties of atoms and the effect of their combination. Next it is explained in book three that the human mind and soul are concrete realities, that their dissolution is death, and so there is no possibility of immortality and no need for fear of death. In book four the operation of our sensory perceptions is also explained on a materialistic basis. Book five is devoted to Epicurean cosmology, and unfolds a beautiful and careful theory of evolution. The final book explains numerous natural phenomena on the basis of Epicurean theories of causation. The poem is a magnificent effort to give to Rome a true picture of the always much maligned and persistently misunderstood Epicurean doctrine. It is the only systematic and complete exposition of the theory of this school which has survived.

ON THE ORIGIN OF SPECIES BY MEANS OF NATURAL SELECTION (1859), by Charles Darwin. In this book the great proponent of evolution aimed to show the probability that every species is a development from previous species, and that all life .is part of a continuous pat tern. His objects of investigation were domestic animals and plants, which vary from generation to generation. All life, plant and animal alike, is engaged in a fierce competition or "struggle for existence." In this conflict an animal or plant which inherits an unfavorable variation will be less likely to survive and have offspring; and, conversely, an animal inheriting a favorable variation will be more likely to survive and have offspring. The severe conditions of life accordingly tend to kill off individuals with unfavorable variations and to favor "the survival of the fittest," the strongest, the most adaptable. From all this Darwin concludes that there exists a "natural selection" of favorable variations which produces new varieties. In the course of thousands of years, the operation of natural selection succeeds in producing a remarkable variety of living things, which are categorized into species, genera, families, orders. All of these classifications are alike subject, in varying degree, to the process of evolution. The first chapter of the book explains the operation of artificial selection in the case of domesticated species, and the second takes up natural selection **in** con sequence of the struggle for existence. Chapter three describes the struggle for existence, chapter four the survival of the fittest, and chapter five the laws of variation. The rest of the book is devoted to a closer examination of some apparent difficulties in the theory of evolution, to questions of geological succession and geographical distribution, and to a recapitulation and conclusion. *The Origin if*

Species, one of the world's greatest books, has deeply influenced biological research since its publication. Subsequent investigation, however, has revealed the inadequacy of some of the author's arguments. In presenting "natural selection" as the effective agent of evolution, Darwin assumes the inheritance of acquired characters in a form scarcely differing from that of Lamarck, which has been discredited. There also are traces of teleology, as the subtitle of the book, Or *the Preservation of Favoured Races* in *the Struggle for Life,* betrays. Darwin was at his best in the investigation of nature, weakest in philosophical interpretation. Through out the long and arduous journey aboard the Beagle from 1831 to 1836, Darwin painstakingly recorded his observations on geology and natural science, publishing them in 1839 in the well-known *Voyages of the Beagle.* It was the data gathered on this expedition which laid the foundation for his later work. The storm of opposition which the theory of evolution occasioned is alluded to by Darwin in very mild terms in the *Descent of Man* (1871). Here he wrote, "The main conclusion arrived at in this work, namely that man is descended from some lowly organized form, will, I regret to think, be highly distasteful to many." In the *Descent if Man* the author shows the special affinities of man to certain lower animals, especially the high apes, and he applies the principle of natural selection in determining the origin and probable line of genealogy of the races of mankind. A large portion of the book is devoted to what Darwin calls "sexual selection," or factors influencing the choice of a mate, both in primitive and modem societies.

PARADISE LOST (1667), by John Milton. This great epic poem is characterized by a sonorous nobility of expression and a compelling moral fervor. Book I. There is a short reference to the fall of man and a statement of the purpose of the work, "to justify the Ways of God to men." The poem opens with Satan and his army of rebellious angels already cast from Heaven into the Abyss of Hell. Satan rises from the Burning Lake and assures his followers that they will have a kingdom rivaling that of Heaven. They build the Palace of Pandemonium. Book II. The rebels meet to determine how they may best revenge themselves upon God. Abandoning the idea of waging further open war, they determine to seek the newly created Earth and God's most favored creation, Man. They hope to pervert him and wreck the great plans made by God for him. Satan alone fares forth on this quest. He escapes from Hell with the connivance of his progeny, Sin and Death, to whom he promises rich feasts upon Earth. Book III. God sees Satan's flight to Earth, and to His Son He foretells the fall and necessary punishment of Man. The Son expresses His desire to sacrifice Himself for Man's redemption. Meanwhile Satan reaches the outskirts of Earth. He flies to the sun, and Uriel, not recognizing him, shows him the pathway to the world. Book IV. In the earthly Paradise of Eden, Adam and Eve are living an idyllic life, unspoiled by Sin, Guilt, or Death. All the fruits of the Earth are theirs, with the exception ot the fruit of the Tree of Knowledge, expressly forbidden by God. Satan steals into the garden, listens to them discussing the forbidden fruit, and seizes upon it as a means of seducing Man from his state of grace. He begins to tempt Eve in disturbing dreams, but is apprehended by the angels and expelled from Paradise. Book V. In order to give Adam and Eve every opportunity for resistance, God sends Raphael, who explains to them the full details of the revolt and war in Heaven, informing them of the person and nature of their foe. Book VI. Raphael tells Adam how the Angels of God fought the Legions of Satan, and of how the Son of God alone finally defeated the enemy. Book VII. Raphael explains that when the ranks of Heaven were depleted by the loss of Satan and his followers, God sent His Son to create a new world, peopled by new creatures. Book VIII. Adam asks Raphael about the movements of the sun, stars, and moon. He speaks of his own creation. Book IX. The wily Satan returns to Eden in the body of a Snake. He subtly seduces Eve to taste of the fruit of the Tree of Knowledge. He tells her God is jealous, and that she and Adam may become as gods. Eve yields, and the Snake slips away. Adam is appalled when he learns of her act, but, nevertheless, deliberately eats of the fruit so that they may share together whatever punishment is visited upon them. Book X. The Son of God judges fallen man, and Sin and Death are allowed to enter the world. The victorious Satan is hailed by his waiting comrades, but they are all transformed into serpents, and doomed to assume such form at stated intervals. Book XI. Michael is commanded to expel Adam and. Eve from Paradise. Their day of death is deferred, and the angel comforts them by giving a vision of what shall happen up to the time of Noah. Book XII. The vision of the future continues. The coming of the Redeemer is predicted by Michael. He tells of the Incarnation, Death, Resurrection, and second coming of Christ. Adam and Eve then leave Paradise.

PILGRIM'S PROGRESS, THE (Part I, 1678; Part II, 1684), by John Bunyan. Probably no other book in the English language, after the Bible, with the possible exception of Defoe's *Robinson Crusoe,* has had such sustained and world-wide popularity as Bunyan's *Pilgrim's Progress.* Since its first appearance it has gone through hundreds of editions, has been translated into more than one hundred languages, and remains a great favorite. The full title of the work is descriptive of its contents: *The Pilgrim's Progress, From This World To That which is to Come: Delivered under the Similitude of A Dream, Wherein is Discovered, The manner if his setting out, His Dangerous Journey, And safe Arrival at the Desired Country.* In the quaintly naive "Author's Apology for his Book," written in doggerel, Bunyan states his moral aim in composing the work: "This Book it chalketh out before thine eyes, The Man that seeks the Everlasting Prize: It shews you whence he comes, whither he goes; What he leaves undone; Also what he does: It also shews you how he runs, and runs, Till he unto the Gate of Glory comes. It shews too, who sets out for Life amain, As if the lasting Crown they would attain: Here also you may see the reason why They lose their labour, and like fools do die." *Pilgrim's Progress* was begun by Bunyan during a prison sojourn in 1675-1676. As a stubborn nonconformist he had been lodged in the Bedford jail to expiate a crime of conscience. While there he experienced his dream, which so shook him that he sat down to record it, together with all his reflections. His prose style is distinguished for its simplicity. Almost the only book he ever read was the King James version of the Bible. In a few words he can sketch a place, such as Vanity Fair, or a character, such as the terrible Apollyon. His description of the Celestial City is memorable, full of piety and poetic rapture. The hero, Christian, is no allegorical shadow, but very much alive; despite the author's moral sensitiveness to "the wilderness of this world" he makes him humorous and ebullient on occasion. There is much natural talk. The names of the characters, places and things are themselves eloquent: Mr. Worldly Wiseman, the Shining One, Faithful, Giant Despair, Mr. By-Ends-of-Fair Speech, Hopeful, Enchanted Ground, House Beautiful, Delectable Mountains, City of Destruction. In the sequel, the Pilgrim's wife, Christiana, and their children make the same journey to salvation, with trials hardly less exciting than those Christian himself experienced.

POETICS, by Aristotle (384-322 B.C.). Of all the works of Aristotle none has had so wide and lasting an influence as the *Poetics.* As we have it, it is fragmentary, dealing only with epic and tragic poetry, but it originally continued with an analysis of comedy. The general principles deduced by Aristotle from popular Greek literature contain much that is of general if not universal application, and his theory of poetry as an imitative art still commands the respect of critic and theoretician. After differentiating the arts according to the character and object of their imitation, he distinguishes between tragedy and comedy. Then he discusses the origin of poetry and gives a brief history of the rise of comedy and tragedy. After his famous definition of tragedy as "an imitation of an action that is serious, complete, and of a certain magnitude; in language embellished with each kind of artistic ornament in the form of action, not of narrative; through pity and fear effecting the proper purgation of these emotions," he proceeds to enlarge upon the details of this definition. In this discussion he is principally concerned with plot, character and diction, and it is here that he advances the theory of dramatic unity which was to affect the composition and criticism of drama even into modern times. The final sections of the treatise as it is preserved contain a comparison of tragedy and epic, and Aristotle's canons of criticism.

PRAISE OF FOLLY, THE (1509), by Desiderius Erasmus. Erasmus wrote *The Praise of Folly* while indisposed with lumbago at the home of his friend Thomas More, in England. He wrote it in seven days. If not the most important of his works, it is the one through which he achieved international renown. It went through forty editions during his lifetime. Holbein illustrated it with pen-and-ink sketches. It is the most popular of all Renaissance classics. Speaking in the name of Folly, Erasmus criticizes the institutions, customs, men and beliefs of his time. The objects of his satire include marriage, self-love, war, the corruption in the Church, national pride, the competition for material goods, the wordiness of the lawyers, the speculations of the scientists, the logic-chopping and hair splitting of the theologians, the ignorance and diversity of the religious orders, the pride of kings and the servility of courtiers, the neglect of spiritual duties and responsibilities to their flocks of bishops, cardinals and popes. All are held up to ridicule; the true duties and interests of all are shown. Erasmus professed a simple, humanistic form of Christianity, and though he was severely critical of the Church, he refused to leave it and join the Protestants.

PRINCE, THE (1513), by Niccolo Machiavelli. A handbook of advice on the acquisition, use, and maintenance of political power, dedicated to Lorenzo de Medici by the Florentine Machiavelli, once active in government, but at the time of writing out of favor. Rules are set down for governing the various kinds of monarchies as well as conquered territory. Methods for insuring military strength are proposed. The young Prince is advised, further, in such matters as the type of personal behavior which will gain him respect without incurring hatred; whom to trust; how to make his ministers competent and faithful; how to be prepared for changes of fortune. The final chapter is an exhortation to liberate Italy from the barbarians. Although written in the formal style of the time, this book maintains an attitude of realism in government and politics. The Prince is urged to make the interests of his subjects his own. However, expediency is the standard for the conduct of a ruler, and "what ought to be" is rejected for "what is." Great importance, moreover, is attached to centralization of power, which Machiavelli saw as an aid to the unification of the Italian city-states. This, in turn, would result in the ending of internecine strife, expulsion of invaders, and enjoyment of the benefits of trade. Therein lay the germs of the nation-state of the modern Western world.

THE REPUBLIC by Plato (427-347 B.C.). This dialogue is in many respects the crown of Plato's works. It is the application of his ethical theories to the delineation of an ideal state. The whole is set forth as a discussion which Socrates reports having had with the sophist Thrasymachus, two of Plato's brothers, Glaucon and Adeimantus, Polemarchus and his aged father, Cephalus, at whose house in the Piraeus they were met in casual and friendly gathering. The conversation drifts to the question of the nature of justice. In the first book attempts are made by several of those present to give a definition, but none of them stand up under Socrates' scrutiny. He suggests that it may be easier to find justice writ large in the state, and so proceeds throughout books two to four to trace the evolution of an ideal state. This state turns out to be an aristocracy, with carefully selected and trained philosophers as its guardians. Socrates then returns to the original question of justice in the individual, but his audience has been intrigued by some of the features of his ideal state; and in book five he is prevailed upon to expound his ideas on the community of women and children among his guardians. In this connection he reminds his listeners that the attempt to sketch an ideal state was undertaken only for experimental purposes, that it may or may not be capable of realization, and that perhaps the most that can be hoped for is an approximation of existing states to this ideal. On this basis he proceeds in books six and seven to discuss the character of his philosopher guardians and the type of education they must have. In the eighth book he returns to the individual, and shows how differences of character correspond to the various types of construction: aristocracy, timocracy, oligarchy, democracy, and despotism, and how these states succeed and replace one another in practice. Thence he comes in the ninth book to conclude that the just man will guide himself with reference to the ideal state. "Perhaps," he says, "in heaven there is laid up a pattern of it for him who wishes to behold it, and beholding to organize himself accordingly. And the question of its present or future existence on earth is quite unimportant." Rather surprisingly in the tenth book Socrates reverts to a subject with which he had dealt in connection with education, i.e., poetry. He finds the influence of poetry wholly bad, and decides reluctantly that it must be excluded, except for hymns to the gods and encomia of great men, from the ideal state. Then turning to the vices he argues that they cannot destroy the soul and that nothing else can, therefore the soul is immortal. The rewards that the just may expect after death are illustrated by the strange and apocalyptic myth of Er, who had witnessed life beyond death and returned to tell man of rewards and punishment and of the governance of the universe.

SONG OF ROLAND, THE (11th c.), Anonymous. This oldest of the French heroic songs *(chansons deoeste)* is the story of a rear-guard action in the Pyrenees. Charlemagne, returning to France from war against the infidel in Spain, leaves Roland at Roncesvalles with his Twelve Peers and 20,000 troops, to cover the withdrawal. Should the Saracens come in great number, Roland is to blow his horn, Oliphant, to recall the Emperor. But Roland is proud and will not blow the horn, although, guided by the traitor Ganelon, the pagan horde threatens to engulf the outnumbered French. Blessed by their Bishop, Turpin, the Peers lay on. Carnage is great. They kill thousands, but other thousands come after, and one by one the noble peers go down. Too late Roland blows his horn. Charlemagne returns, full of grief, to find Roland dead on the field and the Meers long since in flight. Ganelon meets a traitor's end. Extremely popular during the Middle Ages, whole cycles of such epics grew up around the names of such figures as Guillaume of Orange, Doon of Mayence and Charlemagne. They flourished for three centuries. Their vogue was European. It is said that Tallifer the Minstrel entertained William of Normandy in his tent with the singing of the Roland on the eve of the Battle of Hastings.

TRIAL, THE (1925), by Franz Kafka. The novel opens when Joseph K. awakes one morning to be arrested for a crime of which he is completely unaware. Despite the fact that he is under arrest, K. may still go about his daily business. The inquiry to which he is summoned takes place in a dim tenement house garret where nothing is definite but everyone knows of K. "It is only a trial if you recognize it as such" is the pronouncement of the presiding magistrate before a strange crowd of spectators. At home, K. finds it difficult to get to see Fraulein Burstner, a fellow rooming-house lodger. Soon K.'s uncle, Karl, takes him to see a lawyer and judge, who happens to be ill and is attended by a girl, Leni. The lawyer offers no immediate aid but advises resignation to fate. Other quests for advice also seem fruitless. While at the Cathedral, K. observes a prist mount the steps to the pulpit. The cleric turns out to have been sent by the prison to discuss the case. He relates a parable about the guard at the entrance of the law and the newcomer who waits for admittance until the last moment of his life, only to learn just as the door is shut forever that it is meant only for him. In comment the priest states, "It is not necessary to accept everything as true, one must only accept it as necessary." Finally, two plump, formally-dressed men enter K.'s lodgings, escort him to the outskirts of the city, and plunge a knife into his heart. Also in a fragmentary and abstruse, symbolic style are Kafka's two other posthumously published novels *The Castle* (1926) and *Amerika* (1928). Of his shorter prose the most outstanding piece is the nightmarish *Metamorphosis* (1916), the allegorical tale of a man who finds himself one morning transformed into a huge insect, is gradually excluded from human society, and undergoes slow deterioration and disintegration. Prophetic of the scientific, hellishly efficient, frozen inhumanity of the police state and extermination camp is *The Penal Colony* (1919), in which a visitor to a prisoner's island inspects a sadistically ingenious execution apparatus. The Bohemian Jew Kafka, who wrote in German and died almost totally unknown in 1924, gradually is being recognized as one of the most remarkable writers of our time. His work is symbolic of the frustration of modern man.

ULYSSES (1922), by James Joyce. This huge experimental work, the masterpiece of the stream-of-consciousness school, has been regarded as the most important and influential novel of the twentieth century. The time is June 16, 1904--the whole novel covers approximately sixteen hours. The place is Dublin. The framework of the story follows Homer's *Odyssey* closely and ingeniously. The modern allegory tells of Stephen Dedalus (Telemachus) in search of his father, with the Jew Leopold Bloom, typical of the wanderer, as Ulysses. During the day these two cross each other's path twice without recognition. Stephen lives with Buck Mulligan, a medical student, in an old tower near the coast. His conscience is troubled over his conduct at his mother's deathbed; his father is such an aimless drunkard as not to count at all. At the schoolhouse he gets advice from Mr. Deasy. Meanwhile Bloom, of Hungarian origin, prepares breakfast for his unfaithful wife, Marion Tweedy Bloom (Penelope), and then sets out on various errands, including the paying of last respects to Paddy Dignam. At the funeral he thirtks of Rudy, his son, who died eleven days after birth. Among the more striking parts of this day's odyssey of the two characters are Stephen's visit to the library, where he speculates on Shakespeare's relation to his father, and Bloom's temptation by the adolescent Gerty MacDowell, who stands for Circe. Bloom and Stephen meet in a brothel, and suffer various nightmares and fantasies, the latter becoming so drunk that Bloom (who, in bending over him, sees his own child Rudy) must take care of him. They go to Bloom's house, but Stephen refuses to stay the night. The novel ends with Mrs. Bloom's unpunctuated and unexpurgated musings as she lies in bed after midnight. Many techniques are employed, including styles sharply different for the different characters, newspaper headlines, parodies of English authors, dialogue with stage directions, interior monologues, free association, question-and-answer form. The external world, Dublin with its sights and sounds, is often bewilderingly interfused with the thoughts and emotions of the characters. The work was long banned in the United States as obscene. Joyce's experimentalism went still further in his last work, *Finnegans Wake*.